designing with web standards
third edition

Contents at a Glance

Preface, xvii

Part I

Before You Begin, 3

1   99.9% of Websites Are Obsolete, 13

2   Designing and Building with Standards, 33

3   Gentle Persuasion, 61

4   The Future of Web Standards, 69

Part II

5   Modern Markup, 95

6   XHTML and Semantic Markup, 111

7   HTML5: The New Hope, 135

8   Tighter, Firmer Pages Guaranteed: Structure and Semantics, 149

9   CSS Basics, 165

10   CSS Layout: Markup, Boxes, and Floats— Oh My!, 185

11   Working with Browsers Part I: DOCTYPE Switching and Standards Mode, 217

12   Working with Browsers Part II: Bugs, Workarounds, and CSS3's Silver Lining, 229

13   Working with Browsers Part III: Typography, 265

14   Accessibility: The Soul of Web Standards, 295

15   Working with DOM-Based Scripts, 321

16   A Site Redesign, 341

17   NYMag.com: Simple Standards, Sexy Interfaces, 365

Index, 395

designing with web standards
third edition

jeffrey zeldman with ethan marcotte

New Riders

1249 Eighth Street, Berkeley, California 94710
An Imprint of Pearson Education

Designing with Web Standards, Third Edition

Jeffrey Zeldman with Ethan Marcotte

New Riders
1249 Eighth Street
Berkeley, CA 94710
510/524-2178
510/524-2221 (fax)

Find us on the Web at: www.newriders.com
To report errors, please send a note to errata@peachpit.com
New Riders is an imprint of Peachpit, a division of Pearson Education
Copyright © 2010 by Jeffrey Zeldman

Project Editor: Michael J. Nolan
Development Editor: Erin Kissane
Production Editor: Tracey Croom
Copyeditor: Rose Weisburd
Proofreader: Liz Merfeld
Indexer: Fred Leise
Composition: Kim Scott, Bumpy Design
Cover designer: Aren Howell
Interior designer: Kim Scott and Charlene Will
Editorial Assistant: Krista Stevens
Editorial Interns: Henry Li and Nicole Ramsey

Notice of Rights

All rights reserved. No part of this book may be reproduced or transmitted in any form by any means, electronic, mechanical, photocopying, recording, or otherwise, without the prior written permission of the publisher. For information on getting permission for reprints and excerpts, contact permissions@peachpit.com.

Notice of Liability

The information in this book is distributed on an "As Is" basis without warranty. While every precaution has been taken in the preparation of the book, neither the authors nor Peachpit shall have any liability to any person or entity with respect to any loss or damage caused or alleged to be caused directly or indirectly by the instructions contained in this book or by the computer software and hardware products described in it.

Trademarks

Many of the designations used by manufacturers and sellers to distinguish their products are claimed as trademarks. Where those designations appear in this book, and Peachpit was aware of a trademark claim, the designations appear as requested by the owner of the trademark. All other product names and services identified throughout this book are used in editorial fashion only and for the benefit of such companies with no intention of infringement of the trademark. No such use, or the use of any trade name, is intended to convey endorsement or other affiliation with this book.

ISBN 13: 978-0-321-61695-1
ISBN 10: 0-321-61695-2

9 8 7 6 5 4 3 2

Printed and bound in the United States of America

Once again, to Ava. —JZ

To Elizabeth, my impossibly wonderful wife.
We've got a world that swings. —EM

Acknowledgments from Jeffrey

This book is the product of many people to whom I give profoundest thanks.

My gratitude to our fabulous interns, Henry Li and Nicole Ramsey, Microsoft Word wranglers extraordinaire. Without them, this book would be full of burps and hiccups.

To Krista Stevens, who interrupted her frenetic schedule as editor of A List Apart to manage tasks and timings.

To Aaron Gustafson, technical editing colossus. Nobody knows more about anything. The man is a genius. And humble. And lovely. My thanks to him.

The brilliant Ethan Marcotte agreed to co-author this edition, and one mark of his greatness in that capacity is this: in rereading the galleys as this book goes to press, I can't tell where my writing stops and Ethan's begins. My thanks to him, his bride, and all his antecedents.

Despite all the talent mentioned here, this book would be a catastrophic flop if not for the invincible fortitude and strategic verbal cunning of Ms Erin Kissane, editor to the stars. Dear Erin, six words: thank you, thank you, thank you.

This edition and the HTML5 specification have benefited from the thinking of some extremely gifted individuals who flew to Happy Cog's New York studio to review the HTML5 spec, identify its virtues, and tone up its flab. Big thanks to my fellow HTML5 Super Friends (www.zeldman.com/superfriends/), Dan Cederholm, Tantek Çelik, Wendy Chisholm, Aaron Gustafson, Jeremy Keith, Ethan Marcotte, Eric A. Meyer, and Nicole Sullivan (www.flickr.com/photos/zeldman/3813120876/).

Many thanks are due to Michael Nolan, who brought me to New Riders in 2000, and who said to me in 2001, "You ought to write a book about web standards."

Angel trombones of gratitude to John Allsopp, author of Developing with Web Standards, this book's code-rich companion volume.

Hardly least, my thanks and praise to the crew at Peachpit who built the book: Liz Merfeld, Kim Scott, Rose Weisburd, and Tracey Croom.

Lastly, to first-timers and returning readers, thank you for sharing the journey.

—JZ

About Jeffrey Zeldman (author)

Dubbed King of Web Standards by *Business Week*, Jeffrey Zeldman was one of the first designers, bloggers, and independent publishers on the web, and one of the first web design teachers. In 1998, he co-founded and designed—and from 1999 to 2002 he directed—The Web Standards Project, a grassroots coalition that brought standards to our browsers and initiated the web standards movement.

Since 1998, Jeffrey has published and directed the industry-leading magazine *A List Apart* "for people who make websites" (www.alistapart.com). He co-founded the web design conference An Event Apart (www.aneventapart.com) with Eric Meyer, and founded and is executive creative director of Happy Cog™ (www.happycog.com), a high-end web design agency with studios in New York, Philadelphia, and San Francisco. Happy Cog clients include AIGA, Zappos, the U.S. Holocaust Memorial Museum, WordPress, Housing Works, the W3C, Fetch Software, Sundance Festival, W.W. Norton & Co., Mozilla Creative Collective, MICA, Brighter Planet, and The Amanda Project.

Jeffrey has written two books, including *Taking Your Talent to the Web*, a guide for transitioning designers and art directors (New Riders, 2001: now available as a free download at www.zeldman.com/talent). He serves on the Advisory Boards of the SXSW Interactive Festival and Rosenfeld Media, and is a co-founder of The Deck advertising network (www.decknetwork.net), the premier network for reaching creative, web, and design professionals.

Before becoming a web designer, he worked as a composer and performing musician, as a journalist for *The Washington Post* and *City Paper*, and as an advertising copywriter and art director. Jeffrey blogs at www.zeldman.com (since 1995) and www.twitter.com/zeldman. He lives in New York City with his daughter Ava and a small dog named Emile.

Acknowledgments from Ethan

My thanks to the talented Ian Adelman and the design team at New York Magazine, for being one of the finest clients I'll ever work with—finer still for letting me talk about their beautiful site in these pages.

Erin Kissane is the most careful, most thorough, most superlative-exhausting editor I've ever worked with. The English language needs more people like her. Thank you so very much, Erin.

Aaron Gustafson is a miracle of a technical editor, providing careful feedback and thoughtful criticism. He is, as the kids say, a true rockstar.

If I have a career today, it's because I picked up a little orange book several years ago, penned by a fellow whose writing I'd long admired. To work with that fellow on a new edition of that book has been a weird, wonderful dream come true, and I don't have the words to properly thank Jeffrey Zeldman for the opportunity. I don't know if I ever will.

About Ethan Marcotte (author)

Ethan Marcotte is a versatile user experience designer/developer, whose work demonstrates a passion for the intersection of quality code and compelling design. Prior to joining Happy Cog, Ethan worked with such clients as *New York Magazine*, Harvard University, and the W3C. A former steering committee member of The Web Standards Project, his work in the standards space has been covered in several magazines and online publications.

Ethan has acted as a contributing author to *Handcrafted CSS* (New Riders, 2009), *Web Standards Creativity* (friends of ED, 2007) and *Professional CSS* (Wrox, 2005). Ethan is an experienced technical editor, having edited the first edition of *Bulletproof Web Design* (New Riders, 2005), as well as the second edition of *Designing with Web Standards* (New Riders, 2006).

Ethan is a contributing author and technical editor at *A List Apart*, "for people who make websites." He is also a popular educator, and has been a featured speaker at An Event Apart, the SXSW Interactive festival, Harvard University, and AIGA's In Control conference. He spends entirely too much time online, and would like to be an unstoppablerobot ninja (www.unstoppablerobotninja.com) when he grows up. Beep.

Aaron Gustafson (technical editor, third edition)

After getting hooked on the web in 1996 and spending several years pushing pixels for the likes of IBM and Konica Minolta, Aaron Gustafson founded Easy! Designs, LLC (www.easy-designs. net), a boutique web consultancy. Aaron is a member of The Web Standards Project (WaSP), serves as Technical Editor for *A List Apart*, contributes to MSDN, and has written and edited books including *Accelerate DOM Scripting with Ajax, APIs, and Libraries* (Apress, September 27, 2007), *AdvancED DOM Scripting* (Friends of Ed, 2007) and *Web Design in a Nutshell* (3rd Edition, O'Reilly). He is a regular on the web conference circuit and provides web standards and JavaScript training in both the public and private sector. He blogs at www.easy-reader.net.

J. David Eisenberg (technical editor, first edition)

J. David Eisenberg lives in San Jose, California, with his cats Marco and Big Tony. He teaches HTML, XML, Perl, and JavaScript at Evergreen Valley College, and enjoys writing online tutorials. He is the author of *SVG Essentials* (O'Reilly & Associates) and *OASIS OpenDocument Essentials* (Friends of OpenDocument, Inc.). David attended the University of Illinois, where he worked with the PLATO computer-assisted instruction project. He has also worked at Burroughs and Apple.

Eric Meyer (technical editor, first edition)

Eric Meyer is an internationally recognized expert in CSS and the use of web standards, and has been working on the web since late 1993. He is the best-selling CSS author and best-recognized CSS authority in the world. His seven books have been translated into six languages and have sold in the hundreds of thousands. Eric is currently the principal of Complex Spiral Consulting (www.complexspiral.com), which focuses on helping clients use standards to cut costs and improve user experience. In that capacity, he has assisted organizations from universities to government laboratories to Fortune 500 companies; some recent and notable clients include America On-Line, Apple Computer, Macromedia, Sandia National Laboratory, and Wells Fargo Bank.

Table of Contents

Preface   xvii

Part I

Before You Begin   3

Ending the Cycle of Obsolescence   4

No Dogma   5

    A Continuum, Not a Set of Inflexible Rules   6

A Few Important Definitions   6

One Size Does Not Fit All   8

Welcome to the Winning Team   9

1 99.9% of Websites Are Obsolete   13

Modern Browsers and Web Standards   14

New Code for a New Job   15

The "Version" Problem   16

The Junkman Cometh   19

    Bad Markup: The First Bag Is Free   19

Code Forking Can Be Hazardous to Your Site's Long-term Health   21

The Hidden Cost of Bloated Markup   24

Backward Compatibility Is a Lie   27

    Blocking Users Is Bad for Business   28

The Cure   31

2 Designing and Building with Standards   33

Jumping Through Hoops   36

The Cost of Design Before Standards   37

Modern Site, Ancient Ways   38

The Trinity of Web Standards   44

    Structure   44

    Presentation   47

    Behavior   47

Standards In Action   48

The Web Standards Project: Portability in Action   50

    One Document Serves All   50

A List Apart: One Page, Many Views   53
 Design Beyond the Screen   55
 Time and Cost Savings, Increased Reach   56
Where We Go from Here   57

3 Gentle Persuasion   61

4 The Future of Web Standards   69
Findability, Syndication, Blogs, Podcasts, the Long Tail, Ajax
(and Other Reasons Standards Are Winning)   70
 The Universal Language (XML)   71
 A Mother Lode of Inventions   75
 The Future of Standards   85
HTML5: Birth of the Cool   87
 Internet Explorer and Web Standards   89
 Authoring and Publishing Tools   90

Part II

5 Modern Markup   95
The Secret Shame of Rotten Markup   102
 A Reformulation of Say What?   104
 Executive Summary   106
 XHTML 2—For Me and You?   107
Top 5 Reasons to Stick With HTML   109
Top 5 Reasons to Use XHTML 1   110
Top Reason Not to Use XHTML 1   110

6 XHTML and Semantic Markup   111
Converting to XHTML: Simple Rules, Easy Guidelines   113
 Open with the Proper *DOCTYPE* and Namespace   113
 Which *DOCTYPE* Is Your Type?   114
 Strict vs. Transitional: The Great Battle of Our Times   115
 Follow *DOCTYPE* with Namespace   117
 Declare Your Character Set   117
 Write All Tags in Lowercase   120
 Quote All Attribute Values   122
 All Attributes Require Values   123
 Close All Tags   124
 No Double Dashes Within a Comment   125

Encode All < and & Characters 125
Executive Summary: The Rules of XHTML 126
Character Encoding: The Dull, the Duller, and the Truly Boring 126
Structural Healing—It's Good for Me 128
Marking Up Your Document for Sense Instead of Style 128
Visual Elements and Structure 133

7 HTML5: The New Hope 135
HTML5 and Web Applications: the Stakes are High 136
HTML5 vs. XHTML 138
A Pox on Both Your Nomenclatures 138
HTML5 Elements on Parade 140
The Semantics of Page Structure 140
HTML5: Just the Specs 145
Learn More 147

8 Tighter, Firmer Pages Guaranteed: Structure and Semantics 149
div, *id*, and Other Assistants 150
What Is This Thing Called *div*? 151
id Versus *class* 152
Make Your Content Easy to Find and Use 155
Semantic Markup and Reusability 155
Common Errors in Modern Markup 158
*div*s Are Just All Right 161
Loving the id 162
Banish (or Minimize) Inline CSS and Scripting 162
Pause and Refresh 163

9 CSS Basics 165
CSS Overview 166
CSS Benefits 167
Anatomy of Styles 168
Selectors, Declarations, Properties, and Values 168
Alternative and Generic Values 171
Inheritance and Its Discontents 172
Descendant Selectors 173
Class Selectors 176
External, Embedded, and Inline Styles 179
The "Best-Case Scenario" Design Method 183

10 **CSS Layout: Markup, Boxes, and Floats—Oh My!**   **185**

The Dao of Page Flow   186

Meet the Box Model   187

How the Box Model Works   188

Applied Layout 101   191

Humble Beginnings   192

A Touch o' *class*   196

Reworking Our Layout   201

The Content Inventory, Redux   202

Stylin' Out   206

Revisiting Float   209

Clearly Lacking an Eye for Detail   212

Wrapping Up   215

11 **Working with Browsers Part I: DOCTYPE Switching and Standards Mode**   **217**

The Saga of *DOCTYPE* Switching   218

A Switch to Turn Standards On or Off   218

DOCTYPE Switch Basics   220

How Accurate is the Switch?   220

Web Standards and IE 8   221

Web Standards and Gecko   222

Complete and Incomplete DOCTYPEs   223

A Complete Listing of Complete XHTML DOCTYPEs   225

Keep It Simple   227

12 **Working with Browsers Part II: Bugs, Workarounds, and CSS3's Silver Lining**   **229**

CSS Bugs In Slow Motion   230

The Doubled Float-Margin Bug   235

PNG FUBAR SOS   237

The Way Forward   238

Knowing Is (Only) Half the Battle   239

CSS3: The New Hotness   248

Alpha Channels and You   248

Un-Boxing the Boxiness   251

Let the Coder Beware   253

Rethinking "Support"   255

Flash and QuickTime: objects of Desire?   258

Embeddable Objects: A Tale of Hubris and Revenge   258

The Double Vengeance of W3C   259

Twice-Cooked Satay: Embedding Multimedia While
Supporting Standards   259
A Fly in the Ointment: Object Failures   260
A Dash of JavaScript   261
A Workaday, Workaround World   262

13 Working with Browsers Part III: Typography   265
On Typography   266
A-B-Cs of Web Type   269
A Short History of Web Type   271
A Standard Size at Last   274
Arms and the Pixel   275
Sniffing Oblivion   277
Adventures in Font Size   279
Page Zoom: Making Democracy Safe for Pixels   281
Sizing With Ems: The Laughter and the Tears   284
The Font-Size Keyword Method   285
I Want My Franklin Gothic!   286
CSS @font-face: Real Fonts on the Web   287
sIFR—Accessible Type Replacement   289
Cufón—"Fonts For the People"   290
Typekit and its Brothers   291

14 Accessibility: The Soul of Web Standards   295
Five Tips for Creating Accessible Websites   296
1. Get Started   296
2. Use Logical Page Structures   296
3. Provide Keyboard Access   297
4. Provide Alternatives   297
5. Pick a Standard and Stick to It   297
Access by the Books   298
Widespread Confusion   301
The "Blind Billionaire"   301
Access Is Not Limited to the Visually Impaired   302
Section 508 Explained   303
Accessibility Myths Debunked   305
Accessibility Tips, Element by Element   309
Images   309
Tools of the Trade   316
Keeping Tabs: Our Good Friend, the *tabindex* Attribute   317
Planning for Access: How You Benefit   318

15   **Working with DOM-Based Scripts**   321

DOM by the Books   322
What's a DOM?   324
  A Standard Way to Make Web Pages Behave Like Applications   324
  So Where Does It Work?   326
Please DOM, Don't Hurt 'Em   327
  How It Works   327
  Checking for Support   333
  Code Variants   334
  Style Switchers: Aiding Access, Offering Choice   335
Learn to Love Your (JavaScript) Library   338
How Will You Use the DOM?   340

16   **A Site Redesign**   341

Out of the Past   344
Designing from the Content Out   347
  A Little Air   349
  Fonts, Intros, and Drop Caps   350
  The Song Remains the Same   355
  Footer Fetish   356
  Head Out   362

17   **NYMag.com: Simple Standards, Sexy Interfaces**   365

Taking Inventory   367
  From Inventory To Strategy   372
Once More Into the Markup, Dear Friends   375
From Angle Brackets to Curly Braces   378
  Method, Meet Madness   383
Word to Your DOM   386
  Meet the colgroup   386
  Jumping Into jQuery   387
Standards for All Seasons   393

Index   395

Preface to the Third Edition

When my colleagues and I started The Web Standards Project (WaSP) in 1998, we did not know that valid, semantic markup would make your site's content attractive to Google. It does, but that's not what we were concerned about in those pre-Google days. In the late 1990s, a clever web designer was one who could code her client's site in the five ways necessary to make it work and look right in Netscape 3, Netscape 4, IE3, IE4, and whatever else.

If you wanted your site to do anything besides sit there in Netscape and Microsoft's 3.0 and 4.0 browsers, you had to author using two generations of two incompatible scripting languages—four incompatible scripts per page in all, and all of them inline. All those inline scripts sat atop complex HTML table layouts, resulting in pages that were at least 60% heavier than they needed to be. And when it came time to redesign—or when you just needed to repurpose your content—doing so was harder and more costly than it needed to be, because content and layout were all jumbled up together.

Pref 1.
A big benefit of web standards, from a site owner's perspective, is that they make content easy for people and search engines to find. (**www. twitter.com/zeldman/ status/1137456194**)

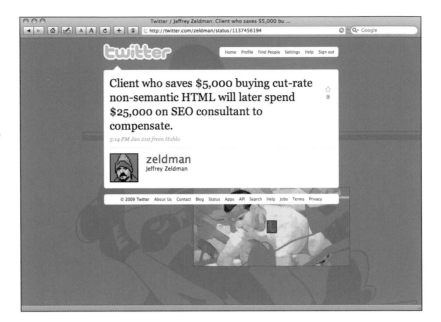

To my fellow WaSP co-founders and me, all that browser-specific coding presented a serious threat to web development. It took at least 25% of every site's development time and thus added at least 25% to the cost of every site. Moreover, if designing the primitive websites of 1998 took five kinds of code, what did the future of web design look like? Would the most thrilling advance in publishing and communication since the printing press be held back by the deliberate incompatibilities of competing browsers? Ten years in the future, would even the simplest websites be burdened by the cost and effort of coding each site twelve ways?

Web standards—semantic (X)HTML markup, CSS layout, and unobtrusive scripting based on JavaScript and the DOM—were the solution to all these problems, and by hammering away at that idea, standards advocates at The Web Standards Project and elsewhere eventually persuaded browser makers to support standards—and many web professionals to use them.

The benefits of designing with web standards, which Part I of this book will explain in detail, are

- Appropriate, semantic markup makes your content easy for people and search engines to find. Merely by converting from nonsemantic table layouts to well-structured semantic markup, sites can often score much higher in search engine listings, bump up their Alexa ranking, and show equal improvement along other findability metrics. (Findability is the *standardista's* preferred term for the promised benefit of *search engine optimization*, or SEO).

- Separating your site's presentation from its structure and behavior makes your site easier and less expensive to develop and test, lowering your overall budget or freeing cash for things like usability testing and content development.

- Separating your site's presentation from its structure and behavior makes your site lighter, thus improving performance.

- Separating your site's presentation from its structure and behavior and using appropriate semantic markup makes your site more accessible to different kinds of browsers and devices, including mobile devices *and* browsing tools used by people with disabilities—from screen readers to alternative input devices. Designing with standards doesn't mean there are no benefits to offering a mobile version. But it makes it easier to pull together a mobile version if you choose to; and in some cases, depending on your site's content, it may remove the need to do so.

- Designing with standards instead of browser-specific code future-proofs your site and its content. If your site is correctly authored in HTML 4.01 or XHTML 1.0 and laid out with CSS2, browsers will support it indefinitely. Even when HTML5, CSS3, and other emerging specifications have been long finalized, and even if they are brilliantly supported in future browsers, the site you author with today's standards will still work perfectly. Sites not authored to web standards have no such guarantee. At best, they will be stuck in time; at worst, they will cease to work.

Translated into fifteen languages from Bulgarian to Korean, the first two editions of this book introduced the notion and methods of standards-based design to hundreds of thousands of designers and developers and their clients worldwide. Since the first edition hit the shelves in 2003, there is scarcely an agency or in-house department that does not have at least one web standards and accessibility evangelist on staff. The industry has grown up, and it is no longer only the leading-edge designer who embraces web standards, no longer just the boutique agency that can claim profound expertise in standards-based design.

This third edition faces a world where web standards are becoming mainstream; where designers and developers argue about CSS3, and more than a few are trying their hand at microformats and HTML5; and where advanced standards compliance is a leading checkbox for software from Apple, Google, Opera, Adobe, Microsoft, and the open source community.

This substantially revised and rewritten edition has been restructured in two parts:

- Part I explains the problems created by old methods of web design and how web standards solve them. It also provides arguments in defense of standards-based design for those who must "sell" these practices to skeptical clients, colleagues, and employers. We next survey the expanding world of web standards, showing how old and new standards are turning the web into a dynamic platform of robust applications and accessible, easy-to-find (and beautifully styled) content. The section ends with a look at the web's future.
- Part II introduces the reader to XHTML, HTML5, and CSS, and (more importantly) to the principles of structured, semantic markup; clean, robust, optimal CSS layout; and unobtrusive scripting. After significant sidebars on typography and accessibility, it ends by taking us deep inside selected web design projects to reveal their standards secrets.

I am beholden to my new coauthor Ethan Marcotte, to our editor Erin Kissane, and to technical editor Aaron Gustafson. No finer team exists. If there is good in this book, thank these folks.

To new friends discovering web standards for the first time, welcome! And to those companions who have journeyed with us before, welcome back.

Part I

Before You Begin   3

1 99.9% of Websites Are Obsolete   13

2 Designing and Building with Standards   33

3 Gentle Persuasion   61

4 The Future of Web Standards   69

Before You Begin

This book is for designers, developers, owners, and managers who want their sites to cost less, work better, and reach more people—not only in today's browsers, screen readers, and wireless devices, but in tomorrow's, next year's, and beyond.

Most of us have gone a few rounds with the obsolescence that seems to be an inescapable part of the web's rapid technological advancement. Every time an improved browser version or new internet device comes onto the scene, it seems to break the site we just finished producing (or paying for).

We build only to rebuild. Too often, we rebuild not to add visitor-requested features or increase usability, but merely to keep up with browsers and devices that seem determined to stay one budget-busting jump ahead of our planning and development cycles. Even on those rare occasions in which a new browser or device mercifully leaves our site unscathed, the so-called "backward-compatible" techniques we use to force our sites to look and behave the same way in all browsers take their toll in human and financial overhead.

We're so used to this experience that we consider it normative—the price of doing business on the web. But it's a cost most of us can no longer afford, if we ever could.

Ending the Cycle of Obsolescence

Technologies created by the World Wide Web Consortium (W3C) and other standards bodies and supported by most current browsers and devices make it possible to design sites that will continue to work, even as those standards and browsers evolve.

What Is the W3C?

Created in 1994, the World Wide Web Consortium (www.w3.org) creates specifications and guidelines that are intended to promote the web's evolution and ensure that web technologies work well together. Roughly 500 member organizations belong to the consortium. Its director, Tim Berners-Lee (www.w3.org/People/Berners-Lee), invented the web in 1989. Specifications developed by the W3C include HTML 4, CSS2, CSS3, XML, XHTML 1.0, XHTML 1.1, HTML5 (created in cooperation with browser makers in the Web Hypertext Application Technology Working Group, or WHATWG), and the standard Document Object Model (DOM), among many others.

Other standards bodies include the European Computer Manufacturers Association (ECMA), which is responsible for the language known as ECMAScript and more familiarly referred to as "standard JavaScript."

This book will teach you how to escape the "build, break, rebuild" cycle without excluding potential visitors or wasting time and money on short-sighted, proprietary "solutions" that contain the seeds of their own doom. It will tell you what you need to know to work around the occasional compliance hiccup in Internet Explorer and other modern browsers, and it will offer strategies for coping with the bad old browsers that might be used by some in your audience, including that stubborn guy in the corner office.

Armed with this book, designers and developers will be able to modify their practices to create websites that work in many browsers and devices instead of a handful, while avoiding perpetual obsolescence born of proprietary markup and coding techniques. Site managers who read this book will be able to stop wasting money on specs that only perpetuate the wasteful cycle and learn instead how to write requirements documents that lead to forward-compatible sites.

No Dogma

This is not a dogmatic book. There is no best way to design a website, no one right way to incorporate standards into your workflow. This book will not advocate strict standards compliance at the expense of transitional approaches that might be better suited to particular sites and tasks. Moreover, this is not a book for theorists or purists, but for people who need to get work done.

I have nothing against the purists whose passion drives the creation of web standards; I admire such people immensely and am lucky enough to have befriended and learned from a number of them. But this book is for working designers and developers and the clients and employers who pay for their expertise, and its exploration of web standards will be rooted in the context of design, content, and marketing issues. Where W3C standards are fuzzy and implementation practices are controversial, I'll share any consensus the standards community has reached and help you make your own decision.

If this book contains one kernel of dogma, or holds one fixed, inflexible view, it's this: the cost of business as usual is too high.

No one reading this book can afford to design today's websites with yesterday's piecemeal methods. Coding every site six ways might have seemed a reasonable practice when the internet boom and grotesquely over-inflated budgets were at their height, but that day is gone. HTML, XHTML, XML, CSS, JavaScript, and the DOM are here to stay—not as ends in themselves, but as components of a rational solution to problems that have plagued site owners and builders since the `blink` tag.

A Continuum, Not a Set of Inflexible Rules

As this book will emphasize, web standards are a continuum, not a set of inflexible rules. In moving to web standards, you might not achieve perfect separation of structure from presentation in your first site or even your fifth. Your first efforts at accessibility might deliver only the minimum required by Web Content Accessibility Guidelines (WCAG) 1.0 Priority 1, and you might not get all of it exactly right. (You'd be in good company; the difficulty of knowing for sure that you've gotten WCAG 1.0 right led the W3C to issue a very different WCAG 2.0 specification in December 2008.)

The point is to begin. Fear of imperfection can immobilize the unwary the same way that shame about our flab might keep us from going to the gym. But we won't begin to lose the excess avoirdupois until we make our first fumbling efforts at physical fitness. Likewise, our sites won't attain forward compatibility if we don't start somewhere. Deleting font tags might be where you start. Or you might replace nonsemantic markup with meaningful h1 and p tags. This is often an excellent place to begin, and as a consequence, this book will spend a fair amount of its time and yours considering modern markup.

A Few Important Definitions

In this book from time to time I refer to *forward compatibility*. What exactly do I mean by that? I mean that, designed and built the right way, any page published on the web can work across multiple browsers, platforms, and internet devices—and will continue to work as new browsers and devices are invented. Web standards make this possible.

What do I mean by web standards? I mean the same thing The Web Standards Project means: namely, structural languages like HTML, XHTML, and XML, presentation languages like CSS, object models like the W3C DOM, and scripting languages like JavaScript, all of which will be explained in this book. (Site owners and managers: Don't worry yourselves over the technical chapters in this book. Just make sure your employees or vendors understand them.)

Hammered out by experts in working groups, these technologies are designed to deliver the greatest benefits to the largest number of web users. Taken together, web standards form a roadmap for rational, sophisticated, and cost-effective web development. As an added attraction, designing with standards also makes sites more accessible to those who have special needs. (Translation: you'll have more customers, lower costs, improved public relations, and a decreased likelihood of accessibility-related litigation.)

What Is The Web Standards Project?

For years, the W3C referred to its specs as "Recommendations," which might have inadvertently encouraged member companies such as Netscape and Microsoft to implement W3C specs less than rigorously. On its launch in 1998, The Web Standards Project (WaSP)—a grassroots coalition of web designers and developers—relabeled key W3C Recommendations "web standards," a guerrilla marketing maneuver that helped reposition accurate and complete support for these specs as a vital ingredient of any browser or internet device.

WaSP (www.webstandards.org) advocates standards that reduce the cost and complexity of site creation and ensure simple, affordable access for all. Thanks to its efforts, today every browser supports web standards as a matter of course. The group also works with the makers of site development tools like Dreamweaver, and with site owners and designers. Today, The Web Standards Project also provides web design and web standards education, as well as outreach beyond the English-speaking Western world.

What do I mean by standards-compliant browsers? I mean Apple's WebKit-based Safari 3 and 4 (which also powers the iPhone's web browser); the open source, Mozilla-powered Firefox 3 and higher; Opera Software's Opera 9+ (and the Opera Mini browser found in many great phones); the WebKit-based Google Chrome; and Microsoft Internet Explorer 8 (and to a lesser extent, IE7—and to a still lesser extent, IE6). What do these products have in common? To varying degrees, they understand and correctly support such standards as XHTML 1.0, CSS2, JavaScript, and the DOM. (All but IE also support tasty bits of CSS3 and some advanced features of HTML5.)

Are these browsers perfect in their support for every one of these standards? Of course they're not. No software yet produced in any category is entirely bug-free. Moreover, standards are sophisticated in themselves, and the ways they interact with each other are complex.

Are some of these browsers better than others where standards compliance is concerned? Every working developer knows the answer to that one. Most of us agree that even the latest version of Internet Explorer, while very good, is not as advanced as Safari, Firefox, and Opera. And of course, many people view the web through old versions of IE that are even less compliant.

But even if your audience hasn't upgraded their PCs since IE6 and Vanilla Ice were hot, cross-browser support is now solid enough that we can discard outdated methods, work smarter, and satisfy more users by designing with standards. And because standards are inclusive by nature, we can even accommodate folks who use older browsers and devices—in a forward-compatible way.

One Size Does Not Fit All

This book is large and has been crafted with care over three editions, yet it barely scratches the surface of what standards mean to the web. There is more to CSS, more to accessible, structured markup, and far more to the DOM and JavaScript than what this book or any single reference could convey. And as I've already mentioned, there are more ways to view the issues covered than the way this author looks at them.

Since the first edition of this book introduced standards to a worldwide audience, a new book with the words "web standards" in its title seems to come out each week. Many of these books offer the same advice as the volume you hold in your hands; others contradict some things said here. Different techniques advance different agendas.

Put two designers in a room and you will hear three opinions. No two designers agree on typography, branding, layout, or color. The same is true with web standards. Not every reader will immediately use every idea discussed in this book. But any thinking designer, developer, or site owner should be able to endorse the general notions advanced in this book. Doing so saves time and money, reduces overhead, extends the usable life of our sites, and provides greater access to our content.

This book will have done its job if it helps you understand how standard technologies can work together to create forward-compatible sites—and provides a few tips to help you along your way. You may disagree with some of what I have to say here, but the point is not to bog down in differences or reject the whole because you're uncertain about one or two small parts. The point is to begin making changes that will help your web projects reach the most people for the longest time, and often at the lowest cost.

Welcome to the Winning Team

After years in which nothing new seemed to be going on at the W3C, the latest browsers support exciting (and still unfinished) specifications like HTML5 and CSS3—and companies as powerful as Google are betting the farm on web applications powered by these technologies (radar.oreilly.com/2009/05/google-bets-big-on-html-5.html). Progressive enhancement techniques made possible by CSS3 are bringing new beauty—and new design thinking—to our medium. Real typography is a heartbeat away (www.zeldman.com/x/16). And organizations as diverse as Apple, MSN, Wikipedia, and WordPress have embraced web standards in their DNA, even if they don't always achieve perfect validation or 100% pure semantic markup (**0.1-0.4**).

0.1
Known for the sophisticated design of its products, Apple has a secret—its site is powered by web standards (**www.apple.com**).

0.2
MSN, #7 in Alexa's
Top 100 sites, validates as
XHTML Strict (**www.msn.
com**).

0.3
When you want answers,
you go to Wikipedia.
When Wikipedia wants
stability, it goes to
XHTML 1.0 Strict markup
and CSS layout (**www.
wikipedia.org**).

0.4
Open source blogging platform WordPress, #22 in Alexa's Top 100 sites, validates as XHTML 1.0 Transitional (**www.wordpress.com**).

Web standards are the tools with which all of us can design and build sophisticated, beautiful sites that will work as well tomorrow as they do today. In this book, I'll explain the job of each standard and how all of them can work together to create forward-compatible sites. The rest is up to you.

chapter one

99.9% of Websites Are Obsolete

An equal opportunity disease afflicts nearly every site now on the web, from the humblest personal home pages to the multi-million-dollar sites of corporate giants. Cunning and insidious, the disease goes largely unrecognized because it is based on industry norms. Although their owners and managers may not know it yet, 99.9% of all websites are obsolete.

These sites might look and work all right in mainstream, desktop browsers. But outside these fault-tolerant environments, the symptoms of decay have already started to appear.

In modern versions of Microsoft Internet Explorer, Opera Software's Opera browser, Apple's Safari, Google's Chrome, and Mozilla (the open source, Gecko-based browser whose code drives Firefox and Camino), carefully constructed layouts have begun to fall apart and expensively engineered behaviors have stopped working. As these leading browsers evolve, site performance continues to deteriorate.

In "off-brand" browsers, in screen readers used by people with disabilities, and in too many mobile phones, large numbers of these sites have never worked and still don't, while others function marginally at best. Depending on their needs and budget, site owners and developers have either ignored these off-brand browsers and devices, or supported them by detecting their presence and feeding them customized markup and code, just as they do for "regular" browsers.

To understand the futility of this outdated industry practice and to see how it increases the cost and complexity of web development without achieving its intended goal, we must consider how modern, standards-compliant browsers differ from the browsers of the past.

Modern Browsers and Web Standards

Throughout this book, when I refer to "modern" or "standards-compliant" browsers, I mean those that understand and support HTML and XHTML, Cascading Style Sheets (CSS), ECMAScript (more commonly referred to as "standard JavaScript"), and the W3C Document Object Model (DOM). Taken together, these are the standards that allow us to move beyond presentational markup and incompatible scripting languages and the perpetual obsolescence they engender.

Such browsers include the award-winning, open source Firefox 3.5+; Microsoft Internet Explorer 7/8 and higher for Windows; Apple's Safari 3.0/4.0+ for Macintosh OS X; Google's Chrome; and Opera Software's Opera 9/10+. (Have I left out your favorite standards-compliant browser? I mean it no disrespect. Any attempt to list every standards-compliant browser would date this book faster than the Macarena.) Although I use the phrase "standards-compliant," please remember that no browser is, or can be, *perfectly* standards compliant.

But lack of browser perfection is no reason to avoid standards. Millions of people still use Internet Explorer 6 for Windows, and that browser's support for standards is decidedly inferior to IE7+, Firefox, Opera, and Safari. Does that mean if your audience includes IE6 users you should forget about web standards? Does it mean you should tell IE6 users to upgrade or get lost? Of course not! Standards-oriented design and development need not and should not mean "designing for the latest browsers only."

Likewise, using XHTML and CSS need not necessitate telling users of older browsers to go take a hike. But a site properly designed and built with standards is unlikely to look the same, pixel-for-pixel, in IE6 as it does in more compliant browsers. In fact, depending on your design method, it might look entirely different—and that's probably OK. Indeed, some designers have gone so far as to recommend serving IE6 users core styles that enhance readability while making no attempt to ape the look and feel of the site as viewed in more compliant browsers. See Andy Clarke's "Universal Internet Explorer 6 CSS" (`www.forabeautifulweb.com/blog/about/universal_internet_ explorer_6_css`) for more about this approach.

New Code for a New Job

Modern browsers are not merely newer versions of the same old thing. They differ fundamentally from their predecessors, and in many cases, they've been rebuilt from the ground up. Mozilla Firefox, Camino, and related Gecko-based browsers are not new versions of the long-extinct Netscape 4. Opera 10 is not based on the same code that drove earlier versions of the Opera browser. These products have been built with new code to do a new job: namely, to comply as well as possible with the web standards discussed in this book.

In contrast, the browsers of the 1990s focused on proprietary (Netscape-only, Microsoft-only) technologies and paid little heed to standards.

Old browsers ignored some standards altogether, but paradoxically this lack of support wasn't much of a headache. If browsers didn't support the Portable Network Graphic (PNG) standard, for example, developers didn't use PNG images. No problem. But these old browsers also provided partial and incorrect support for some standards. This slipshod, inconsistent support for standards as basic as HTML created an untenable web-publishing environment.

When a patient's appendix bursts, a qualified surgeon performs an appendectomy. But what if, instead, a drunken trainee were to remove half the appendix, randomly stab a few other organs, and then forget to sew the patient back up? That's what standards support was like in old browsers: incompetent, incomplete, and hazardous to the health of the web.

If Netscape 4 ignored CSS rules applied to the body element and added random amounts of whitespace to every structural element on your page, and if IE4 got body right but bungled padding, what kind of CSS was safe to write? Some developers chose not to write CSS at all. Others wrote one style sheet to compensate for IE4's flaws and a different style sheet to compensate for the blunders of Netscape 4. To compensate for cross-platform font and UI widget differences, some developers also served different style sheets for different operating systems.

CSS wasn't the only trouble spot: browsers couldn't agree on HTML, on table rendering, or on scripting languages used to add interactivity to the page. There was no fully supported correct way to structure a page's content, produce the design of a page, or add sophisticated behavior to a site.

Struggling to cope with ever-widening incompatibilities, designers and developers authored customized versions of (nonstandard) markup and code for each differently deficient browser that came along. It was all we could do at the time if we hoped to create sites that would work in more than one browser or operating system. It's the wrong thing to do today, because all modern browsers support the same open standards. Yet the practice persists, needlessly gobbling resources, fragmenting the web, and leading to inaccessible and unusable sites.

The "Version" Problem

The creation of multiple versions of nonstandard markup and nonstandard code is the source of the perpetual obsolescence that plagues most sites and their owners. But although it's costly, futile, and unsustainable, the practice persists.

Faced with a browser that supports web standards, many developers treat it like one that doesn't. Thus, they'll write detection scripts that sniff out IE6 and feed it Microsoft-only code even though IE6 can handle standard JavaScript and the DOM. They then feel compelled to write separate detection scripts (and separate code) for modern Mozilla-based browsers that can also handle standard JavaScript and the DOM.

The Perils of Browser Sniffing

All browsers have a user agent (UA) string, a short string of text that contains the browser's name, version, and platform, and acts as a digital fingerprint for the browser. Web servers frequently log the UA, providing valuable information to site owners hoping to better understand their audience. But all too frequently, site owners use JavaScript or server-side code to parse the UA string so they can serve platform-appropriate or version-specific content. The problem with this approach is that the user agent string is unreliable. Depending on the user's security or network settings, a browser may not relay its UA to the server, causing these browser-sniffing scripts to fail, preventing users from reaching their destination.

Furthermore, all modern browsers allow the user to change the UA, whether through user-installed extensions (Firefox) or as part of its native feature set (Safari and Opera). In fact, prior to version 8.02, Opera identified itself as Internet Explorer *by default* to avoid being blocked by the many sites that lock out everyone who doesn't use IE.

The fallibility of UA sniffing was underscored during the recent release of Opera 10, the first browser release to reach double digits. This happy milestone was soured during the browser's beta release, when a legion of shoddily written browser detection scripts failed to properly register the second digit in Opera 10's version number, instead misidentifying the browser as "Opera 1." This problem was so widespread that Opera changed its browser to identify itself not as "Opera 10.00", but "Opera 9.80", the number of its last single-digit release (`dev.opera.com/articles/view/opera-ua-string-changes`).

Unfortunately, this Y2K-like version rollover fate awaits all browsers that have yet to reach version 10, unless we do away with browser sniffing, and adopt a more standards-aware approach.

With multiple versions come ever-escalating costs and conundrums. Sites produced to the proprietary scripting specifications of long-extinct browsers don't work in modern browsers and devices. Should the site owner throw more money at the problem, asking developers to create a fifth or sixth version of the site? What if there's no budget for such a version? Many users will be locked out.

Even when they embrace standard web technologies like XHTML and CSS, designers and developers who cut their teeth on old-school methods often miss the point. Instead of using standards to *avoid* multiple versions, many old-school developers create multiple browser- and platform-specific CSS files that are almost always self-defeating [**1.1**, **1.2**].

1.1

In 1999, the MSN Game Zone (**zone.msn.com/blog.asp**) sported three external style sheets and still didn't render properly in most modern browsers. It also contained multiple scripts (most of them inline), including heavy-duty browser detection. And it still didn't work. Throwing more versions of code at a problem rarely solves it.

1.2

To be fair, the preceding screen shot is four years old. Today, the same web page is even worse, as yet more code gets thrown at it. Six years after Microsoft brought the first standards-compliant browser to market, parts of the Microsoft site still don't know the first thing about designing with standards.

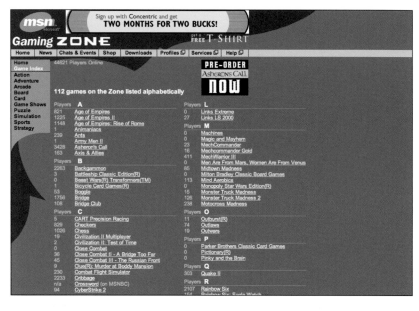

These practices waste time and money. Neither commodity has ever been abundant. Creating multiple site versions nobody can afford does nothing to advance the cause for which so much time and treasure have been squandered. Sites are still broken, and users are still locked out.

The Junkman Cometh

Peel the skin of major commercial sites like Amazon.com and eBay.com. Examine their tortuous nonstandard markup, their convoluted JavaScript (often including broken detection scripts), and their ill-conceived use of CSS. It's a wonder such sites work in any browser.

Often, non-standards-compliant sites work in yesterday's browsers because their owners have invested in costly publishing tools that accommodate browser differences by generating multiple, nonstandard versions tuned to the biases of specific browsers and platforms, as described earlier in "The 'Version' Problem." The first four generations of Netscape Navigator and Microsoft Internet Explorer did not merely tolerate nonstandard markup and browser-specific code; they actually encouraged sloppy authoring and proprietary scripting in an ill-conceived battle to own the browser space.

Bad Markup: The First Bag Is Free

Early in a computer programmer's education, he or she learns the phrase "Garbage In, Garbage Out." Likewise, among the first things a graphic designer learns is that the quality of source materials determines the effectiveness of the end product. Start with a high-resolution, high-quality photograph, and the printed piece or web graphic will look good. Try to design with a low-quality snapshot or low-resolution web image, and the end result won't be worth viewing. Garbage in, garbage out.

But old browsers don't work that way. Lax to the point of absurdity, they gobble up broken markup and bad links to JavaScript source files without a hiccup, in most cases displaying the site as if it were authored correctly. This laxity has encouraged front-end designers and developers to develop bad habits—and also persuaded middleware and backend developers to view technologies like XHTML, CSS, and JavaScript as contemptibly primitive.

Those who do not respect a tool are unlikely to use it correctly. Consider the following snippet, lifted from the costly e-commerce site of a company competing in a tough market, and reprinted here in all its warty glory:

```
<td width="100%"><ont face="verdana,helvetica,arial" size="+1"
color="#CCCC66"><span class="header"><b>Join now!</b></span>
</ont></td>
```

The nonsensical ont tag is a typo for the deprecated font tag—a typo that gets repeated thousands of times throughout the site, thanks to a highly efficient publishing tool. That error aside, this markup might look familiar to you. It might even resemble the markup on your site. In the context of this web page, all that's actually necessary is the following:

```
<h3>Join now!</h3>
```

Combined with an appropriate rule in a style sheet, the preceding, simpler markup will do exactly what the cumbersome, nonstandard, invalid markup did, while saving server and visitor bandwidth and easing the transition to a more flexible site powered by semantic markup (possibly including machine-readable code such as microformats, discussed later in this book). The same e-commerce site includes the following broken JavaScript link:

```
<script language=JavaScript1.1src=
"http://foo.com/Params.richmedia=yes&etc"></script>
```

Among other problems, the unquoted language attribute erroneously merges with the source tag. In other words, the browser is being told to use a nonexistent scripting language ("JavaScript1.1src").

By any rational measure, the site should fail, alerting the developers to their error and prompting them to fix it pronto. Yet until recently, the JavaScript on this site worked in mainstream browsers, thus perpetuating the cycle of badly authored sites. Little wonder that skilled coders often view front-end development as brain-dead voodoo unworthy of respect or care.

As newer browsers comply with web standards, they are becoming increasingly intolerant of broken code and markup. Garbage in, garbage out is beginning to take hold in the world of browsers, making knowledge of web standards a necessity for anyone who designs or produces websites.

Code Forking Can Be Hazardous to Your Site's Long-term Health

More than one company I know has spent over a million dollars on an overly complex, not-terribly-usable content management system (CMS). The makers of this software behemoth partially justify its sickening cost by pointing to its ability to grind out all manner of nonstandard code versions. In addition to wasting obscene truckloads of cash, the practice hurts findability by drowning meaningful content in a sea of nonsemantic tags [1.3]. Unfairest of all, it taxes the dial-up (or smart phone) user's patience by wasting bandwidth on code forking, deeply nested tables, spacer pixels and other image hacks, and out-dated or invalid tags and attributes.

1.3

Quick! Find "Information on Volkswagen models and services" in the convoluted, nonstructural HTML markup of Volkswagen.com. Tip: If you have a hard time finding it, so do readers and search engines. (**www.volks wagen.com**)

What Is Code Forking?

Code is the stuff programmers write to create software products, operating systems, or pretty much anything else in our digital world. When more than one group of developers works on a project, the code might "fork" into multiple, incompatible versions, particularly if each development group is trying to solve a different problem or bend to the will of a different agenda. This inconsistency and loss of centralized control is generally regarded as a bad thing.

As used in this book, *code forking* refers to the practice of creating multiple versions of incompatible code to cope with the needs of browsers that do not support standard JavaScript and the DOM (see "The 'Version' Problem," above).

At the same time, code forking squanders the site owner's bandwidth at a cost even the bean counters might be at a loss to calculate. The bigger the site and the greater its traffic, the more money is wasted on server calls, redundancies, image hacks, and unnecessarily complex code and markup.

Hard numbers are hard to come by, but in general, if a site reduces its markup weight by 35%, it reduces its bandwidth costs by the same amount. An organization that spends $2,500 a year on bandwidth would save $875. One that spends $160,000 a year would save $56,000.

Consider the front page of Volkswagen.com [1.4]. Despite a straightforward, elegant design, the page's markup is weighted down by antiquated, table-bloated markup, inefficient JavaScript, and pages of inline CSS. Now, this is no amateur website: the international portal for one of the world's most recognizable brands is served millions of times per day. Multiply each wasted byte of outdated HTML design hacks by the site's staggering number of page views, and the result is gigabytes of bandwidth that both tax Volkswagen's servers and add Pentagon-like costs to its overhead. If Volkswagen simply replaced its inefficient, bandwidth-gobbling markup [1.3, **1.5**] with lightweight, CSS-styled semantic HTML, the cost of serving each page would greatly diminish—and this would, in turn, increase the company's profits.

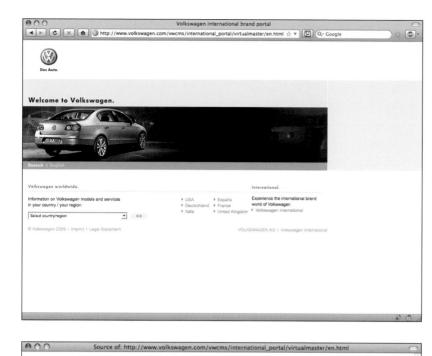

1.4
What Volkswagen (**www.volkswagen.com**) looks like—stark, compelling, beautiful.

1.5
Beautiful, that is, until you look under the hood. Peel back Volkswagen's skin (with your browser's "view source" feature), and you'll discover that the code and markup used to create this simple-looking website are unbelievably convoluted and perplexing.

So why hasn't Volkswagen made the switch? Presumably, the company wishes its site to look exactly the same in long-extinct browsers that don't support CSS as it does in modern, standards-savvy browsers that do. The irony is that no one using a ten-year-old browser is likely to care what Volkswagen's website looks like. And they're certainly not going to compare how the Volkswagen site looks in IE5 with how it looks in Firefox 3 or IE8. By constructing their pages using techniques outlined in this book, Volkswagen's design team could ensure that their content is accessible to all devices and browsers, even when niceties of the site design are not.

That a company as smart as Volkswagen misses this opportunity says everything you need to know about the entrenched mindset of brand managers who treat the web as if were a print ad, and of developers who hold "backward compatibility" in higher esteem than reason, usability, or their own profits.

The Hidden Cost of Bloated Markup

Suppose the code and markup on one old-school web page weighs in at 60K. Say that, by replacing outdated font tags and other presentational and proprietary junk with clean, structural markup and a few CSS rules, that same page can weigh 30K. (In our agency's practice, we can often replace 60K of markup with 22K or less. But let's go with this more conservative figure, which represents bandwidth savings of 50%.) Consider two typical scenarios, detailed next.

T1 Terminator

Scenario: A self-hosted business or public sector website serves a constant stream of visitors—several hundred at any given moment. After cutting its page weight in half by converting from presentational markup to lean, clean, structural XHTML, the organization saves $1,000 a month.

How it works: To serve its audience prior to the conversion, the self-hosted site requires four T1 lines, each of which is leased at a cost of U.S. $500 per month (a normal cost for a 1.544-megabit-per-second T1 line). After shaving file sizes by 50%, the organization finds it can get by just as effectively with two T1 lines, thus removing $1,000/month from its operating expenses. In addition to savings on bandwidth, there will also be fewer hardware expenses, plus lowered storage costs and energy use for large data centers, both in running the machines and cooling the room. That's right: web standards can help save the earth.

The simpler the markup, the faster it's delivered to the user. The faster it's delivered, the less stress is placed on the server—and the fewer servers you need to buy, service, and replace. This is particularly true for servers that must cope with dynamic, database-driven content—that is, all commerce and most modern content sites (even most blogs).

Metered Megabytes

Scenario: As a commercially hosted site grows popular, its owners find themselves paying an unexpected file transfer penalty each month, to the tune of hundreds, or even thousands, of unexpected dollars. Cutting file sizes in half restores the monthly bill to a manageable and reasonable fee.

How it works: Many commercial hosting services allot their users a set amount of "free" file transfer bandwidth each month—say, up to 3GB. Stay below that number, and you'll pay your usual, monthly fee. Exceed it, and you must pay more. Sometimes *much* more.

In one infamous case, a hosting company slapped designer Al Sacui with $16,000 in additional fees after his noncommercial site, Nosepilot.com, exceeded its monthly file transfer allowance. It's an extreme case, and Sacui was able to avoid paying by proving that the host had changed the terms of service without notifying its customers, but only after a lengthy legal fight. Who wants to risk outrageous bills or protracted legal battles with an ornery hosting company?

Not every hosting company charges outrageous amounts for excess file transfers, of course. Whether your site is large or small, visited by millions or just a handful of community members; the smaller your files, the lower your bandwidth. (By the way, it's best to choose a hosting company that permits unlimited or "unmetered" file transfers rather than one that penalizes you for creating a popular site.)

Condensed Versus Compressed Markup

After delivering a lecture on web standards, I was approached by a developer who claimed that the bandwidth advantages of clean, well-structured markup didn't amount to a hill of beans for companies that compress their HTML.

In addition to *condensing* your markup by using semantic structures, you can digitally *compress* your markup in some server environments. For instance, the Apache web server includes a `mod_gzip` module that squeezes HTML on the server side. The HTML expands again in the user's browser.

The developer I spoke with gave this example: If Amazon.com wastes 40K on outdated font tags and other junk but uses `mod_gzip` to compress it down to 20K, Amazon's bloated markup represents less of an expense than my lecture (and this book) would suggest.

As it turns out, Amazon does not use `mod_gzip`. In fact, the tool is used little on the commercial web, possibly due to the extra load required to compress pages before sending them. But that quibble aside, the smaller the file, the smaller it will compress. If you save money by compressing an 80K page down to 40K, you'll save even more by compressing a 40K page down to 20K. Savings in any given page-viewing session might seem small, but their value is cumulative. Over time, they can substantially reduce operating costs.

Bandwidth savings are only one advantage to writing clean, well-structured markup, but they're one that accountants and clients appreciate, and they hold as true for those who compress their HTML as they do for the rest of us.

Backward Compatibility Is a Lie

What do developers mean by "backward compatibility"? If you ask them, they'll say they mean "supporting all our users." And who could argue with a sentiment like that?

In practice, however, backward compatibility means using nonstandard, proprietary (or deprecated) markup and code to ensure that every visitor has the same experience, whether they're sporting IE2 or Opera 10. Backward compatibility sounds great in theory. But the cost is too high and the practice has always been based on a lie. The truth is, there is no real backward compatibility. There is always a cut-off point. For instance, neither Mosaic (the first visual browser) nor Netscape 1.0 supports HTML table-based layouts. By definition, then, those who use these ancient browsers cannot possibly have the same visual experience as folks who view the web through slightly less ancient browsers like Netscape 1.1 or MSIE2.

Developers and clients who claim to strive for backward compatibility inevitably specify a "baseline browser" such as Internet Explorer 6 and agree that that's the earliest browser their site will support. (In this scenario, Internet Explorer 5.5 users are out of luck.) To achieve baseline browser support, developers layer their markup with browser-specific, nonstandard hacks, write multiple scripts to accommodate "supported" browsers, and use UA sniffing to feed each browser the code it likes best. In so doing, they further increase the girth of their pages, pump up the load on their servers, and ensure that the race against obsolescence will continue.

Blocking Users Is Bad for Business

While some companies undercut their own profitability trying to ensure that even the oldest browsers display their sites exactly as new browsers do, others have decided that only one browser matters. In a misguided effort to reduce expenses, many sites are designed to work only in Internet Explorer, and sometimes only on the Windows platform, thus locking out 15–25% of their potential visitors and customers [**1.6**, **1.7**, **1.8**, **1.9**, **1.10**].

1.6

The home page of KPMG (**www.kpmg.com**), circa 2003, as seen in Netscape Navigator. Or rather, as not seen in Navigator, thanks to IE-only code.

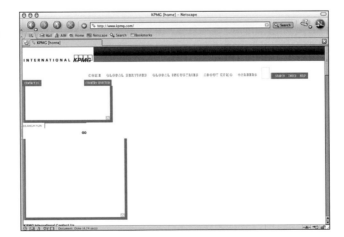

1.7

The site was equally useless in Netscape 7.

1.8

Well, if the site was for IE only, how did it work in IE5/Mac? Apparently, not well at all.

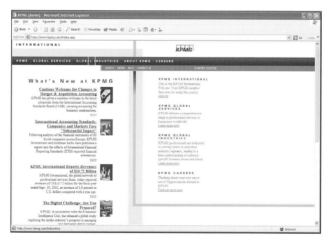

1.9

The same site as seen in IE6/Windows, where it finally deigned to work.

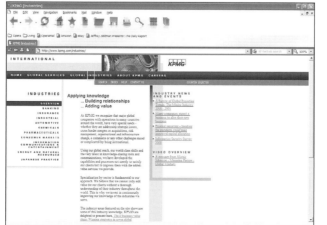

1.10

To be fair, the site kind of worked in Opera 7 for Windows when Opera was set to identify itself as IE. (When Opera identified itself as Opera, the site failed.)

1.11
After a redesign, today KPMG's site looks OK and works right across multiple browsers and platforms. There's still much room for improvement under the hood, but updated, non-IE-only markup makes all the difference.

I won't pretend to understand the business model of a company that would say no to up to a quarter of its potential customers. And the sheer number of customers lost by this myopic approach should boggle the mind of any rational business owner or noncorporate agency with a mandate to serve the public. According to recent statistics (www.internetworldstats.com), nearly 1.6 billion people used the web in May 2009. You do the math.

Say you don't mind losing up to 25% of the people who choose to visit your site. The "IE-only" approach still makes no sense because there's no guarantee that IE (or even desktop browsers as a category) will continue to dominate web space. As I write these words, Firefox continues to take market share away from IE, and ever more people are getting their internet fix via mobile devices powered by Webkit and Opera Mini. As ubiquitous computing gains acceptance and creates new markets, the notion of designing to the quirks of *any* individual desktop browser seems more and more 20th century and less and less intelligent.

Besides, as this book will show, standards make it possible to design for *all* browsers and devices as easily and quickly as for just one.

In our efforts to deliver identical experiences across incompatible browsing environments, we've lost sight of its true potential as a rich and multilayered medium accessible to all. We lost it when designers and developers, scrambling to keep up with production demands during short-lived internet booms, learned deeply flawed ways of creating sites, thus bringing us to our current pass, whose name is obsolescence.

But the obsolescent period of web development is dying as you read these words, taking countless sites down with it. If you own, manage, design, or build websites, the bell tolls for you.

The Cure

"Write once, publish everywhere," the promise of web standards, is more than wishful thinking; it is being achieved today, using methods we'll explore in this book. Although today's leading browsers finally support these standards and methods, the message has not yet reached many designers and developers, and new sites are still being built on the quicksand of nonstandard markup and code. This book hopes to change that.

Crafted by the members of the World Wide Web Consortium (W3C) and other standards bodies and supported in all post-2000 browsers, technologies like CSS, XHTML, standard JavaScript, and the W3C DOM enable designers to do the following:

- Attain more precise control over layout, placement, and typography in graphical desktop browsers while allowing users to modify the presentation to suit their needs.

- Develop sophisticated behaviors that work across multiple browsers and platforms.

- Comply with accessibility laws and guidelines without sacrificing beauty, performance, or sophistication.

- Redesign in hours instead of days or weeks, reducing costs and eliminating grunt work.

- Support multiple browsers without the hassle and expense of creating separate versions, and often with little or no code forking.

- Support nontraditional and emerging devices, from wireless gadgets and smart phones to Braille output devices and screen readers used by those with disabilities—again without the hassle and expense of creating separate versions.
- Deliver sophisticated printed versions of any web page, often without creating separate "printer-friendly" page versions or relying on expensive proprietary publishing systems to create such versions.
- Transition from the tag soup of the past to the real semantic web of the present and future.
- Ensure that sites so designed and built will work correctly in today's standards-compliant browsers and perform acceptably in old browsers, even if they don't render pixel-for-pixel the same way in old browsers as they do in newer ones.
- Ensure that sites so designed will continue to work in tomorrow's browsers and devices, including devices not yet built or even imagined. This is the promise of forward compatibility.
- … and more, as this book will show.

Before we can learn how standards achieve these goals, we must examine the old-school methods they're intended to replace and find out exactly how the old techniques perpetuate the cycle of obsolescence. Chapter 2 reveals all.

Not in the mood for a history lesson? Skip ahead to Chapter 3 for a quick blast of fresh air.

chapter two

Designing and Building with Standards

How did designers and developers produce sites before web standards were created and before browsers supported them? Any which way they could. Consider the late Suck.com, one of the web's earliest and wittiest independent periodicals [2.1]. Suck possessed a sharp writing style and had the smarts to slap its daily content right on the front page, where readers couldn't miss it. It sounds obvious today, when everyone and their brother has a blog featuring continually updated front-page stories, but in the mid-1990s when Suck debuted, most sites buried their content behind splash screens, welcome pages, mission statements, and confusing "Table of Contents" pages.

Suck's straight-ahead emphasis on text felt refreshingly direct in an era when most commercial sites wrapped their content in overwrought, literal metaphors ("Step Up To Our Ticket Counter," "Enter the Web Goddess's Lair"). Likewise, Suck's spare, minimalist look and feel stood out at a time when many sites were over-designed

Suck didn't. A decidedly bright site from the pioneering days of the commercial web (www. suck.com).

exercises in metallic bevels and high-tech, Gothy glows, or non-designed messes flung together by systems administrators and self-taught HTML *auteurs*. Many site builders at the time used every primitive device Netscape 1.1 offered the would-be layout artist, from the repeating background tile to the proprietary center tag, and some web pages still showcase these techniques [2.2]. In a web where more was more, Suck stood out by daring to do less.

To achieve Suck's distinctively spare, content-focused appearance, co-creators Carl Steadman and Joey Anuff had to jump through hoops. HTML lacked design tools, and for good reason: as conceived by Tim Berners-Lee, the physicist who invented the web, HTML was a structured markup language (www. w3.org/MarkUp/html-spec) derived from SGML, not a design language like Adobe's PostScript or the Cascading Style Sheets standard. (CSS had yet to be approved as a W3C standard, and once approved, it would take four long years before browsers supported the standard with anything close to accuracy.)

So how did Steadman and Anuff control their site's presentation? They did it with creativity, invention, and many rolls of digital duct tape.

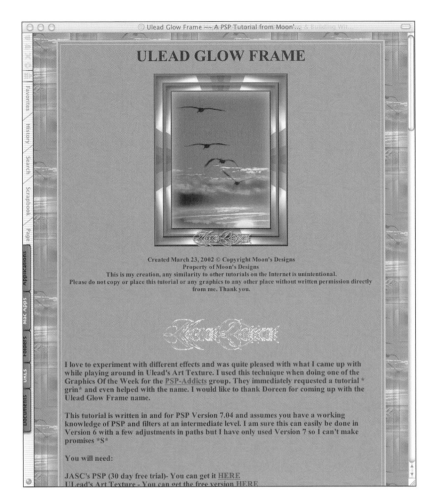

2.2

The Ulead Glow Frame tutorial at Moon's Designs exemplifies mid-1990s web design (**www.moonsdesigns. com/tutorials/ frames/glow.html**). Content is centered in an HTML table that is also centered. One repeating background tile is applied to the table and another to the page that contains it.

Jumping Through Hoops

To create the look of Suck, Steadman and Anuff wrote a Perl script that counted the characters in their text, inserting a p paragraph tag as a carriage return when a set number of characters had elapsed:

```
<p>One of the strange-but-truisms of
<p>minor peddling is that using the
<p>computer and other Fetish fodder
<p>somehow empowers children - plug
<p>in, log on, attend a good
<p>college on full scholarship, and
<p>get the hell out of the house.
```

The entire production was then wrapped in "typewriter" tt tags to force early graphical browsers (mainly Netscape 1.1) into styling the text in a monospace font like Courier or Monaco.

The result was rudimentary typographic control and a brute-force simulation of leading. Such HTML hacks offered the only way to achieve design effects in 1995. (The visual example shown in Figure **2.1** is from 1996, after a somewhat more graphic-intensive Suck redesign—still fairly minimalist. The original design is lost to the sands of internet time.)

Equally creative methods of forcing HTML to produce layout effects were widely practiced by web designers and were taught in early web design bibles by authors like Lynda Weinman and David Siegel—pioneers to whom all web designers owe a lasting debt. The creators of HTML clucked their tongues at this wholesale deformation of HTML, but designers had no choice as clients clamored for good-looking web presences.

Many designers still use methods like these, and many books still teach these outdated—and in today's web, counterproductive—techniques. One otherwise excellent recent web design book straight-facedly advised its readers to control typography with font tags and "HTML scripts." font tags have long been deprecated (W3C parlance for "please don't use this old junk") and HTML is not a scripting language. But bad or nonsensical advice of this kind continues to appear in best-selling web design books, perpetuating folly and ignorance.

The Cost of Design Before Standards

By creatively manipulating HTML, Suck had achieved a distinctive look, but at a double cost: the site excluded some readers and was tough for its creators to update.

In early Mom-and-Pop screen readers (audio browser interfaces for the visually disabled), the voice that read Suck's text aloud would pause every few words in deference to the ceaseless barrage of paragraph tags, disrupting the flow of Suck's brilliantly argumentative editorials:

```
One of the strange-but-truisms of ... [annoying pause]
minor peddling is that using the ... [annoying pause]
computer and other Fetish fodder ... [annoying pause]
somehow empowers children—plug ... [annoying pause]
in, log on, attend a good ... [annoying pause]
college on full scholarship, and ... [annoying pause]
get the hell out of the house.
```

Hard enough to parse under ideal conditions, Suck's convoluted sentence structures devolved into Zen incomprehensibility when interrupted by non-semantic paragraph tags. These audio hiccups presented an insurmountable comprehension problem for screen reader users and made the site unusable to them.

If the HTML tricks that made Suck's layout work in graphical browsers thwarted an unknown number of readers, they also created a problem for Suck's authors each time they updated the site.

Because their design depended on Perl and HTML hacks, it was impossible to template. Hours of production work had to go into each of Suck's daily installments. As the site's popularity mushroomed, eventually leading to a corporate buyout, its creators were forced to hire not only additional writers but also a team of producers. The manual labor involved in Suck's production was inconsistent with the need to publish on a daily basis.

In a more perfect world, these difficulties would have been confined to the era in which they occurred. They would be anecdotes of early commercial web development. While admiring pioneering designers' ingenuity, we'd smile at the thought that development had ever been so screwy. But in spite of the emergence of standards, most commercial production still relies on bizarrely labor-intensive workarounds and hacks and continues to suffer from the problems these methods engender. The practice is so widespread that many designers and developers never even stop to think about it.

Modern Site, Ancient Ways

Leap from 1995 to 2003 and consider a little movie called *Hooked: The Legend of Demetrius "Hook" Mitchell*. While *Hooked* might not be on your top ten list, the independent documentary was featured at over twenty film festivals, and garnered not a few awards. As part of the film's marketing campaign, the makers of *Hooked* built a website to help them better promote the film (www.hookmitchell.com) [**2.3**]. It was (and is) a well-designed site, but was assembled using labor-intensive table layout techniques that had outlived their usefulness on the modern web.

Hooked told the story of a legendary amateur basketball player whose hard life on the streets eventually derailed his career. And while the site's design effectively captured the film's grittiness, the *Hooked* website had plenty of grime under the hood, too. Its table-heavy markup and spacer-GIF–ridden layout had more than a few drawbacks:

2.3

The Hook Mitchell website (**www.hookmitchell.com**), built in 2003 with 1998-era markup. A compelling design powered by contorted code.

- If the filmmakers needed to make any changes to the site—even something as small as the addition of a single link—the markup for the homepage would need to be completely scrapped and rebuilt. Changing the size of even one component image would cause the entire HTML table that combined the various image slices [2.4] to burst apart.

- Thus, even the smallest changes to the site would incur a significant cost. The graphics would have to be redesigned, resliced, and reoptimized, and the table markup would have to be rewritten, along with the JavaScript that powered the rollovers. When a task as basic as adding a link requires hours of work, something is wrong.

- The site excluded many potential visitors. As implemented, the site was inaccessible to users of screen readers, text browsers, and mobile devices. Viewed in a nongraphical browsing environment [2.5], the page's total content read as follows:

```
spacer.gif
spacer.gif spacer.gif
spacer.gif
spacer.gif spacer.gif
[And so forth...]
spacer.gif spacer.gif
bottom.jpg
```

2.4
The same film site, with table borders activated to reveal construction methods (and potential maintenance headaches).

2.5

In a text browser like Lynx (**lynx.isc.org**), the Hook Mitchell website provides no information: images are missing their required `alt` attributes, so filenames are displayed instead of human-readable link titles. To see how your web pages appear in a nongraphical environment, test them in Lynx, a Lynx emulator, or a screen reader like JAWS or OS X's VoiceOver. A free online Lynx emulator (**www.delorie.com/web/lynxview.html**) is available but can be used only on sites for which you are the "webmaster."

2.6

Because there is no content to be found on the *Hooked* homepage beyond nonsensical image filenames, its search engine results are polluted, and its ranking no doubt suffers. If you were searching for information on the movie, would "spacer.gif. bottom.jpg" compel you to visit? (I didn't think so.)

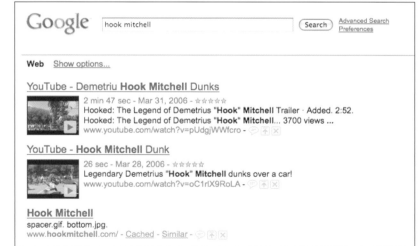

Without a lick of nongraphical content to be found on their homepage, even the site's search results return nothing useful about the movie it was designed to promote [**2.6**]. Was "spacer.gif" the message that the producers of *Hooked* hoped to convey to the site's visitors? We doubt it.

I'm not saying images are bad, or intricate design is a liability. To the contrary, images are vital, beauty is needed, and the *Hooked* site is indeed a well-crafted aesthetic online experience. But that experience need not have been inaccessible.

Though visually attractive, the *Hooked* site epitomizes the secret shame of old-school page layouts: their code reveals a hidden ugliness in the form of inaccessibility and a reliance on inefficient and expensive production techniques. Thankfully, much of the web has long abandoned these techniques in favor of a more standards-driven approach. But despite the progress we've made, many sites are still being built with outdated techniques (see sidebar "No Room at the Inn"). Those of us forced to rely on broken markup will find that our carefully constructed layouts break when the client wishes to make changes, as all clients do all the time. We either bill the client or eat the cost—or implement visually confusing workarounds that damage the site's credibility and usefulness. (For example, we might add three plain links to the top of the *Hooked* site to make newly added sections accessible, but this addition would degrade the site's carefully controlled aesthetic effect, and could confuse users as well.)

No Room at the Inn

Sadly, nonstandard production techniques like those used to build the Hook Mitchell site are still in use today.

Onward but not upward we fly to present day, to Hilton's hotel search (www. hilton.com/en/hi/hotels/search/index.jhtml). Looking to make a reservation? Good luck. Over a decade after the introduction of CSS and in the era of the standards-compliant browser, Hilton's search form still relies on nonsemantic table layouts, obsolete font tags, 1995-style spacer GIF images, and other long-stale crusts. As if all that nonstructural markup didn't waste enough bandwidth, whopping JavaScripts embedded into each page (instead of being externalized) further swell the site's bloat, slowing

(continues on next page)

(continued from previous page)

page display. Worst of all, the content is an accessibility nightmare. Missing alt attributes on images will cause audio browsers to read gibberish. And if JavaScript is disabled, large swaths of the page will cease to work. So if you don't meet Hilton's stringent technical requirements, you'll have to find another hotel to put you up.

Model of worst practices though it may be, Hilton's poorly produced search engine is scarcely unique. Plenty of dinosaurs just as big and just as dumb still roam the cooling planes of cyberspace [2.8]. All the more reason to advocate for smarter techniques based on web standards, so that mistakes like these stay in the past.

2.7

Hilton's hotel search (www.hilton.com/en/ hi/hotels/search/ index.jhtml), directly accessible from hilton. com, is a simple form weighted down by over-wrought presentational markup: spacer GIFs, nested tables, and—can it be?—heaps of obso-lete tags. So make your reservation, and 1999'll leave a light on for you.

2.8

In 2009, Smartronix, Inc. (`www.smartronix.com`) was awarded $9.5 million (`www.bizjournals.com/washington/stories/2009/07/06/daily78.html`) to oversee the redesign of recovery.gov, a site dedicated to preventing government waste. Judging from Smartronix's invalid markup, much of that budget will be spent on bandwidth.

FIGHT BACK!

Tired of outdated, non-standards-based redesigns that make sites harder for customers to use while also making web standards harder to sell to your clients? Accessibility expert and standardista Joe Clark, whose name will pop up more than once in this book, created a Failed Redesigns campaign (`blog.fawny.org/category/web-standards/failed-redesigns`*) to spread standards awareness while shaming those who produce new or redesigned sites that act as if "the 21st century is frozen in the amber of the year 1999."*

As the creators of the sites above might have learned by now, desktop-centric layouts don't travel well. They might look fine in aging browsers under "average" conditions. But beyond those borders, our sites might cease to communicate. At the very least, such inaccessibility cuts off potential customers.

When they drowned their content in tag soup and locked out users and browsers, these designers were using long-established (if painfully outdated) techniques. But why would they do so? It may be a matter of education: perhaps they were using the most modern technologies they were familiar with. The designers may also have been hampered by outdated content management systems, or by a client's equally outmoded respect for long-dead browsers.

But whatever the motive, the problems generated by these techniques are not unique to Hilton or Hook Mitchell. They're the problems faced by any site crafted to the quirks of a few visual browsers instead of being designed to facilitate universal access via web standards. They are also the problems of any site that yokes presentation to structure by forcing HTML to deliver layouts, a job it was not built to do.

Fortunately, there's another way to design and build websites—a way that solves the problems created by old-school methods without sacrificing the aesthetic and branding benefits the old methods deliver: web standards.

The Trinity of Web Standards

Figure **2.9** indicates how web standards solve the problems we've been discussing by breaking any web page into three separate components: structure, presentation, and behavior.

Structure

A *markup language* (HTML 4.01: www.w3.org/TR/html401; XHTML 1.0: www.w3.org/TR/xhtml1) contains text data formatted according to its structural (semantic) meaning: headline, secondary headline, paragraph, numbered list, definition list, and so on.

2.9
Structure, presentation, and behavior: the three components of any web page in the world of web standards.

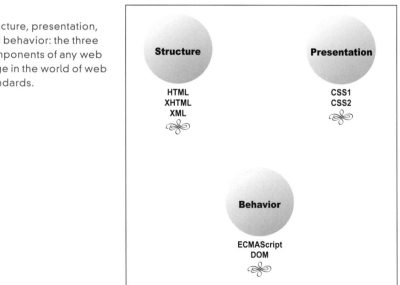

On the web, this text would likely be part of a definition list dl. The subhead, "Structure," would be marked up as a definition title dt. The paragraphs you're now reading would be wrapped in definition data dd tags:

```
<dl>
<dt>Structure</dt>
<dd>A <em>markup language</em> (<a href="http:// www.w3.org/
TR/html401">HTML 4.01</a>; <a href="http://www.w3.org/TR/
xhtml1">XHTML 1.0</a>) contains text data formatted according
to its structural (semantic) meaning: headline, secondary
headline, paragraph, numbered list, definition list, and so
on.</dd>
<dd>On the web, this text would likely be part of a definition
list &lt;dl&gt;. The subhead, &#8220;Structure,&#8221; would be
marked up as a definition title. The paragraphs you&#8217;re
now reading would be wrapped in definition data tags.
</dd>
</dl>
```

Alternately, if it made better semantic sense for your document, the two paragraphs might simply follow a single headline element:

```
<h3>Structure</h3>
<p>A <em>markup language</em> (<a href="http:// www.w3.org/
TR/html401">HTML 4.01</a>; <a href="http://www.w3.org/TR/
xhtml1">XHTML 1.0</a>) contains text data formatted according
to its structural meaning: headline, secondary headline,
paragraph, numbered list, definition list, and so on.</p>
<p>On the web, this text would likely be part of a definition
list &lt;dl&gt;. The subhead, &#8220;Structure,&#8221; would
be marked up as a definition title. The paragraphs you&#8217;re
now reading would be wrapped in definition data tags.</p>
```

THE 411 ON ’

If you're one of the five people who will actually take the time to read the text in the XHTML examples, you might wonder what ’ *means. Quite simply, it is the standard Unicode character sequence encoding a typographically correct apostrophe. Likewise,* “ *is Unicode for typographically correct double open quotation marks, while* ” *is the code that closes those double quotation marks.*

XML (www.w3.org/TR/REC-xml), the extensible markup language, provides considerably more options than this, but for now we'll limit ourselves to XHTML 1.0, a transitional markup language and stable W3C standard since 2000 that works just like HTML in nearly every browser or internet device.

When authored correctly (containing no errors, and no illegal tags or attributes), standards-compliant XHTML or HTML is completely portable. It works in web browsers, screen readers, text browsers, wireless devices—you name it.

The markup can also contain additional structures deemed necessary by the designer. For instance, content and navigation might be marked as such and wrapped in appropriately labeled tags:

```
<div id="content">[Your content here.]</div>
<ul id="navigation">[Your navigational menu here.]</ul>
```

Markup can also contain embedded objects such as images, Flash presentations, or video clips, along with tags and attributes that present text equivalents for those who cannot view these objects in their browsing environment.

Valid? Semantic? Say what?

- Markup is *valid* when it contains no errors (example: forgetting to close a tag's bracket) and no illegal tags or attributes (example: the `height` attribute, applied to a table, is not legal in XHTML). Validation can be tested via free online software (`validator.w3.org`).

- Markup is *semantic* when tags are chosen according to what they mean. For example, tagging a headline `h1` because it is the most important headline on the page is a semantic authoring practice. Tagging a headline `h1` "to make it look big" is not. In this book I sometimes use the phrase "structural markup" to mean pretty much the same thing as "semantic markup." ("Structural markup" takes its name specifically from the idea that each web document has an outline-like structure.)

A web page can be valid yet not be semantic. For example, an HTML page could be layed out with table cells and no structural markup. If the table markup contains no errors and no illegal tags or attributes, the page is valid. Likewise, a page can be semantic and invalid. Typically, professionals who practice standards-based design strive to create pages whose markup is both valid and semantic.

Presentation

Presentation languages (CSS 2.1: `www.w3.org/TR/CSS21`; CSS 3: `www.w3.org/Style/CSS/current-work`) format the web page, controlling typography, placement, color, and so on. CSS can take the place of old-school HTML table layouts. In all cases, it replaces nonstandard font tags and bandwidth-wasting, outdated junk like this:

```
<td bgcolor="#FFCC00" align="left" valign="top"><br><br><br> </td>
```

We could strike such junk from our markup by applying the `border` property to the element via a single CSS rule.

Because presentation is separated from structure, it is possible to change one without negatively affecting the other. For instance, you can apply the same layout to numerous pages or make changes to text and links without breaking the layout. You or your clients are free to change the XHTML at any time without fear of breaking the layout because the text is just text; it does not serve double duty as a design language.

Likewise, you can change the layout without touching the markup. Have readers complained that your site's typeface is too small? Change a rule in the global style sheet, and the entire site will reflect these changes instantly. Need a printer-friendly version? Write a print style sheet, and your pages will print beautifully, regardless of how they appear on the screen.

Behavior

A standard object model (the W3C DOM at `www.w3.org/DOM`) works with CSS, XHTML, and ECMAScript 262 (`www.ecma-international.org/publications/standards/Ecma-262.htm`), the standard version of JavaScript, enabling you to create sophisticated behaviors and effects that work across multiple platforms and browsers. No more browser-specific scripting.

Standards In Action

If Suck were produced today, web standards like (X)HTML and CSS would allow the staff to concentrate on writing. A basic (X)HTML template would semantically describe the document. CSS would control the look and feel without requiring additional design work for every issue. Paragraph tags would denote the beginnings and ends of paragraphs rather than force vertical gaps between each line of text. (CSS would do that job.)

In graphical browsers like IE, Firefox, Opera, and Safari, style sheets would ensure that Suck looked as its designer intended. Semantic markup would deliver Suck's content not only to these browsers but also to mobile devices, screen readers, and text browsers without the accompanying hiccups of fake paragraphs and similar hostages to markup-as-a-design-tool.

As a content-focused site, Suck.com would be a prime candidate for a strict XHTML/CSS makeover in which substance and style would be delivered via the appropriate technology: CSS for layout and XHTML for structured content.

Similarly, the Hook Mitchell site could deliver their layout with CSS, conserving bandwidth while enabling the design team to change one section of the page without recooking the whole tamale. The site's designers could use the CSS `background` property to position its primary image as a single JPEG or PNG file instead of a dozen image slices [2.4] and could easily overlay one or more menu graphics using any of several time-tested CSS positioning methods.

In addition to abstracting the presentational logic out of their markup and into their CSS, the designers could also use valid XHTML or HTML and accessibility attributes such as `alt` and `title` to ensure that the site's content would be accessible to all instead of meaningless to many [2.5]. And a single style sheet could control the design on countless interior pages, lowering maintenance overhead, as well as the cost of future design tweaks.

Thankfully, since the first edition of this book went to press, countless sites have embraced these technologies. Consider the website for the Maryland Institute College of Art (MICA), a recent redesign by Happy Cog. Underneath its striking design you'll find some equally attractive code, as MICA uses web standards to deliver its content to all [**2.10, 2.11**].

2.10
The homepage for MICA (**www.mica.edu**), an art school that places the striking work of its students front and center. And web standards like XHTML and CSS make it happen.

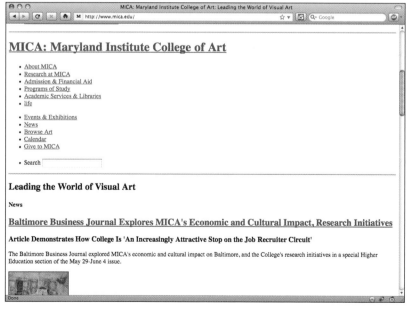

2.11
With style sheets disabled, MICA's content is still perfectly accessible, its semantically rich markup easily read. The experience in a text-only browser would be similar.

The Web Standards Project: Portability in Action

The Web Standards Project (WaSP) [**2.11**] launched in 1998 to persuade
Netscape, Microsoft, and other browser makers to thoroughly support the
standards discussed in this book. It took time, persistence, and strategy (aka
yelling, whining, and pleading), but eventually browser makers bought into
WaSP's view that interoperability via common standards was an absolute
necessity if the web was to move forward.

LIP SERVICE...

*One of the ironies of the struggle for standards compliance in browsers was that
Microsoft, a W3C member that has contributed significantly to the creation of web
standards, had to be bullied into fully supporting the very technologies it helped to
create. Go figure.*

After browsers finally began meaningfully supporting standards, The Web
Standards Project relaunched in 2002 to encourage designers and developers to learn about and harness the power of these hard-won technologies. To
denote the enlargement of the group's mission from bully pulpit to educational
resource, the site was rewritten and redesigned.

As expected, the site looked nice in standards-compliant browsers [**2.12**]. It
also looked acceptable in older, less-compliant browsers [**2.13**]. But the site
transcended the PC-based browsing space without requiring additional or
alternative markup, code, or device detection. (Look, Ma, no versions!)

One Document Serves All

The Web Standards Project was built with XHTML 1.0 Strict. CSS was used for
layout. There is no Palm version or WAP version, although creating such versions was common practice at the time. Multiple versions were not needed;
when you design and build with standards, one document serves all.

Figure **2.14** shows webstandards.org as seen in a Palm Pilot. Figure **2.15**
shows how it looks in Microsoft's PocketPC. Most uncannily of all, Figure **2.16**
shows the site working just as fine as you please on a Newton handheld, Apple's
long-discontinued proto-PDA. (Think of it as the iPhone's great-grandfather.)
Grant Hutchinson, who captured the Newton screenshot, told us: "There's
nothing like viewing a modern site using a piecemeal browser on a vintage
operating system."

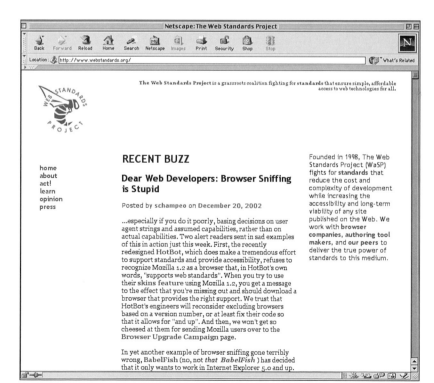

2.12
The Web Standards Project's CSS-powered homepage in 2002, as seen in an early version of the Camino (Mozilla) browser for Mac OS X (`www.webstandards. org`).

2.13
The same site looks decent and works acceptably in creaky old Netscape 4, our poster child for non-standards-compliance. A special "Netscape 4 version" was not needed.

2.14

(left) The same site on a different day, as seen in a Palm Pilot. Look, Ma, no WAP! Screenshot courtesy of Porter Glendinning (**www.g9g.org**).

2.15

(right) The same site as seen in Microsoft's PocketPC. Screenshot courtesy of Anil Dash (**www.dashes.com/ anil**).

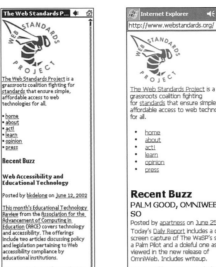

2.16

Webstandards.org again, this time as viewed in Apple's long-discontinued Newton handheld. Screenshot courtesy of Grant Hutchinson (**www. splorp.com**).

That should be music to the ears of any designer or site owner who wants to reach the greatest number of visitors with the least effort. Strict compliance with (X)HTML and intelligent use of CSS frees designers and developers from the need to create multiple versions.

By the time you see this book, The Web Standards Project will have redesigned again, and these screenshots will be obsolete—although the points they prove will still be true.

A List Apart: One Page, Many Views

Published by our agency Happy Cog since 1998, *A List Apart* (www.alistapart.com) "for people who make websites" has long taught and promoted standards-based design. In February 2001, as the last of the standards-compliant browsers came to market, my cohorts and I converted the magazine to pure CSS layout and encouraged other designers to do likewise on sites they were designing. Hundreds of thousands have since done so.

A List Apart's form and structure demonstrate advantages of the powerful combination of semantic markup and CSS layout. The combination lets us support old browsers and other non-CSS-compliant devices without the need to create separate versions: devices that understand CSS see the layout [**2.17**]; those that don't understand CSS see the content, formatted by their browser in accordance with document structure [**2.18**].

Indeed, some readers prefer it this way; immediately following *A List Apart*'s initial CSS redesign, Netscape 4 usage by *ALA* visitors temporarily increased. It seems these visitors preferred a plain page their browser could handle to the previous layout whose gymnastics only underscored Netscape 4's weaknesses. Those who hold that standards hurt users of old browsers might consider this story an indicator of just the opposite: when properly used, standards help everyone.

Further, in most cases this combination of semantic markup and CSS layout frees you from the need to create separate, "printer-friendly" page versions [**2.19**].

2.17

A List Apart (**www. alistapart.com**), "for people who make websites." Jason Santa Maria's beautiful layout shines when the site is viewed in a standards-compliant browser.

2.18

The same site in a 4.0 browser. No CSS layout, no problem. The site is still readable and usable; markup, filtered through browser defaults, provides the basic layout.

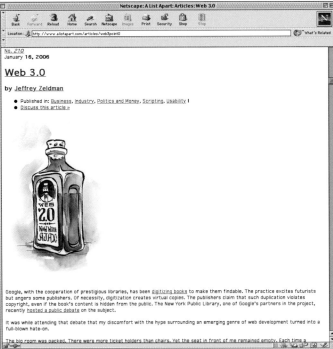

2.19
From web to print: *ALA* articles become printer friendly on the fly, thanks to print style sheets.

Design Beyond the Screen

Figure 2.19 shows what an *A List Apart* article looks like when printed. As you can see, the sidebar has been removed, as readers of the printed piece don't need the navigational links the sidebar contains. The site's strong issue number bullet has been replaced by a simple link. Fonts have been optimized for printing, and the URL of every link is usefully displayed, whether said URL appears on the screen version or not. This magic is accomplished via a print style sheet designed by Eric Meyer, author of *Eric Meyer on CSS* (New Riders, 2002) and a half dozen other CSS masterworks. In an article (`www.alistapart.com/articles/goingtoprint`), Eric explains the rationale and techniques for creating a print style sheet.

The important concept to grasp for now is that with a single, lightweight document—a print style sheet—*A List Apart* no longer needs to produce separate, "printer-friendly" versions. In all probability, neither will your sites. A possible exception: sites that use multipage article formats, like `www.nytimes.com` or the O'Reilly Network (`www.oreilly.com`), will still require a printer-friendly page simply to stitch the whole story together into a single document. But they, too, can still benefit from using a print style sheet, because the output of that stitched-together page can use a print style sheet.

Let's review the benefits reaped by the two sites we've just looked at.

Time and Cost Savings, Increased Reach

If designing with standards means you no longer need to create multiple versions of every site, it's easy to see that time and cost savings can be enormous:

- No more browser-specific versions
- No more "basic" versions for old browsers
- In many cases, no more separate mobile-specific versions
- In many cases, no more printer-friendly versions
- No more browser and platform sniffing, and no more straining of the server to fetch various browser or device-optimized components

Much as they might want to accommodate users of mobile devices, many organizations simply cannot afford to build separate mobile versions. Thanks to the XHTML and CSS standards, they don't have to. Without lifting a finger, these organizations will still reach new readers and customers, whose numbers are legion.

Strict standards compliance also provides a huge head start on solving the accessibility problem. If your site works in an old Palm Pilot, it most likely works in a screen reader like JAWS, although, of course, you need to test to be sure, and you might need to do a bit more work to be truly accessible. We'll look deeper into accessibility in Chapter 14 and in other sections of Part II.

Where We Go from Here

We can't get to tomorrow's web by following yesterday's design and development norms. Our way ahead is one of forward compatibility, of hewing closely to the spirit of web standards. What does this entail? Let's take a look.

Forward Compatibility Ingredients

- Full separation of structure from presentation and behavior
- Valid CSS used for layout. Tables used only for their true and original purpose: the presentation of tabular data such as that found in spreadsheets, address books, stock quotes, event listings, and so on
- Valid XHTML 1.0 Strict or Transitional (or HTML 4.01 or 5) used for markup
- Emphasis on structure. No presentational hacks in markup (Strict) or as few as possible presentational hacks in markup (Transitional)
- Structural labeling/abstraction of design elements—"Menu" rather than "Green Box"
- DOM-based scripting for behavior: if you need to fork your code, then sniff for object support, not browser versions
- Accessibility attributes and testing

Why You Should Care

Strict forward compatibility—CSS layout plus valid, semantic markup—is recommended for today's web, and the wide array of standards-compliant browsers that populate it. By adopting the techniques outlined above, you'll allow noncompliant browsers to access your content, but perhaps not every element of your site's branding and behavior. The US Navy site designed by Campbell-Ewald [2.20] combines pure CSS layout and XHTML 1.0 Strict markup with bits of Flash content to keep things interesting.

Benefits

- Forward compatibility: increased interoperability in existing and future browsers and devices (including mobile devices).
- Reaches more users with less work.
- No versioning.

2.20

The U.S. Navy (**www. navy.com**) is strict. XHTML 1.0 Strict, that is. Its site, designed by Campbell-Ewald, uses CSS, not tables, for lay-out (and mixes in a little Flash).

2.21

And just because we're apparently on a patriotic kick, the 2009 incarnation of the White House web-site (**www.whitehouse. gov**) is code we can believe in. XHTML 1.0 Transitional structures the content, CSS drives the presentation, and some DOM-based JavaScript adds a touch of behavior.

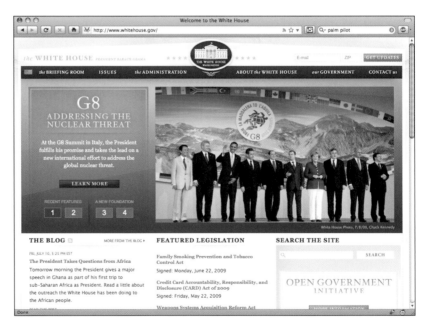

- Fewer accessibility problems. The content of sites so designed is generally accessible to all.

- Restores elegance, simplicity, and logic to markup.

- Restores document structure to documents.

- Faster, easier, less expensive production and maintenance—because sites cost less to produce and maintain, low budgets can avoid strain, while higher budgets (if available) can be put into writing, design, programming, art, photography, editing, and usability testing.

- Easier to incorporate into dynamic publishing and template-driven content-management systems.

- CSS layout makes possible some designs that cannot be achieved with HTML tables.

- Sites will continue to work in future browsers and devices.

Things to Consider

- Sites are likely to look quite plain in old browsers.

- Even in 2009, browser support for CSS is imperfect: some workarounds ("CSS hacks") may be required, mostly for older versions of Internet Explorer.

- DOM-based behaviors will not work in 4.0 and earlier mainstream browsers or in screen readers, text browsers, and most wireless devices; but if you're building with an eye toward progressive enhancement, then users without JavaScript will still be able to benefit from your content (more on this later).

Part II explains how standards work (individually and collectively) and offers tips and strategies to solve design and business problems related to various types of web development. But before we delve in, let's pause to consider some questions that might already have occurred to you.

If standards increase interoperability, enhance accessibility, streamline production and maintenance, reduce wasted bandwidth, and lower costs, why aren't all designers and developers using web standards correctly and consistently on every site they create?

Why aren't all clients clamoring for standards compliance the way inmates in old prison movies rattle tin cans against the bars of their cells when they want better chow? Why was it necessary for me to write this book or for you to read it, let alone beg your clients, colleagues, bosses, and vendors to read it? Why, six years later, was it necessary to write a third edition, and why were there still plenty of non-standards-compliant sites being created? Why aren't web standards more widely understood and used?

One reason is lack of knowledge. You can counter this ignorance and become a superb ambassador for web standards simply by building lean, accessible, fast-loading sites whose content can be easily found by search engines. Showing by doing—advocating by delivering results—will win you respect from team-mates, managers, and clients. Creating sites that work harder for more users, more easily accomplish business goals, and are simpler and less expensive to maintain and update will not only help you evangelize web standards, it may also lead to a promotion and new clients.

The other reason many sites on the web still don't seem to have grokked standards is that some site owners, managers, and IT directors object to the use of web standards, typically on dubious grounds that don't stand up to the light of investigation and reason. If your boss or client tells you that you can't use web standards for one ridiculous reason or another, it's your job to persuade them otherwise. Fortunately, the next chapter tells you how.

chapter three

Gentle Persuasion

This may be the shortest book chapter you'll ever read. It is certainly the shortest thing I've written, if you don't count that note apologizing for eating all the blueberries. But although it is brief, this chapter is value packed, for in it you will find the objections employers, colleagues, and clients raise to designing with standards—and the things you can say and do in response. I can't promise that your boss or client's objections to standards-based web design will melt like ice cream on a hot grill, but at least they'll thaw. The rest is up to you.

Objection: "We are standardized on IE6."

What to say: "Wonderful! Then we can use standard HTML, CSS, and JavaScript in our site."

What to do: Design with web standards, as this book advises. Develop your layout in a competent browser such as Firefox 3+, IE8+, Opera 10+, or Safari 4+, and then add the minimum number of workarounds necessary to make the design—or a close proximity of the design—work in older versions of IE. (Such workarounds are described in Part II of the book.) By "close proximity of the design," I mean make sure the general look and feel render accurately in IE6, and don't worry about niceties like rounded corners, indented paragraphs, and drop-caps. Alternately, craft a simple design that works the same way in all browsers (including IE6), then layer in additional flourishes, such as rounded corners, indented paragraphs, and drop-caps for more capable browsers—a design process known as *progressive enhancement*. As a third possibility, in some cases you may wish to craft a simple IE6 visual experience that differs from the design you show every other browser. For details on this approach, turn back to the discussion of "Universal Internet Explorer 6 CSS" in the "Modern Browsers and Web Standards" section of Chapter 1.

Objection: "We are standardized on IE7."

What to say: "Wonderful! Then we can use standard HTML, CSS, and JavaScript in our site."

What to do: Do the same thing as in the preceding example, but with less worry about IE6.

Objection: "We need to save our money for SEO (search engine optimization)."

What to say: "Wonderful! That's what lean, audience-appropriate copy and clean, semantic markup deliver best."

What to do: Explain how structured, accessible markup delivers search engine results. (If you can't explain it, photocopy a few pages out of this book—just don't tell my publisher.)

Objection: "Isn't Flash (or other proprietary technology) better supported across platforms?"

What to say: "That's a common misconception. Flash certainly has its place as a video delivery system or as a component in the experience layer, but you can't beat (X)HTML, CSS, and JavaScript for maintainability and extensibility. In today's browsers, design and scripting are as well supported across platforms with standards as they are in Flash. And you can't beat web standards for SEO and accessibility."

What to do: Show a complex site rendering beautifully in IE, Firefox, Safari, and Opera, on Linux, Mac OS, and two generations of Windows. That will knock down the belief that only Flash can do this. Pick a site with sophisticated interactivity, and show how that same site, unobtrusively scripted via web standards, can perform well in the absence of JavaScript—something a Flash site can't do in the absence of Flash. As for SEO (findability) and accessibility, let Google's search results tell that story for you. Although it is possible to make Flash sites findable and accessible, few Flash developers bother to do so. By contrast, even marginally talented HTML-slingers can use semantic markup and good title authoring to score with search engines. To all but the most biased eyes, the win is clear.

Objection: "Our site has to look the same in all browsers."

What to say: "What research are we basing this requirement on, and how far back do we go?"

What to do: Be smoothly yet firmly persuasive. Marketing people, brand directors, and CEOs are most likely to put out this mandate. You can reason with all of them, as long as you base your arguments on business rationales, not standards evangelism.

First, gently find out what the advertising director actually means when he says the site must look the same in all browsers. In some rare, fortunate cases, all he really means is that the logo has to display correctly. Most often, of course, brand folks really do mean that the site has to look and work exactly the same way in IE6 as it does in IE8. (Why IE? People who make this argument are unlikely to talk about Firefox, Opera, or Safari.)

If they're only talking about IE6—not Netscape 4 or IE5—then design with standards as described above, using progressive enhancement to add details in newer, more capable browsers, and secure your client or boss's permission to omit those tiny details from the IE6 user's experience. If the site looks good and works well in IE6, and if you are honest and clear about the small details that are being omitted (and can explain the decision to withhold those details on the grounds of site maintenance and bandwidth) an executive who is a grownup will grant approval.

Of course, that grownup executive may need your help moving from "no" to "OK." For instance, you might need to show the same page coded two ways: first lean and semantic, and then with loads of meaningless markup required to make things like rounded corners work in IE6. Calculate the additional bandwidth used by the less semantic version. Multiply the waste by the site's stats, and create a dollars-and-cents cost per year. It won't guarantee that the executive sees things your way, but it's a start, and you'll be speaking language the executive understands.

Create a spreadsheet showing the potential difference in page load time for every user, paying particular attention to dial-up and slow DSL users. Point to studies showing that the more slowly a page loads, the more likely the user is to leave without reading the company's message (Jakob Nielsen calls slow load time "the number one design mistake") and ask if it makes sense to lose page views and customers merely to enforce the same pixel-for-pixel details in every browser.

Study the site's logs to see how many people are using IE6; if it's under 20%, you can make the argument that it's silly to punish 80% of users with a slower-than-necessary experience in order to show 20% of users a few minor visual details they probably don't care about anyway. (Don't spend too much time pushing the point that users don't care about small visual details, though; after all, at other stages of the design process, you'll doubtless make the point that small visual details matter a lot.)

If your executive is still not sold, ask her how many IE6 users she thinks are likely to open the site in Firefox 3.5 and IE6 and compare visual details in side-by-side browser windows. No one but a web developer is likely to engage in that kind of visual quality assurance test. Clearly, those who insist on pixel-for-pixel sameness across browsers are designing to meet the needs of less than 1% of their users—namely the freaks who consciously compare site design rendering in multiple browsers. To squander time, money, and bandwidth catering to such a minority—and to risk losing customers by doing so—does not make business sense.

Remind her, too, that as more of her customers access the web via mobile phones, they are becoming accustomed to seeing different versions of the same site: mobile.nytimes.com versus nytimes.com, m.flickr.com versus flickr.com, and so on [**3.1**, **3.2**]. Seen in this light, an outdated browser merely becomes one of a range of possible site viewing tools.

3.1
Readers accept that the mobile version of the New York Times online looks and behaves differently...

3.2
...from the "desktop browser" version of the same website. The ever wider use of mobile devices has trained people to accept differing versions of the same website. This is good news for developers fighting the client mindset that every site must look identical in all browsers.

If users accept that your site is different in an old phone, a smart phone, and a modern browser, they should also shrug off (or not even notice) a slightly different visual experience in an old browser.

With a sophisticated executive, you might even raise the subtler point that every site user always has a unique experience based on his interests and choices. A pleasing range of possible visual experiences is simply par for the course—or should be. Assuming you've used a standard information architecture/user experience process to develop the site in the first place (or to drive the latest redesign), the executive signed off on the notion that different users have different needs when she embraced user personas leading to different user pathways. In the same way that a university site is designed to offer "Student," "Teacher," "Alumnus," and "Donor" different experiences, it's equally logical that people using old and new browsers might have somewhat different visual experiences. Most people who own or manage a site understand and accept user personas because the practice, although rooted in the psychology of needs, has connections to marketing and demographics. It's a short gap from "different user experiences are okay" to "different visual experiences may be okay, too." A wise businessperson, brought along respectfully, can probably make the jump.

If none of this helps—if your boss or client insists on standing athwart the axis of history—two options remain:

- Consider a simpler design—one that will work in multiple platforms without requiring endless reams of meaningless markup. If platform discussion and the demand for pixel precision are part of the initial requirements discovery, then it's good environmental stewardship to aim for a look and feel that can be coded with a minimum of waste. (Such a design may actually be preferable to an overwrought drop-shadow and gradient-fest anyway.)

- If a simpler design is also out of the question, use as many semantic hooks and as few hacks as you can, and carefully document every dumb `div` in your markup, so that next year, or two years from now, when the percentage of people using old browsers has changed, you can go back in and replace the crud with lean, clean code.

What do you do if the person telling you the site has to look and behave the same in all browsers means anything older than IE6? For instance, what do you do if the client tells you he has "standardized" on Netscape 4 or IE5? Obviously, you find another client. And in your resignation letter, be sure to include a link to dowebsitesneedtolookexactlythesameineverybrowser.com [**3.3**].

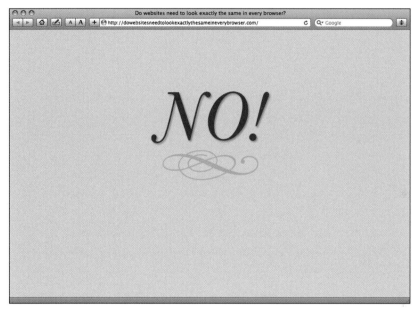

3.3
This lovely site answers the musical question, "do websites need to look exactly the same in every browser?"

chapter four

The Future of Web Standards

Like the chapter we've just read, the first part of this chapter is for bosses, clients, the head of IT, the new director of marketing, and anyone else who doesn't yet see the connection between web standards and their organization's long-term health. For this is where we connect the dots between web standards, "Web 2.0," Search engine optimization (SEO), and other industry-leading ideas that can make even a businessperson who is indifferent to technology sit up and roll over.

This chapter is also for web designers and developers who want to understand what the best web standards have in common, where they came from, and where they (and we) are going. If you're excited (or worried) about HTML5, if you're relieved (or disappointed) that activity on XHTML 2 has ceased, or if you're a hard-working professional who has no idea what I'm talking about, this chapter is for you.

Let's start with the stuff your boss or client needs to know.

Findability, Syndication, Blogs, Podcasts, the Long Tail, Ajax (and Other Reasons Standards Are Winning)

Are you bosses, clients, IT folks, and marketers listening? Here's what you need to know: despite misunderstandings that stymie their adoption in some quarters, standards are winning on many fronts and are rapidly changing technology, business, and publishing on and off the web. Indeed, web standards have played a defining role in just about every market-changing, money-making digital innovation of the past five years.

Take podcasts. Or take blogs (please!). Even the assistant to the lower middle manager of marketing has heard of *those*. What makes them run? RSS—an XML application. What else does this XML application do? It helps traditional newspapers and magazines migrate their content to the one place more and more people are reading it—namely, the web.

Maybe the new director of marketing has been reading about "long-tail" marketing, where small sales add up to big bucks. In October 2004, *Wired* editor-in-chief Chris Anderson, who is also the curator of the TED conference, discovered that "more than half of Amazon's book sales come from outside its top 130,000 titles…. [Thus] the market for books that are not even sold in the average bookstore is larger than the market for those that are" (www.wired. com/wired/archive/12.10/tail.html).

The web is where people with obscure tastes can find niche products the local shop can't afford to carry. Who will best ride the long tail? Those whose content is most easy to discover. Peter Morville, co-creator of modern information architecture, calls this success-fueling quality "findability."

To make their products findable on the web, companies spend millions on search engine optimization. Yet some companies that can't afford to spend a dime on SEO nevertheless do brilliantly with search engines and long-tail sales. Their secret? They write lean, keyword-rich, buzzword-free content that's actually relevant to their customers—and let semantic markup as described in this book push their text to the top of the digital data pile. Coupled with appropriately written and edited copy, CSS layout and structural XHTML are the golden keys to findability. Companies that know this are prospering.

Those that don't are falling behind. (For the fate of those who worship SEO but ignore the value of semantic markup, see the Twitter screen shot in this book's preface—and feel free to print those words on T-shirts, mugs, and bumper stickers.)

If the web looked moribund in 2000, it and the internet are once again blossoming—and, in spite of turmoil in other economic sectors, sprouting pretty flowers of cash—thanks to new ideas and new technologies powered by web standards. Not least of these technologies is Extensible Markup Language (XML), an all-embracing data format that's been almost universally adopted and adapted to meet complex needs.

The Universal Language (XML)

The Extensible Markup Language standard (www.w3.org/TR/REC-xml) took the software industry by storm when it was introduced in February 1998. For the first time, the world was offered a universal, adaptable format for structuring documents and data, not only on the web, but everywhere. The world took to it as a lad in his Sunday best takes to mud puddles. Although the "XML web" anticipated by futurists has not come to pass (in hindsight, the prediction that XML will replace HTML looks rather like flying cars and time machines), specific XML applications *have* transformed and revitalized the medium, and XML has supercharged the consumer and professional software businesses.

XML HAS THREE DADDIES

Tim Bray, Jean Paoli, and C. M. Sperberg-McQueen gave the world XML. An annotated version (www.xml.com/axml/testaxml.htm) *by Mr. Bray provides deep insights into XML and SGML and even a few chuckles.*

XML and HTML Compared

Although it's based on the same technology that gave rise to HTML (and though, just like HTML, it uses tags, attributes, and values to format structured documents), XML is quite different from the venerable markup language it was intended to replace.

HTML is a basic language for marking up web pages. It has a fixed number of tags and a small set of somewhat inconsistent rules. In HTML, you must close some tags, mustn't close others, and might or might not want to close still others, depending on your mood. This looseness makes it easy for anyone to create a web page, even if they don't quite know what they're doing—and that, of course, was the idea.

It was a fine idea in the early days, when the web needed basic content and not much else. And at heart, it will always be a fine idea, for the democratizing power of the web consists precisely in its low access barrier. But for today's larger, more sophisticated sites, where pages are assembled via publishing tools and content must flow back and forth from database to web page to mobile device to print, the lack of uniform rules in HTML may impede data repurposing. It's easy to convert text to HTML, but it's difficult to convert data marked up in HTML to any other format.

Likewise, HTML is merely a formatting language, and not a particularly self-aware one. It contains no information about the content it formats, again limiting your ability to reuse that content in other settings. (Microformats, discussed later, represent one fairly successful attempt to enrich the semantics of HTML.) And, of course, HTML is strictly for the web.

XML-based markup, in contrast to HTML, is bound by consistent rules and is capable of traveling far beyond the web. When you mark up a document in XML, you're not merely preparing it to show up on a web page. You're encoding it in tags that can be understood in any XML-aware environment.

One Parent, Many Children

Specifically, XML is a language for creating other languages. As long as they adhere to its rules, librarians are free to create XML markup whose custom tags facilitate the needs of cataloging. Music companies can create XML markup whose tags include artist, recording, composer, producer, copyright data, royalty data, and so on. Composers can organize their scores in a custom XML markup language called MusicML. (To avoid carpal tunnel syndrome, I'll refer to "creating XML markup" as "writing XML" from here on.)

These custom XML languages are called *applications*, and because they are all XML, they are compatible with each other. That is, an XML parser can understand all these applications, and the applications are able to easily exchange data with one another. Thus, data from a record company's XML database can end up in a library's catalog of recordings without human labor or error and without bogging down in software incompatibilities.

An Essential Ingredient of Professional and Consumer Software

This power to format, understand, and exchange data has made XML as ubiquitous as Coca-Cola. XML not only stores content housed in online and corporate databases, but it also has become the *lingua franca* of database programs like FileMaker Pro and of much non-database-oriented software, from high-end design applications to business products like Microsoft Office and OpenOffice, whose native file formats are XML-based.

Print design powerhouses Quark XPress and Adobe InDesign import and export XML and support the creation of XML-based templates. Web editors such as Dreamweaver are likewise XML-savvy, making it easier (or at least possible) to bounce data back and forth between the printed page, the web layout, and the database that runs your online store or global directory.

Not content to merely parse XML, some products are actually made of the stuff. Dreamweaver has long been built with XML files that are available to the end user, making it possible to modify the program by rolling up your shirtsleeves and editing these files. As far back as 2002, a popular *A List Apart* article by Carrie Bickner (www.alistapart.com/articles/dreamweaver) explained how to make Dreamweaver 4 (yes, Dreamweaver 4) generate valid XHTML by editing the XML files on which the software was built. Selling customized versions of Dreamweaver is something of a cottage industry. Heck, it's more than a cottage. I know a guy who bought a house with the money he made doing it.

Consumer software loves XML, too. The Personal Information Manager on your PC, Mac, or PDA reads and writes XML or can be made to do so via third-party products. When your digital camera time-stamps a snapshot and records its dimensions, file size, and other such information, it most likely records this data in XML. Each time your dad emails you those pipe-clobbering 7MB vacation photo sets, he's likely sending you XML-formatted data along with the beauty shots of lens caps at sunset. Hey, your dad's into web standards.

Image management software like Apple's iPhoto understands XML, too. And when you print a family photo, the print comes out right thanks to presets stored as XML data by the Macintosh OS X operating system. (Indeed, the whole UNIX-based OS X operating system stores its preferences as XML.) Apple's iTunes for Windows and Mac is hip to the jive as well. Export a playlist? XML.

More Popular Than a White Rapper

Why has XML seized the imagination of so many disparate manufacturers and found its way into their products? XML combines *standardization* with *extensibility* (the power to customize), *transformability* (the power to convert data from one format to another), and relatively seamless data exchange between one XML application (or XML-aware software product) and another.

As an open standard unencumbered by patents or royalties, XML blows away outdated, proprietary formats with limited acceptance and built-in costs. The W3C charges no fee when you incorporate XML into your software product or roll your own custom XML-based language. Moreover, acceptance of XML is viral. The more vendors who catch the XML bug, the faster it spreads to other vendors, and the easier it becomes to pass data from one manufacturer's product to another's.

Plus, XML works. Gone are the days when your officemates considered you a guru if you were able to beat plain, tab-delimited text out of one product and import it into another (often with some data loss and much manual reformatting). XML helps vendors build products whose interoperability empowers consumers to work smarter, not harder. Consumers respond with their pocketbooks.

Not a Panacea, But Plays One on TV

I'm not saying that XML is a panacea for all software problems. The data in a JPEG is much better expressed in binary format than as text. Nor do I claim that every software package on the market "gets" XML, although most professional applications and many consumer products do, and their numbers are continually growing. I'm not even saying that all software that claims to support XML does so flawlessly. (Not even on the web. As mentioned elsewhere in this book, the chief gripe against XHTML, the XML version of HTML, is that Internet Explorer treats it as HTML.) But flawlessly implemented or not, XML is the web standard that has most transformed the software industry and the hardware we use in our homes and workplaces.

Even the makers of products that don't support XML seem to believe they should. In April 2002, distressed by lackluster sales and a fragmented middleware market, a group of interactive television and technology providers banded together under the banner of the iTV Production Standards Initiative (www. itvstandards.org). Its mission: to unveil—and shore up support for—an XML-based standard intended to "allow producers to write interactive content once and distribute it to all major set-top box and PC platforms." Sound familiar? It's exactly what The Web Standards Project had to say about W3C standards during the browser wars of the mid- to late 1990s.

Builds Strong Data Five Ways

On the web, XML is increasingly the format of choice for IT professionals, developers, and content specialists who must work with data housed in large corporate or institutional systems. Choosy mothers choose XML for five reasons, many of which will be familiar from the preceding discussion:

- Like ASCII, XML is a single, universal file format that plays well with others.

- Unlike ASCII (or HTML), XML is an intelligent, self-aware format. XML not only holds data; it can also hold data about the data (metadata), facilitating search and other functions.

- XML is an extensible language: it can be customized to suit any business or academic need, or used to create new languages that perform specific tasks, such as data syndication or the delivery of web services.

- XML is based on rules that ensure consistency as data is transferred to other databases, transformed to other formats, or manipulated by other XML applications.

- Via additional XML protocols and XML-based helper languages, XML data can be automatically transferred to a wide variety of formats, from web pages to printed catalogs and annual reports. This transformational power is the stuff developers could only dream about before XML came along. Nor do corporate bean counters fail to appreciate the cost-saving efficiencies that XML facilitates.

A Mother Lode of Inventions

While a complete discussion of XML is outside the scope of this book, the examples that follow will suggest the depth of XML acceptance on and beyond the web and illustrate how the continual emergence of new XML-derived languages and protocols solves problems that once daunted even the brainiest developers.

Resource Description Framework (`www.w3.org/RDF`)

This XML-based language provides a coherent structure for applications that exchange metadata on the web. In practical terms, RDF integrates library catalogs and directories; collects and syndicates news, software, and all kinds of content; and facilitates communication and sharing between various types of collections (such as personal photo and music collections, to steal an example from the write-up on W3C's site). The power of RDF can also drive software. If you happen to have the Mozilla browser available on your desktop, open its folders and sniff around. You'll find RDF (and CSS) files that help the browser do its job. Specifically, dig around in the profile folders. Each profile has its own set of XML-based files.

RDF can be a frustrating, obtuse language—but in the right hands, it empowers beautiful creations. Jo Walsh (`frot.org`) has done remarkable work annotating geospatial relationships with RDF (`space.frot.org`). And in a single essay on RDF-powered taxonomies, writer Paul Ford made the notion of a "semantic" web real to thousands of designers for whom it had previously seemed so much airy piffle (`www.ftrain.com/arbs_and_all.html`). For more RDF fun facts, see Tim (Mr. XML) Bray's "What Is RDF?" at XML.com (`www.xml.com/pub/a/2001/01/24/rdf.html`).

RDFa (`www.w3.org/TR/xhtml-rdfa-primer`)

The W3C intends RDFa to serve as a bridge between the "human and data webs." Like microformats (although disliked by some in the microformats community), RDFa adds semantics to (X)HTML using existing elements such as `a` and `rel`. For a friendly overview, spend a pleasant half hour with Mark Birbeck's "Introduction to RDFa" (`www.alistapart.com/articles/introduction-to-rdfa`) and "Introduction to RDFa Part II" (`www.alistapart.com/articles/introduction-to-rdfa-ii`).

Extensible Stylesheet Language Transformations (`www.w3.org/TR/xslt`)

This XML-based markup language can extract and sort XML data and format it as HTML or XHTML, ready for immediate online viewing. If you prefer, XSLT can transform your data to PDF or plain text or use it to drive a continuously updateable chart or similar business image rendered in the Scalable Vector Graphics (SVG) format. XSLT can even do all these things simultaneously. For a hands-on tutorial, see J. David Eisenberg's "Using XML" (`www.alistapart.com/articles/usingxml`).

Rich Site Summary 2.0 (`blogs.law.harvard.edu/tech/rss`)

I see the marketing folks are with us again. Rich Site Summary (RSS) is a lightweight XML vocabulary for describing websites. I can use it to tell you when I update my site's content. More radically (and more appealingly to a marketer), I can also use it to send you the content. Remember those meetings you slept through, where people yakked about making your site "sticky"? This is way better. Instead of you hoping your readers will stick around your site, with RSS your content sticks to your readers.

In ancient times, Dan Libby developed RSS to populate AOL/Netscape's "My Netscape" portal. (No, I don't remember it either.) After AOL lost interest in April 2001, Dave Winer's UserLand Software Company carried the spec forward. Winer later left UserLand for academic pastures, and the RSS spec is now housed under a Creative Commons license at Harvard's Berkman Center (`cyber.law.harvard.edu`).

Today RSS 2.0 is streamed from millions of personal and corporate sites, blogs, and social media networks, making it possibly the most widely accepted XML format on the web [4.1, 4.2, 4.3]. Its simple, powerful syndication empowers both blogging and podcasting (see sticky note "You Got Your Podcast in My Webcast!"). All blog-authoring software supports RSS 2.0 along with a competing specification called Atom. There are aggregators (sites or products that "harvest" RSS feeds) and there are services that alert search engines when you update (`www.pingomatic.com`).

YOU GOT YOUR PODCAST IN MY WEBCAST!

Podcasts are audio programs that can be downloaded to your computer for your Apple iPod (hence the name), iPhone, or MP3 player for listening in the gym, in the car, or while flying between continents. While you're online, RSS 2.0 alerts your receiving device to the presence of updated content you've subscribed to, typically also initiating the download and triggering the erasure of the previous podcast. Like blogs, podcasts can be created by anyone; "amateurs" are responsible for some of the most popular podcasts, just as they are also behind some of the most-read blogs.

4.1

Standards-compliant blogging platforms such as WordPress support RSS out of the box (**www. wordpress.org**).

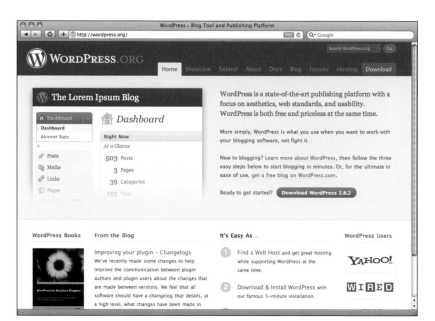

4.2

Same goes for Movable Type (**www. movabletype.org**).

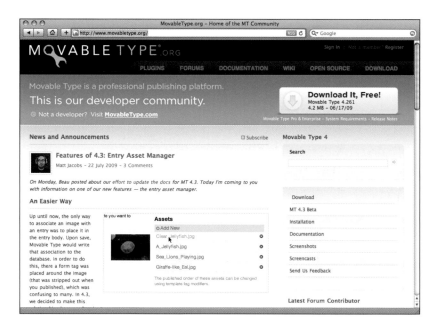

4.3
Social media media
networks from Twitter
to Flickr (shown here)
allow friends to "fol-
low" each other via RSS
(**www.flickr.com**).
When I publish a photo,
my friends who've sub-
scribed to my feed see
the new photo in their
RSS reader. OK, I just
wanted to get a picture
of my kid into this edition.
Do you blame me?

Publishers use RSS to stay in contact with existing readers and continually
reach new ones. And not just small, forward-thinking independent publishers do this. The *USAToday* website publishes RSS feeds (content.usatoday.
com/marketing/rss/index.aspx). So do the BBC [4.4], Amazon, and Yahoo
(developer.yahoo.com/rss/#biglist). *Wired News* and the *New York Times*
(www.nytimes.com/services/xml/rss/index.html) do it. Even birds in the
trees do it. There are RSS feeds for individual sections of newspapers and blogs
[4.5] and for the discussions of individual articles (www.alistapart.com/
feed/hattrick/rss.xml).

It's a publisher's dream, a marketer's joy, and a salesperson's revenue stream.
(To the disgust of many and the relief of salespeople and advertisers who see
their traditional TV and newspaper outlets declining, more and more RSS
feeds include paid advertisements.)

XMLHttpRequest — It's not just for Ajax any more (en.wikipedia.org/ wiki/XMLHttpRequest)

Created by Microsoft as part of ActiveX for Internet Explorer/Windows but now
also supported as a native object in Apple's Safari and in Mozilla and Opera
browsers, the XMLHttpRequest Object works with JavaScript to fetch XML
data from servers without forcing a page refresh. Rich user experiences can be

4.4
Like all modern news sites, that of the BBC enables readers to subscribe to a variety of feeds from News Front Page and World to Sci-Tech (a video feed) and Latest Published Stories. The BBC site is salutary in not merely dumping these feeds on a page, but actually explaining them to the uninitiated (**news.bbc.co.uk/2/hi/help/rss/default.stm**).

4.5
Choose which part of Jason Santa Maria's website you wish to subscribe to (**www.jasonsantamaria.com**).

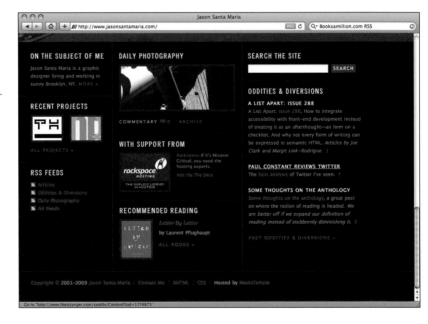

fashioned from the uninterrupted interactivity this combination of technologies provides. In a widely read essay, consultant Jesse James Garrett named this approach to application development *Ajax* (`www.adaptivepath.com/publications/essays/archives/000385.php`); the acronym helped the method gain traction in the marketplace.

When you hear marketers, investors, and developers discussing "Web 2.0" applications, they most often mean products built using XMLHttpRequest, XML, and JavaScript and displayed in pages designed in CSS and structured in XHTML. As the third edition goes to press, Ajax has pretty much cornered the rich applications market; it is also the power behind social networking sites from Facebook to Flickr.

And XMLHttpRequest is not just for Ajax any more. HTML, JSON, text, and more can be sent asynchronously, providing hours of fun for geeks of all ages (`www.hedgerwow.com/360/ajax/rss-json/demo.php`). In fact, they always could be—we just didn't bother until Ajax made it sexy by bringing the feeling of desktop applications to the web. Note that Ajax helped JSON take off as an alternative to XML. JSON is now spoken natively by most backend web technologies, including PHP and Ruby on Rails.

XML-RPC (`www.xmlrpc.com`)

Another UserLand Software innovation, XML-RPC is "a spec and a set of implementations that allow software running on disparate operating systems [and]… in different environments to make procedure calls over the internet." Among other things, XML-RPC can be used to automate site-management tasks in web publishing tools like those described next.

Web Publishing Tools for the Rest of Us

As this brief survey shows, that which the XML-aware software products described earlier do at a price, XML-based languages in the hands of clever developers do for free. In turn, these developers often create new products to facilitate the needs of their fellow designers, developers, and authors.

Personal publishing products like WordPress [4.1] and Movable Type [4.2] employ XML-RPC to facilitate site management and XML RSS to automatically syndicate and distribute content to other XML-aware sites. If WordPress and Movable Type grant their users the power to publish, XML gives these products the ability to exist.

As personal publishing (including podcasting—see sticky note "You Got Your Podcast in My Webcast!") spreads, so does XML, not only among sophisticated developers but also among those who've never heard of the XML standard and would be hard pressed to write XML (or sometimes, even HTML) on their own.

At Your Service(s)

The logic of XML drives the web services market, too. The XML-based Simple Object Access Protocol (www.w3.org/TR/soap) facilitates information exchange in a decentralized, platform-independent network environment, accessing services, objects, and servers, and encoding, decoding, and processing messages. The underlying power of XML allows SOAP to cut through the complexity of multiple platforms and products.

SOAP is only one protocol in the burgeoning world of web services (www. w3.org/2002/ws). David Rosam (www.dangerous-thinking.com) defines web services thusly:

> Web Services are reusable software components based on XML and related protocols that enable near zero-cost interaction throughout the business ecosystem. They can be used internally for fast and low-cost application integration or made available to customers, suppliers, or partners over the Internet.

That's excellent from a business point of view, but what makes web services magical is their inclusion of libraries called APIs (en.wikipedia.org/wiki/API) that let one web service spawn an endless number of derivative works—most often supported by GNU (www.gnu.org/copyleft/gpl.html) or Creative Commons (www.creativecommons.org) licensing to ensure that the "child" products will be free of legal encumbrance.

Because Google Maps (maps.google.com), Flickr [4.3], and Amazon.com sport APIs, independent developers can spin decentralized services using centralized data. In 2005, Chicago-based journalist and web developer Adrian Holovaty, co-creator of the open-source Django Web framework (www. djangoproject.com) created one of the first, pre-API Google Map mashups, chicagocrime.org [4.6]. The site played a small part in influencing Google to open its map API. Holovaty took things a step further with EveryBlock [4.7], "an experiment in microlocal news." Taking the idea of decentralization one

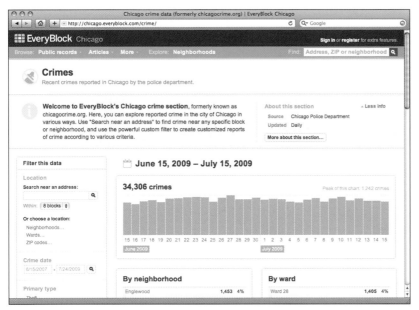

4.6
They stand on the APIs of giants. EveryBlock's Chicago Crime section (**chicago.everyblock.com/crime**), formerly at chicagocrime.org, connects crimes reported by the Chicago police department to their locations, mapped by Google. Invented by Adrian Holovaty, it was one of the first, pre-API Google Map mashups, and helped encourage Google to open its map API.

4.7
EveryBlock (**www.everyblock.com**), the natural extension of chicagocrime.org, combines the worlds of data and journalism via the power of web standards. Is this the newspaper of the future?

step further, Apple's Dashboard Widgets are consumer-written applications—built with XHTML, XML, CSS, and standard JavaScript—that pull remote data to your desktop (`www.apple.com/downloads/dashboard`).

What makes Widgets and sites like EveryBlock so exciting is our knowledge that they are only the beginning of a great creative outpouring. They are like the one-reel silent movies of the late 19th century: interesting in themselves, explosive in their implications for the future.

XML Applications and Your Site

XML is the language on which Scalable Vector Graphics (`www.w3.org/TR/svg`) and Extensible Hypertext Markup Language (`www.w3.org/TR/2002/REC-xhtml1-20020801`) are based. Illustrators who export their client's logo in the SVG format and web authors who compose their pages in XHTML are using XML, whether they know it or not.

The rules that are common to all forms of XML help these formats work together and with other kinds of XML—for instance, with XML stored in a database. An SVG graphic might be automatically altered in response to a visitor-generated search or continuously updated according to data delivered by an XML news feed.

The site of a local TV news channel could use this capability to display live metro traffic in all its congested glory. As one traffic jam cleared and another began, the news feed would relay this information to the server, where it would be formatted as user-readable text content in XHTML and as an updated traffic map in SVG. At the same time, the data might be syndicated in RDF or RSS for sharing with other news organizations or used by SOAP to help city officials pinpoint and respond to the problem.

Although based on XML, SVG graphics are easy to create in products like Adobe Illustrator (`www.adobe.com/illustrator`). Like Flash vector graphics, images created in SVG can fill even the largest monitors while using little bandwidth. And SVG graphics, like other standard web page components, can be manipulated via Standard JavaScript and the DOM. Not to mention that SVG textual content is accessible by default, and can even be selected with the cursor no matter how it's been stretched or deformed. Firefox supports SVG natively.

Compatible by Nature

Because they share a common parent and abide by the same house rules, all XML applications are compatible with each other, making it easier for developers to manipulate one set of XML data via another and to develop new XML applications as the need arises, without fear of incompatibility.

Ubiquitous in today's professional and consumer software, widely used in web middleware and backend development, and essential to the web services market, XML has succeeded beyond anyone's wildest dreams because it solves everyone's worst nightmares of incompatibility and technological dead ends.

Software makers, disinclined to risk customer loss by being the odd man out, recognize that supporting XML enables their products to work with others and remain viable in a changing market. Executives and IT professionals, unwilling to let proprietary systems continue to hold their organizations' precious data hostage, can solve their problem lickety-split by converting to XML. Small independent developers can compete against the largest companies by harnessing the power of XML, which rewards brains, not budgets.

In today's data-driven world, proprietary formats no longer cut it—if they ever did. XML levels the playing field and invites everyone to play. XML is a web standard, and it works.

And that is the hallmark of a good standard: that it works, gets a job done, and plays well with other standards. Call it interoperability (the W3C's word for it), or call it cooperation between components. Whatever you call it, XML is a vast improvement over the bad old days of proprietary web technologies. Under the spell of web standards, competitors, too, have learned to cooperate.

The Future of Standards

Thanks to The Web Standards Project, browser makers learned to support the same standards. As an unexpected consequence of their technological cooperation, these once-bitter competitors have also learned to play nicely together in other, often surprising ways.

In July 2002, Microsoft submitted to the W3C's HTML Working Group "a set of HTML tests and testable assertions in support of the W3C HTML 4.01 Test Suite Development" (lists.w3.org/Archives/Public/ www-qa-wg/2002Jul/0103.html). The contribution was made on behalf of

Microsoft, Openwave Systems, Inc., and America Online, Inc., then-owners of Netscape and Mozilla. Opera Software Corporation (makers of the Opera browser) and The Web Standards Project also reviewed it.

Test Suites and Specifications

W3C test suites enable browser makers to determine if their software complies with a standard or requires more work. No test suite existed for HTML 4.01 (the markup language that is also the basis of XHTML 1.0). In the absence of such a test suite, browser makers who wanted to comply with those standards had to cross their fingers and hope for the best.

Moreover, in the absence of a test suite, the makers of standards found themselves in an odd position. How can you be certain that a technology you're inventing adequately addresses the problems it's supposed to solve when you lack a practical proving ground? It's like designing a car on paper without having a machine shop to build what you've envisioned.

In the interest of standards makers as well as browser builders, a test suite was long overdue.

How Suite It Is

When Microsoft took the initiative to correct the problem created by the absence of a test suite, it chose not to act alone, instead inviting its competitors and an outside group (WaSP) to participate in the standards-based effort. Just as significantly, those competitors and that outside group jumped at the chance. The work was submitted free of patent or royalty encumbrance, with resulting or derivative works to be wholly owned by the W3C. Neither Microsoft nor its competitors attempted to make a dime for their trouble.

In the ordinary scheme of things, Microsoft was not known for considering what was best for Netscape, nor was Netscape overly interested in helping Microsoft—and neither wasted many brain cells figuring out what was good for Opera. And these companies didn't go into business to lose money on selfless ventures. Yet here they were, acting in concert for the good of the web, and focusing not on some fancy new proprietary technology, but on humble HTML 4.

Ignored by the trade press, the event signified a sea change. The "set of HTML tests" quietly presented to the W3C by Microsoft and its staunchest business foes signaled a permanent shift in the way the web would now evolve. No longer ignored in deference to proprietary "innovations," web standards now bind browser makers together.

It was only natural and logical that the next step would be for browser makers to take "joint innovation" to the next level by creating web standards together instead of passively waiting for the W3C. Combine uncertainty about the direction of XHTML 2.0, impatience with the W3C process, and a Web 2.0-driven preference for *applications* over *documents*, and what happened next was inevitable.

HTML5: Birth of the Cool

In 2005, under the leadership of Ian Hickson, engineers from the Mozilla Foundation and Opera Software formed the Web Hypertext Application Technology (WHAT) Working Group (www.whatwg.org), "a loose, unofficial, and open collaboration of Web browser manufacturers and interested parties" whose goal is "to address the need for one coherent development environment for Web applications, through the creation of technical specifications that are intended to be implemented in mass-market Web browsers."

Although its parent organizations, including the Mozilla Foundation and the Opera Software company, are among the W3C's greatest contributors, the engineers who formed WHAT were frustrated by the sometimes slow pace of W3C standards development. The group's emphasis on practical, browser-related issues, and its preference for HTML over XML, initially set it apart from the W3C. But WHAT chose to work with the W3C, not against it, quickly submitting the first draft of its proposed HTML5 language to the W3C for approval.

By working across company lines and tackling focused areas—for instance, specifying how all browsers should handle RDF controls, menus, and toolbars—the WHAT group hopes to fast-track web standards and rationalize browser development so all browsers uniformly support ever-more-advanced standards.

We'll explore the *mechanics* of HTML5 in Chapter 7, "HTML5: The New Hope." For now, it's sufficient to discuss some of the language's goals and the way they break from the markup of the present.

A New Semantics in Town

Although CSS is a layout language, it is not a semantic one, and nothing about it suggests page structure. HTML and XHTML are document languages that contain outline structure but no hint of page structure. HTML5 (www.whatwg.org/html5) sets out to change that—and to rid the world of "div soup"—by introducing page layout elements such as header, nav, footer, section, and aside. Lachlan Hunt's "A Preview of HTML 5" (www.alistapart.com/articles/previewofhtml5) explains with simple, elegant clarity the intention behind such elements. In the same article, he explains how HTML5's proposed enhancements to form controls, APIs, and multimedia will "give authors more flexibility and greater interoperability."

Lachlan Hunt is a fan of HTML5; John Allsopp is on the fence. In "Semantics in HTML 5" (www.alistapart.com/articles/semanticsinhtml5), he explains why:

> We need mechanisms in HTML that clearly and unambiguously enable developers to add richer, more meaningful semantics—not pseudo semantics—to their markup. This is perhaps the single most pressing goal for the HTML 5 project.
>
> But it's not as simple as coming up with a mechanism to create richer semantics in HTML content: there are significant constraints on any solution. Perhaps the biggest one is backward compatibility. The solution can't break the hundreds of millions of browsing devices in use today, which will continue to be used for years to come. Any solution that isn't backward compatible won't be widely adopted by developers for fear of excluding readers. It will quickly wither on the vine.
>
> The solution must be forward compatible as well. Not in the sense that it must work in future browsers—that's the responsibility of browser developers—but it must be extensible. We can't expect any single solution we develop right now to solve all imaginable and unimaginable future semantic needs. We can develop a solution that can be extended to help meet future needs as they arise.
>
> These two constraints in tandem, present a huge challenge. But in the context of a language whose major iterations arrive a decade apart, and whose importance as a global platform for communication is paramount, this is a challenge that must be solved.

Additional concerns about HTML5 include worries that its tolerance of bad HTML will stymie the movement toward the kind of clean, structured, semantic markup which this book advocates and many developers now practice; concerns that it places the future of the web in the hands of a small group with fairly (or unfairly) fixed ideas; and questions about the process. (Presently, two groups are working on HTML5 simultaneously: the WHATWG, chaired by Mr. Hickson, and a W3C working group, also chaired by Mr. Hickson. If Mr. Hickson adds an element to HTML5 in the WHATWG, the W3C group also chaired by Mr. Hickson may take it out again. The classic "Who's On First?" routine is funny when presented by Abbott and Costello, but troubling when the future of markup hangs in the balance.)

The July 2, 2009, announcement by the W3C that it was discontinuing all work on XHTML 2 (`www.w3.org/News/2009#item119`) was humane in that it put XHTML 2 out of its misery. But it made those who find parts of HTML5 questionable all the more uneasy, and left some standardistas wondering whether XHTML had been a dead end (`www.zeldman.com/2009/07/07/in-defense-of-web-developers`). (It hasn't been: XHTML 1.0 will still be working long after you and I retire, and the best ideas from XHTML 2.0 are being incorporated into HTML5. Moreover, HTML5 will support HTML *and* XHTML syntax—although even that bothers some people.)

While this book still cheerfully recommends XHTML 1.0 Transitional or Strict (as it did in the first two editions), it behooves every designer to learn HTML5 and start working with those parts of it that all modern browsers support. Whether you confine your HTML5 exploration to a personal project or use it on a "real" website (as we have on aneventapart.com) is up to you, your client, your browser stats, and the kinds of sites you design. Those who work chiefly on web applications are most likely to desire the power of HTML5.

Internet Explorer and Web Standards

As companies go, only Apple is more secretive than Microsoft. Thus it represented a hopeful break from the past in 2005 when, instead of developing its next browser version in secret, Microsoft worked with The Web Standards Project to ensure that IE7 supported web standards more accurately than any Microsoft browser had before.

Microsoft worked with The Web Standards Project again as it prepared to release its masterpiece of standards compliance, IE8. Comedy ensued as the company vacillated between shipping the browser in standards-compliance mode by default (at the risk of causing scripting and CSS errors in old-school websites optimized for IE only) and using a `meta` declaration to toggle Standards mode on (thus failing to support standards unless developers explicitly treat IE as a special case and opt in). There were reasonable arguments to be made on both sides, but when it comes to Microsoft and web standards, nobody feels like arguing reasonably. Sacrificing a goat in a roomful of kindergarteners would have gone down with less protest than has attended this on-again, off-again toggle tug-of-war.

For details, see Aaron Gustafson's "Beyond DOCTYPE: Web Standards, Forward Compatibility, and IE8" (`www.alistapart.com/articles/beyonddoctype`), the article that announced that IE8 would provide advanced standards support on an opt-in basis. Follow it, if you wish, with Eric Meyer's "From Switches To Targets: A Standardista's Journey" (`www.alistapart.com/articles/fromswitchestotargets`), Jeremy Keith's "They Shoot Browsers, Don't They?" (`www.alistapart.com/articles/theyshootbrowsers`), and Jeffrey Zeldman's (hey, that's me!) "Version Targeting: Threat or Menace?" (`www.alistapart.com/articles/minorthreat`). On a positive note, all major browsers now beautifully support HTML 4.01, XHTML 1.0, CSS1, CSS2.1, standard JavaScript, and the DOM—the very things The Web Standards Project demanded (but little expected to see come to pass) when we formed the group in 1998.

Where IE is concerned, the trick for standards-based designers and developers is to decide precisely what "supporting" IE6 users means on the one hand, and determining whether to use CSS 3, which Firefox, Safari, and Opera support (but even IE8 does not), on the other. Your decision and your mileage may vary. We'll have more to say about all this in Part II.

Authoring and Publishing Tools

Developed at the height of the browser wars, a market-leading, professional visual editor like Adobe Dreamweaver initially addressed the problem of browser incompatibility by generating markup and code optimized for 3.0 and

4.0 browsers. When browsers ran on nonstandard, invalid HTML tags, that's what Dreamweaver created. As browsers shored up their standards support, tools like Dreamweaver needed to do likewise. In 2001, with help from The Web Standards Project, it did.

The Web Standards Project's Dreamweaver Task Force, led by Drew McLellan and Rachel Andrew, was created in 2001 to help Dreamweaver's engineers improve the standards compliance and accessibility of sites the tool produces. The Task Force's history can be found at `www.webstandards.org/act/ campaign/dwtf`. Among the group's objectives were these:

- Dreamweaver should produce valid markup "out of the box." (Valid markup uses only standard tags and attributes and contains no errors.)

- Dreamweaver should allow the choice between XHTML and HTML versions, inserting a valid DTD for each choice. (A DTD, or Document Type Definition, tells the browser what kind of markup has been used to author a web page. See Chapter 5.)

- Dreamweaver should respect a document's DTD and produce markup and code in accordance with it.

- Dreamweaver should enable users to easily create web documents accessible to all.

- Dreamweaver should render CSS 2 to a good level of accuracy so that pages formatted with CSS can be worked on within the Dreamweaver visual environment.

- Dreamweaver should not corrupt valid CSS layouts by inserting inline styling without the user's consent.

- Dreamweaver users should feel confident that their Dreamweaver-created pages will validate and have a high level of accessibility.

Released in May 2002, Dreamweaver MX achieved these objectives, and the product's standards support has improved ever since.

In 2006, Molly Holzschlag of The Web Standards Project worked with Microsoft to ensure the standards compliance of its visual web editor, Expression Web Designer (`www.microsoft.com/products/expression`). The product supports XHTML out of the box and provides CSS comparable to Dreamweaver's.

No visual editor can match hand coding for smart CSS and semantic markup. But pros who like working with visual editors have two standards-compliant options to choose from. (WaSP also worked with Microsoft to improve the compliance of Visual Basic Studio.)

The Road to Joy Is Paved with Validation

Today, more and more designers are using web standards to create sites that are beautiful, usable, and accessible. More and more developers are using them to bring new products and new ideas to the digital marketplace. Ajax is the new black, findability trumps animation, and the modern social contract is written in (X)HTML, CSS, and JavaScript. Yet (X)HTML/CSS validation is rarely achieved on large-scale commercial sites, even when the initial templates validate and the client and designers are fully committed to supporting W3C specifications.

Outdated content management systems and compromised databases cause many of these validation errors. Others come from third-party ads served with invalid methods and improper URL handling. But understanding why an otherwise responsible standards-based site fails to achieve perfect validation is not the same as condoning the neglect of web standards by CMS makers and advertising services.

For the web to progress to its full potential, publishing tools must become standards compliant. Site owners and managers must tell CMS vendors and ad-service managers that compliance matters, just as designers and developers once told browser makers. When enough customers do this, the vendors will upgrade their products, and 99.9% of websites will be begin to leave obsolescence behind.

Part II

5   Modern Markup   95

6   XHMTL and Semantic Markup   111

7   HTML5: The New Hope   135

8   Tighter, Firmer Pages Guaranteed:
Structure and Semantics   149

9   CSS Basics   165

10   CSS Layout: Markup, Boxes, and Floats—Oh My!   185

11   Working with Browsers Part I:
DOCTYPE Switching and Standards Mode   217

12   Working with Browsers Part II:
Bugs, Workarounds, and CSS3's Silver Lining   229

13   Working with Browsers Part III: Typography   265

14   Accessibility Basics: The Soul of Web Standards   295

15   Working with DOM-Based Scripts   321

16   A Site Redesign   341

17   NYMag.com: Simple Standards, Sexy Interfaces   365

chapter five

Modern Markup

Part I outlined the creative and business problems engendered by old-school web design methods, sketched the benefits of designing with standards, and painted a cheery picture of standards-powered advances in the medium. The rest of this book will move from the general to the particular. The best way to start is by taking a second look at the fundamentals of web markup—including which language we should use, and just how we should mark up such familiar elements as headlines, paragraphs, and lists (hint: semantically).

Many designers and developers will balk at the thought of reconsidering markup. Surely those of us who've spent more than a few weeks designing professional sites know all there is to know about dumb old HTML. Shouldn't we spend our limited free time learning newer, more powerful languages? For instance, isn't it more important to study server-side technologies like PHP, Ruby on Rails, ASP, or Cold-Fusion (see sidebar) than to piddle away precious hours rethinking rudiments like the HTML table or paragraph tag?

The answer is yes and no. Server-side technologies are essential to the creation of dynamic sites that respond to user queries. Even traditional informational sites often benefit from storing their content in databases and fetching it as needed via PHP or similar technologies. Nearly every modern site, including the humblest personal blog, functions this way. Like the standards this book discusses, server-side scripting languages and web-based frameworks such as Ruby on Rails, CakePHP, Django, and Symfony abstract data from the interface. Just as CSS frees the designer from the need to imprison each snippet of content in semantically meaningless table cells, languages like PHP and relational database management systems like MySQL free site creators from the drudgery of creating each page by hand.

What Is This Thing Called PHP?

PHP (www.php.net) is an open source, general-purpose scripting language that is well suited to web development and can be embedded in HTML and XHTML (the reverse is also true). Its syntax draws upon C, Java, and Perl and is comparatively easy to learn. PHP (which stands, rather confusingly, for PHP: Hypertext Preprocessor) has many capabilities but has become vastly popular for one: when used in combination with a MySQL (www.mysql.com) database, it lets designers and developers easily author dynamic sites or build web applications.

PHP is free, which is one reason for its popularity. Another is the language's wide array of profiling and debugging tools. Open source developers and independent designers are enamored of the language—or were, until they got a load of its hot young cousin Ruby—and use it to push pages and power products [5.1, 5.2]. Because of its scalability (not to mention the free price) big companies, rarely known for embracing open source, have come to love PHP. For example, PHP has powered Yahoo.com since 2002 (most recently via the Symfony open source PHP framework [www.symfony-project.org]), and IBM has thrown its might behind PHP via Zend and the CakePHP framework (www.internetnews.com/ent-news/article.php/3485806).

PHP can run with Microsoft's server software, but it's most often used in combination with the Apache server. Apache works on both Windows and (most commonly) UNIX. Apple's UNIX-based Mac OS X operating system includes PHP and the Apache server, as do almost all Linux distributions.

PHP does not require that the front end of a website be built with CSS layout and valid, semantic markup, but where you find standards-based web pages, you will also often find PHP behind them.

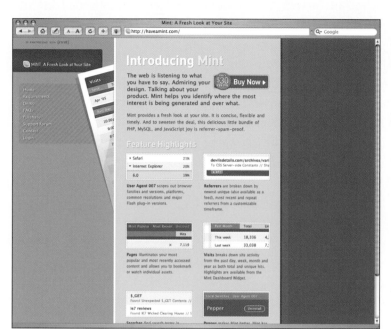

5.1
Designer/coder Shaun Inman used PHP, MySQL, JavaScript, and CSS to make Mint (**www. haveamint.com**), an extensible reporting tool that tells you who's visiting and linking to your site, what browser they're using, and much more.

5.2
A typical Mint installation. (This one is from the An Event Apart conference site.)

But those dynamically generated web pages won't be much use if they are inaccessible, incompatible with a broad range of browsers and devices, or cluttered with junk markup. If those dynamic pages don't render in some browsers and devices, or if they take sixty seconds to load over dial-up when ten seconds might suffice, the server-side technologies won't be doing all they can for you or your users. And if people and search engines can't find your site because you've buried your content in semantically meaningless junk markup, all your fine editorial work and design and all those clever backend capabilities will be like brilliant musicians playing to an empty hall.

What is Rails?

Ruby on Rails (www.rubyonrails.org) is an open source web framework optimized for fast, productive, sustainable coding [5.3]. What's Ruby? Glad you asked. Ruby is an object-oriented programming language created by Yukihiro Matsumoto in 1995 and distributed as free software under an open source license. It combines Perl- and Ada-inspired syntax with object-oriented features, and also shares features with Lisp and Python.

So what's Rails? Rails is an MVC (model-view-controller) framework, written in Ruby by David Heinemeier Hansson, that was extracted from 37signals's Basecamp project management application [5.4] in July 2004. (Version 1.0 was released as open source in December 2005.) Developers have jumped on it because they believe that its guiding principles liberate them to write better code, faster.

In most programming environments, you'd write a dozen lines of code to move a variable onto (or off of) the screen. And you'd do this every time you sit down to create a new program, for every little thing your program might need to do. It's like having to build a word processor every time you want to write a business letter. Ruby on Rails junks that model. Within Rails, developers no longer need to code every tiny detail; they only configure what is unconventional. Like PHP, Rails does not require a standards-compliant front end, but the two go together more often than not. A combination of XHTML, CSS, JavaScript, and Ruby on Rails powers popular web applications like Twitter [5.5]. Traditional web application sites like yellowpages.com [5.6] are also Ruby on Rails (and XHTML) fans. Other languages, such as PHP and Python, offer MVC frameworks similar to Rails (as mentioned above).

5.3
Ruby on Rails (**www.rubyonrails.org**), an open source development framework. Its guiding principles include "DRY—Don't Repeat Yourself" and "Convention Over Configuration."

5.4
37signals's Basecamp (**www.basecamphq.com**) is the gift that keeps on giving. Not only is it a dandy project management application, it's also the app from which Rails was abstracted.

(continues on next page)

(continued from previous page)

5.5
Twitter (**www.twitter.com**), an insanely popular messaging service, is built with CSS, XHTML 1.0 Strict, and Ruby on Rails.

5.6
Let your fingers do the walking through the Yellow Pages (**www.yellowpages.com**), powered by Ruby on Rails and XHTML 1.0 Transitional.

In short, it's not an "either/or," but a "both." Server-side technologies and databases facilitate smarter, more powerful sites, but what those sites deliver is content that works best when it is semantically and cleanly structured. And that's where many of us (and many of the content management systems we rely on) fall short.

Other Platforms, Other Rooms

Microsoft Active Server Pages .NET 2.0 (www.asp.net) and Adobe Cold-Fusion 8 (www.adobe.com/products/coldfusion) are two other scripting platforms used to deliver dynamic web content and build sexy web apps. Each has its own strengths and its own passionate user community. JavaServer Pages (JSP), another dynamic technology, is most commonly found in huge enterprise systems and is way beyond the scope of this book.

Publishing systems built in some of these languages can break your standards-compliant templates unless you take care. In one application with which my agency was involved, ASP (pre .NET 2.0) rendered everything invalid until we inserted HTML Tidy (tidy.sourceforge.net) into the flow. This was like throwing mud at clean clothes and then hosing them down, but it enabled us to beat valid web pages out of a system that was inimical to good, clean code. Apart from Tidy, using custom tools such as TinyMCE (tinymce.moxiecode.com) or WYMEditor (www.wymeditor.org) as part of your CMS can help a great deal on the content entry end. Quasi-markup languages like Dean Allen's Textile (www.redcloth.org/hobix.com) and John Gruber's Markdown (www.daringfireball.net/projects/markdown) can also help site owners who aren't HTML wizards avoid writing standards-unfriendly markup.

The Secret Shame of Rotten Markup

During our industry's first decade, designing for the web was like feeding a roomful of finicky toddlers. To build sites that worked, we dutifully learned to accommodate each browser's unique dietary requirements. Today's browsers all eat the same nutritious stuff, and have done since 2001; but many professionals *still* haven't grasped this and continue crumbling M&Ms into the soufflé.

Bad food hardens arteries, rots teeth, and diminishes the energy of those who consume it. Bad markup is equally harmful to the short-term needs of your users and the long-term health of your content. But until recently, this fact was hidden from many of us by the high junk-code tolerance of most popular browsers, as discussed in Chapter 1.

In this chapter and those that follow, we'll investigate the forgotten nature of clean, semantic markup and learn to think structurally instead of viewing web markup as a second-rate design tool. At the same time, we'll examine XHTML 1.0, the current standard language for marking up web pages, discussing its goals and benefits and developing a strategy for converting from HTML to XHTML. We'll also begin considering HTML5 (www.w3.org/TR/htm15), the new kid on the block.

BAD URL SYNDROME

Scripting languages often generate long URLs that include raw ampersands, an HTML/ XHTML no-no. In HTML and XHTML, the ampersand character (&) is used to denote entities, such as ’, *which is Unicode for the typographically correct apostrophe. This can be fixed by using a ColdFusion function called* URLEncodedFormat(). *ASP has a similar function called* HTMLEncode. *And PHP offers* urlencode() (us3.php. net/manual/en/function.urlencode.php), rawurlencode() (us3.php.net/ manual/en/function.rawurlencode.php)*, and* htmlentities() (us3.php. net/manual/en/function.htmlentities.php)*. In all cases, developers can (and should) avoid the problem by passing their URLs through the function before outputting them.*

By a strange coincidence, proper XHTML authoring encourages structural markup and discourages presentational hacks. In XHTML 1.0 Transitional, such hacks are "deprecated," which means you can use them if you must, but you are encouraged to achieve the same design effects in other ways—for instance, by using CSS. In XHTML 1.0 and 1.1 Strict, presentational hacks are actually forbidden: use them and your page will no longer pass muster when you run it through the W3C's Markup Validation Service, familiarly known as "the Validator" [5.7]. (If it's not familiar to you now, it will become so as you learn to design and build with standards. See the "Validate This!" sidebar.)

5.7
Designers and developers may use the W3C's free online Validation Service (**validator. w3.org**) to make sure their pages comply with standards.

5.8
It may not be lovely to look at, but Validator.nu is a powerful validation tool that can validate XML, HTML5, etc. (**www.validator.nu**).

Validate This!

The W3C's Validation Service (validator.w3.org) can test web pages built with HTML 4.01, XHTML 1.0, and XHTML 1.1 to be certain they conform to spec. Its CSS Validation Service (jigsaw.w3.org/css-validator) does the same for your style sheets. The Web Design Group at htmlhelp.com maintains an equally reliable markup validation service (www.htmlhelp.com/tools/validator). All three services are offered at no charge.

Tip: Advanced geeks, if you're getting busy with HTML5, not every validation service will be up to the task of accurately validating your work. One service that is capable of validating HTML5 is at validator.nu [**5.8**]. The W3C's Validation Service now validates HTML5 as well. Enjoy!

Whether you choose XHTML Strict or Transitional, time and again you'll have the humbling experience of discovering that "everything you know is wrong." Line breaks (br) you've scattered like snowflakes to simulate a list; headers you've deployed "to force a display issue" instead of to convey hierarchical stature within an implied outline; transparent spacer pixel GIF images you've used to create whitespace: you'll find yourself shucking off these husks and many others.

Instead of presentational hacks, you'll begin to think structurally. You'll let markup be markup. Even in transitional layouts that use a few presentational tables or other deprecated elements, you'll learn to do more with CSS, such as banishing complex and redundant table cell color and alignment attributes from your XHTML and replacing them with one or two rules in a global style sheet. As we relearn web markup, we can also unlearn years of bad habits. So let's delve in, shall we?

A Reformulation of Say What?

According to the W3C, "XHTML (www.w3.org/TR/xhtml1) is a reformulation of HTML in XML." In plainer if slightly less precise English, XHTML is an XML-based markup language that works and looks like HTML with a few small but significant differences. To web browsers and other user agents, XHTML 1.0 works exactly the same way as HTML, although some sophisticated modern browsers might treat it a bit differently, as we'll see in the next chapter. To designers and developers, writing XHTML 1.0 is almost the same as writing HTML, but with slightly tighter house rules and one or two new elements, to be covered next.

Earlier in this book, we described XML, aka Extensible Markup Language, as a "super" markup language from which programmers can develop other custom markup languages. XHTML (Extensible Hypertext Markup Language) is one such markup language. XHTML 1.0 is the first and most backward-compatible version of XHTML, hence the most comfortable version to learn and the least troublesome to browsers and other user agents.

Additional applications and protocols based on XML are legion, and their popularity is partially due to their ability to exchange and transform data with relatively little effort and few (if any) compatibility hassles—a virtue they share with XHTML. Among these protocols are Rich Site Summary—better known simply as RSS (`blogs.law.harvard.edu/tech/rss`), Scalable Vector Graphics (`www.w3.org/TR/SVG`), Synchronized Multimedia Integration Language (`www.w3.org/TR/SMIL`), and Resource Description Framework (`www.w3.org/RDF`). (More about these languages may be found in Chapter 4.)

Each of these protocols plays a role in the emerging web, but none has been as vital to designers and developers as XHTML—and none is as easy to learn.

Why "reformulate" HTML in XML or anything else? For one thing, XML is consistent where HTML is not. In XML, if you open a tag, you must close it again. In HTML, some tags never close, others always do, and still others can close or not at the developer's discretion. This inconsistency can create practical problems. For instance, some browsers might refuse to display an HTML page that leaves table cells unclosed even though HTML says it is okay not to close them. XHTML compels you to close all elements, thereby helping you avoid browser problems, save hours of testing and debugging, and stop wasting valuable neurons trying to remember which tags close and which don't.

More importantly, if you author your markup in an XML-based language, your site may work better with other XML-based languages, applications, and protocols.

If XML is that important, why create an XML-based markup language that works like HTML? XML is powerful and pervasive, but you can't serve raw XML data to most web browsers and expect them to do anything intelligent with it, such as displaying a nicely formatted web page. Indeed, older browsers would tinkle all over themselves if faced with raw XML. In essence, then, XHTML is a bridge technology, combining the power of XML (kind of) with the simplicity of HTML (mostly).

Executive Summary

Loosely speaking, XHTML is XML that acts like HTML in old and new web browsers and also works as expected in most internet devices, from ancient (1990s) Newtons to Palms and iPhones, making it portable, practical, and efficient.

XHTML is as easy to learn and use as HTML—a little easier for newcomers who have no bad habits to unlearn, and perhaps a little harder for old hands who embraced web design and development in the wild and wooly 1990s.

XHTML is the current markup standard (replacing HTML 4), and it's designed to return rigorous, logical document structure to web content, to work well with other web standards, such as CSS and the DOM, and to play well with other existing and future XML-based languages, applications, and protocols. We'll look at the benefits of XHTML after the short, but important, detour that follows.

STRICT OR TRANSITIONAL?

In the first two editions of this book, we recommended XHTML 1.0 Transitional, which is the most forgiving flavor of XHTML, the most compatible with traditional web development methods, and the easiest to learn and transition to. If you are unlearning old habits or gently updating an old site, XHTML 1.0 Transitional may be a good choice.

On the other hand, at this late date, most standardistas prefer to submit their markup to the more rigorous discipline of XHTML 1.0 Strict—or even, if they can work out a way to serve the proper MIME type to all browsers except Internet Explorer, XHTML 1.1 Strict. Choosing Strict as a default is partly a matter of fashion — it's a way to show the world (or at least that segment of the world that Views Source) that you're hardcore about web standards. Not that there's anything wrong with that.

XHTML 2—For Me and You?

As of the first edition of this book, a draft XHTML 2.0 specification had been presented to the development community for comment. As I began the third edition six years later, XHTML 2.0 was still a draft specification (www.w3.org/TR/xhtml2), and it had not been updated in three years. This might suggest that the world is not clamoring for XHTML 2, and in fact the specification, while it contained some fascinating ideas, never gained traction with the development community. On July 2, 2009, the W3C put XHTML 2 out of its misery (www.w3.org/News/2009#item119) and the web standards community went berserk (www.zeldman.com/2009/07/07/in-defense-of-web-developers).

XHTML 2.0 was about moving closer to a semantic ideal, even if it meant dumping existing development methods in the orphanage. Its initial draft was purist indeed. By design, XHTML 2.0 was not backward compatible with HTML or XHTML 1.0. It abandoned familiar conventions including the img element (object was to be used instead), the br tag (replaced by a new line element, which later became just l), and the time-honored anchor link, in whose stead we were offered a technology called hlink.

Developers complained so much about that one that in a later draft the a (anchor) element came back to us. But in revised XHTML 2, *any* page element or group of elements could have an href attribute. Many developers, it should be pointed out, *love* the idea that any element on a page can have an href; indeed, the same idea has made its way into HTML5, an XHTML 1.0 replacement that some of the kids actually like. The only trouble, so far, is that most browsers do not support an href on anything other than an a element.

As for img, it finally came back in XHTML 2 (www.w3.org/TR/xhtml2/mod-image.html#sec_20.1) but it was deprecated. We were still supposed to use object, even though object would not work in any version of Internet Explorer prior to IE8. (The polite way of viewing this is that IE8 finally supports object. Cool!)

Some greeted the initial XHTML 2 specification with little yelps of joy. Others complained that it smelled too much of ivory towers and too little of the trenches where sites get built. (Okay, that was probably me who said that.) Most designers paid it no mind at all. Six years later, all but a handful of bleeding-edge types were still ignoring it. Rather than support two "future of markup" languages, only one of which interested web developers, the W3C made the sensible decision to cease work on XHTML 2.0.

XHTML 2.0 may be dead, but don't let that worry you. No browser maker will stop supporting XHTML 1. For that matter, no browser maker intends to stop supporting HTML 4. Sites correctly authored to the HTML 4.01 specification will keep working for years to come. The same is true for sites properly authored in XHTML 1.

On the other hand, if HTML5 is to be the future language of website construction, why use XHTML? It's a fair question, and one that those of us who spent a decade promoting XHTML have asked ourselves in quiet watches of the night. If a final version of HTML5 were imminent, and if all of next year's browsers were going to support all the new elements in HTML5 (from page structure elements like `footer` to `hrefs-on-anything`), there might be little sense in bothering to learn XHTML on any grounds other than a slightly increased compatibility with XML applications on your site. But HTML5 is still unfinished, and Internet Explorer in particular does not support most of what is new in that language. So, for now, the choice between HTML and XHTML comes down to ten key points summarized in the following lists:

Top 5 Reasons to Stick With HTML

1. HTML works in all browsers, and all browsers (including IE) correctly support the HTML MIME type.

2. While HTML5 may not be finalized for years to come, parts of it work now in all modern browsers—making now a great time to begin learning about this powerful, upcoming version of HTML.

3. HTML is more forgiving of errors than XHTML.

4. HTML does not require as many formal closing elements as XHTML, and is therefore slightly lower in bandwidth. (And the HTML5 DOCTYPE uses the least bandwidth of any DOCTYPE.)

5. HTML5 is the first markup language designed with rich internet applications in mind, which is why huge internet companies like Google are prepared to bet the farm on it. If you work in the web application space, and if you're comfortable with the direction HTML5 is taking, now's the time to dive in.

As a bonus, the presence of an HTML DOCTYPE no longer automatically triggers Quirks mode in any current browser. While not an advantage over XHTML, the use of HTML no longer puts developers at a disadvantage by increasing the risk of unwanted Quirks mode. In Chapter 7, we'll survey the goals of HTML5, explore how it differs from XHTML, and take a closer look at its elements, rules, and syntax.

Top 5 Reasons to Use XHTML 1

1. XHTML is the current markup standard, replacing HTML 4.

2. XHTML is designed to work well with other XML-based markup languages, applications, and protocols—an advantage that HTML lacks.

3. XHTML is more consistent than HTML, so it's less likely to cause problems of function and display.

4. Authoring in XHTML can assist you in breaking the habit of writing presentational markup, and that in turn can help you avoid accessibility problems and inconsistencies of display between different manufacturers' desktop browsers. (If you write structural XHTML and place all or most of your visual flourishes in CSS, where they belong, you'll no longer be overly concerned about differences in the way Firefox and IE treat, say, empty table cells to which widths have been applied.)

5. Just as practicing to a metronome makes you a better musician, XHTML's emphasis on well-formedness and rules provides a perfect *social education platform* for designers and developers who have spent years writing semantically meaningless "tag soup" HTML. Even if you switch to HTML5 two or three years from now, you'll write cleaner, stronger markup for having learned semantics under strict conditions.

Top Reason Not to Use XHTML 1

1. You don't know the rules of XHTML.

Fortunately, we can do something about that. See Chapter 6.

chapter six

XHTML and Semantic Markup

I could have titled this chapter, "XHTML: Simple Rules, Easy Guidelines." For one thing, the rules and guidelines discussed in this chapter are simple and easy. For another, "simple" and "easy" are to web design books what "new!" and "free!" are to supermarket packaging—namely, hackneyed but effective attention-getting devices that stimulate interest and encourage trial.

And I certainly want to stimulate interest in and encourage trial of this chapter. Why? Because after you've grasped the simple, easy ideas it contains, you'll rethink the way web pages work—and begin changing the way you build them. And I don't mean you'll write this year's tags instead of last year's tags. I mean you'll genuinely think (and work) differently. "Simple Rules, Easy Guidelines" doesn't begin to cover all that.

On the other hand, "Attain Oneness with the One True Way in a Blinding Flash of Enlightenment," another chapter title I kicked around, seemed a bit too thick for its pants. And increasing the semantic richness and *findability* of web content is chiefly what XHTML (and this chapter) is about. So, "XHTML and Semantic Markup" it is.

In this chapter, we'll learn the ABCs of XHTML and explore the mechanics and implications of *semantic* versus *presentational* markup. If you've been incorporating web standards into your design/development practice, some of this material will be familiar to you. But even old hands might feel a *frisson* of surprise as they unlock the hidden treasures of this chapter.

Reading List

- *Ambient Findability: What We Find Changes Who We Become* by Peter Morville (O'Reilly, 2005) introduces the concept of findability and examines the convergence between information and connectivity from an information architecture and business perspective (www. amazon.com/Ambient-Findability-What-Changes-Become/ dp/0596007655). The author is a founding father of modern user experience design, having coauthored the groundbreaking and best-selling *Information Architecture for the World Wide Web* with Louis Rosenfeld.

- *Building Findable Websites: Web Standards, SEO, and Beyond* by Aarron Walter (New Riders, 2008) provides practical, web-standards-based techniques to help more people find your site, help users find content within your site, and encourage return visits (www. buildingfindablewebsites.com). It's a beautifully and simply written teaching tool, filled with practical, hands-on design and code examples. The author is a web designer, developer, college instructor, and lecturer, and a member of The Web Standards Project.

Converting to XHTML:
Simple Rules, Easy Guidelines

Converting from traditional HTML to XHTML 1.0 is quick and painless, as long as you observe a few simple rules and easy guidelines. (I really can't get enough of that phrase.) If you've written HTML, you can write XHTML. If you've never written HTML, you can still write XHTML. Let's zip through the basics, shall we? Here are the rules of XHTML.

Open with the Proper *DOCTYPE* and Namespace

XHTML documents begin with elements that tell browsers how to interpret them and validation services how to test them for conformance. The first of these is the DOCTYPE (short for "document type") declaration. This handy little code snippet informs the validation service which version of XHTML or HTML you're using. For reasons known only to a W3C committee member, the word DOCTYPE is always written in all caps—just like your dad's e-mail messages.

Why a *DOCTYPE*?

XHTML allows designers/developers to author several different types of documents, each bound by different rules. The rules of each type are spelled out within the XHTML specifications in a long piece of text called a document type definition (DTD). Your DOCTYPE declaration tells validation services and modern browsers which DTD you followed in crafting your markup. In turn, this information tells those validation services and browsers how to handle your page.

DOCTYPE declarations are a key component of compliant web pages; your markup won't validate unless your XHTML source begins with a proper DOCTYPE. In addition, your choice of DOCTYPE affects the way most modern browsers display your site. The results might surprise you if you're not expecting them.

XHTML 1.0 offers three yummy choices of DTD and three possible DOCTYPE declarations:

- **Transitional**—The comfortable, slightly frowsy DTD whose motto is "live and let live"

- **Strict**—The whip-wielding, mysteriously aloof DTD that flogs you for using presentational markup elements or attributes
- **Frameset**—The one with the 90s haircut; also the one that gives you the ability to use frames in your design, which comes to the same thing

Which *DOCTYPE* Is Your Type?

Of the three flavors listed in the previous section, XHTML 1.0 Transitional is the one that's closest to the HTML we old-time web designers know and love. That is to say, it's the only one that forgives presentational markup structures and deprecated elements and attributes.

The `target` attribute to the `href` link is one such bit of deprecated business. If you want linked pages to open in new windows—or even if you don't want that but your client insists—Transitional is the only XHTML DTD that lets you do so with the `target` attribute:

```
<p>Visit <a href="http://www.whatever.org" target=
"_blank">whatever.org</a> in a new window.</p>
```

```
<p>Visit <a href="http://www.whatever.org/" target=
"bob">whatever.org</a> in a named new window.</p>
```

To open linked pages in new windows under XHTML 1.0 Strict, you would need to write JavaScript, and you'd also need to make sure the links work in a non-JavaScript-capable environment. Whether you *should* force linked pages to open in new windows is beside the point here. The point is that XHTML 1.0 Transitional lets you do so with a minimum of fuss.

XHTML 1.0 Transitional also tolerates background colors applied directly to table cells and other such stuff you really ought to do with CSS instead of in your markup. If your DOCTYPE declaration states that you've written XHTML 1.0 Strict but your page includes the deprecated `bgcolor` attribute, validation services will flag it as an error—and some compliant browsers will ignore it (that is, they will not display the background color). By contrast, if you declare that you're following the XHTML 1.0 Transitional DTD, `bgcolor` will not be marked as an error, and browsers will honor it instead of ignoring it. (See? You're already beginning to learn how the presence of a particular DOCTYPE can affect what content is displayed, and *how* it is displayed, in a given browser.)

Strict vs. Transitional: The Great Battle of Our Times

Now, few readers of this book—especially of this third edition—have any great motivation to use the deprecated `bgcolor` attribute. (You'd only use something like that if you had to support, say, a large group of Netscape Navigator 3 users, and nobody reading this book should have to do that.) So why not just use XHTML 1.0 Strict on every project? The answer is, you can—if your project and process support standards all the way.

XHTML 1.0 Strict is a *great* choice when you know what you're doing, have complete control over your site, and are writing only structural, semantic markup—using CSS for presentation, and unobtrusive scripting to control behavior.

But Transitional is better when your partners have the ability to ding your beautiful standards-based canvas. For instance, Transitional may be better when you know that a poorly authored third-party content feed, such as an advertising or news feed, is going to sully your pristine structural markup with bad HTML. In 2009, alas, this still happens. Transitional is also a safer choice when a bad content management system (or a bad job of template integration in a good CMS) is going to spray your beautiful markup with ugly, invalid HTML. It may also be the best choice when your site's editorial staff has the power to dump bad HTML into your beautiful templates. (Depending on the CMS, and the way permission settings are configured, you can sometimes prevent Joe the Editor from turning into Joe the Template Butcher.)

To sum up, XHTML 1.0 Transitional is a perfect DTD for designers who are making the transition to modern web standards (they don't call it "transitional" for nothing) or when systems and people beyond your control have the power to damage your work. And Strict is for those who…

- Know what they're doing;
- Work to ensure their markup contains only structural and semantic elements—nothing presentational (no font tags, table layouts, or deprecated presentational elements and attributes) or behavioral (i.e., no inline JavaScript, no "JavaScript links"); and
- Enjoy the luxurious certainty of knowing that their work will not be tampered with by editors, clients, marketers, standards-unaware CMS systems, and inept future developers.

Hey! What About Frameset?

The Frameset DOCTYPE is used for those documents that have a frameset element in them; in fact, you *must* use this DOCTYPE with your frameset documents. Whether any developer should use frames is another great debate of our age, and the answer is no.

Hey, Where Do You Want This *DOCTYPE*?

The DOCTYPE declaration must be typed into the top of every XHTML document, before any other code or markup. It precedes the html element, the head element, the title element, the meta elements, and the links to style sheet and JavaScript files. It also, quite naturally, comes before your content. In short, the DOCTYPE declaration precedes everything.

(Standards-savvy readers might wonder why I haven't mentioned a scrap of code that can come before the DOCTYPE declaration: namely, the optional XML prolog. I'll get to it in a few paragraphs.)

XHTML 1.0 *DOCTYPE* Quick Guide

Here are the three XHTML 1.0 DOCTYPEs, along with typical use cases:

XHTML 1.0 Transitional

```
<!DOCTYPE html PUBLIC "-//W3C//DTD XHTML 1.0 Transitional//EN"
"http://www.w3.org/TR/xhtml1/DTD/xhtml1-transitional.dtd">
```

Use when transitioning to standards; when you need to use a few presentational HTML elements or inline scripts; or when systems or people outside your control have the power to damage your beautiful markup.

XHTML 1.0 Strict

```
<!DOCTYPE html PUBLIC "-//W3C//DTD XHTML 1.0 Strict//EN"
"http://www.w3.org/TR/xhtml1/DTD/xhtml1-strict.dtd">
```

Use when authoring pure semantic markup on a site over which you have full control.

XHTML 1.0 Frameset

```
<!DOCTYPE html PUBLIC "-//W3C//DTD XHTML 1.0 Frameset//EN"
"http://www.w3.org/TR/xhtml1/DTD/xhtml1-frameset.dtd">
```

Use when someone holds a gun to your head and forces you to use frames.

Follow *DOCTYPE* with Namespace

The DOCTYPE declaration is immediately followed by an XHTML namespace declaration that enhances the old-fashioned html element:

```
<html xmlns="http://www.w3.org/1999/xhtml" xml:lang="en"
lang="en">
```

A namespace in XML is a collection of element types and attribute names associated with a specific DTD, and the namespace declaration allows you to identify your namespace by pointing to its online location, which in this case is www.w3.org/1999/xhtml. The two additional attributes, in reverse order of appearance, specify that your document is written in English, and that the version of XML you're using is also written in English. The additional attributes are optional; your document will validate without them.

With the DOCTYPE and namespace declarations in place, your XHTML Transitional 1.0 page would start out like this:

```
<!DOCTYPE html PUBLIC "-//W3C//DTD XHTML 1.0 Transitional//EN"
"http://www.w3.org/TR/xhtml1/DTD/xhtml1-transitional.dtd">
<html xmlns="http://www.w3.org/1999/xhtml" xml:lang="en"
lang="en">
```

Cut, Paste, and Go!

If you dislike trying to type markup and code out of books, feel free to view the source at zeldman.com or *A List Apart* (www.alistapart.com) and copy and paste to your heart's content. (I don't mean feel free to copy and paste those sites' content and design, which are copyrighted, I just mean feel free to grab dull stuff like DOCTYPE and namespace declarations.)

Declare Your Character Set

To be correctly interpreted by browsers and to pass markup validation tests, all XHTML documents must declare the type of character encoding that was used in their creation, be it Unicode, ISO-8859-1 (also known as Latin-1), or what have you.

If you're unfamiliar with character encoding, or if ISO-8859-1 isn't ringing any bells, never fear: we'll discuss that stuff later in this chapter. (See the later section, "Character Encoding: The Dull, The Duller, and the Truly Boring.") For now, all you need to know is this: there are three ways to tell browsers what kind of character encoding you're using, but only one works reliably as of this writing, and it's not one the W3C especially recommends.

The XML Prolog (And How to Skip It)

Many XHTML pages begin with an optional XML prolog, also known as an XML declaration. When used, the XML prolog precedes the DOCTYPE and namespace declarations described earlier, and its mission in life is to specify the version of XML and declare the type of character encoding being used in the page.

The W3C recommends beginning any XML document, including XHTML documents, with an XML prolog. To specify ISO-8859-1 (Latin-1) encoding, for example, you would use the following XML prolog:

```
<?xml version="1.0" encoding="ISO-8859-1"?>
```

Nothing complicated is going on here. The prolog tells the browser that XML version 1.0 is in use and that the character encoding is ISO-8859-1. About the only thing new or different about the prolog is the question mark that opens and closes it, imbuing it with a lovely Spanish flavor.

Unfortunately, several browsers, even those from nice homes, can't handle their XML prolog. After imbibing this XML element, they stagger and stumble and soil themselves, bringing shame to their families and eventually losing their place in society.

Actually, the browsers go unpunished, and it's your visitors who suffer when the site fails to work correctly. In some cases, your entire site might be invisible to the user. It might even crash her browser. In other cases, the site does not crash, but it displays incorrectly. (This is what happens when IE6 encounters the prolog.) IE7 does better, in that it ignores the prolog, allowing valid XHTML sites with the proper DOCTYPE to display correctly (i.e. in Strict rather than Quirks mode—see Chapter 11, "DOCTYPE Switching and Standards Mode").

These days, IE6 (and older versions of IE) is just about the only browser that still chokes on or ignores the XML prolog. If your audience includes no (or nearly no) IE6 users, feel free to use the prolog. Otherwise, ignore the W3C recommendation to insert the troublesome prolog. Instead, specify character encoding by inserting a Content-Type `meta` element into the `head` of your document. To specify ISO-8859-1 encoding, type the following:

```
<meta http-equiv="Content-Type" content="text/html;
charset="ISO-8859-1" />
```

The beginning of your XHTML document would then look something like this:

```
<!DOCTYPE html PUBLIC "-//W3C//DTD XHTML 1.0 Transitional//EN"
"http://www.w3.org/TR/xhtml1/DTD/xhtml1-transitional.dtd">
<html xmlns="http://www.w3.org/1999/xhtml">
  <head>
<title>Transitional Industries: Working for Change</title>
<meta http-equiv="Content-Type" content="text/html;
charset="ISO-8859-1" />
  </head>
```

If you're working on an international site that will include a plethora of non-ASCII characters, you might author in Unicode and insert the following Content-Type element into your markup:

```
<meta http-equiv="Content-Type" content="text/html;
charset=UTF-8" />
```

Software developer/blogger Joel Spolsky recommends putting the `meta` element before the title; otherwise, the browser may parse the entire page, then re-parse it with the instructed encoding (`www.joelonsoftware.com/articles/unicode.html`). This isn't a problem if your web server is sending the proper `Content-Type` header.

You might also want to forget all the geeky details of the preceding discussion. Many designers know nothing about these issues aside from which tags to copy and paste into the tops of their templates, and they seem to live perfectly happy and productive lives.

Aside from one even geekier topic to be touched upon with merciful brevity a few pages from now, you have now waded through the brain-addling, pocket-protector-equipped portion of this chapter. Congratulations! The rest will be rich, moist cake.

Write All Tags in Lowercase

Unlike HTML, XML is case sensitive. Thus, XHTML is case sensitive. All XHTML element and attribute names must be typed in lowercase, or your document will not validate. (Validation ensures that your pages are error free. Flip back to Chapter 5, "Modern Markup," if you've forgotten about the free markup validation services offered by the W3C and the Web Design Group.)

Let's look at a typical HTML element:

```
<TITLE>Transitional Industries: Our Privacy Policy</TITLE>
```

You will recognize this as the TITLE element, and you will recognize the Privacy Policy page as the one nobody outside your legal department ever reads. Translating this element to XHTML is as simple as switching from uppercase to lowercase:

```
<title>Transitional Industries: Our Privacy Policy</title>
```

Likewise, P becomes p, BODY becomes body, and so on.

Of course, if your original HTML used lowercase element and attribute names throughout, you won't have to change them. But most of us learned to write our HTML element and attribute names in all caps, so we'll have to change them to lowercase when converting to XHTML.

HTML editors like Panic Coda (www.panic.com/coda), BareBones BBEdit (www.barebones.com/products/bbedit), and Optima System PageSpinner (www.optima-system.com/pagespinner), as well as visual editors like Adobe Dreamweaver, let you automatically convert tag and attribute names to lowercase, and the free tool HTML Tidy (see the upcoming sidebar, "Tidy Time") will do this for you as well.

Don't Worry About the Case of Attribute Values or Content

In the preceding example, notice that only the element name (title) converted to lowercase. "Transitional Industries: Our Privacy Policy" could stay just the way it was, initial caps and all. For that matter, the title element's content could be set in all caps (TRANSITIONAL INDUSTRIES: OUR PRIVACY POLICY) and would still be valid XHTML, although it would hurt your eyes to look at it.

Element and attribute names must be lowercased; attribute values and content need not be. All the following are perfectly valid XHTML:

```
<img src="/images/whopper.jpg" alt="Big John catches a
whopper." />
<img src="/images/WHOPPER.JPG" alt="Big John catches a
whopper." />
<img src="/images/whopper.jpg" alt="Big John catches a
Whopper and fries." />
```

Note that, depending on your server software, the filename mentioned in the src attribute might be case sensitive, but XHTML doesn't care. class and id values, on the other hand, are case sensitive.

Tidy Time

By far, the easiest method of creating valid XHTML pages is to write them from scratch. But much web design is really *re*design, and you'll often find yourself charged with updating old pages. Redesign assignments provide the perfect opportunity to migrate to XHTML, and you don't have to do so by hand. The free tool HTML Tidy (tidy.sourceforge.net), created by standards geek Dave Raggett and maintained as open source software by SourceForge, can quickly convert your HTML to valid XHTML.

There are online versions of Tidy as well as downloadable binaries for Windows, UNIX, various Linux distributions, Mac (OS 9 and OS X), and other platforms. Some versions work as plug-ins to enhance the capability of existing web software. For instance, BBTidy is a plug-in for BareBones Software's BBEdit (X)HTML editor. Each version offers different capabilities and consequently includes quite different documentation. Tidy might look simple, but it is a power tool, and reading the manual can save you grief.

Macromates TextMate (www.macromates.com) for Mac OS X includes Tidy as well as direct connections to the validator services in the HTML bundle. Lastly, the euphoniously named Jeffrey Zeldman's Web Standards Advisor (www.zeldman.com/x/19) offers semantic and structural advice while flagging errors and running validation services.

Be careful with mixed-case attribute names. If you use a WYSIWYG tool like Adobe Dreamweaver or an image editor like Adobe Fireworks or Adobe Photoshop's ImageReady to generate JavaScript rollovers, you may need to change the mixed-case onMouseOver to the lowercase onmouseover. Yes, really.

The following will get you into trouble:

```
onMouseOver="changeImages();"
```

But *this* is perfectly OK:

```
onmouseover="changeImages();"
```

(While this onmouseover example is OK from an XHTML validation point of view, it is *not* OK from the point of view of separating your site's structure from its behavior. To separate structure from behavior, use unobtrusive scripting and progressive enhancement, as described in Chapter 15.)

Quote All Attribute Values

In HTML, you needn't quote attribute values, but in XHTML, they *must* be quoted (height="55", *not* height=55). That's pretty much all there is to say about this one. Nice weather we're having.

OK, here's something else worth mentioning. Suppose your attribute value includes quoted material. For instance, what if your alt attribute value must read, "The Happy Town Reader's Theater Presents 'A Christmas Carol.'" How would you handle that? You would do it like this, of course:

```
<img src="/images/carol.jpg" alt="The Happy Town Reader's
Theater presents 'A Christmas Carol.'" />
```

If you preferred to get fancy and use the escape character sequences for typographically correct apostrophes and single and double quotation marks, you would do that like this:

```
<img src="/images/carol.jpg" alt="The Happy Town Reader&#8217;s
Theater presents &#8216;A Christmas Carol.&#8217;" />
```

Now that you are quoting attributes, you must separate your attributes with blank spaces. The following is an error:

```
<hr width="75%"size="7" />
```

This should, of course, be written as...

```
<hr width="75%" size="7" />
```

Note: The W3C validator flags the missing space error with the user-friendly, clear-as-day message, "XML Parsing Error: attributes construct error." And they wonder why the kids are on pot.

If, for some strange reason, you need straight quotes in an attribute value, use ", as in the following:

```
<img src="/images/hello.jpg" alt="Mrs. O&#8217;Hara says,
&quot;Hello&quot; to us." />
```

Quoting attribute values was optional in HTML, but many of us did it, so converting to XHTML often represents no work at all in that area. In an effort to trim their bandwidth, some commercial sites avoided quoting attribute values. Those sites will have to start quoting those values when they convert to XHTML.

HTML Tidy can quote all your attribute values automatically. In fact, it can automatically perform every conversion task mentioned in this chapter.

All Attributes Require Values

All attributes must have values; thus, the attributes in the following HTML:

```
<td nowrap>
<hr noshade>
<input type="checkbox" name="shirt" value="medium" checked>
```

...must be given values. The value *must* be identical to the attribute name.

```
<td nowrap="nowrap" />
<hr noshade="noshade" />
<input type="checkbox" name="shirt" value="medium" checked=
"checked" />
```

I know, I know. Looks weird, feels weird, takes getting used to—and runs directly counter to the principle of lean, structured, bandwidth-saving markup. HTML5, discussed in the next chapter, runs leaner. For instance, the following is valid HTML5:

```
<input disabled>
```

But, of course, it isn't valid XHTML.

Close All Tags

In HTML, you have the option to open many tags such as p and li without closing them. The following is perfectly acceptable HTML but bad XHTML:

```
<p>This is acceptable HTML but would be invalid XHTML.
<p>I forgot to close my Paragraph tags!
<p>But HTML doesn't care. Why did they ever change these darned
rules?
```

In XHTML, every tag that opens must close:

```
<p>This is acceptable HTML and it is also valid XHTML.</p>
<p>I close my tags after opening them.</p>
<p>I am a special person and feel good about myself.</p>
```

This rule—every tag that opens must close—makes more sense than HTML's confusing and inconsistent approach, and it might help avoid trouble nobody needs. For instance, if you don't close your paragraph tags, you might run into CSS display problems in some browsers. XHTML forces you to close your tags, and in so doing, helps ensure that your page works as you intend it to.

Close "Empty" Tags, Too

In XHTML, even "empty" tags such as br and img must close themselves by including a forward slash /> at the end of the tag:

```
<br />
<img src="zeldman.jpg" />
```

Note the slash /> at the end of the XHTML break tag. Then note the slash /> at the end of the XHTML image tag. See that a blank space precedes each instance of the slash to avoid confusing browsers that were developed prior to the XHTML standard. None of this is rocket surgery.

Nor does it require much (if any) work. Since 2001 or so, BBEdit, PageSpinner, and HomeSite have automatically added the required space and slash to "empty" tags if you tell these editors you're working in XHTML. Coda, Text-Mate, and visual web editing tools Adobe Dreamweaver (www.adobe.com/products/dreamweaver) and Microsoft Expression Web (www.microsoft.com/expression/products/Overview.aspx?key=web) do likewise.

Naturally, to remain valid and accessible, the image element in the second example would also include an `alt` attribute, and an optional `title` attribute wouldn't hurt:

```
<img src="zeldman.jpg" alt="Jeffrey Zeldman, author of
Designing with Web Standards." title="Jeffrey Zeldman, debonair
web designer and billionaire author of Designing with Web
Standards, now in its 400th printing." />
```

Now that is good XHTML.

No Double Dashes Within a Comment

Double dashes can occur only at the beginning and end of an XHTML comment. That means that these are no longer valid:

```
<!--Invalid -- and so is the classic "separator" below. -->
<!----------------------------------->
```

Either replace the inner dashes with equal signs, or put spaces between the dashes:

```
<!-- Valid - - and so is the new separator below -->
<!--===================================-->
```

Encode All < and & Characters

Any less-than signs (<) that aren't part of a tag must be encoded as `&lt;`, and any ampersands (&) that aren't part of an entity must be encoded as `&amp;`. Thus,

```
<p>She & he say that x < y when z = 3.</p>
```

must be marked up as this:

```
<p>She &amp; he say that x &lt; y when z = 3.</p>
```

Note: I recommend that you always encode > as `&gt;`. Even though you never *have* to encode it (with the exception of one highly esoteric circumstance), it is there for symmetry, and your markup will be easier for others to read if you use it.

Let's review the XHTML rules we've learned.

Executive Summary: The Rules of XHTML

- Open with the proper DOCTYPE and namespace.
- Declare your character encoding using the META Content element.
- Write all element and attribute names in lowercase.
- Quote all attribute values.
- Assign values to all attributes.
- Close all tags.
- Close "empty" tags with a space and a slash.
- Do not put double dashes inside a comment.
- Ensure that less-than and ampersand are < and &.

Viewed as a short list, the rules of XHTML look few and simple enough—and they are. One sadly dull additional point must be made before we move on to the good stuff.

Character Encoding: The Dull, the Duller, and the Truly Boring

In reading the second rule of XHTML in the preceding section ("Declare Your Content Type"), you might have asked yourself, "Why should I declare my content type?" You might even have asked yourself, "What is a content type?" The answers to these dull questions appear next. Perhaps you're asking yourself, "Must I really read this tedious stuff?" The answer, of course, is yes. If I had to write it, you have to read it. That's only fair. Plus, you might learn something.

Unicode and Other Character Sets

The default character set for XML, XHTML, and HTML 4.0 documents is Unicode (www.w3.org/International/0-charset), a standard defined, oddly enough, by the Unicode Consortium (www.unicode.org). Unicode is a comprehensive character set that provides a unique number for every character, "no matter what the platform, no matter what the program, no matter what the language." Unicode is thus the closest thing we have to a universal alphabet, although it is not an alphabet but a numeric mapping scheme.

Even though Unicode is the default character set for web documents, developers are free to choose other character sets that might be better suited to their needs. For instance, American and Western European websites often use

ISO-8859-1 (Latin-1) encoding. You might be asking yourself what Latin-1 encoding means, or where it comes from. OK, to be honest, you're not asking yourself any such thing, but I needed a transition.

What Is ISO 8859?

ISO 8859 is a series of standardized multilingual single-byte coded (8 bit) graphic character sets for writing in alphabetic languages, and the first of these character sets, ISO-8859-1 (also called Latin-1), is used for Western characters. ISO 8859 character sets include Latin-2 (East European), Turkish, Greek, Hebrew, and Nordic, among others.

The ISO 8859 standard was created in the mid-1980s by Ecma (www.ecma-international.org) and endorsed by the International Standards Organization (www.iso.org). Now you know.

Declaring Your Character Set

Regardless of which character set you've chosen, you must declare your character encoding, as discussed in the second rule of XHTML presented earlier. (You see, there was a point to all this.) Sites can declare their character encoding in any of three ways:

- A server administrator ("systems guy") might set the encoding via the HTTP headers returned by the web server. The W3C recommends this approach, but it is rarely followed—maybe because systems guys would rather play networked games than muck around with HTTP headers.

- For XML documents (including XHTML), a designer/developer might use the optional XML prolog to specify the encoding. This, too, is a W3C recommendation, but until the corpse of IE6 has rested in its tomb for many a year, I can't recommend it.

- In HTML or XHTML documents, a designer/developer might also specify the encoding via the "Content-Type" meta element. As opposed to the server administrator method (which fails when the server administrator forgets to do his job) and the XML prolog method (which fails when IE chokes on it), the "Content-Type" method can be counted on to work. That is the approach I recommended earlier in this chapter. Now you know why.

Congratulations! You have now read the dullest section of this book, or at least of this chapter, or anyway of this page. Let the healing begin! From here on in, we begin the interesting work of rethinking the way we design and build websites.

Structural Healing—It's Good for Me

Developing in XHTML goes beyond converting uppercase to lowercase and adding slashes to the end of br tags. If changing "tag fashions" were all there was to it, nobody would bother, and instead of web standards, this book would be filled with delicious tofu recipes. But I digress. To benefit from XHTML, you need to think about your markup in structural rather than visual terms.

Making this one change—marking up your page structurally and your content semantically—will shrink your page size while awakening Google (and human beings) to your site's rich, lovely content. Indeed, if you learn nothing from this book except to write structural, semantic markup styled with CSS, you will have gained the world. You will certainly have gained an advantage over competitive sites (and designers), as every site you design will be relatively lightweight, portable, *findable*, and fairly or completely accessible.

Here comes the good stuff!

Marking Up Your Document for Sense Instead of Style

Remember: you will use CSS for layout. In the world of web standards, XHTML markup is not about presentation; it's about core document structure and the semantics of individual elements. Well-structured documents make as much sense to a screen reader (or Newton!) user as they do to someone who's viewing your page in Google's Chrome on a 32-inch monitor. Well-structured documents also make visual sense in old desktop browsers that don't support CSS and in modern browsers whose users have turned off CSS for one reason or another.

What do we mean by *semantic*? We mean that we choose an XHTML element to match the meaning of the content it contains—a list if the content is a series of items in a list, a p if the content is a paragraph, an h1 if it is the most important headline on the page, and so on. What do we mean by *structural*? We mean, we write XHTML that assembles semantic elements in a logical and orderly structure (as opposed to table layouts, font tags, and other junk).

As rudimentary as this is, it was considered radical and was far from the norm when I wrote the first edition of this book. Alas, it is still not the norm. That's where you come in.

Here are some tips to help you start to think more structurally.

Color Within the Outlines

In grammar school, most of us were forced to write essays in a standard outline format. Then we became designers, and, oh, how free we felt as we cast off the dead weight of restrictive outlines and plunged boldly into unique realms of personal expression. OK, so maybe our brochure and commerce sites weren't that unique or personal. But at least we didn't have to worry about outlines any more. Or did we?

Actually, according to HTML, we should *always* have structured our textual content in organized hierarchies (outlines). We couldn't do that and deliver marketable layouts in the days before browsers supported CSS, but today we can deliver good underlying document structure without paying a design penalty.

When marking up text for the web or when converting existing text documents into web pages, think in terms of traditional outlines:

```
<h1>My Topic</h1>
<p>Introductory text</p>
<h2>Subsidiary Point</h2>
<p>Relevant text</p>
```

Avoid using deprecated HTML elements such as font tags or meaningless elements like br to visually simulate a logical structure where none exists. For instance, don't do this:

```
<font size="7">My Topic</font><br />
Introductory text <br /><br />
<font size="6">Subsidiary Point</font><br />
Relevant text <br />
```

Use Elements According to Their Meaning, Not Because of the Way They "Look"

Some of us have gotten into the habit of marking text as an h1 when we merely want it to be large or as li when we just want to stick a bullet in front of it. As discussed in Part I, browsers have traditionally imposed design attributes on HTML elements. We are all used to thinking that h1 means big, li means bullet, and blockquote means "indent this text." Most of us old-time web designers have scribbled our share of HTML that uses structural elements to force presentational effects.

Along the same lines, if a designer wants all headlines to be the same size, she might set all her headlines as h1, even though doing so makes no structural sense:

```
<h1>This is the primary headline, or would be if I had
organized my textual material in outline form.</h1>
<h1>This isn't the primary headline but I wanted it to be the
same size as the previous headline and I don't know how to use
CSS.</h1>
<h1>This isn't a headline at all! But I really wanted all the
text on this page to be the same size because it's important
to my creative vision. If I knew about CSS, I could achieve my
design without sacrificing document structure.</h1>
```

We must put our toys aside and start using elements because of what they mean, not because of the way they "look." In reality, h1 can look like anything you want it to. Via CSS, h1 can be small and roman (normal weight), p text can be huge and bold, li can have no bullet (or can use a PNG, GIF, or JPEG image of a dog, cat, or the company logo), and so on. My colleague Eric Meyer has given a presentation in which he overrides a browser's internal style sheet and uses CSS to style "invisible" elements of an HTML page, such as the HTML title and meta data. Although browsers have defaults, HTML does not. There is nothing in HTML or XHTML that says that an h2 must be large, or even visible. These are merely conventions, like the idea that spaghetti requires tomato sauce.

From today on, we're going to use CSS to determine how our XHTML elements look. We can even change the way they look according to where they appear on a page or in a site. There is no longer a need, if there ever was, to use li for any reason except the one for which it was created (to indicate that the element is one in a list of several items).

CSS completely abstracts presentation from structure, allowing you to style any element as you wish. In a CSS-capable browser, all six levels of headline (h1–h6) can be made to look identical if the designer so desires:

```
h1, h2, h3, h4, h5, h6   {
  font-family: Georgia, Palatino, "New Century Schoolbook",
Times, serif;
  font-weight: normal;
  font-size: 2em;
  margin-top: 1em;
  margin-bottom: 0;
  }
```

Why might you do this? You might do it to enforce a branded look and feel in graphical browsers while preserving the document structure in text browsers, old or feature-limited mobile devices, and opt-in HTML mail newsletters.

We don't mean to get ahead of ourselves by showing CSS techniques in a chapter about XHTML. We simply wanted to show that document structure and visual presentation are two distinctly different beasts, and that elements should be chosen for their semantic value in a logically structured content presentation. Elements should not be chosen to force display.

RESIST TEMPTATION, YOU MUST

Black-hat search engine optimization dudes take advantage of CSS's ability to trump visual conventions by marking keywords (or whole pages) as h1 *and using CSS to make that* h1 *content look like ordinary text. People who do this will someday answer to a higher authority. Don't give in to the Dark Side, Luke!*

Prefer Semantic Elements to Meaningless Junk

Because we've forgotten—or never knew—that HTML and XHTML elements are intended to convey structural meaning, many of us have acquired the habit of writing markup that contains no semantics or structure at all. For instance, many HTML wranglers will insert a list into their page by using markup like this:

```
item <br />
another item <br />
a third item <br />
```

Use an ordered or unordered list instead:

```
<ul>
<li>item</li>
<li>another item</li>
<li>a third item</li>
</ul>
```

"But li gives me a bullet, and I don't want a bullet!" you might say. Refer to the previous section. CSS makes no assumptions about the way elements are supposed to look. It waits for you to tell it how you want them to look. Turning off bullets is the least of what CSS can do. It can make a list look like ordinary text in a paragraph—or like a graphical navigation bar, complete with rollover effects [**6.1**].

6.1

John Allsopp duplicates Apple's navigation bar using only CSS and a semantic list—no images (**www.westciv.com/ style_master/blog/ apples-navigation- bar-using-only-css**).

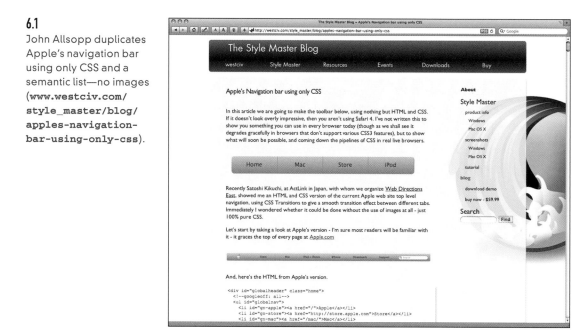

So use list elements to mark up lists. Similarly, prefer strong to b, em to i, and so on. By default, most desktop browsers will display strong as b and em as i, creating the visual effect you seek without undermining your document's structure.

Although CSS makes no assumption about the display of any element, browsers (via built-in style sheets) make lots of assumptions, and we've never encountered a browser that displayed strong as anything other than bold (unless instructed to display it some other way by a designer's creative CSS). If you're worried that some strange browser won't display your strong text as bold, you can write a CSS rule like this one:

```
strong  {
  font-weight: bold;
  font-style: normal;
  }
```

Using structural markup such as `strong` also protects people using text browsers and other alternative devices from downloading markup that is meaningless in their browsing environment. (What does `b` mean to a Braille reader?)

There are exceptions to every rule, of course. Here are a few times when you might want to use `b` instead of `strong` or `i` instead of `em`:

- You're marking up an unordered list, which you will later style in CSS to look like a navigation bar in CSS-capable, graphical browsers. You want to highlight the nav bar's Home "button" to indicate that the user is on the home page, and you want this "you are here" information to come across even in non-CSS environments. Wrapping the Home link in `b` tags will do the trick while avoiding false semantics. It'll save you a few bytes of markup, too. That's why some of us use `b` and `i` instead of `span` when adding semantic hooks for CSS. (More on that in another chapter.)

- In Paul Ford's famous example (`www.ftrain.com/ProcessingProcessing.html`), "when I'm publishing content from 1901 and it's in italics, it's in italics, not emphasized. Typography has a semantics that is subtle, changing, and deeply informed by history."

For more deep thoughts and passionate bickering on `b` versus `strong`, see Matthew Paul Thomas (`mpt.net.nz/archive/2004/05/02/b-and-i`), Joe Clark (`blog.fawny.org/2004/05/16/ubu`), and James Craig (`cookiecrook.com/2004/05/#cc108424449201351713`). Note too that HTML5 redefines `b` and `i` in non-visual (medium-neutral) terms that more or less replicate the semantics of `strong` and `em` anyway.

Visual Elements and Structure

Web standards abide not only in the technologies we use, but also in the way we use them. Writing markup in XHTML and using CSS to handle some or all layout chores doesn't necessarily make a site any more accessible or portable or any less of a bandwidth buster. XHTML and CSS can be misused or abused as easily as earlier web technologies were. Verbose XHTML markup wastes every bit as much of the user's time as verbose HTML ever did. Long-winded, overwrought CSS is not an adequate replacement for presentational HTML; it's simply one bad thing taking the place of another.

The guidelines in the earlier "Structural Healing—It's Good for Me" section can help avoid overly complex, semantically meaningless interior structures (body copy and so on). But what do we do about branded visual elements, such as site-wide navigation bars, which typically include a logo? Can these elements be treated semantically?

And how about page structure? It's all well and good to talk about p and h1, but you've got a sexy and complex visual layout to render, and if you can't do it with tables any more, surely you'll need hundreds of divs just as semantically meaningless and bloated as any table layout ever was. Right?

We'll find out in Chapter 8. But first, we need to consider an emerging alternative to XHTML—namely, HTML5. The next chapter reveals all.

chapter seven

HTML5: The New Hope

HTML5 represents the first significant change to web markup since, well, forever. For one thing, it is the first web markup language crafted by browser makers rather than scientists alone: as discussed in Chapter 4, the "Web Hypertext Application Technology Working Group" (WHATWG) (www.whatwg.org), founded by employees of Apple, Opera, and Mozilla and led by Google's Ian Hickson, pioneered the spec. They now develop it jointly with the W3C HTML Working Group (www.w3.org/html), led by software developer Sam Ruby and Microsoft Internet Explorer development lead Chris Wilson. You'd be hard-pressed to find an academic or pure theorist in either group—and you'll find Mr. Hickson in both groups.

It's also the first markup language to be created during a period of web standards acceptance (you're welcome), when browser makers, as well as many web designers, are finally paying strict attention to standards. At the same time, and rather paradoxically, it is the first markup standard since the widespread acceptance of XML and XHTML to walk away from well-formedness—the dotted i's and crossed t's that the W3C has recommended and web standards evangelists (not to mention all editions of this book) have taught for a decade.

HTML5 and Web Applications: the Stakes are High

Most importantly, HTML5 is the first web markup language to be conceived in the era of the *web application*. Scientists designed prior web markup languages to deliver document structure. Browser makers are designing HTML5 to do that, too, of course. They've even given us additional semantic elements to help us write smarter and more sophisticated documents. But they also (and primarily) see HTML5 as a platform to jump-start web application development.

With web apps an accepted fact of life—powerful enough to replace desktop calendar, contact, and project management software, and to threaten the dominance of Microsoft Office and Adobe Photoshop—and with proprietary platforms such as Microsoft Silverlight (`www.microsoft.com/silverlight`) and Adobe Flex (`www.adobe.com/products/flex`) striving to take the rich internet application space back from Ajax and web standards, the rewards and stakes are as high as could be.

And you thought this was going to be just another dull chapter about markup.

What's New in HTML5

HTML5 approaches the acceleration of web application development by

- Introducing shiny new app-focused elements such as `canvas`, a live drawing surface, and `video`, a replacement for plug-ins,

- Working directly with APIs,

- Proposing standardized error handling that works the same way in all browsers,

- Supporting location awareness via the W3C GeoLocation API,

- Introducing multi-threaded JavaScript so web apps can respond to user activity while the browser is still processing previously triggered scripts, and

- Facilitating user-editable pages via such attributes as `contenteditable`, `draggable`, and `spellcheck`.

Even its DOCTYPE is built for speed:

```
<!DOCTYPE HTML>
```

That's all she wrote, and it's all you need to write. The framers of HTML5 would probably have omitted the `DOCTYPE` altogether if it weren't needed to prevent browsers from going into Quirks mode (discussed in Chapter 11). By the way, the string is case insensitive; you could also write `<!doctype html>`, `<!DOCTYPE html>`, and so on.

But Does It Work in Browsers?

Although the ink on HTML5 is not dry, many browsers already support some of the most advanced new features it makes possible. Opera, Firefox, and Safari, including Mobile Safari in the iPhone, support GeoLocation as well as `canvas`, and Firefox supports `video`—presently only for one codec, but the commitment is there. Indeed, the involvement of browser makers in every aspect of specification development means HTML5 will not languish as XHTML 2.0 did, but will be adopted correctly, completely, and soon. Under the current timetable, HTML5 is to be finalized in 2011, and all browsers are expected to support every jot and tittle correctly by 2022. That sounds a long way off, and it is, but most browser makers anticipate supporting everything in HTML5 within the next few years.

Indeed, all modern browsers including IE8 already let us write HTML5 page structure elements like `nav` and `section` (discussed next) and style them in CSS. It doesn't work in IE7 or 6 by default, of course, but Remy Sharp has shown how you can use JavaScript to trick older versions of IE into supporting HTML5 (`www.slideshare.net/remy.sharp/html5-js-apis`), and Dean Edwards has created a JavaScript library that plugs the holes in browsers' HTML support (`www.blip.tv/file/2299313`).

Details of the programming opportunities created by HTML5 are outside the scope of this introduction to standards-based *design*, but will undoubtedly find their way into the best of the next generation of web development and web programming books. It's an exciting time to be a web developer. A complete list of HTML5 elements and how they are to be used may be found at `www.whatwg.org/specs/web-apps/current-work/multipage/semantics.html#semantics`. In the rest of this chapter, we'll look at those elements of HTML5 that most concern web designers—particularly at the new page structure elements. We begin by examining how HTML5 differs from the language we just studied.

HTML5 vs. XHTML

If you seek a plausible water-cooler summary of how HTML5 compares to XHTML, you might say this: *HTML5 is like XHTML 1.0, but with more relaxed rules about tag closure, and with new elements designed to facilitate application development and create a semantics of page layout, or deepen the semantics of page structure, if you prefer.* You might also say that XHTML 1.0 is stable and well supported in browsers (MIME type peccadilloes in XHTML 1.1 aside) and will work for decades to come, whereas HTML5, although nearly finalized as I write these words, is still in development and subject to change. You might end by observing that while browsers including IE8 comfortably support the vanilla bits, they do not yet support all of HTML5's new elements.

There's more to it, but those are the headlines.

A Pox on Both Your Nomenclatures

Where XHTML, inspired by the XML virtue of "well-formedness," imposed strictness on web markup, HTML5 tolerates an HTML-like looseness about such questions as whether every element that opens must close. This laxness incenses many developers who know about such things, and will be ignored by developers who don't—a paradox I call the Hickson Uncertainty Principle, in honor of the editor of the WHATWG and co-editor of the W3C HTML group HTML5 specs.

Fortunately for code neatniks like us, HTML5 offers two kinds of syntax (or, in WHATWG-speak, two modes of serialization): HTML5, which is simple and works like HTML, and XHTML5, which offers an XHTML-like syntax. In other words, if you want to keep using strict XHTML syntax, you can.

At present, validation services—principally the validator.nu service incorporated into the W3C validator—can tell you if your HTML5 is valid, but they *cannot* tell you if your HTML syntax (or XHTML syntax) is properly formed. Thus you could write valid HTML5 served as `text/html` that uses both HTML and XHTML syntax, and no validator will tell you you're doing anything wrong. It's nice that browsers will handle this kind of mixed-syntax HTML5 without a hiccup—their doing so will enable you to include third-party content, for instance, without worrying that mixed authoring styles will create validation errors or cause a browser to shut down. But validation services should provide advanced web designers and developers with the option to check the validity of their HTML or XHTML syntax. Some colleagues and I have requested that Henri Sivonen, the designer of the HTML5 validation service (about.validator.nu), add this feature; by the time you read this, he may have done so.

New elements aside, HTML5, in its HTML5 incarnation, is compatible with old browsers. According to the intentions of HTML5's creators, a document served with the MIME type text/html will be processed as HTML5 by browsers. As XHTML5 uses XML in its syntax, a web page with the MIME type application/xhtml+xml will be processed as XHTML5 in browsers. If you write valid HTML5, using valid XHTML5 syntax, but serve it as text/html, browsers will display it just fine.

The specification makes no bones about which syntax it prefers: HTML5 served as text/html, and with relaxed rules about tag closing:

> Authors are reminded that the processing for XML and HTML differs; in particular, even minor syntax errors will prevent an XML document from being rendered fully, whereas they would be ignored in the "HTML5" syntax.
>
> — www.w3.org/TR/html5/introduction.html#html-vs-xhtml

As well as a not-so-subtle dig against Mr. Hickson's bugbear of XHTML served as text/html (discussed elsewhere in this book), this is a fair defense of browser looseness in regard to syntax errors, with which the web runs rife. After all, even the tightest, most semantically structured website can develop validation errors due to an unclosed em in a reader's comment, a CMS hiccup, badly written ad-serving software, an application or document section pulled in from a content partner's site, or simple human error. It would be wrong, and would shut down 99.9% of the web, if browsers quit or froze upon encountering a simple, and all-too-common, validation error. By contrast, browser makers are encouraged to impose Draconian error handling on HTML5 when it is served as application/xhtml+xml. As web designers may use HTML or XHTML syntax in web pages served as text/html, and as browsers are instructed to wink at errors in pages served as text/html, it's hard to imagine a situation in which you'd want to serve your website as anything other than text/html.

HTML5 Elements on Parade

Beyond relaxing the rules that XHTML tightened, the big news in HTML5 is of course the creation of new elements. Some of these are long overdue application-focused shiny bits such as `video` and `audio`. As indicated earlier in the chapter, these elements allow video and audio to play in browsers without plug-ins, without previously invalid `embed` elements, and without nested `object` elements intermingled with scripts and fallbacks. In "A Preview of HTML5" (www.alistapart.com/articles/previewofhtml5), Lachlan Hunt provides these examples:

```
<video src="video.ogv" controls poster="poster.jpg"
width="320" height="240">
    <a href="video.ogv">Download movie</a>
</video>

<audio src="music.oga" controls>
    <a href="music.oga">Download song</a>
</audio>
```

Note the attributes `controls`, which tells the browser to create playback controls, and `poster`, which tells the browser what image to use as a placeholder until the user decides to play the video. Also note the use of simple fallback links for those whose browsers don't support `video` or `audio`.

Sophisticated web page markup doesn't get much simpler than that, nor will we miss all the nested tags, scripts, and workarounds. Experimental builds of Opera, Firefox, and Webkit (Apple Safari, Google Chrome) are beginning to support these new HTML5 multimedia elements, so do yourself a favor and practice using them. As this book goes to press, Firefox only supports the Ogg codec (www.xiph.org/downloads). No matter! You can find Ogg music files for Firefox via www.vorbis.com/music_links.

The Semantics of Page Structure

More interesting (and more controversial) are HTML5's new page-structure elements, `section`, `article`, `header`, `nav`, `footer`, `figure`, and `aside`. What do they do? Glad you asked.

- **Section:** Like a `div`, a `section` contains and organizes related content, including headings, paragraphs, images, and so on. It normally has a `header` and may also have a `footer`. `section` does not replace `div`, which remains a block-level organizer. A `div` contains items that may or may not relate to one another. A `section`, in contrast, may *only* contain thematically related items, such as an `h1` headline advertising a house for sale, a photograph of the house, several paragraphs of text describing the house, a list containing the realtor's contact information, and so on. The enclosing section conveys the semantic information that the content of these items is related. In the hands of a standards-based designer, this relationship was implicit with the items contained in a `div` in XHTML. But HTML5 makes the connection explicit, and removes such a connection if a `div` is used. In HTML5, a `div` becomes simply a junk drawer (or "flow content" container in WHATWG parlance), and web designers are strongly encouraged to use `section` instead.

- **Article:** self-contained content such as a blog post, news article, or reader comment. Like `section`, it may contain a `header` and `footer`. Although the specification doesn't explicitly call it this, an `article` may be viewed as a specialized form of a `section`. A blog post or news article would be marked up as an `article`, not as a `section`. Neither `section` nor `article` is "higher" in the stack. An `article` may contain sections; a `section` may contain `articles`. Like anything new, `section` and `article` may initially strike you as strange and unnecessary. But they are a good idea, for they create additional and probably overdue page structure semantics; make it easier to create page outlines that go far beyond the traditional `h1-h6`; and clear away all kinds of formatting and validation problems bequeathed to us by HTML 4. For example, in HTML 4 and XHTML 1.0, if I copy all the content from an article page into my home page, I'll probably have to strip out and reformat its markup to avoid having multiple `h1`s on the same page and so on. But in HTML5, I can include the content as-is inside an `article` container. The description of the `header` element, next, explains why.

- **Header:** intended (but not required) to contain the `section`'s heading (an `h1`–`h6` element). "The `header` element can also be used to wrap a `section`'s table of contents, a search form, or any relevant logos." In HTML5, for the first time, we can have more than six levels of heading, as a page might have a section that begins with `h1` and contains a subsection that *also* begins with `h1`, thus creating up to twelve heading levels in this simple example. Theoretically, an infinite number of heading levels is possible by nesting one `section` containing heading levels `h1-h6` inside another, inside another, and so on.

- **Nav**: "A section… that links to other documents or to parts within the document itself; that is, a section of navigation links." Intended for "primary navigation blocks," not just any group of links on the page. As of this writing, breadcrumbs and footer links can't be used in the nav section.

- **Aside**: think sidebars (the kind used in magazines, not the kind found in three-column layouts) and pull-quotes.

- **Figure**: As in this book, (well, not in this chapter, but in the "pretty" ones), a figure is a chart, a movie, an image, a graph, a code sample, or other information that aids understanding of the section or article but can be removed from the "flow" (repositioned) without affecting meaning. The figure element also gives the legend element another venue (besides forms). The element is not exactly new to HTML5. W3C team member Dave Raggett introduced it in HTML 3 as fig, but the element was removed in HTML 3.2. We will never know what the web's history would have been if Raggett's semantically advanced HTML 3.0 had won widespread support.

- **Footer**: "A footer typically contains information about its section such as who wrote it, links to related documents, copyright data, and the like. May not contain heading or sectioning elements." So read the specification in August, 2009. This seemed needlessly restrictive to many of us, who typically include navigation elements such as "About us" and "Contact" in our footers. But here again, the framers of HTML5 were using a familiar word (*footer*) that conveys a specific meaning to millions of web developers, and putting it to a different use than what we expect. In HTML5, footer was mainly a container of metadata. Alerted to the problem by the HTML5 Super Friends (www.zeldman.com/superfriends), the framers of HTML5 have since removed the restriction about heading and sectioning elements. footer's content model now matches that of header, enabling designers to use it in the way its name implies (without preventing others from using it the way HTML5's framers recommend).

Worth noting: HTML5 takes its element names from practices revealed by an analysis of millions of web documents. In theory this is great, because familiarity with the name should make the new element easy for developers to understand and use. The problem arises when the familiar name is put to an unfamiliar use, as is the case with aside, and especially with header and footer.

It's All About the Markup

Before we discuss why some folks are unhappy with these new page structure elements, let's see what they're intended to achieve. In "The Power of HTML5 and CSS 3" (www.perishablepress.com/press/2009/07/19/power-of-html5-css3), designer/developer Jeff Starr contrasts the "div soup" of XHTML with the structured clarity of HTML5. Here's Starr's (X)HTML example:

```
<div id="news">
    <div class="section">
        <div class="article">
            <div class="header">
                <h1>Div Soup Demonstration</h1>
                <p>Posted on July 11th, 2009</p>
            </div>
            <div class="content">
                <p>Lorem ipsum text blah blah blah.</p>
                <p>Lorem ipsum text blah blah blah.</p>
                <p>Lorem ipsum text blah blah blah.</p>
            </div>
            <div class="footer">
                <p>Tags: HMTL, code, demo</p>
            </div>
        </div>
        <div class="aside">
            <div class="header">
                <h1>Tangential Information</h1>
            </div>
            <div class="content">
                <p>Lorem ipsum text blah blah blah.</p>
                <p>Lorem ipsum text blah blah blah.</p>
                <p>Lorem ipsum text blah blah blah.</p>
            </div>
            <div class="footer">
                <p>Tags: HMTL, code, demo</p>
            </div>
        </div>
    </div>
</div>
```

Hoo, boy, that's a lot of divs. And a designer's eyes could easily cross while trying to edit such a file, leading to errors that break layouts and validation when one too few or one too many closing (</div>) tags gets removed by mistake.

(I've done that.) Next, Starr shows us how it would look in HTML5, using that language's new page-structural elements:

```
<section>
   <section>
      <article>
         <header>
            <h1>Div Soup Demonstration</h1>
            <p>Posted on July 11th, 2009</p>
         </header>
         <section>
            <p>Lorem ipsum text blah blah blah.</p>
            <p>Lorem ipsum text blah blah blah.</p>
            <p>Lorem ipsum text blah blah blah.</p>
         </section>
         <footer>
            <p>Tags: HMTL, code, demo</p>
         </footer>
      </article>
      <aside>
         <header>
            <h1>Tangential Information</h1>
         </header>
         <section>
            <p>Lorem ipsum text blah blah blah.</p>
            <p>Lorem ipsum text blah blah blah.</p>
            <p>Lorem ipsum text blah blah blah.</p>
         </section>
         <footer>
            <p>Tags: HMTL, code, demo</p>
         </footer>
      </aside>
   </section>
</section>
```

The second example is certainly easier to scan and understand, and less likely to lead to errors during a wee-hours coding session.

Too Few Elements, or Too Many?

It turns out that people have a lot to say about HTML5. John Allsopp, author of this third edition's companion volume, *Developing with Web Standards* (New Riders, 2009), doesn't have a problem with the new elements per se. He has a problem with their lack of forward compatibility, in that HTML5 presents us with a finite number of new elements and no extensibility mechanism for adding new elements in the future. See the section entitled "A New Semantics in Town" in Chapter 4 of this book for details.

My view, and that of some of my smartest colleagues, is that adding only a limited number of new elements to HTML is the right decision. A *small, limited set of new elements* is easier to teach and use, and more likely to be used intuitively and correctly, than a heap of new elements. Consider the simplicity of your favorite applications and websites; now think of all the applications you must use but wish you didn't because they're overloaded with confusing features you rarely need. The challenge for HTML5 is not to come up with more elements, but to be certain that these new elements are the *right* elements, with names that indicate exactly how they are to be used.

HTML5: Just the Specs

The specs of the HTML5 draft standard may be found at `www.whatwg.org/html5`. Remember that it is a work in progress. Before coding in HTML5, check this URL for any details that may have changed since this book went to press.

The spec opens with a brief declaration of principles (`www.whatwg.org/specs/web-apps/current-work/multipage/introduction.html#background`):

> The World Wide Web's markup language has always been HTML. HTML was primarily designed as a language for semantically describing scientific documents, although its general design and adaptations over the years have enabled it to be used to describe a number of other types of documents.

> The main area that has not been adequately addressed by HTML is a vague subject referred to as *web applications*. This specification attempts to rectify this, while at the same time updating the HTML specifications to address issues raised in the past few years.

Having stated its goals, the specification quickly gets down to details.

Most of the specifications of HTML5 as detailed at `www.whatwg.org/html5` will be familiar from your experience with HTML and this book's discussion of XHTML. HTML elements have a start tag such as `<body>` and an end tag such as `</body>`. As in HTML, but contrary to XHTML, start and end tags can be omitted in some cases. You can even omit the `html` and `body` elements in some cases. This is where some of us reach for the Drano.

As in all web markup languages, tags must be nested correctly.

```
<p>This is <em>so <strong>wrong</em>!</strong></p>
<p>This <em>is <strong>right</strong>.</em></p>
```

Elements can have attributes, such as the `href` attribute to the a (anchor) element:

```
<a href="#">
```

Attributes are placed inside the start tag, and consist of a name and a value, separated by an "=" character. The attribute value can be left unquoted if it doesn't contain any special characters. (In XHTML, all attributes must be quoted.)

In HTML5, this is valid:

```
<input name=address maxlength=200>
```

So is this:

```
<input name=address maxlength="200">
```

Neither would be valid in XHTML.

As we work our way through the elements (www.whatwg.org/specs/web-apps/current-work/multipage/dom.html#elements), we encounter familiar entities such as the `id` attribute, the `title` attribute, the `class` attribute, and so on. Some ancient elements have been gently redefined to be less visual and more presentation-neutral. For instance, `i` now means "stressed" instead of italic, making it as appropriate for a voice browser as it is for a visual web page. There are also new attributes such as `dir`, which "specifies the element's text directionality." Possible values are `ltr` (left-to-right) and `rtl` (you guessed it: right-to-left). You might use this when writing in a right-to-left language such as Hebrew, encoded in Unicode. (The *old* HTML `dir` element, which had nothing to do with direction, has been deleted.)

In the "Embedded content" section, we encounter old and new friends such as `svg`, `audio`, `canvas`, and `embed` (finally legal! and it only took fifteen years).

Under "Interactive content," we find traditional elements such as `input`, `button`, and `textarea`, as well as `video` and `datagrid` (www.whatwg.org/specs/web-apps/current-work/multipage/interactive-elements.html#datagrid), a new element that "represents an interactive representation of tree, list, or tabular data," facilitating such things as sortable data tables and canvases on which content may be drawn.

Elsewhere in the specification, scripters will find familiar constructs such as `innerHTML` and `document.write()`. There is also support for microdata (www.whatwg.org/specs/web-apps/current-work/multipage/microdata-0.html#microdata-0), for standards like vCard (familiar from contact programs) (www.whatwg.org/specs/web-apps/current-work/multipage/microdata-0.html#vcard), and for converting HTML to other formats (www.whatwg.org/specs/web-apps/current-work/multipage/microdata-0.html#converting-html-to-other-formats) including JSON, RDF, vCard, iCalendar, and Atom—but, strangely, not Atom's older brother RSS.

Unlike in previous markup languages other than XHTML 2, in HTML5 just about any element or group of elements can be wrapped in a link. Supported link types (using the `rel` attribute) include `nofollow`, `license`, `archives`, `author`, `bookmark`, `external`, `icon`, and many more. In short, to the delight of librarians and information specialists everywhere, the humble link now contains metadata that can make your content friendlier to machines and search engines as well as scripts and applications, and that can provide additional and simpler hooks for CSS. Just don't expect these CSS 2 attribute selectors (www.w3.org/TR/CSS2/selector.html#attribute-selectors) to work correctly in IE6.

Learn More

As this too-brief introduction suggests, HTML5 offers a lot to be excited about, including increased semantic richness, new elements upon which to hang deeper CSS, greater control over forms, faster prototyping of web applications, more powerful and faster (because multi-threaded) scripting, and more. The specification runs to more than 600 pages on the web and over 900 in PDF. It's almost an insult to try to capture even a part of that richness in a single chapter of a design book. No doubt, when the specification is finalized, the next edition of this book (or perhaps a new book altogether) will have loads more to say about HTML5. Until then, see...

- *Developing with Web Standards*, Chapter 5 ("HTML5")
- HTML5 Doctor (www.html5doctor.com), maintained by the ever-reliable Bruce Lawson
- "Canvas Tutorial" (developer.mozilla.org/en/Canvas_tutorial)
- HTML5 Gallery (www.html5gallery.com)
- HTML5 Reset Stylesheet by Richard Clark (www.html5doctor.com/html-5-reset-stylesheet)
- Topics: Code: HTML and XHTML (www.alistapart.com/topics/code/htmlxhtml)
- "A Preview of HTML5" (www.alistapart.com/articles/previewofhtml5)
- "Semantics in HTML5" (www.alistapart.com/articles/semanticsinhtml5)
- "HTML5: Could it Kill Flash and Silverlight?" (www.infoworld.com/d/developer-world/html-5-could-it-kill-flash-and-silverlight-291)
- "Google Bets Big on HTML5" (radar.oreilly.com/2009/05/google-bets-big-on-html-5.html)
- "HTML5: A Story in Progress" by Burningbird (www.burningbird.net/node/28)
- "Accessible Drag and Drop with WAI-Aria" (dev.opera.com/articles/view/accessible-drag-and-drop)
- "Can HTML5 Make Accessibility Usable?" (my.opera.com/jax/blog/can-html5-make-accessibility-usable)
- "HTML5: Features You Want Desperately But Still Can't Use" (www.youtube.com/watch?v=xIxDJof7xxQ)

chapter eight

Tighter, Firmer Pages Guaranteed: Structure and Semantics

Whatever you do, don't skip this chapter. Reading it will improve your skills, trim unwanted fat from your web pages, and sharpen your understanding of the difference between markup and design. The ideas in this chapter are easy to follow, but can make a profound difference in the performance of your sites and the facility with which you design, produce, and update them.

In this chapter, you'll learn how to write logical, compact markup that can lower your bandwidth by 50% or more, restoring pep and vigor to your sites' loading times while reducing server aches and stress. We'll achieve these savings by banishing presentational elements from our (X)HTML and learning to avoid common practices that, frankly, stink.

These malodorous practices afflict many sites on the web, even those that have largely or completely converted from table-based layout to CSS. As this third edition goes to press, CSS layout, once considered as relevant to corporate site building as coffeehouse poetry, is now the norm. (You're welcome.) Yet many CSS layouts are produced wastefully and ineptly, even when the designers are extremely skilled in everything else they do. It is an equal opportunity problem, as likely to appear in Ajax-powered web applications and sophisticated social networks as in MySpace pages and mom-and-pop sites spun by the neighbor's kid. (No offense to the neighbor's kid; indeed, kids today are more likely to use structural, semantic markup than some senior designers who've created websites for years. For that matter, no offense to MySpace, which employs some of the best web developers around, regardless of what users' pages may look like.) The source of this muddle can most often be traced not to CSS, but to the markup that provides hooks for it.

In this chapter, we'll name these common markup mistakes so you can recognize and guard against them, and learn what to do instead. We will also make friends with the unique identifier (id) attribute, which allows you to write ultra-compact, semantic markup; serve the correct layout to a specific page type without backend scripting; and show users, without JavaScript, where they are in the site's hierarchy. And we'll add semantic richness to our sites via the class attribute, while avoiding the gross misuse of that attribute that wreaks semantic havoc on far too many modern sites.

div, id, and Other Assistants

This chapter and those that follow make much reference to the div element and the id attribute. Used correctly, div is the Hamburger Helper of structured markup, while id is an amazing little tool that permits you to write highly compact (X)HTML, apply CSS wisely, and add sophisticated behavior to your site via standard JavaScript. The W3C, in "The Global Structure of an HTML Document," defines div and two other important HTML/XHTML components thusly:

> The DIV and SPAN elements, in conjunction with the id and class attributes, offer a generic mechanism for adding structure to documents. These elements define content to be inline (SPAN) or block-level (DIV) but impose no other presentational idioms on the content. Thus, authors may use these elements in conjunction with style sheets... to tailor HTML to their own needs and tastes (www.w3.org/TR/ REC-html140/struct/global.html#h-7.5.4).

What Is This Thing Called *div*?

This is as good a place as any to explain that `div` is short for *division*. When you group a bunch of links together, that's one division of a document. Content would be another, the legal disclaimer at the foot of the page would be still another, and so on. In XHTML, it is a best practice to group related elements together, thus giving the `div` element a semantic value of conveying related-ness. As we've seen in Chapter 7, HTML5 removes that semantic value, apply-ing it instead to new semantic elements such as `section` and `article`.

A Generic Mechanism for Specific Structures

All HTML jockeys are familiar with common elements like `p` or `h1`, but some might be less familiar with `div`. The key to understanding the `div` element is found in the W3C's phrase, "a generic mechanism for adding structure."

When marking up a page in HTML 5 (at least as that spec is defined as I write this chapter), I would create page navigation using the `nav` element that markup language introduces (www.zeldman.com/x/36). In HTML 4.01 or XHTML, I might mark up my navigation using `div class="navigation"` or `div id="navigation"`. I'd choose a `div` if the navigation section of the page contained multiple elements, such as an unordered list (`ul`) for the primary navigation, a second unordered list for site tools, and so on. The `div` could con-tain all those elements while conveying their shared semantic value as naviga-tion, and clarifying for machines as well as human source code readers that this entire section of the page—*this page division*—is devoted to navigation.

If my navigation were sufficiently simple—if it contained no sub-elements—I'd mark it up as `ul class="navigation"` or `ul id="navigation"` instead of via a `div` element. (Some *very* semantics-oriented developers do this even when their navigation contains numerous sub-elements.) The choice of `class` or `id` depends on what else happens on the page. If there is one navigation section on the page, `id` is the appropriate choice; if more than one, `class` is the way to go. I'll have more to say about the difference between `class` and `id` in the next section.

Must we label our `class` or `id` `navigation`? Indeed not. Names like "Gladys" or "orangebox" would be perfectly kosher within the rules of (X)HTML. But structural names (names that explain the function performed by elements contained within) are best. You would feel pretty silly having labeled a part of your site "orangebox" when the client decides to go with blue. You would feel sillier still revising your style sheets under a deadline six months from now and trying desperately to remember whether "Gladys" was a navigational area, a sidebar, a search form, or what. In the pioneer days, we had fun crafting nonsensical labels, inserting Easter egg comments in source, and in various other ways revealing that we had no lives. But in the mature web of teams and processes, sensible, structural labels that convey the semantics of grouped content help when it's time for you (or another teammate) to dive back in and update the site.

Plus, crafting structural identifiers like "menu" or "content" or "search_form" helps you remember that markup is not layout, and that a well-structured page can be made to look any way you desire. If you cultivate the habit of assigning structural names to core page components (such as the navigation, content, and search areas), you will wean yourself from the habit of authoring and thinking in presentational markup.

id Versus *class*

The id attribute is not new to XHTML or HTML5; neither are the class attribute or the div and span elements. The id attribute assigns a unique name to an element. Each name can be used only once on a given page. For example, if your page contains a div whose id is "content", it cannot have another element with that same identifier. In short, id is for *identification*. You wouldn't share your passport or Social Security number—they are used to identify you, and only you. The id attribute works the same way.

The class attribute, by contrast, can be used over and over again on the same page, because it's for *classification*. For example, five paragraphs on the page might share a class name of "small" or "footnote". The following markup will help clarify the distinction between id and class:

```
<div id="search">
<!-- Search form components go here. This section of the page
is unique. -->
. . .
</div>

<div class="blog_entry">
  <h2>Today's blog post</h2>
  <p>Blog content goes here.</p>
```

```
    <p>Here is another paragraph of blog content.</p>
    <p>Just as there can be many paragraphs on a page, so too
there may be many entries in a blog. A blog page could use
multiple instances of the class "blog_entry" (or any other
class).</p>
</div>

<div class="blog_entry">
    <h2>Yesterday's blog post</h2>
    <p>In fact, here we are inside another div of class "blog-
entry".</p>
    <p>They reproduce like rabbits.</p>
    <p>If there are ten blog posts on this page, there might be
ten divs of class "blog_entry" as well.</p>
</div>
```

In these examples, div id="search" would be used to block out that area of the page containing the search form, while div class="blog_entry" would block out each entry on a blog. There is only one search form on the page, so id is chosen for that unique instance. But a blog may have many entries, so the class attribute is used in that instance. Likewise, a news site might have multiple divs of class "news_entry" (or "news_item" or "news_story").

These divs aren't needed on every site. A blog might get along just fine with nothing but headlines (h1, h2, h3, etc.) and paragraphs (p). A news site could do likewise. divs of class "blog_entry" are shown not to encourage you to fill your page with divs, but merely to demonstrate the principle that multiple items can use the same class attribute (they can have the same *classification*), but only one item per page can use each id attribute (no two items can share the same *identification*).

The Sticky Note Theory

It might be helpful to think of the id attribute as a sticky note. I slap a sticky note on the fridge to remind me to buy milk. A sticky note stuck to the phone reminds me to call a late-paying client. Another, applied to a folder of bills, reminds me they must be paid by the fifteenth of the month (which also reminds me to call the late-paying client).

The id attribute is similar in that it labels a particular area of your markup, reminding you what purpose that part of the markup serves, and helping you also remember that the area will likely require special consideration during later design phases in which you work on presentation and behavior via CSS and JavaScript. For instance, your CSS file might have special rules that apply only to elements within the specific div whose id is "search." Or your style sheet might contain rules that apply only to a div whose id is "navigation."

When an id attribute's value is used as a magnet for a specific set of CSS rules, it is called a CSS selector. There are many other ways of creating selectors, but id is particularly handy and versatile.

The Power of id

The id attribute is incredibly powerful. Among other tasks, it can serve in the following capacities:

- As a style sheet selector (see the preceding section), permitting you to author tight, minimal (X)HTML.

- As a target anchor for hypertext links, replacing the outdated name attribute (or coexisting with it for the sake of backward compatibility).

- As a means to reference a particular element via DOM-based standard JavaScript.

- As the name of a declared object element.

- As a tool for general purpose processing (in a W3C example, "for identifying fields when extracting data from HTML pages into a database, translating HTML documents into other formats, and so on").

Rules of *id*

In CSS, identifiers (including element names, classes, and ids in selectors) can contain only the characters a-z, A-Z, 0-9, and ISO 10646 characters U+00A1 and higher, plus the hyphen (-) and the underscore (_); they cannot start with a digit, or a hyphen followed by a digit. Identifiers can also contain escaped characters and any ISO 10646 character as a numeric code (see next item). For instance, the identifier "B&W?" may be written as "B\&W\?" or "B\26 W\3F."

Also, if you intend to use an id with JavaScript in the form document.idname .value, you must name it as a valid JavaScript variable; that is, it must begin with a letter or an underscore, followed by letters, digits, and underscores. No blanks, and especially no hyphens, are allowed. (This no-hyphen rule applies only if you use document.idname, which is not recommended, anyway; use document.getElementById() instead.)

Make Your Content Easy to Find and Use

The elements and attributes discussed here are often misused and abused, quadrupling the weight of pages instead of reducing them, and removing all traces of structure instead of adding a logical outline structure to the generic structural elements of (X)HTML.

A logical outline structure, when applied correctly, *helps search engines find your content*; its absence helps search engines find someone else's content instead. I'll make this point over and over in this book, but it can't be overstated. If you want people to find your content, the first thing you must do is write great content, and the second thing you must do is mark up that content semantically. There is no third thing to do, although fiddling with page titles can help.

Likewise, *an outline helps people who use screen readers navigate your site*; its absence makes your site harder to use. Visually impaired people are the chief users of screen readers; the screen reader software enables them to "scan," say, all the h2s on your page, the same way people with "normal" eyesight scan headlines visually. When you use structural HTML elements like h1, h2, p, and li properly, and when you support those elements with semantic class and id attributes, you leave the old web of inaccessible content and keyword hucksterism for a new world where sites are findable, usable, and accessible.

After reading this chapter, you will be well on your way to this new world, and you will recognize and avoid the nonsemantic slop that makes pages fat, unfindable, and unfriendly to people with (permanent or temporary) disabilities.

Semantic Markup and Reusability

Now that we've discussed general-purpose (X)HTML elements (particularly div and id), let's look at some HTML.

```
<div id="masthead">
<h1>Feed the Hungry Project</h1>
  <ul class="navigation">
    <li>Home</li>
    <li>About Us</li>
    <li>Get Involved</li>
</ul>
</div>
```

Any reader who is still awake can translate this. We're in the "masthead" (or "header") section of the imaginary Feed the Hungry Project's website. The simple site contains three main sections, accessible from the navigation bar: Home, About Us, and Get Involved. The standardista who marked up this page has kept bandwidth to an absolute minimum while making her site's content friendly to people as well as to Google and Bing.

In contrast, an old-school web designer would create a visual layout in Photoshop or Fireworks, slice it into component GIFs or JPEGs, use table cells to position the component images on the web page, and apply visual effects such as rollovers via JavaScript (possibly inline). The result would look the same but take longer to download and would be inaccessible to many users and invisible to search engines because it substitutes image files for structured data.

Old-school table layouts waste bandwidth and have no semantic value. (Non-semantic "CSS layouts," as we'll explain in a moment, are nearly as bad.) The markup above presents the ideal we should strive for and can easily achieve. Notice that this markup contains no `img` tags, and thus no associated `width`, `height`, `background`, or `border` attributes. It is also free of table cells, with their associated `height`, `width`, background color (`bgcolor`), `rowspan`, and `colspan` attributes. It is as clean as a whistle and as minimal as a 1980s bass line, and yet it provides all the information a browser, a search engine, a screen reader, or (for that matter) a web designer on your team would need to make sense of it.

In all likelihood, the CSS that supports this markup displays the `h1` headline as a clickable image of the organization's logo via image replacement and CSS rollover techniques. And the unordered list, marked up as "navigation," undoubtedly looks like a navigation bar, again thanks to the magic of CSS. As a bonus, the page's structure will be readily comprehensible even in limited environments such as an outdated mobile phone that doesn't support CSS, or in a browser whose user has turned off CSS and images (possibly because he or she has only slow and limited internet access, as might be the case in a poor or politically repressed country). Without CSS and images, it is still clear that *Feed the Hungry Project* is the title of the page, and *Home*, *About Us*, and *Get Involved* are navigational links. Structured markup communicates even when there are no other elements to support it.

Removing all those nonsemantic `img` elements from the markup does more than just lower bandwidth costs and make content findable and accessible. Because we've decoupled page structure from presentation (separated content from look and feel), we can use JavaScript or backend scripting to encourage visitors to customize the reading experience—for instance, by selecting a smaller or larger type size, or by increasing page contrast to improve legibility. I'm not talking about the late 1990s-style "personalization" craze, which nobody ever cared about, and which only betrayed a lack of design commitment from the short-lived portals and dog-food vendors that offered this useless service. I'm talking about useful page layout adjustments such as that pioneered by *A List Apart* (www.alistapart.com/articles/alternate) and now a standard feature of any good newspaper website [**8.1**].

8.1

Enabling readers to change text size (and remembering their preference via a cookie) is a feature of many modern newspaper sites. Separating structure from presentation via web standards encourages this kind of reader-focused thoughtfulness (www.washingtonpost.com).

And because the markup is free of images or table cells and their associated effluvia—because it concerns itself purely with structural elements of the page—as long as the site's architecture doesn't change, the next team to redesign this site could use this same markup as the basis of an entirely fresh layout. Reduce, reuse, recycle.

This is how standards-based design outperforms table-based layouts while delivering identical visual results.

Common Errors in Modern Markup

Alas, not every site that uses `divs` for structure and CSS for layout achieves anything like this kind of performance. Indeed, the opposite is too often true. In this section, we'll look at the dumb ways too many sites are built and explain why these methods are counterproductive. We'll also concoct denigrating labels for several especially unsavory techniques that are used too often. Reading this section will not only banish these bad habits from your work, but it will also help you spot these errors in the work of your colleagues and vendors.

After you've read this section of the chapter and engraved its simple lessons on your heart, when colleagues or vendors try to get away with certain kinds of foolish markup, you will call them on it, using the chillingly apt descriptive labels invented in this chapter. Your colleagues and vendors will develop a newfound respect for markup, a newfound respect for you, and above all, a profound discomfort whenever you're around them.

Actually, I named the bad authoring practices described next not to make fun of anyone, but simply to identify and banish these practices from my own work. Since the first edition was published, they have entered the lexicon of web design and helped scores of designers and developers clean up their act and their markup. I hope they help you, too.

Classitis: The Measles of Markup

Modern designers use CSS instead of table layouts with outmoded presentational markup tools like `bgcolor` and `font`. Today, even web designers living under a Siberian rock know we don't want stuff like this on our pages:

```
<td align="left" valign="top" bordercolor="black"
bgcolor="white">
<font family="verdana, arial" size="2">Shoot me</font></td>
```

But the results are no better if structure and semantics are abandoned in favor of the quick fix. Even on "famous" sites like Facebook, we see far too much tripe like this:

```
<div class="leftandtopalign"><p class="small"><span
class="blackborder">
Shoot the developer, then shoot me</span></p></div>
```

I call this style of markup *classitis*. In a site afflicted by classitis, every element, whether structural or not, breaks out in its own swollen, blotchy `class`. Consider this example:

```
<p class="bodycopy">Text goes here.</p>
<p class="bodycopy">More text goes here.</p>
<p class="bodycopy">Still more goes here.</p>
```

What should our markup look like instead?

```
<p>Text goes here.</p>
<p>More text goes here.</p>
<p>Still more goes here.</p>
```

If we think we need a `class` to style each paragraph in a given page section, what we probably need to do is wrap our paragraphs in a `div` that conveys the structure of that section of the page, and style all paragraphs in that section by using the containing block as a targeting mechanism—a technique explained later in the book, when we dive into CSS. Here's what the resulting markup might look like:

```
<div id="maincontent">
  <p>Text goes here.</p>
  <p>More text goes here.</p>
  <p>Still more goes here.</p>
</div>
```

Classitis obscures meaning as it adds needless weight to every page. The affliction dates back to the early days of semi-CSS-capable browsers and to many designers' initially childish comprehension of how CSS works.

Alas, many have not yet outgrown that misunderstanding of CSS, either because they moved on to study some other technology or because their visual editing tool applies a `class` to every tag it generates, and they have "learned" CSS by studying the source their tool produces. Classitis is as bad in its own way as the `font` tag ever was; rarely does good markup require it.

Visual Editors and Classitis

Even the best, most sophisticated visual web editors tend to cough up needless classes like so many cold germs—primarily because they are visual editors, not people. People can abstract from the specific to the general. When you style a paragraph in CSS, you know that you intend all paragraphs to be styled the same way. But a visual editor cannot know what you intend. If, while working in such an editor, you create five paragraphs that all use 0.75em Verdana, the tool might assign a class to each of these paragraphs. Even when using as sophisticated a tool as Adobe Dreamweaver or Microsoft Expression, you'll want to edit its output to avoid classitis and divitis.

The Heartbreak of Divitis

In its better moments, classitis can be grafted onto otherwise structural markup:

```
<p class="noindent">This is a bad way to design web pages.</p>
<p class="indentnomargintop">There is no need for all these
classes.</p>
<p class="indentnomargintop">Classy designers avoid this
problem.</p>
<p class="indentnomargintop">Class dismissed.</p>
```

The previous example is the kind of thing that even a sophisticated and standards-aware visual-editing tool might generate (see sidebar, "Visual Editors and Classitis"). At other times classitis is exacerbated by a still more serious condition. We have named this condition *divitis*:

```
<div class="primarycontent"><div class="yellowbox"><div
class="heading"><span class="biggertext">Welcome</span> to
the Member page!</div><div class="bodytext">Welcome returning
members.</div><div class="warning1">If you are not a member <a
href="/gohere/" class="warning2">go here</a>!</div></div></div>
```

Here we have no structure whatsoever—only many bytes of nonstructural and hence nonsensical junk markup. Visit such a website with a text browser or last year's mobile phone, and you'll have no idea how the various elements relate to each other. For the fact is, they *don't* relate to each other.

Classitis and divitis replace the nutrition of structure with the empty calories of sugary junk. They are weeds in the garden of meaning.

Prune classitis ruthlessly from your markup and you will see overgrown web pages shrink to half their size. Avoid divitis and you will find yourself writing clean, compact, primarily structural markup that works as well in a text browser as it does in your favorite desktop browser. Do these things rigorously, and you will be well on your way to smarter, more compliant web pages. Only you can prevent divitis.

divs Are Just All Right

Some of you are thinking: "Hey, Mister Fancy Pants Standards Book Fellow, you say div elements are bad, yet you yourself used a div element in the very first example in this chapter. I have caught you in a big fat lie, you bad, bad man."

Actually, I never said div elements are bad and neither did the W3C, which after all created these elements. (If you skipped it, refer back to "div, id, and Other Assistants" earlier in this chapter.) div is an entirely appropriate unit of markup for blocking out structural areas of your site.

Divitis kicks in only when you use div to replace perfectly good (and more appropriate) elements. If you've written a paragraph, then it's a paragraph and should be marked up as such—not as a div of the "text" class. Your highest-level headline should be h1, not div class="headline". See the difference? Sure you do.

Why a div?

Many designers use nonstructural divs to replace everything from headlines to paragraphs. Most who do so, and who've been designing sites for a good long while, acquired the habit when they discovered that 4.0 browsers, particularly Netscape's, wrapped layout-destroying, unwanted white space around structural elements like h1, but managed not to ruin layouts that used only nonstructural divs.

Having learned in the bad old days to use nonstructural div elements to the exclusion of standard paragraphs, headlines, and so on, many designers still do so today. The cost of so doing is high. The practice renders sites semantically impenetrable to an ever-growing group of mobile and screen reader users. And it doubles the bandwidth for every site visitor, regardless of what browser or device they're using. Not worth it.

Another classic example of divitis kicks in when a designer catches the "tables are bad, CSS is good" virus and righteously replaces 200 tons of table markup with 200 tons of nested divs. They haven't gained a thing (except a smug, self-satisfied feeling) and they may even have made their document harder to edit.

Loving the id

So if presentational HTML is out, and classitis and divitis are out, how can we convey that an element is "special," and requires special treatment? We can do it through the wizardry of id. Assign a unique label to items that are unique, such as ul id="navigation" or div id="search". Later, when you write your style sheet, you'll create a selector such as ul#navigation or div#search and an associated set of CSS rules that can control the appearance of these elements and their children, down to the pixel if you wish. You can then use these same selectors in your standard JavaScript to control how these elements and their children behave.

Banish (or Minimize) Inline CSS and Scripting

If we are to create lean, semantic pages, the final thing we must do is banish inline CSS and scripting. Markup like the following adds needless bandwidth and will make it harder for us to update our design or migrate our content to the next CMS:

```
<div style="float: left; width: 500px;"><p style="font-family:
'Helvetica Neue', Arial, Helvetica, sans-serif;">Got some
Helvetica, y'all!</p></div>
```

If you've paid attention, you know that this CSS belongs in a style sheet, not in the page's markup. And what's true for the visual goose is true for the behavioral gander:

```
<span id="somebehavior" onclick="SomeFunction();">Some text</
span>
```

Although this is the way we all learned to code JavaScript (and although the first edition of this book contained JavaScript written in precisely this way), it's the wrong way to do things today. Chapter 15 will have more details, but the problems with inline JavaScript include:

- Like inline CSS, divitis, classitis, and old-school table layout techniques, it adds needless weight, and thus wait;
- Like inline CSS, inline scripts are not cached, forcing the user to download them each time and adding further weight;
- Like inline CSS, inline JavaScript is hard to maintain, because your code is scattered everywhere instead of being stored in a single, logical location;
- Last but hardly least, inline JavaScript lacks a fallback interaction handler, making it inaccessible to some users. By contrast, unobtrusive scripting, explained in Chapter 15, works even when JavaScript is not supported.

Pause and Refresh

We have now learned all we need to know to create lean, vigorous markup—markup that is purely structural and semantic (at least, as semantic as a child of SGML can get). Now comes the fun part: adding design through the beauty and elegance of CSS. Turn the page when you're ready to begin.

chapter nine

CSS Basics

In this chapter, we'll move swiftly through the rudiments of CSS grammar, cover a few not-so-basic ideas, and end by describing a CSS design method. Even if you're familiar with CSS, you might want to stick around.

CSS Overview

The W3C rather crisply defines CSS as "a simple mechanism for adding style (for example, fonts, colors, spacing) to web documents" (`www.w3.org/Style/css`). A few details omitted from that summary are worth noting:

- CSS is a standard layout language for the web—one that controls colors, typography, and the size and placement of elements and images.

- Although precise and powerful, CSS is easy to author by hand, as this chapter will show. Indeed, CSS framers Håkon Lie and Bert Bos designed the web's layout language to be easy to learn, teach, implement, maintain, and (eventually) extend, choosing ease of understanding over advanced power at the cost of profound complexity (`www.zeldman.com/2009/07/24/why-standards-fail`).

- CSS is bandwidth friendly: a single CSS file can control the appearance of an entire site comprising thousands of pages and hundreds of megabytes.

- CSS was intended by its creators (the W3C) to replace HTML table-based layouts, frames, and other presentational hacks, leaving markup to its original purpose: semantically describing our content.

- Pure CSS layout, combined with structural XHTML, can help designers separate presentation from structure, making sites more accessible and easier to maintain, as described in the next section.

CSS Benefits

A Russian proverb states, "Repetition is the mother of learning." So forgive us if we wax a tad repetitive in reminding you that CSS, like other web standards, was not created for abstract purposes and was not intended for some distant future. Used well, right now, CSS provides practical benefits including (but not limited to) these:

- Conserves user bandwidth, thus speeding page load times, especially over dial-up.

- Reduces site owner's server and bandwidth requirements, saving money. (See Chapter 1.)

- Once mastered, reduces design and development time, facilitating dynamic prototyping. This makes CSS eminently suitable for agile development and web application design. (These savings pertain only to time spent on development, of course: user experience design, content strategy, interface design, and artistic development still take as long as they take.)

- Reduces updating and maintenance time.

- Content folks no longer need to worry about complex tables, font tags, or other old-school layout components that can break when text is updated. Because there are no (or fewer) such elements, there is little or nothing to break.

- Designers, developers, and agencies no longer need to worry about clients breaking the site.

- Global changes can be accomplished in minutes. Text too dark? Tweak a rule or two in the CSS file and the entire site instantly reflects the change.

- Increases interoperability by adhering to W3C web standards.

- Increases accessibility by removing presentational elements from markup.

Anatomy of Styles

In this section, we'll introduce you to the thighs, wings, and drumsticks of CSS. Well, we'll introduce you to the thighs and drumsticks. This book is not a full-blown CSS reference manual. A CSS reference manual could exceed the length of this book, although our favorite CSS reference is small enough to fit in your pocket—see the sidebar, "CSS by the Book(s)." On the other hand, how many full-blown CSS reference manuals use the word *thighs* three times in one paragraph? Your money was well spent on this book. Our anatomy of styles begins next.

CSS by the Book(s)

- *The CSS Pocket Reference* (Eric Meyer: O'Reilly & Associates, Inc., 2001), as its name suggests, fits in your pocket or purse. But don't let the small size or publication date fool you. It is the clearest and most complete guide I know to the ins and outs of CSS1.

Also very highly recommended:

- *Bulletproof Web Design* (New Riders: Dan Cederholm)
- *Handcrafted CSS* (New Riders: Dan Cederholm and Ethan Marcotte)
- *Transcending CSS: The Fine Art of Web Design* (New Riders: Andy Clarke)
- *CSS Mastery: Advanced Web Standards Solutions* (Friends of Ed: Andy Budd)
- *Web Standards Creativity* (Friends of Ed: Budd, Weychert, Lloyd, Rubin, et. al)
- *Stylin' with CSS: A Designer's Guide* (New Riders: Charles Wyke-Smith)
- *The Zen of CSS Design* (New Riders: Dave Shea, Molly E. Holzschlag)

Selectors, Declarations, Properties, and Values

A style sheet consists of one or more rules that control the way selected elements should be displayed. A CSS rule set consists of two parts: a selector and a declaration block:

```
p { color: red; }
```

In the preceding rule, p is the selector, whereas color: red;, contained within the curly braces, is a declaration. Declarations, in turn, also consist of two parts: a property and a value. In the earlier declaration, color is the property, red the value.

Choices and Options

Instead of the English word "red," we might have written the hexadecimal (web color) value of #ff0000:

```
p { color: #ff0000; }
```

As the hexadecimal color is made up of three matching pairs ("FF" for the red value, "00" for the blue and green values), we might save a few bytes by using CSS shorthand that means exactly the same thing:

```
p { color: #f00; }
```

We could also have used RGB in either of two ways:

```
p { color: rgb(255,0,0); }
p { color: rgb(100%,0%,0%); }
```

Zero Is Optional, Except When It's Not

Notice that when you're using RGB percentages, the percent sign appears even when the value is zero. This is untrue in other CSS situations. For instance, when specifying a size of 0 pixels, the 0 need not be followed by px.

Many of us consider it bad form to write 0px or 0in or 0pt or 0cm. Zero is zero. Who cares what the unit of measurement is when its value is zero? But when specifying RGB percentages, the value of zero requires a percentage sign. Don't ask me, I just work here.

Multiple Declarations

It is bad form to specify a color without also specifying a background color, and vice-versa:

```
p { color: #f00; background-color: white; }
```

Notice that a rule can consist of more than one declaration and that semicolons are used to separate one declaration from the next.

Semicolon Health

Here we go again with the inconsistencies and exceptions. The last rule in any declaration need not end in a semicolon, and some designers leave out the final semicolon in a series of declarations. (That's because, as in the English language, the semicolon functions as a separator, not a terminator.)

But most experienced CSS authors add the semicolon to the end of every declaration anyway. They do this partly for consistency's sake, but mainly to avoid headaches when adding and subtracting declarations to and from existing rules. If every property/value pair ends in a semicolon, you don't have to worry when you move declarations from one place to another.

Whitespace and Case Insensitivity

Most style sheets naturally contain more than one rule set, and most rule sets contain more than one declaration. Multiple declarations are easier to keep track of, and style sheets are easier to edit when we use whitespace:

```
body {
    color: #000;
    background: #fff;
    margin: 0;
    padding: 0;
    font-family: Georgia, Palatino, serif;
    }

p {
  font-size: small;
    }
```

Whitespace, or its absence, has no effect on the way CSS displays in browsers, and unlike XHTML, CSS selectors are not case sensitive; the selectors above could be written as BODY and P, and the browser would play along. Naturally, there is an exception: class and id names are case sensitive when they're associated with an HTML document. myText and mytext are not matches in such a situation. CSS itself is case insensitive, but the document language might not be.

Alternative and Generic Values

A web designer might specify fonts for an entire site as follows:

```
body {
     font-family: "Lucida Grande", Verdana, Lucida, Arial,
Helvetica, sans-serif;
     }
```

Notice that multi-word font names (Lucida Grande) must be enclosed within straight ASCII quotation marks, and that the comma follows rather than precedes the closing quotation mark, to the annoyance of literate American designers accustomed to placing the comma inside the quotation marks.

Fonts are used in the order listed. If the user's computer contains the font Lucida Grande, text will be displayed in that face. If not, Verdana will be used. If Verdana is missing, Lucida will be used. And so on. Why these fonts in this order?

Using Order to Accommodate Multiple Platforms

Order matters. Lucida Grande is found in Mac OS X. Verdana is found in all modern Windows systems, in Mac OS X, and in older ("Classic") Mac operating systems. If Verdana were listed first, OS X Macs would display Verdana instead of Lucida Grande.

With the first two fonts—Lucida Grande and Verdana—the designer has met the needs of nearly all users (Windows and Macintosh users). Lucida follows for UNIX folks, and then Arial for users of old Windows systems. Helvetica will be used in old UNIX systems. If none of the listed fonts is available, the generic sans-serif assures that whatever sans-serif font is available will be pressed into service. In the unlikely event that the user's computer contains no sans-serif fonts, the browser's default font will be used instead. If the browser has no default font, the teeth of a small chimp will be used. Just kidding with that last part.

Not a Perfect Science

No one pretends that Lucida, Verdana, Arial, and Helvetica are equivalent in their beauty, elegance, width, x-height (desktoppub.about.com/od/glossary/g/xheight.htm), or fitness for screen service—or even that all pressings of Helvetica are equally good. Our goal is not to create identical visual experiences for all users; platform, browser, monitor size, monitor resolution, monitor quality, gamma, and OS anti-aliasing settings make that quite impossible. We simply try to ensure that all visitors have the best experience their conditions permit, and that those experiences are fairly similar from one user to the next. It should be noted, however, that `font-size-adjust` is a good way to get equivalent x-height across your fallback fonts. Technical editor Aaron Gustafson employed this very approach when coding the Brighter Planet social media network designed by Happy Cog (`www.brighterplanet.com`).

CSS `@font-face`, which embeds real fonts on your page, is an exception to this general principle, and will be discussed in a separate chapter.

Grouped Selectors

When several elements share stylistic properties, you can apply one declaration to multiple selectors by ganging them together in a comma-delimited list:

```
p, td, ul, ol, ul, li, dl, dt, dd {
   font-size: 1.2em;
   }
```

When coupled with style sheets' natural inheritance, discussed in the next section, this grouping of selectors can be a powerful technique indeed.

Inheritance and Its Discontents

According to CSS, properties inherit from parent to child elements. But it doesn't always happen that way. Consider the following rule:

```
body {
   font-family: Verdana, sans-serif;
   }
```

Having come this far in Chapter 9, you know as well as I do what this rule says. The site's body element will use Verdana if that font is found on the visitor's system; otherwise, it will use a generic sans-serif font.

All Its Children

Per CSS inheritance, what's true for the highest-level element (in this case, the `body` element) is true for its children (such as `p`, `td`, `ul`, `ol`, `ul`, `li`, `dl`, `dt`, and `dd`). Without the addition of even one more rule, all of `body`'s children should display in Verdana or a generic sans-serif, as should their children and their children's children. And that's exactly what happens in modern browsers.

(Because ancient browsers like Netscape 4 didn't understand inheritance, previous editions of this book recommended writing "Be Kind to Netscape 4" rules that explicitly listed every child of the body. Nobody needs to write such rules today, and if you're cleaning up CSS you or someone else wrote years ago, a great place to start is by deleting these redundancies and trusting browsers to respect inheritance.)

Is Inheritance a Curse?

What if you don't want `Verdana, sans-serif` to be inherited by every child element? What if, for instance, you want your paragraphs to display in Times? No problem. Create a more specific rule for `p` (highlighted in bold in the following code), and it will override the parental rule:

```
body {
    font-family: Verdana, sans-serif;
  }
p {
    font-family: Times, "Times New Roman", serif;
  }
```

And a good Times will be had by… OK, I won't do that.

Descendant Selectors

You can avoid classitis and keep your markup neat and clean by making the style of an element dependent upon the context in which it appears. Selectors that apply rules in this way are called contextual selectors in CSS1 because they rely on context to apply a rule or refrain from doing so. CSS2 calls them descendant selectors, but their effect is the same no matter what you call them. (As this edition goes to press, pretty much anyone who's anyone calls them descendant selectors.)

To italicize text that's marked `strong` and prevent it from displaying in bold-face when it occurs within a list item, you would type:

```
li strong {
    font-style: italic;
    font-weight: normal;
  }
```

What does a rule like that do?

```
<p><strong>I am bold and not italic because I do not appear in
a list item. The rule has no effect on me.</strong></p>
<ol>
<li><strong>I am italic and of Roman (normal) weight because I
occur within a list item.</strong></li>
<li>I am ordinary text in this list.</li>
</ol>
```

Or consider the following CSS:

```
strong {
    color: red;
    }
h2 {
    color: red;
    }
h2 strong {
    color: blue;
    }
```

and its effect on markup:

```
<p>The strongly emphasized word in this paragraph is
<strong>red</strong>.</p>
<h2>This subhead is also red.</h2>
<h2>The strongly emphasized word in this subhead is
<strong>blue</strong>.</h2>
```

You probably won't use descendant selectors to slim down and italicize normally boldface text in lists. You might use these selectors to create sophisticated design enhancements, such as adding a background image to an
ordinary (X)HTML element, along with sufficient whitespace (padding) to
prevent the text from overlapping the image. But more likely, you would create
those kinds of effects using id or class selectors.

id Selectors and Descendant Selectors

In modern layouts, id selectors, introduced in Chapter 6, are often used to set
up descendant selectors.

```
#sidebar p {
    font-style: italic;
    text-align: right;
    margin-top: 0.5em;
    }
```

The preceding style will be applied only to paragraphs that occur in an element whose id is "sidebar". That element will mostly likely be a div, although it could also be a table or some other block-level element. It could even be an inline element, such as <em></em> or <span></span>, although such usages would be as bizarre as a rat in spats, not to mention invalid—you can't nest a p inside a span. Regardless of which element is used, it must be the only element on that page to use an id of "sidebar". Flip back to Chapter 6 if you've forgotten why.

One Selector, Multiple Uses

Even though the element identified as "sidebar" will appear only once per page in the markup, the id selector can be used in descendant selectors as many times as needed:

```
#sidebar p {
    font-style: italic;
    text-align: right;
    margin-top: 0.5em;
    }
#sidebar h2 {
    font-size: 1em;
    font-weight: normal;
    font-style: italic;
    margin: 0;
    line-height: 1.5;
    text-align: right;
    }
```

Here, p elements in sidebar get a special treatment distinct from all other p elements on the page, and h2 elements in sidebar get a different, special treatment distinct from all other h2 elements on the page.

The Selector Stands Alone

The id selector need not be used to create descendant selectors. It can stand on its own:

```
#sidebar {
    border: 1px dotted #000;
    padding: 10px;
    }
```

According to this rule, the page element whose id is "sidebar" will have a dotted black (#000) border that's one pixel thick, with padding (inner whitespace) of 10 pixels all the way around.

Class Selectors

Discrimination on the basis of class is a terrible thing in life but a fine thing in style sheets. In CSS, class selectors are indicated by a dot:

```
.fancy {
    color: #f60;
    background: #666;
    }
```

Any element classified (get it?) as "fancy" will sport orange (#f60) text on a gray (#666) background. Thus, both <h1 class="fancy">Boy Howdy!</h1> and <p class="fancy">Yee haw!</p> will share this striking color scheme.

Like id, classes can also be used in descendant selectors:

```
.fancy td {
    color: #f60;
    background: #666;
  }
```

In the preceding example, table cells within some containing element whose class name is "fancy" will have orange text with a gray background. (The larger element whose name is "fancy" might be a table row or a div.)

Elements can also be selected based on their classes:

```
td.fancy {
    color: #f60;
    background: #666;
    }
```

In the preceding example, table cells of class "fancy" will be orange with a gray background.

```
<td class="fancy">
```

You can assign the class of "fancy" to only one table cell or to as many as you want. Those so classified will be orange with a gray background. Table cells that are not assigned a class of "fancy" will not be influenced by this rule. Just as significantly, a paragraph of class "fancy" will not be orange with a gray background, nor will any other element of class "fancy" be orange with a gray background. The effect is limited to table cells classified as "fancy" because of the way we wrote the rule (using the td element to select the "fancy" class).

Combining Selectors to Create Sophisticated Design Effects

Class, id, and descendant selectors can be combined to create subtle or striking visual effects. Housing Works is a nonprofit organization that works to end homelessness. In the Housing Works site designed by Happy Cog, the brand-appropriate image of a house's roof (bullet-std.png) replaces the boring black dot found in ordinary unordered lists [9.1].

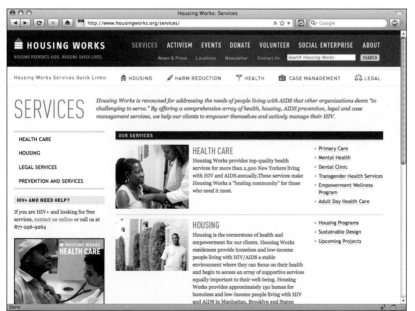

9.1
Descendant, class, and **id** selectors can be combined to create visual effects. On certain sections of their site (**www. housingworks.org/ services**), the boring dot found in most unordered lists is replaced by a pink triangle, a subtle nod to their logo.

Following are the CSS rules that tell unordered lists of class "std" to display an image instead of a plain dot:

```
ul.std {
    list-style: none;
}
ul.std li {
    background: url(../i/screen/bullet-std.png) no-repeat 0
.5em;
    margin: 0;
    padding: 0 0 5px 10px;
}
```

And here, abbreviated to fit on this page, is the markup it rides in on:

```
<ul class="microlist std">
<li><a href="/services/health-care/1-primary-care/">Primary
Care</a></li>
<li><a href="/services/health-care/2-mental-health/">Mental
Health</a></li>
<li><a href="/services/health-care/3-dental/">Dental Clinic</
a></li>
</ul>
```

If you've been following along, you'll understand that an unordered list of a different class will not show the pink triangle, nor will the triangle appear if the class is applied to anything other than an unordered list.

However, the live rule on the Housing Works site actually includes a grouped selector:

```
.secondary-content ul li,
ul.std li,
.full-col ul.std li li,
.home .col ul.std li {
    background: url(../i/screen/bullet-std.png) no-repeat 0
.5em;
    margin: 0;
    padding: 0 0 5px 10px;
    }
```

Why bulk up our CSS rule in this way? With a rule grouping multiple selectors together, we can apply this style to multiple elements of our design without peppering our markup with the "std" class. This means our markup stays lean, leaving our CSS to do the heavy lifting.

Moving Ahead

We will learn more about CSS grammar in the next chapter, but at this point, we must pause to consider a query: Where do we stick our CSS? Does it get tucked into the (X)HTML somewhere? Is it a separate file, or what? (Hint: Keep reading.)

External, Embedded, and Inline Styles

Style sheets can be applied to a web page in any of three ways: external, embedded, or inline. We'll start with the best first.

External Style Sheets

An external style sheet (CSS file) is a text document that lives separately from the (X)HTML pages it controls. An (X)HTML page uses that CSS file by referring to it via a `link` element in the head of the document or by importing it into a `style` element (also in the head of the document). A style sheet link looks like this:

```
<link rel="stylesheet" href="/styles/mystylesheet.css"
type="text/css" media="screen" />
```

The `@import` directive, used to import a style sheet, looks like this:

```
<style type="text/css" media="screen">
@import "/styles/mystylesheet.css";
</style>
```

or this:

```
<style type="text/css" media="screen">
@import url("/styles/mystylesheet.css");
</style>
```

Whether linked or imported, external style sheets provide the greatest power at the lowest cost. After an external style sheet has been downloaded to the user's cache, it remains active and can control the design of one, dozens, hundreds, or even hundreds of thousands of pages on the site without requiring an additional download. That's mighty handy.

The benefits of greatly lowered user and server bandwidth are available only when you use external style sheets.

Embedded Style Sheets

Instead of linking to or importing one or more separate style sheet files, a designer can embed the style sheet rules in the head of an XHTML 1.0 page, using the `style` element as shown (and highlighted in bold) next:

```
<!DOCTYPE html PUBLIC "-//W3C//DTD XHTML 1.0 Transitional//EN"
    "http://www.w3.org/TR/xhtml1/DTD/xhtml1-transitional.dtd">
<html xmlns="http://www.w3.org/1999/xhtml">
<head>
<meta http-equiv="Content-type" content="text/html;
charset=utf-8" />
<title>Site Title</title>
<style type="text/css">
<!--
body {
    background: #FFF;
    color: #000;
    }
-->
</style>
</head>
```

Unlike linked or imported styles, embedded styles offer no bandwidth benefit because the user must load a new embedded style sheet each time she opens a new page. Even if the embedded style sheet is the same on every page, the user still has to download it. You might wonder, then, why a designer would ever use an embedded style sheet. Here are a few reasons:

- The site consists of only one page. I didn't say it was likely—I just said it was possible.

- The designer's audience lives in a time warp and is using IE3 to visit the site. IE3 was the first browser to begin supporting bits and pieces of CSS. It did not support external style sheets. Okay, come to think of it, that's not a very likely reason either.

- The designer has used external style sheets to control the entire site, but she needs to create additional rules for just one page. That is an excellent reason to create an embedded style sheet.

- The designer is still creating the style sheet and needs to immediately see the effect of changes made to it. This is the other excellent reason to create an embedded style sheet.

When you're designing a site, it makes perfect sense to embed the style sheet in the head of the page you're working on. Then, when your design is just the way you like it, you can copy the styles to an external CSS file and delete the embedded style from your markup. I do this every time I design a website. (Note: many full-time front-end web developers set up a local server and use absolute paths instead of this technique.)

An @import of Some Import

There's an additional technique available to the standards-savvy style sheet slinger: namely, CSS files can @import other CSS files. (We'll let that sink in for a moment. Still with us? Good.) Let's say we've included a single link to a main.css file:

```
<!DOCTYPE html PUBLIC "-//W3C//DTD XHTML 1.0 Transitional//EN"
    "http://www.w3.org/TR/xhtml1/DTD/xhtml1-transitional.dtd">
<html xmlns="http://www.w3.org/1999/xhtml">
<head>
<meta http-equiv="Content-Type" content="text/html;
charset=utf-8" />
<title>Your Title Here</title>
<link rel="stylesheet" href="/css/main.css" type=
"text/css" media="screen, projection" />
</head>
```

If we opened up that main.css file, we might find the following:

```
@import url("reset.css");
@import url("core.css");
@import url("lib/sIFR.css");
@import url("lib/lightbox.css");
@import url("2009-fall-colors.css");
```

Each of those imported style sheets are linked to our XHTML document through the main.css "container" file, their style rules each evaluated and applied in turn. What's the benefit of this approach?

- If you're working on a respectably sized website, or perhaps on a suite of applications, you might partition shared components into their own CSS files.
- Some third-party UI widgets like Lightbox (www.huddletogether. com/projects/lightbox) and sIFR (wiki.novemberborn.net/sifr3) require you to include a CSS file before they will function. In those cases,

keeping those style sheets separate from your own can help with future upgrades.

- Or maybe you'd simply like to partition your CSS into files that speak to different elements of the design—`typography.css`, `colors.css`, and so on.

Including multiple style sheets through a single linked style sheet can often be helpful. But keep in mind that each style sheet referenced by your document is an extra "hit" on your server, which could impact a high-traffic server's performance. Then, too, Microsoft's browsers don't cache imported styles beyond a few depth levels. Furthermore, creating a truckload of CSS files might create maintenance headaches. On the other hand, those with backend expertise can have the best of both worlds by using the server to merge multiple CSS files into a single one when requested. Experiment with these techniques to determine what works best for you and your users.

Inline Styles

CSS can be applied to an individual element by using the style attribute to that element, as in the examples that follow:

```
<h1 style="font-family: Verdana, Arial, sans-serif;">
Headline</h1>
<img style="margin-top: 25px;">
```

As you might expect, inline styles save no bandwidth—indeed, they add bandwidth to every page that uses them and are generally as wasteful as `font` tags in that regard.

Web pages should never be styled primarily with inline CSS. It's as absurd as painting your house with a bottle of Wite-Out. But used with respect and discretion, inline CSS can be a helpful tool. Inline styles are the touch-up paint of CSS, and they have saved many a dented digital fender. For example, if you absolutely have to change the positioning of an often-used element just once on one page, you might save bandwidth by doing it with inline CSS, rather than writing an embedded style that references a one-time class name, and then applying that class name to the element in question.

The "Best-Case Scenario" Design Method

In the old days, when we created layouts almost entirely with presentational markup, we would test our work in the oldest, crummiest browser on our hard drive. To make it look right in that old browser, we'd build deeply nested tables; use nonstructural `divs` in place of structural elements like `h1, h2, li,` and `p`; and do all the other things we don't want to do any more.

When the site looked right in the bad old browser, we would test it in a new browser, where it also quite likely looked good—but at a terrible cost to bandwidth and semantics. Many web designers still follow this practice of designing for the worst browser they can get their hands on. But the cost is too high; the method is no longer productive.

Instead, write your CSS in an embedded style sheet and preview your work in a browser you trust, such as the latest versions of Firefox, Opera, or Safari. In this way, you'll create accessible, low-bandwidth, compliant pages that let markup be markup and that use CSS correctly.

When you're satisfied with what you've designed, test the page in other good, compliant browsers, such as IE8. It should look the same in all of them. If it doesn't, you have more work to do. One of your CSS rules might be incorrectly written, yet your favorite browser understood what you intended, as a friend sometimes understands you when you talk with your mouth full. The W3C's markup and CSS validators (`validator.w3.org` and `jigsaw.w3.org/css-validator`, respectively) can help you catch these faux pas before you begin your testing.

Of course, not all browsers are 100% standards compliant—as we've said before, none of them are. So what happens when bad browsers meet good code? If your site works correctly and looks great in good browsers, but has problems in less compliant ones, you need to at least consider using hacks or workarounds. Fortunately, such things are addressed in our very next chapter. Read on, MacDuff.

chapter ten

CSS Layout: Markup, Boxes, and Floats— Oh My!

In this chapter, you'll finally be bringing your standards savvy to bear on a proper page layout. Your skills will be focused on a single page design like some sort of white-hot standards laser thing. And my similes may falling be flat, but *you* won't: nine chapters of knowledge, theory, and standards know-how have you well prepared for the simple exercises contained in this chapter. Trust me. You just have that look about you.

But first, to better understand the finer points of CSS, let's examine the mechanics of page layout and how our style sheets can influence them.

The Dao of Page Flow

Every element in a web page occupies a position within the document's *flow*, and affects the position of the elements around it. No matter the tag, each element creates a "box" in the document flow, whose properties can then be manipulated by our CSS.

There are two kinds of boxes:

1. *Block boxes* stretch horizontally to occupy the full width of their containing element, and push subsequent elements down to the next line. Paragraphs, lists, tables, divs, and heading elements like h1 and h2 are all fine examples of this blocky behavior.

2. By contrast, *inline boxes*—such as those generated by a, img, em, span, and strong—are laid out horizontally within their containing box, resting comfortably (you guessed it) in a line with their neighboring inline elements. If the inline elements' container isn't wide enough to accommodate them, they'll wrap onto the next line.

Without any CSS applied to it, every HTML element in your page's flow will fall squarely into one of these two formatting models. That's why your paragraphs and headings stack on top of each other, and why multiple links fit on one line inside an h2, which in turn sits below the h1 that precedes it. However, as you'll see throughout the rest of this chapter—and throughout your time designing with web standards—this behavior is merely a default. It can be overridden completely by your CSS.

Let's take a closer look at these boxes, and their different component parts. They'll be crucial to the layouts built in this chapter, later in this book, and throughout your standards-focused career.

Meet the Box Model

Figure **10.1** illustrates the four areas of the CSS box model. Every box, be it inline or block, has a *content area* in the middle, which is surrounded by *padding* and a *border*. The entire box is then offset from other elements by a *margin* on each of its four sides.

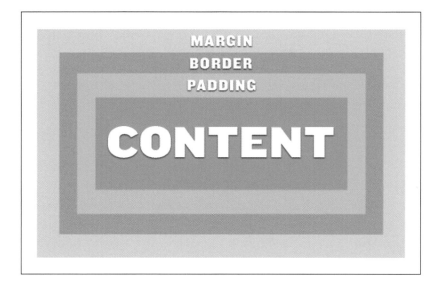

10.1

The four areas of the generic CSS box: content, padding, border, and margin. (The margin was artificially darkened for your viewing pleasure.)

We can easily alter each of these four properties with a few modest lines of CSS:

```
#content {
    border: 5px solid #000;
    height: 200px;
    margin: 10px;
    padding: 20px;
    width: 400px;
}
```

In this rule, we've selected an element with an `id` attribute of "content" and assigned a width and height to its content area, which is bounded by a 20px-wide padding and a 5px-wide black border. Notice that we didn't write this:

```
content: 400px;
```

We also didn't write anything like this:

```
content-area-width: 400px;
content-area-height: 75px;
```

There are no such properties in CSS. Border, margins, and padding are assigned their values by name; the content area is not. In beginning to learn and use CSS, you might understandably assume that `width: 400px` applies to the entire box (excluding the margin). After all, that is how page layout programs work, it is how designers think, and it is how users understand layouts. If you create a CSS layout containing two `divs` side by side and assign each a width of 50% of the visitor's browser window, you might expect the two to retain that value as you add padding and borders. But that is not how CSS works.

In fact, the CSS box model is more sophisticated than what common sense and graphic design norms would lead you to expect.

How the Box Model Works

According to CSS, each of the four areas (content, padding, border, and margin) can be assigned values, and these values are additive. To determine the overall width of the box, add the content, padding, and border values together [**10.2**]. If the content width is 400px, the padding is 50px on each side, and the border is 2px per edge, the box's overall width would be 504px (400 content + 2 left border + 50 left padding + 50 right padding + 2 right border = 504 total).

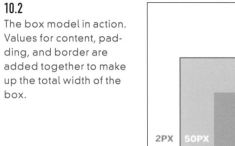

10.2

The box model in action. Values for content, padding, and border are added together to make up the total width of the box.

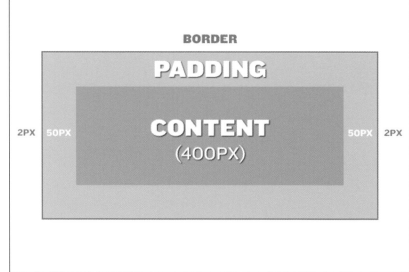

CSS doesn't care how you choose to play chef or which kinds of values you choose to mix and match. For instance, you might specify that the content width is 67% of the visitor's browser window width at the time the page is viewed, the padding is 5em, and the border is 1px thick. The overall size in pixels would then be…uh, pretty hard to figure out, and it would depend on the width of the visitor's browser window and the default (1em) size of text.

When changing the value of a box's margins or padding, we can avail ourselves of shorthand CSS properties for each. For example, we could write this into a rule:

```
margin: 25px 0;
```

This tiny line applies vertical margins of 25px to an element and removes the horizontal margins by setting them to zero. It is a shorthand version of this rule:

```
margin: 25px 0 25px 0;
```

The preceding two rules are, in turn, shorthand versions of this:

```
margin-top: 25px;
margin-right: 0;
margin-bottom: 25px;
margin-left: 0;
```

In CSS, values are assigned in the order of the main numbers on a clock: 12 o'clock (the top margin), 3 o'clock (the right margin), 6 o'clock (the bottom margin), and 9 o'clock (the left margin). If we wanted our page to have a top margin of 25px, a right margin of 5px, a bottom margin of 10px, and a left margin of 3em, our rule *could* be written like this:

```
margin-top: 25px;
margin-right: 5px;
margin-bottom: 10px;
margin-left: 3em;
```

But instead, it's much more efficient to use the margin shorthand property, and set each of the four values in one simple list:

```
margin: 25px 5px 10px 3em;
```

When the vertical margins are the same at the top and bottom (as they are in our first example—namely, 25px) and when the horizontal margins are the same at left and right (again, as they are in the first example—namely 0), we can save a few bytes by typing this:

```
margin: 25px 0;
```

Note: As mentioned in Chapter 9, the 0 value does not require a unit of measurement. 0px is the same as 0cm, 0in, or 0bazillionmiles. (There is no "bazillion miles" unit of measurement in CSS, but if there were, we wouldn't need to use it when the value is zero.)

Of course, if the values for all four margins are the same—say, 25px on each side—we could condense the rule to a single value:

```
margin: 25px;
```

Shorthand properties allow us to gain critical efficiencies in our code, which means our users will download leaner files. This in turn means they'll use less bandwidth when browsing our sites, and therefore lower server overhead for us. Everybody wins.

Now, margin is not the only shorthand CSS property available to us. If the design had called for it, the above examples could easily have been written with padding and its component parts (padding-top, padding-right, padding-bottom, and padding-left). And border can be similarly expanded to border-top, border-right, and so on. But there are shorthand properties that have nothing to do with the box model, some of which we'll use later in this chapter and throughout the rest of this book.

While we've explored quite a bit of the box model, there is more to it than what we've seen so far. For one thing, upper and lower margins of vertically adjacent elements collapse into each other. (Andy Budd, UK designer and standardista extraordinaire, wrote a wonderful essay explaining this very thing. Browse over to www.andybudd.com/archives/2003/11/no_margin_for_error for edification galore.)

But for now, let's put theory aside and see how this whole "box model" thing works in practice.

Applied Layout 101

Consider the following design, breathtaking in its modest aesthetic and eloquent copywriting [**10.3**]. (Okay, we're being generous.) Our designer has sent over a new page mockup, and you've been tasked with converting it into standards-compliant code.

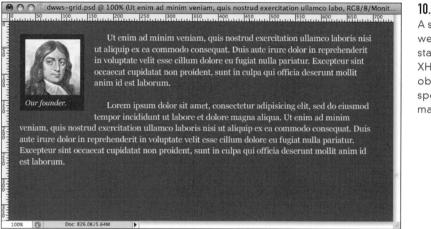

10.3

A simple page mockup we'll be converting into standards-compliant XHTML and CSS. (It's obvious the designer spent weeks on this masterpiece.)

As you review the file that's been dropped in your lap, you might be inclined to start sampling color values, or analyzing typefaces and font sizes. But before we even consider how to implement the *design*, we need to take a mental inventory of the kind of *content* we're looking at, without worrying about how it should look. From there, we'll choose the most semantically appropriate markup first, and introduce CSS to handle the presentation once that semantic foundation is in place.

To build this foundation, we'll use a static XHTML 1.0 Transitional template, like so:

```
<!DOCTYPE html PUBLIC "-//W3C//DTD XHTML 1.0 Transitional//EN"
"http://www.w3.org/TR/xhtml1/DTD/xhtml1-transitional.dtd">

<html xmlns="http://www.w3.org/1999/xhtml" xml:lang="en"
lang="en">
<head>

<meta http-equiv="Content-Type" content="text/html;
charset=utf-8"/>
```

```
<title>My Page Title</title>

<link rel="stylesheet" href="styles.css" type="text/css"
media="screen, projection" />

</head>

<body>


</body>
</html>
```

You could easily use any flavor of HTML 4.01 (or if you're feeling experimental, HTML5) instead, but we like the extra consistency in the markup required by XHTML 1.0. Whatever DOCTYPE you select, the fundamentals will stay the same: we'll be writing valid, semantic HTML into the document's body, and writing our CSS in an external style sheet called styles.css, which is linked to our markup through (surprise!) the link tag in the head of our page.

Let's begin.

Humble Beginnings

Since our mockup contains two paragraphs with a captioned image inset to the left, we'll simply use three p elements to mark up our content:

```
<p><img src="j-milt.jpg" alt="" /> Our founder.</p>

<p>Ut enim ad minim veniam, quis…</p>

<p>Lorem ipsum dolor sit amet, consectetur...</p>
```

These three p elements are simply contained within the body element, and the result [10.4] is simple indeed. Without any style applied, our three paragraphs render within the page's flow as full-width, block-level boxes, vertically stacked atop each other. And the img within the first paragraph sits inline with the text beside it. Now of course, this won't work for our designer: where are the sublime serifs, the captivating color palette?

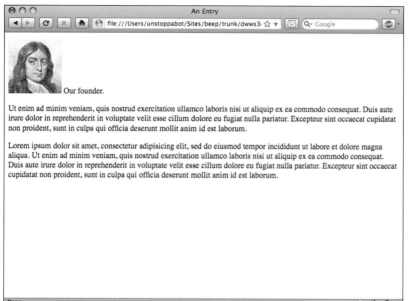

10.4
Without any styles applied, our paragraphs are humble looking indeed. But with this modest foundation in place, exciting stuff lies ahead.

That's easily fixed with a few short lines of CSS. Reviewing the comp, we know that our page's background color is a deep slate (specifically, a hex color of #48505A), with text set in white Georgia at 16px. So let's add the following to our styles.css file:

```
body {
    background: #48505A;
    color: #FFF;
    font: normal 16px/1.375 Georgia, Times, serif;
}
```

As we saw in Chapter 9, each style sheet rule begins with a selector that determines which element (or elements) the rule applies to. So the first rule selects the body element, setting its background to #48505A and the page's text color to white (color: #FFF), while the font property establishes the type parameters for our design. We'll cover the nuances of web typography in Chapter 13, but for now let's behold Figure **10.5** in all its (ahem) glory.

10.5
One style rule later, and we've got color and basic typography in place. Take that, **font** tags.

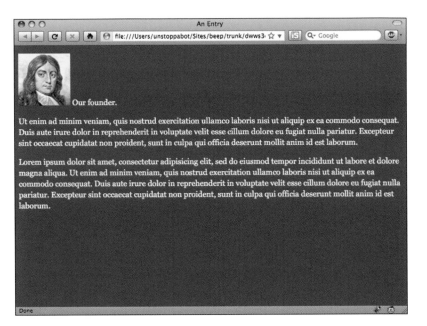

Our template is evolving nicely, but our work's not done yet. With these basic style parameters in place, let's turn our attention to the meat of our meager design: the paragraphs.

```
body {
    background: #48505A;
    color: #FFF;
    font: normal 16px/1.375 Georgia, Times, serif;
}

p {
    margin: 0 0 1em;
    text-indent: 1.5em;
}
```

While the first rule selects our document's sole body element, the second rule applies to all paragraphs on the page—all three of them [**10.6**]. We've used the text-indent property (www.w3.org/TR/CSS21/text. html#indentation-prop) to indent the first line of each paragraph by 1.5 ems. The shorthand margin property zeroes out the top, right-, and left-hand margins from our paragraphs, and sets the bottom margin to 1em. (You'll notice that we didn't need to re-declare either color or font values on our paragraph

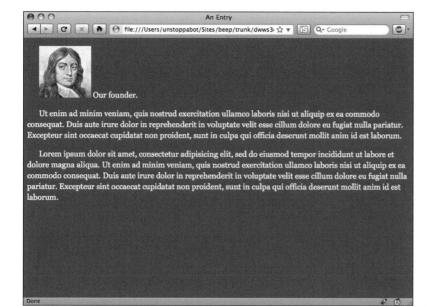

10.6
One more rule, and
we've typographically
tuned all our document's
paragraphs.

Shorthand Rox! (omg srsly)

You may have noticed that our page's font color is described in hex shorthand—I've written #FFF instead of #FFFFFF. As noted in Chapter 9, this shorthand notation can only be used to replace paired characters: #FC0 is the same as #FFCC00. Color shorthand cannot be used in the absence of paired characters. There is no shorthand for a non-websmart color like our body element's #48505A, for example. It also cannot be used unless all three character sets are pairs. For example, #FFCC09 cannot be replaced by #FC09.

Web typography is covered in greater detail in Chapter 13, but you may have noticed that the font property is more verbose than the other properties in our body rule. That's because it's another shorthand property like margin or padding, and

does the work of four separate CSS properties. We could have written the following instead:

```
body {
    background: #48505A;
    color: #FFF;
    font-weight: normal;
    font-size: 16px;
    line-height: 1.375;
    font-family: Georgia, Times,
serif;
}
```

This would, however, have unnecessarily bulked up our CSS, and our users' bandwidth would pay the price. Since each of those four properties (font-weight, font-size, line-height, and font-family) can be set by a single font declaration, the old adage holds true: less is truly more.

rule. That's because both of these properties are inherited from the values we set on our body element, saving us time and bandwidth in the process. See "All Its Children" in Chapter 9 for more information about CSS inheritance, and say a silent prayer of thanks for this time-saving feature.)

So we've slightly tweaked the properties of these elements' box model, and our template is quickly coming together. However, one design detail still needs some attention: how do we convert that topmost paragraph into an inset image?

A Touch o' *class*

The p element containing our image will be styled differently than its siblings, so we'll need some sort of "hook" in our markup for our CSS to identify that particular paragraph. To that end, we can add a class attribute to the element, and assign the appropriately descriptive value of "figure" to it:

```
<p class="figure"><img src="j-milt.jpg" alt="" /> Our
founder.</p>
```

(If we knew this design element was going to be unique to the page, we could have used an id attribute instead. But we've erred on the side of caution—and of possible style reuse—so the class remains.)

With our new class attribute in place, let's add the following rule to our style sheet:

```
p {
    margin: 0 0 1em;
    text-indent: 1.5em;
}

p.figure {
    background: #2B3036;
    font-size: 14px;
    font-style: italic;
    margin-right: 1em;
    padding: 10px;
    text-indent: 0;
}
```

As Figure **10.7** shows, this new rule drastically alters the look of our first paragraph. We've applied a new background color (#2B3036), set the type in an italic face at 14px, and turned off text-indent for this class of paragraphs.

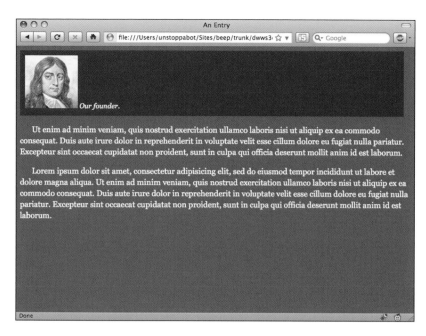

10.7
Our image and caption
pair get a new lick of
paint.

We've added a `10px`-wide `padding` around the inside of the paragraph, and added a right-hand margin that's `1em` thick. And since our second rule's selector is limited only to p elements with a `class` of "figure", our other two paragraphs are untouched.

Next, let's see about getting our caption to sit underneath the image, as it does in the mockup. In figure 10.7, the image and the text adjacent to it in the markup share a line, because `img` elements create inline boxes in the page flow. A new rule, however, can easily override that default:

```
p.figure {
    background: #2B3036;
    font-size: 14px;
    font-style: italic;
    margin-right: 1em;
    padding: 10px;
    text-indent: 0;
}

p.figure img {
    display: block;
    margin-bottom: 0.4em;
}
```

This seems so simple that many of you will skip over it without thinking about it, but explicitly assigning block or inline status to an element is an incredibly powerful tool. With this single rule, we've turned our inline image into a block level box that behaves as a p or div might, pushing the adjacent text down to the subsequent line [10.8]. (We've also added a slight bottom margin to the img as well, creating a bit of air between the image and its corresponding caption, but the display: block is the interesting bit here. Don't you think?)

10.8
The powerful **display** property can turn our inline **img** into a block-level box to be reckoned with.

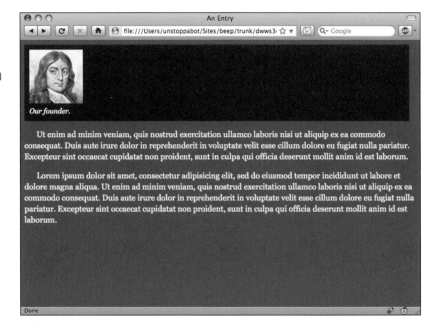

While the display property accepts many values, the entire list is far too long to list here (for the completists in the audience, be sure to check out www.w3.org/TR/CSS21/visuren.html#display-prop).

Our colors are in place, the type is set, and the image is sitting proudly atop the caption. All that's left is to inset our image off to the left. For that, we'll bring the float property into play:

```
p.figure {
    background: #2B3036;
    float: left;
    font-size: 0.875em;
    font-style: italic;
    margin: 0 1em 1em 0;
    padding: 10px;
    text-indent: 0;
}
```

As the name implies (and as Figure **10.9** demonstrates), invoking `float: left` causes our "figure" paragraph to change pretty drastically. First, it causes the element to "float" all the way to the left of its container (the `body` element). Floating an element also has a kind of shrink-wrap effect on it, reducing its width to match the width of the elements it contains. That's why the floated element's width has been reduced to the width of our image, plus the ten pixels of padding we've applied to the left and right sides.

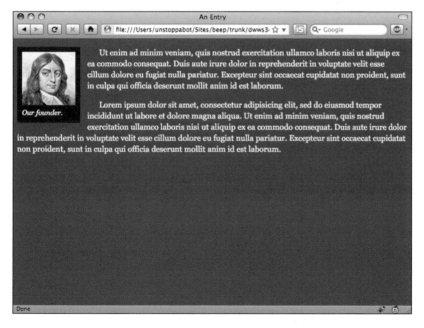

10.9
Meet **float**, a versatile way to alter the page's flow.

It's just as important to note that floated elements are *partially removed* from the document flow. The subsequent non-floated paragraph completely ignores the floated element that precedes it and moves up in the page flow to occupy its position. If we were to put a background and border on that non-floated paragraph, you'd see that our floated paragraph perfectly overlaps it [**10.10**]. However, the *contents* of the paragraph are aware of the position of the floated paragraph, as the text does its best to flow around it.

10.10

We've turned on some fake backgrounds to show how our float has been partially removed from the document flow. Its non-floated neighbors rise up to occupy the space vacated by their floated sibling, while their text reflows around the float.

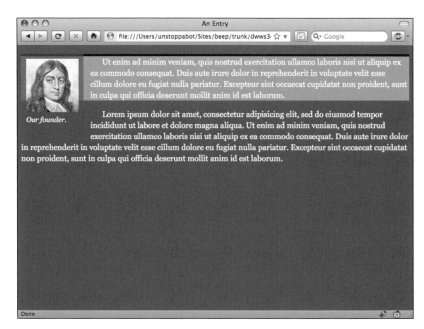

And with that, we've completed our template. With nothing more than a foundation of semantically rich XHTML and a pinch of CSS, we've converted our designer's comp to a pixel-perfect template. And though twenty lines of CSS might seem like a lot, remember that they're housed in an external style sheet that can be included on countless templates. Let's see table cells and spacer GIFs do *that*.

So our assignment's done, right? Time to schedule that coffee break, right?

Reworking Our Layout

Let's not rest on our proverbial laurels quite yet. Here's the skinny: seems your designer (and his bosses) were impressed with how quickly you turned around that last template, and they need some modifications made. In fact, they've sent over a new comp altogether [**10.11**], which bolts a few new modules onto the work you've already done.

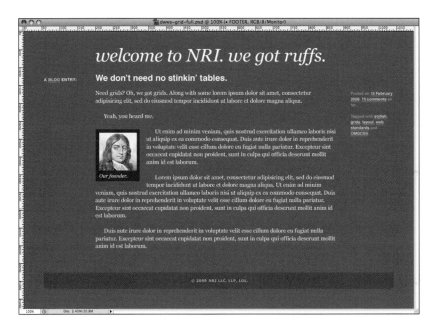

10.11

Our revised page design. The center should look familiar by now, but there've been a few more elements added.

But that's OK—there's no need to hyperventilate (or strangle your designer). Granted, there are a few more elements on the page, but the workflow you've learned in our simple paragraph exercise will see you through. As we did with our three-paragraph template, we'll follow these three easy steps:

1. We'll step back from the design, and put aside aesthetics as we perform an inventory of the kinds of content on the page.

2. Once we've determined those content types, we'll translate them into lightweight, semantic markup.

3. With our finished markup, we'll layer CSS in as needed, making judicious use of `class` and `id` selectors to target specific areas of our design. We'll also lean a bit more heavily on the float model to get the different columns of our design in place.

Sound familiar? That's because you've already mastered this workflow. All standards-based designs are built using some slight variation on the above, so you're already in a great position to dive in.

So let's do just that.

The Content Inventory, Redux

Our first step is to review the kinds of content on our page—to ask what we're actually looking at. As I see it, the design can be broken into a few different content components, which I've outlined in figure **10.12**. Working from the top down, we've got:

1. A prominent headline that titles the entire page.

2. Immediately beneath the main headline is a blog entry, which contains:

    1. The title of the entry, as well as an introductory "intro" headline off to the left.

    2. Two content columns are nested within the entry:

        1. The blog entry's primary content on the left, and

        2. Some meta information off to the right.

3. A footer that spans the entire width of the page, sitting neatly beneath our blog entry.

10.12
We'll review the different content areas of our design, before thinking about how to implement it in CSS.

All of this is contained within a grid-based layout that's 988 pixels wide, and centered horizontally within the page.

Hey, hey, hey—what did we say about not hyperventilating? I realize this seems like quite a departure from our last template, and there *is* more content than before. However, we can reuse much of our earlier work and avoid starting a new template from scratch.

Let's start with our lonely little paragraphs.

```
<p class="figure"><img src="j-milt.jpg" alt="" /> Our
founder.</p>

<p>Ut enim ad minim veniam, quis…</p>

<p>Lorem ipsum dolor sit amet, consectetur…</p>
```

Those three p elements are still at the heart of our page, but they have a few extra layers of content wrapped around them. In fact, if we insert semantically named divs around them that correspond to the content areas we've outlined above, our template will look something like this:

```
<div id="page">

   <div class="entry">
      <div class="content">
         <div class="main">
            <p class="figure"><img src="j-milt.jpg" alt="" />
Our founder.</p>

            <p>Ut enim ad minim veniam, quis…</p>

            <p>Lorem ipsum dolor sit amet, consectetur…</p>
         </div><!-- /end .main -->

         <div class="meta">

         </div><!-- /end .meta -->
      </div><!-- /end .content -->
   </div><!-- /end .entry -->

   <div id="footer">

   </div><!-- /end #footer -->
</div><!-- /end #page -->
```

I've highlighted the original three paragraphs, so you can see just how far we've come. By using the class and id attribute as descriptive labels, our various content types are well represented in our markup: the blog entry has a class of "entry", its meta information is classified as such, and our lone footer has an id of…well, you get the point. And all of these descriptive divisions are sitting pretty within a "page" container, which neatly cordons off all of our content.

As you can see, we're just staring at an empty collection of divs. They're well-named, sure, but there's no content to be had here, which makes our markup pretty meager indeed. Let's do something about that.

First, let's look at the headlines on our page [10.13]. We've got three to work with: the prominent, primary headline at the top of the page; the title of our blog entry; and finally, the informational headline that describes the content immediately to its right. Three headlines, ranked in terms of their priority in the page's content hierarchy. What's a standards-savvy coder to do?

```
<div id="page">
    <h1>Welcome to <abbr title="Neck Ruffs International">NRI</
abbr>. We Got Ruffs.</h1>

    <div class="entry">
        <h2>We don&#8217;t need no stinkin&#8217; tables.</h2>

        <h3 class="info">A <a href="#">Blog</a> Entry:</h3>

        <div class="content">…
```

10.13
Three different head-lines sit at the top of our design. Visually, they're quite different—but let's consider their semantic hierarchy before we get into aesthetics.

If you guessed h1, h2, and h3, you'd be so very right. (Leave your name and address with the man out front, if you don't mind. We've a lovely door prize to send you.) Remember: heading elements don't mean "big, bold, and ugly." They have a semantically appropriate use: namely, weighting headlines according to their relative importance on the page. We've also added a class value of "info" to our new h3, which will help our CSS distinguish it from any other h3s that might appear on the page.

With our headlines sorted, the rest of the content is fairly easy to convert into HTML. In fact, we just need to go a little p-happy in the remaining modules.

```
<div class="main">
    <p>Need grids? Oh, we got grids…</p>
</div><!-- /end .main -->

<div class="meta">
    <p>Posted on 15 February 2009. <a href="#">15
comments</a> so far.</p>

        <p>Tagged with <a href="#">stylish</a>, <a
href="#">grids</a>, <a href="#">layout</a>, <a href="#">web
standards</a> and <a href="#">OMGCSS</a>.</p>
    </div><!-- /end .meta -->
    </div><!-- /end .content -->
  </div><!-- /end .entry -->

  <div id="footer">
    <p>&copy; 2009 <abbr title="Neck Ruffs
International">NRI</abbr> <abbr title="Limited Liability
Corporation">LLC</abbr>, <abbr title="Limited Liability
Partnership">LLP</abbr>, <abbr title="Laugh Out Loud">LOL</
abbr>.</p>
    </div><!-- /end #footer -->
</div><!-- /end #page -->
```

The content in both the blog entry's meta information (contained in div class="meta") and in the page's footer (in div id="footer") is nothing more than paragraphs, so p is really the best element to use here. Full stop, end of paragraph. Onward!

Stylin' Out

OK, so "onward" might have been a bit overenthusiastic. If you look at our template [**10.14**], now replete with proper content, you can see that all the elements are just sitting within the page flow, stacked on top of each other. The exception is, of course, our ever-lovely p class="figure" image, which is floated off to the left of our other paragraphs. But otherwise, it's one big linear mess in need of a proper layout. Where do we begin?

10.14
Our page's markup is complete. But right now, it's all just sitting in the page flow, begging to be properly positioned.

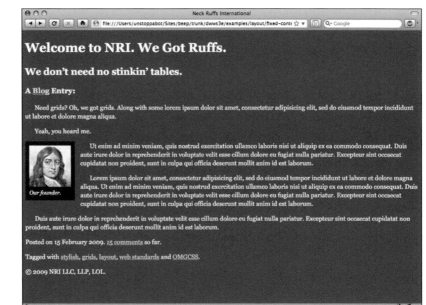

While I did say that we can build on our first template's styles, there's one tiny modification we'll need to make. Our three paragraphs from before are now contained within our blog's "entry" block—specifically, the innermost div class="main"—and our CSS should reflect that, so that we're not applying those rules to *every* paragraph in our document. So let's change our paragraph rules to use this new markup structure, and make our old rules more specific:

```
.entry .main p {
    margin: 0 0 1em;
    text-indent: 1.5em;
}
```

(continues)

```
.entry .main p.figure {
    background: #2B3036;
    float: left;
    font-size: 0.875em;
    font-style: italic;
    margin: 0 1em 1em 0;
    padding: 10px;
    text-indent: 0;
}

.entry .main p.figure img {
    display: block;
    margin-bottom: 0.4em;
}
```

We've just chained a few class selectors together to create a new descendant selector, which narrows the scope for these rules as we pair them to the new markup structure. Whereas the previous rules applied to all paragraph elements in our document, we're now choosing only the paragraphs that are descendants of an element that has a class of "main," and which is, in turn, contained within an element that has a class of "entry." Bet you can't say that five times fast.

As we noted above, our design is 988 pixels wide, and will be horizontally centered within the browser window. Since we've wrapped our content in a "page" div, let's apply a few choice styles directly to the div:

```
#page {
    margin: 0 auto 40px;
    width: 988px;
}
```

The width property's a pretty obvious choice, as we're carrying over the pixel value from our comp. The margin property is, as we've discussed, a shorthand property that lets us assign values to all four of the box's margins in one concise line. Here, we've set the div's top and bottom margins to 0 and 40px, respectively, while setting its left and right margins to auto. By applying a value of auto to a block-level element's right- and left-hand margins, it horizontally centers the element within its container (www.w3.org/TR/CSS21/visudet.html#blockwidth). No matter how wide the browser window is, our content will stay fixed squarely in the middle [10.15].

10.15

Assigning horizontal **auto** margins to an element centers it within its container.

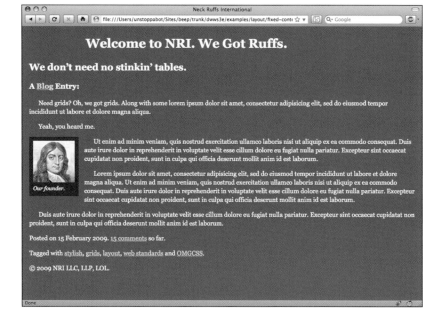

10.16

Assigning a **width** and a left-hand margin to our **h1** snaps it into place.

While we're dusting up the easy work, let's maneuver our primary headline into place. In the comp [**10.16**], we can see that the headline is 700px wide and is offset from the left edge of our content by 144px. So with a quick touch-up of margin-left and width properties, we're practically done.

```
h1 {
   margin-left: 144px;
   width: 700px;
}
```

Two easy little CSS rules, and our layout's already begun to take shape. I love this job.

Revisiting Float

For the rest of our content, we'll need to slightly change our tack. With the exception of the h1 and our p class="figure" inset, all of our content is still sitting within the document flow: the paragraphs and divs are simply stacked on top of each other, behaving like true block-level boxes.

The last time we needed to skirt around that darn page flow, we simply floated a paragraph off to the left. Can we do the same with our h2 and h3?

```
.entry h2 {
  float: right;
  width: 844px;
}

.entry .info {
  float: left;
  width: 124px;
}
```

Now that's interesting. As figure **10.17** shows, our two headlines form a horizontal row above the rest of the blog entry's content. What's more, while the h3 comes after the h2 in our markup order, floating it to the left caused it to appear first on the CSS-styled page. Neat, huh? This is the key to finishing up our page's layout: we can use the float property to partially remove our various content divs from the document flow, allowing them to sit horizontally next to other columns in the design.

First, we can float the div class="content" element, which contains all of our entry's copy:

```
.entry .content {
   float: right;
   width: 844px;
}
```

10.17
Floating our two sub-headlines causes them to share a row, which is the key to finishing our multi-column layout.

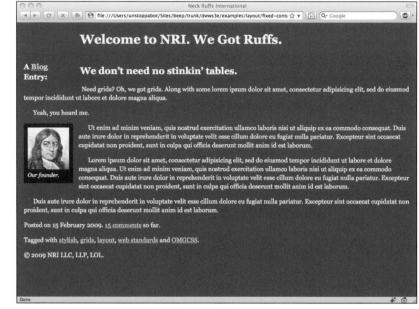

Floats: Dubious Hack or Elegant Layout Technique?

Some standardistas have decried using floats for layout, comparing the practice to the old-school method of abusing `spacer.gif`. Strictly speaking, they're right: floats were never intended to control page layout, but rather to control the flow of text around an object, much as `align="left"` or `align="right"` would wrap text around an image. As such, floats can definitely be seen as a hack, albeit one elegantly appropriated for an altogether different purpose. But still, they're the most reliable way to create CSS-driven page layouts, and offer us much more flexibility than tables ever could.

The W3C has acknowledged that CSS needs a more robust layout model, and plans to provide exactly that in the CSS3 specification. While the Grid Positioning Module (`www.w3.org/TR/css3-grid`) is still very much a work in progress, it's a promising alternative to floats and their idiosyncrasies. But until that day, `float` to your heart's content.

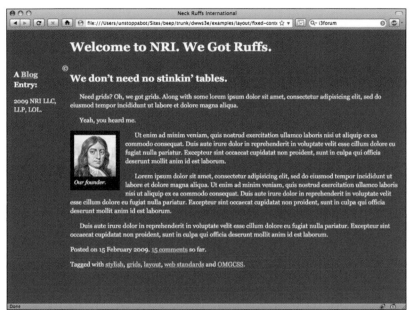

10.18
We've floated the content area off to the right, creating a basic two-column structure.

We've floated it off to the right and assigned it a width from our design, ensuring that it shares the same row as our h3 [**10.18**].

What's more, we can apply float to the children of a floated element, which we'll do to the "main" and "meta" divs found inside the "entry" block:

```
.entry .main {
    float: left;
    width: 700px;
}

.entry .meta {
    float: right;
    width: 124px;
}
```

By floating "main" to the left and "meta" to the right, our now-floated inner columns share a row. We've moved the errant divs into their proper positions along the design's grid: "main" occupies the first 700px of the blog's content area, while "meta" is draped across the final 124px [**10.19**]. And with that, we're done at last—or are we?

10.19
The innermost columns are properly floated, and our page layout's (mostly) completed.

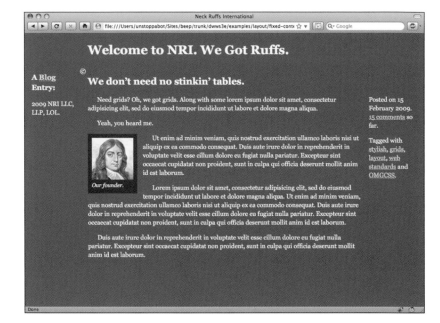

Clearly Lacking an Eye for Detail

You might have noticed something slightly odd about our last few figures. In fact, you might have been hopping up and down, pointing madly at one rather egregious bug in all of them, in the hopes that I'd stop blathering on about "floats" and "columns" and just *fix* our poor footer.

And you would have been right. Our page's final `div` is behaving oddly [**10.20**], with its content lodged beneath our `h3`. Heck, the poor © is yanked away from its subsequent text and left hovering above our entry's title `h2`. What gives?

10.20
Our footer seems mis-placed (and as a result, somewhat misnamed).

To answer the first question, we need to look back to our inset image from the first template (we'll wait here while you flip back a few pages). When we floated our p class="figure", we partially removed it from the document flow. [10.9, 10.10]. As a result, those non-floated p elements shifted into the space formerly occupied by our float, as though we'd never coded our inset image at all. But the text within those paragraphs was still aware of our float, and flowed around it.

And that's all that's happening here. Our footer is the only non-floated div on the page—in fact, every major structural markup element is floated, with the exception of the h1 at the very top of our page. In fact, as far as our footer's box is aware, the h1 is the only other element on the page, which is why it's lodged near the top of the page. However, just as with the text in our previous template's paragraphs, the text *inside* our footer does its best to reflow around the floats that precede it. So what we need is some way to tell CSS that our footer should sit beneath the floats before it.

Cue the cavalry trumpets, as clear enters stage left:

```
#footer {
    clear: both;
}
```

The clear property accepts four values: none, left, right, and both. When applied to an element via CSS, clear tells the browser to position that element beneath all left-hand floats (if clear: left was applied), right-hand floats (if we'd used clear: right), or floats on both sides (clear: both). Since we've got both left- and right-hand floats before our footer, we've instructed our style sheet to position our footer beneath both types of float, putting it squarely at the bottom of our page [**10.21**].

And with that, our layout's finally finished. With a few additional typographic flourishes and a couple dabs of color, our page is at last ready for our designer's review [**10.22**].

10.21

With `clear: both` applied, our footer's position is restored.

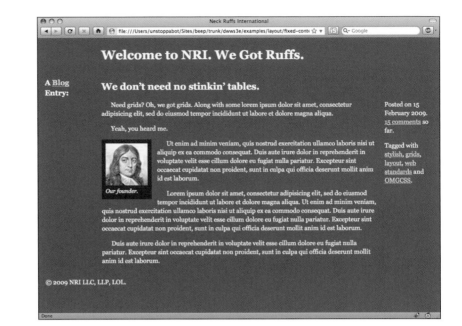

10.22

With the layout complete, we can clean up the design's details, our job finally finished.

Wrapping Up

So. You've finally had the chance to apply web standards to a living, breathing design. More importantly, you've gained a clearer understanding of the process behind building a standards-compliant page, a process we'll be revisiting in future chapters as we explore more CSS-driven layouts. With these fundamentals under your belt, the road ahead should be a fun one to walk.

There are, of course, the occasional potholes. Even the most widely implemented standards fall afoul of web browsers and their occasionally "idiosyncratic" behavior. But have no fear: in the next few chapters, we'll learn more about how to work around those quirks without resorting to hair-pulling and/or drastic career shifts.

chapter eleven

Working with Browsers Part I: DOCTYPE Switching and Standards Mode

How do today's browsers *know* when you've created a forward-compatible site? How can they display your standards-based site correctly when they must also do a decent job of supporting antiquated sites built with outdated methods?

The answer is that most modern browsers use our old friend the DOCTYPE, whose acquaintance we made in Chapter 6, to toggle between Standards mode (where your site works as W3C specs say it should) and backward-compatible Quirks mode (so named because old-school sites are authored to the quirks of variously incompatible browsers). If you want to control the way your site looks and behaves, this chapter is for you.

This chapter explains how the modes work and provides a simple method of ensuring that your site looks the way you want it to despite differences in the way good browsers interpret CSS and other specs.

The Saga of *DOCTYPE* Switching

In the late 1990s, as leading browser makers recognized that complete and accurate support for web standards was important to web designers and developers, they asked themselves how they could fashion new browsers that supported standards correctly without ruining millions of old, noncompliant sites in the process.

After all, the 3.0 and 4.0 browsers had persuaded legions of designers to learn their particular quirks, including their proprietary extensions to HTML, partial and incorrect CSS implementations, and manufacturer-specific scripting languages. Microsoft and Netscape—at the time, equal shareholders in the web's future—were willing to do a much better job of supporting standards, but not if it meant breaking billions of dollars worth of existing sites. For a browser maker, that would be suicide.

An example might help explain the browser makers' dilemma.

In the mid-1990s, when early versions of Internet Explorer began to partially support CSS1, they naturally got a few things wrong, such as the box model (explained in Chapter 12). First drafts are always rough, and Microsoft is to be commended for beginning to support CSS at the dawn of 1997.

But commendable or not, Microsoft's early misinterpretation of the CSS box model posed a problem. Tens of thousands of designers had already "learned" the incorrect box model used by IE4.x and IE5.x and had tailored their CSS to display appropriately in those versions of IE. If later versions of IE, let alone other manufacturers' browsers, supported the box model more accurately, existing designs would surely fall apart. What to do?

A Switch to Turn Standards On or Off

Even before Netscape and Microsoft agreed to build browsers that supported standards more accurately and completely, an unsung hero had solved the problem of gently handling sites built with noncompliant methods. That hero was user interface technologist Todd Fahrner (`style.cleverchimp.com`), a contributor to the W3C's CSS and HTML working groups and cofounder of The Web Standards Project. In early 1998, on an obscure W3C mailing list (all W3C mailing lists are fairly obscure, of course, but the adjective lends a certain mystique to our story), Fahrner proposed that browser makers incorporate a switching mechanism capable of toggling standards-compliant rendering on or off. He suggested that the presence or absence of a DOCTYPE be used as the on/off switch.

If a web page's markup began with a DOCTYPE, Fahrner reasoned, the odds were high that its author knew about and had made an attempt to comply with standards. Browsers should parse such a web page according to W3C specs. By contrast, a DOCTYPE-free page could not pass W3C validation tests (validator. w3.org), and would most certainly have been built using old-school methods. Browsers should treat it accordingly; that is, they should display that web page the way older, noncompliant browsers handled such pages.

One problem remained: there were no standards-compatible browsers. The world would have to wait two years to see if DOCTYPE switching held the key to forward *and backward* compatibility. (But you don't even have to wait two paragraphs.)

Throwing the Switch

In March 2000, Microsoft released IE5 Macintosh Edition, whose Tasman rendering engine, created by Microsoft engineer and W3C standards geek Tantek Çelik, provided substantially accurate and mostly complete support for standards including CSS1, XHTML (as text/html), and the DOM. IE5/Macintosh included Text Zoom to enhance accessibility, and it was the first browser to use DOCTYPE switching to toggle between Quirks and Standards modes.

The engineers who were working on Gecko-based browsers knew two good things (DOCTYPE switching and Text Zoom) when they saw them. Contemporary Gecko browsers including Netscape 6+, Mozilla, and Chimera, released soon after IE5/Mac, included DOCTYPE switching and Text Zoom, along with the rigorous and detailed standards support made possible by the Gecko/Mozilla rendering engine (www.mozilla.org/newlayout). Mozilla begat today's Firefox, Chimera begat Camino, and Cain moved East of Eden, to the land of Nod. When IE6/Windows joined its standards-compliant peers, it likewise supported DOCTYPE switching and added a DOM property that could show whether or not Standards mode was switched on for a given web document.

DOCTYPE Switch Basics

Today in nearly all browsers, DOCTYPE switching works exactly as it did when Todd Fahrner proposed it back in 1998, before standards-compliant browsers were a gleam in developers' eyes:

- In Standards mode, the browser assumes that you know what you're doing. An XHTML DOCTYPE that includes a full URI (a complete web address) tells browsers to render your page in Standards mode, treating your CSS, XHTML, and standard JavaScript per W3C specs. Some complete HTML 4 DOCTYPEs also trigger Standards mode, as discussed a few pages from now. So does an HTML5 DOCTYPE (with no URI required).

- Using an incomplete or outdated DOCTYPE—or no DOCTYPE at all—throws these same browsers into Quirks mode, where they assume (probably correctly) that you've written old-fashioned, invalid markup and browser-specific, nonstandard code. In this setting, browsers attempt to parse your page in backward-compatible fashion, rendering your CSS as it might have looked in IE5 and reverting to a proprietary, browser-specific DOM.

To control which tack the browser takes, simply include or omit a complete DOCTYPE. It's that easy.

Almost.

How Accurate is the Switch?

In 2000, when browsers first began implementing DOCTYPE switching, it served as a reliable indicator of whether or not the people who authored the site knew what they were doing where web standards were concerned. After all, only those who knew about standards-based design would begin their markup with an XHTML DOCTYPE.

Then The Web Standards Project persuaded the makers of such web authoring tools as Adobe Dreamweaver to include a valid DOCTYPE by default, and to create valid XHTML markup when the user is in WYSIWYG mode. This speeds the workflow for Dreamweaver-using designers who "get" web standards, but it also causes DOCTYPEs to begin web documents created by people who may not be at all standards-savvy.

In some cases, those people are lucky, and their authoring tool corrects their mistakes. In other cases, non-standards-aware developers may write invalid markup and CSS and IE-only scripts—but browsers will be fooled by the presence of a DOCTYPE into trying to present those noncompliant websites as if they were standards-based. Particularly with scripting, the unintended consequences could be serious.

Web Standards and IE8

It's for this reason that Microsoft—the last browser maker to fully join the standards party (with IE8)—argued in 2008 that DOCTYPE was no longer a reliable gauge of standards compliance, and that an additional toggle was needed. For details on the standards community's reaction, flip back to the section entitled "Internet Explorer and Web Standards" in Chapter 4. The additional toggle is a meta element that looks like this:

```
<meta http-equiv="X-UA-Compatible" content="IE=8" />
```

(Alternately, an X-UA-Compatible HTTP header set by the author can replace the meta element.)

Ultimately, to the joy of standards-oriented web designers and developers, Microsoft decided that the additional toggle would be *opt-out*. This means that if you want Internet Explorer 8 to recognize a *noncompliant* website for what it is, you have to opt out of Standards mode by inserting the meta element in the head of your document. If you want Standards support, you do what you would do for any other browser: write valid markup, and include a modern DOCTYPE (HTML 4.01 and higher) with a complete URI.

The optional toggle does serve one purpose for standardistas: it can be used to lock IE8 in Standards mode, overriding a user's request to have the browser operate in another mode. What do I mean by another mode? Glad you asked.

The Four Modes of IE8

For compatibility purposes, IE8 has four rendering modes:

Valid markup and a modern DOCTYPE (HTML 4.01 and higher) with a complete URI (discussed in the section "Complete and Incomplete DOCTYPEs," below) puts IE8 in *Standards mode*, where it renders your site as a standards-oriented designer expects, complete with superb DOM support. This is the browser's default mode; it's what it was built to do.

An invalid document with no DOCTYPE puts the browser into *IE5.5 Quirks mode*, where IE8 renders the page the way IE5.5 would have.

In *IE7 Standards mode*, also called *IE8 Compatibility View*, IE8 behaves almost exactly like IE7. This mode is triggered when a user requests it by adjusting a preference that asks the browser to render the page the way IE7 would. Typically, a user will only do this if the site looks or acts funny when it loads in the default Standards mode. Microsoft added this feature to support web standards by default while not penalizing web users if they come upon a site that was authored with the behavior of IE7 in mind—a clever solution to a difficult problem. When a number of people request IE7 mode on a given site, if those people have opted to notify Microsoft about their usage data, IE8 will render the website in IE7 Standards mode by default. This sounds like a blacklist (or whitelist, depending on your point of view), but it really isn't—it just makes sense. In addition, when a site is added to the IE7 compatibility list, Microsoft tries to contact the site's owners, so they can challenge the listing or let Microsoft know when they are ready to be removed from it. Moreover, Microsoft constantly monitors and updates the list. When a site that was previously rendered in IE7 Standards mode converts to pure standards, users will request that the browser render the site in IE8 mode. A sufficient number of these requests, from people who've opted to share their usage data, will change the site's default rendering back to IE8 Standards mode.

IE8 Almost Standards mode is similar to the Almost Standards Mode in Mozilla/Firefox, described next.

Web Standards and Gecko

Microsoft is not alone in offering multiple modes. Modern Gecko browsers such as Firefox toggle between three modes: *Quirks* (described earlier), *Almost Standards* (discussed below), and *Standards* (complete, strict, accurate standards support). Also, some DOCTYPEs that trigger Standards mode in early Gecko browsers such as Netscape 6 and 7 and Mozilla 1.0 instead trigger Almost Standards mode in later Gecko browsers. As those browsers are outdated, and as Firefox/Mozilla fans tend to update their browser almost as soon as a new version comes out, that wrinkle needn't bother us. It is, however, important to understand Almost Standards mode.

Almost Standards Mode in Mozilla/Firefox

To better serve transitioning designers, Mozilla engineers created an Almost Standards mode that behaves like IE6/7's Standards mode. For instance, in Standards Mode, Gecko treats images as inline unless you specify in your CSS that they are block level. All inline elements, such as text, live on a baseline to make room for the descending shapes of lowercase letters such as *y, g,* and *j.* That baseline's size and placement depends on the size and font family of the containing element—for instance, on the size and family of text in a paragraph that contains the inline image.

A designer who is transitioning to standards might create a hybrid layout (part table layout, part CSS layout), and expect his images to fit together in Firefox as they do in IE6. But in Standards mode, the baseline and line-height of the containing text element will create gaps between images, breaking the designer's table layout.

To avoid this, Mozilla engineers determined that XHTML Transitional DOCTYPEs would invoke Gecko's Almost Standards mode, while Strict DOCTYPEs would continue to trigger Gecko's more rigorous Standards mode. After all, if you're writing Strict, non-presentational markup, you are probably not sticking images in table cells.

As Transitional DOCTYPEs trigger Almost Standards mode in Gecko, readers of this book who are creating standards-based CSS layouts may prefer to use XHTML Strict—and that's certainly a sensible option, if you can be assured that your client and their CMS will leave your markup and CSS intact. But designers who prefer Transitional should use it; all you need to do to work around Gecko's Almost Standards mode is be sure your CSS declares that images are block level.

Complete and Incomplete DOCTYPEs

Where XHTML is concerned, browsers that use DOCTYPE switching look for complete DOCTYPEs. That is to say, they look for DOCTYPEs that include a complete web address such as `http://www.w3.org/TR/xhtml1/DTD/xhtml1-strict.dtd`. The following DOCTYPE triggers Standards mode in any modern browser that employs DOCTYPE switching:

```
<!DOCTYPE html PUBLIC "-//W3C//DTD XHTML 1.0 Strict//EN"
    "http://www.w3.org/TR/xhtml1/DTD/xhtml1-strict.dtd">
```

Yes, this is a Strict DOCTYPE, and yes, I've been promoting the use of XHTML 1.0 Transitional so far. I use Strict here because it makes my point without a heap of caveats, which we'll get to soon enough. The point right now is that a complete DOCTYPE like the preceding one will trigger Standards mode.

Alas, many of us write—and many of our authoring programs insert by default—incomplete DOCTYPEs that trigger backward-compatible Quirks mode instead of the desired Standards mode. For instance, many authoring tools insert DOCTYPEs like the following, which they derive from the W3C's own site:

```
<!DOCTYPE html PUBLIC "-//W3C//DTD XHTML 1.0 Strict//EN"
    "DTD/xhtml1-strict.dtd">
```

How does this string of geeky text differ from the one that preceded it?

If you look closely at the last part of the previous DOCTYPE (DTD/xhtml1-strict.dtd), you'll see that it is a relative link rather than a complete URI. In fact, it is a relative link to a DTD document on W3C's website. Unless you've copied the W3C's DTD and placed it on your own server in the directory indicated—and nobody does that—the relative link points to nothing at all. Because the DTD resides on W3C's site but not yours, the URI is considered incomplete, and the browser displays your site in Quirks mode.

(Do current browsers actually try to locate and load the DTD? No, they simply recognize the incomplete DOCTYPE from their database and go into Quirks mode. Does this mean that pages at w3.org that use this relative URI DOCTYPE will also be rendered in Quirks mode? It seems like it would mean exactly that. Although the irony is delicious to contemplate, I don't know for sure, and in any case, it's not my problem or yours.)

Now let's look again at the complete version that will trigger the desired Standards mode:

```
<!DOCTYPE html PUBLIC "-//W3C//DTD XHTML 1.0 Strict//EN"
    "http://www.w3.org/TR/xhtml1/DTD/xhtml1-strict.dtd">
```

Notice that it includes a complete URI at the end of the tag. You could copy and paste that URI into the address bar of any web browser, and if you did so, you would be able to read the XHTML 1.0 Strict DTD in all of its incomprehensibly geeky glory. Because the URI at the tail end of this DOCTYPE indicates a valid location on the web, DOCTYPE-switching browsers consider this DOCTYPE to be full and complete and render your page in Standards mode.

In an additional wrinkle, please note that Internet Explorer pre-IE8 switches into Standards mode in the presence of any XHTML DOCTYPE, whether or not that DOCTYPE includes a full URI. However, an XHTML DOCTYPE that does not include a full URI is technically invalid. Thus, in the discussion that follows, I will encourage you to use a full URI in your XHTML DOCTYPE. (After all, why switch into Standards mode if your web page is not valid?)

If all this complexity seems counter to the simple spirit of standards, you'll be happy to know that browsers (including IE8) go into Standards mode in the presence of the HTML5 DOCTYPE, which is brief as a kiss and requires no URI:

```
<!DOCTYPE html>
```

PROLOG QUIRKS IN IE6

There's an exception to every rule. Even with a complete XHTML DOCTYPE, IE6 will kick back into Quirks mode if you include the optional XML prolog. No, really. Opera 7 suffers from the same bug. Actually, IE6 slips into Quirks mode if anything, not just the prolog, precedes the DOCTYPE declaration. It's crazy, right? That is why I advised you to skip the prolog way back in Chapter 6. You see? I've got your back.

A Complete Listing of Complete XHTML DOCTYPEs

Listed next are the complete XHTML DOCTYPEs that trigger Standards or Mozilla's Almost Standards modes in DOCTYPE-switching browsers.

XHTML 1.0 DTD

XHTML 1.0 Strict—Triggers full-on Standards mode in all browsers that support DOCTYPE switching. Has no effect in Opera pre-7.0 or in versions of IE before 6.0.

```
<!DOCTYPE html PUBLIC "-//W3C//DTD XHTML 1.0 Strict//EN"
     "http://www.w3.org/TR/xhtml1/DTD/xhtml1-strict.dtd">
```

XHTML 1.0 Transitional—Triggers full-on Standards mode in compliant IE browsers (IE6+/Windows, IE5/Macintosh). Triggers full-on Standards mode in first-generation Gecko browsers (Mozilla 1.0, Netscape 6) and Almost Standards mode in updated Gecko browsers (Mozilla 1.01+, Netscape 7+,

Firefox 1.0+, Camino). Has no effect in Opera pre-7.0 or in versions of IE/Windows before 6.0.

```
<!DOCTYPE html PUBLIC "-//W3C//DTD XHTML 1.0 Transitional//EN"
    "http://www.w3.org/TR/xhtml1/DTD/xhtml1-transitional.dtd">
```

XHTML 1.0 Frameset—Triggers full-on Standards mode in compliant IE browsers (IE6+/Windows, IE5/Macintosh). Triggers full-on Standards mode in first-generation Gecko browsers (Mozilla 1.0, Netscape 6) and Almost Standards mode in updated Gecko browsers (Mozilla 1.01, Netscape 7+, Chimera 0.6+). Has no effect in Opera pre-7.0 or in versions of IE/Windows before 6.0. DOCTYPE switching might affect the way frames are rendered, but if it does so, no browser maker seems to have documented these variants.

```
<!DOCTYPE html PUBLIC "-//W3C//DTD XHTML 1.0 Frameset//EN"
    "http://www.w3.org/TR/xhtml1/DTD/xhtml1-frameset.dtd">
```

XHTML 1.1 DTD

XHTML 1.1 (Strict by definition)—Triggers full-on Standards mode in all browsers that support DOCTYPE switching. Has no effect in Opera pre-7.0 or in versions of IE/Windows before 6.0.

```
<!DOCTYPE html PUBLIC "-//W3C//DTD XHTML 1.1//EN"
    "http://www.w3.org/TR/xhtml11/DTD/xhtml11.dtd">
```

SAVE YOUR PRETTY FINGERS

If you dislike trying to type stuff like this out of a book (and who can claim to enjoy it?), feel free to copy and paste from A List Apart's *"Fix Your Site with the Right DOCTYPE"* (www.alistapart.com/articles/doctype).

DOCTYPE Switching: The Devil Is in the Details

DOCTYPE switching is not limited to XHTML or HTML5. As mentioned earlier, some complete HTML 4 DOCTYPEs also trigger Standards mode. For instance, IE toggles into Standards mode (and 21st century Gecko-based browsers toggle into Almost Standards mode) in the presence of a complete HTML 4.01 Strict DOCTYPE:

```
<!DOCTYPE HTML PUBLIC "-//W3C//DTD HTML 4.01//EN"
    "http://www.w3.org/TR/html4/strict.dtd">
```

But in both IE and Gecko-based browsers, a complete HTML 4.0 DOCTYPE triggers backward-compatible Quirks mode instead. What a difference a 0.01 makes. If these inconsistencies suggest that you might be better off authoring your site in XHTML than HTML 4, hey, I've been saying that all along.

Keep It Simple

Standards-based design thrives in Standards mode. To trigger it, use an XHTML 1.0 Strict or Transitional DOCTYPE with a complete URI, or an HTML5 DOCTYPE. In your CSS, specify that images are block elements to work around Gecko's Almost Standards mode. If you want to lock IE8's behavior into Standards mode, even if the user requests IE7 mode, include the X-UA-Compatible toggle.

chapter twelve

Working with Browsers, Part II: Bugs, Workarounds and CSS3's Silver Lining

"Create once, publish everywhere" is the grail of standards-based design and development. We don't learn proper (X)HTML authoring to win a gold star. We do it so that our sites will work in desktop browsers, text browsers, screen readers, and handheld devices—today, tomorrow, and ten years from now. Likewise, we don't use CSS exclusively for short-term rewards like reducing bandwidth to save on this month's server costs. We do it primarily to ensure that our sites will look the same in Internet Explorer 14.0 as they do today, and that unneeded presentational markup won't impede user experience in non-CSS environments. To save breath and time, I have labeled this *raison d'être* of standards-based design "forward compatibility." (I have labeled my underwear "Jeffrey," but for a different reason.)

Standards-compliant user agents move forward compatibility from the realm of wishful thinking to the forefront of rational, sustainable design strategies. If the web were still viewed mainly in the previous decade's broken browsers, forward compatibility would be unattainable by all but the most rudimentary sites. If the leading user agents that succeeded 4.0 browsers had continued to promote proprietary technologies at the expense of baseline standards, the web's future as an open platform would be open to doubt. Thankfully, all leading and many niche browsers released within the past few years can justifiably be called standards-compliant. But some are more compliant than others. Coping with compliance hiccups is what this chapter is about.

CSS Bugs in Slow Motion

Imagine, if you will, that you're working on a simple content module. Handed another comp by your designer [12.1], you've been asked to help build an alert box. So, remembering our standards workflow from Chapter 10, we begin not with code but content, taking inventory of the different content types in the design. Once we've completed that inventory, we'll turn them into semantically appropriate markup.

Thankfully, this assignment is looking like it'll be over quickly. A quick scan of the mockup reveals two types of content:

1. A heading at the top of the module.
2. A paragraph immediately beneath it.

12.1
A simple little warning dialog begs to be templated. Let's oblige it, shall we?

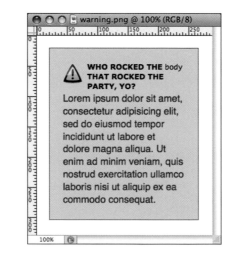

With this short list in mind, we can drop the following into a blank (X)HTML template:

```
<div id="warning">
  <h2>Who rocked the <code>body</code> that rocked the party,
yo?</h2>
  <p>Lorem ipsum dolor sit amet…</p>
</div><!-- /end #warning -->
```

Simple markup for a simple assignment: our paragraph is marked up as a p, our headline as an h2. I've even tossed in a code element to denote a bit of HTML element-*cum*-unfortunate pun in our headline. And we've cordoned off our markup with a div, with an appropriately descriptive id of "warning," which we can target with our CSS.

Note: Why did I use an h2 element? Since this hypothetical module will be part of a larger page, I'm assuming that its headline isn't the most important one on the page—for the sake of this exercise, I'm putting it immediately below the h1 in terms of importance. If this were a real module, I'd need to evaluate the headline's importance relative to the rest of the page's content, and choose the HTML element that best fits that priority level. But let's stick with h2 for now.

This markup foundation might not look that attractive at first [**12.2**]. But as you know by now, this unadorned HTML is all we need to apply a layer of style:

```
body {
  background: #FFF;
  color: #333;
  font: normal 100%/1.3 Helvetica, Arial, sans-serif;
  margin: 0;
  padding: 0;
  }

code {
  font: normal 1em/1.3 Monaco, "Lucida Console", "Bitstream
Vera Sans Mono", monospace;
  text-transform: none;
  }
```

```
#warning {
  background: #FCC;
  border: 1px solid #C00;
  float: left;
  padding: 1.4em;
  margin: 20px;
  width: 200px;
  }

#warning h2 {
  background: url("alert.png") no-repeat 0 0.3em;
  color: #000;
  font: bold 0.75em/1.3 Verdana, sans-serif; /* 12px / 16px =
0.75em */
  margin: 0 0 0.3em;
  min-height: 40px;
  padding-left: 40px;
  text-transform: uppercase;
  }

#warning p {
  margin: 0;
  }
```

12.2
Unstyled markup, but not for long.

While some of the properties may be new to you, the general syntax should hopefully feel familiar after our work in Chapter 10. I'll spare you a complete breakdown of the entire style sheet (we're here for the bugs, after all), but there are a few items of note:

- You've likely become an old hand at spotting this by now, but our first order of business was establishing default typographic properties on the `body` element. In the following rule, we've set page-wide parameters for the document's `code` elements as well.

- The bulk of our work is done on the "warning" element itself: we've set its `width` to `200px`, applied a `margin` of `20px` to each side of the element's box, and set its `background-color` to `#FCC` (using the less verbose `background` shorthand property). We've floated it to the left because our hypothetical designer told us to; apparently it'll be inset within the page's content area, with text flowing around its right side as needed.

- In the next rule, we're using the `background` property to affix a kicky icon (`alert.png`) to our headline (`#warning h2`). Much like `margin`, `padding`, and `font`, `background` is a shorthand CSS property and contains values for `background-image` (providing the URL for our image), `background-repeat` (since we don't want this image to tile, we've assigned a value of `no-repeat`), and `background-position` (the two values, `0` and `0.3em`, are x- and y-coordinates for positioning the image within the element's box). We could have declared a `background-color` at the beginning (`background: #FCC url("alert.png") no-repeat 0 0.3em`), but we've left it out to keep the property's default value, `transparent`.

- Coupled with our `background` property, we've set a `padding-left` value of `40px` on our headline. Without it, the headline's text would overlap the background image, since background graphics—like our little icon—don't occupy any space in the page flow.

- Similarly, we've used the `min-height` property to ensure that even if the headline were drastically shortened, the headline would always have a minimum height of `40px`. Without this threshold, a single word headline would drastically reduce the height of the element, clipping off the bottom of the graphic. And nobody wants that. (Trust me.)

- And finally, you may have noticed that our headline is displayed in capital letters in the browser, but not in our HTML source. We have the `text-transform` property to thank for that—setting it to `uppercase` sets our headline in caps, without changing our markup. What's more, we can set `text-transform: lowercase` on the `code` element to selectively turn off those angry-looking capitals.

Once we link that style sheet up to our unremarkable markup, *voilà*: web standards sexiness in action [**12.3**]. Your markup validates, your CSS was coded to spec, and it's looking *mahvelous* in such browsers as Safari, Firefox, and Opera. Even Internet Explorer 7 and 8 like it—in short, nice work! You've completed yet another standards-based design, and all with a few scraps of CSS and (X)HTML. Can we rest on our laurels yet?

12.3

Our little "warning" **div** looks great in most modern browsers. But we're not done yet.

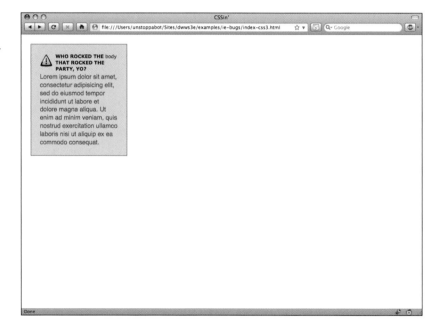

Not quite yet, unfortunately. Despite what these popular modern browsers might tell you, it's not quite time to ship that code, but to test it further in a few other browsers. Unglamorous though it may be, thorough browser testing is critical to launching a project successfully, as important as getting sign-off on your artwork or writing valid code. For although your CSS and (X)HTML might perfectly conform to a specification, any given browser may fail to implement a certain feature in some way—or at least, a browser might implement it differently than you expect, filling in a specification's ambiguities with its own unique (read: incompatible) solution.

And sometimes a browser just plain fails, and fails *hard*. If we open up our simple little template in IE6—breaker of hearts, destroyer of layouts—we'll see just that. Let's take a look at three little bugs that plague our poor module.

Hi Ho, Hi Ho, It's Off to Install Myriad Browser Versions I Go

In the early, turbulent days of the web, vetting our work against different browser/platform combinations was often frustrating. And when dealing with browsers integrated into their native operating systems, like IE/Windows or Safari, such testing was often impossible. Updates for those browsers were frequently rolled out with their respective OS, so reviewing code on older versions required separate machines or disk partitions, one for each version.

Thankfully, that's all changed. Independent developers have found unofficial ways of working around these restrictions, providing us with Multi-Safari (www.michelf.com/projects/multi-safari) and Internet Explorer Collection (www.finalbuilds.edskes.net/iecollection.htm). When used in conjunction with resources such as evolt.org's Browser Archive (browsers.evolt.org), it's never been easier to set up a proper testing environment.

The Doubled Float-Margin Bug

Actually, on first glance, our layout doesn't look too bad [12.4]. Our colors are in place, our type set to our specification, and our "warning" block looks pretty OK. Maybe this whole "standards" thing does work after all. The warm fuzzies begin to set in.

However, if you look at the left edge of our box, those fuzzies begin to feel decidedly un-warm. You'll notice that its margin on that side is grotesquely large in IE6—in fact, it's exactly *double* the 20px we specified in our CSS, and twice what more standards-compliant browsers display [12.5]. A bit of research online reveals that we've stumbled across IE6's Doubled Float-Margin Bug (www.positioniseverything.net/explorer/doubled-margin.html), which afflicts any elements that share the following characteristics:

12.4

Here's what "warning" **div** looks like in IE6. Not *too* horrible, but we can do better.

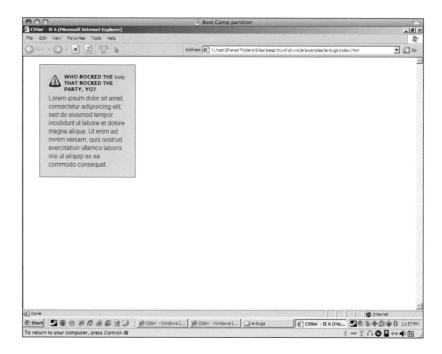

12.5

See the difference between Firefox (above) and IE6 (below)? Meet the Doubled Float-Margin Bug. I'd like to tell you you'll never see this bug again, but I like you too much to lie.

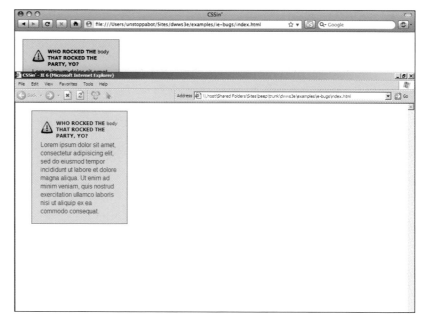

1. The box has been floated, to either the left or the right.

2. There's a margin applied in the same direction as the float (so `margin-left` on boxes with `float: left`, or `margin-right` on `float: right` elements).

When both of these conditions are met, the problematic margin is doubled in IE6. So despite having declared `20px` explicitly in our CSS, IE6 thinks we wrote `40px`—and all because we declared a `margin` in the same direction as our float. (If you can explain why this happens, the web design community will likely chip in and buy you a pony.)

So congratulations! You've uncovered your first browser bug. But we're not done yet—IE6 has a few more to throw our way.

PNG FUBAR SOS

Moving inward to the center of our box, you'll notice that our `alert.png` icon looks a bit off. Rather than being bounded by the "warning" box's pink background (`#FCC`), IE6 shows a mysterious gray box around our icon [**12.6**]. Unfortunately, the problem lies in our file extension: rather than using a simple GIF for our icon, we opted instead for a 24-bit PNG file with a transparent background, which would allow us to update our module's background color without re-exporting a new image to match. (More information on PNGs than you ever thought you needed is available at `www.mywebsite.force9.co.uk/png`.)

But wonderfully versatile though PNGs are, there's no support for their alpha transparency in IE6 and lower. Instead, IE6 translates the transparent pixels to a solid gray, possibly because it enjoys the sounds of our screams.

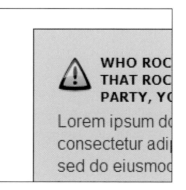

12.6
Our PNG icon is decidedly less transparent than it should be. Gosh, thanks IE6.

The Way Forward

So here we have a simple error module that displays properly in all modern desktop browsers, save for two noticeable bugs in Internet Explorer 6, one of the oldest, most popular, and semi-standards-compliant browsers in use today. Does IE6's impressive market share (and equally impressive bugginess) mean that web standards are a flight of theoretical fancy, a clever bit of academic fluff not fit for real-world design?

Not by half. For every browser idiosyncrasy or imperfect CSS implementation, there's a workaround to address it. But while there are more CSS bugs in browsers than this chapter or ten like it could cover (most of them, to Microsoft's undoubted shame, occurring in Internet Explorer 6 and lower), this handy list outlines a few sites that can get you up to speed:

- Position is Everything (www.positioniseverything.net). "Modern browser bugs explained in detail." And they mean it. Bookmark this or die.

- CSS-Discuss (www.css-discuss.org). Founded by CSS guru Eric Meyer, CSS-Discuss is a popular mailing list dedicated to "talking about CSS and ways to use it in the real world." Indispensible to budding standards designers and veterans alike, CSS-D can provide help in your darkest hour.

- Browser Bugs at CSS-Discuss (css-discuss.incutio.com/ ?page=BrowserBugs). The motherlode! Everything you need to know about CSS flaws in all major browsers, curated by the users of CSS-D.

- WordPress CSS Codex—Fixing Browser Bugs (codex.wordpress.org/ CSS_Fixing_Browser_Bugs). Just like it says.

- Honorable Mentions—IE Blog (blogs.msdn.com/ie/default.aspx) and Surfin' Safari (www.webkit.org/blog). Apple, typically known for secrecy, let Safari browser chief engineer Dave Hyatt blog about Safari's bugs and fixes to foster a sense of openness—and persuade Mac users to switch to Safari. It worked. Microsoft is doing the same thing here. Neither are "bug blogs" per se, but both are excellent places to read up on two prominent browsers' development while interacting with their creators.

Fortunately, most Internet Explorer bugs were stamped out in IE7; and IE8, released in the first half of 2009, is remarkably stable. But not every IE user will update—or as we'll discuss later, *can* update—past version 6, so you still need to know about the bugs in this chapter and the bugs left out of it. With these resources to back us up, let's begin ironing out our minor CSS issues.

Knowing Is (Only) Half the Battle

First, let's look to closing up IE6's doubled `margin-left`. According to Position Is Everything's exhaustive article on the Doubled Float-Margin Bug (`www.positioniseverything.net/explorer/doubled-margin.html`), adding `display: inline` to our CSS rule will make our inflated margin disappear. (We, and they, are at a loss to explain why this happens.) So if that's the case, is this all we need to write?

```
#warning {
  background: #FCC;
  border: 1px solid #C00;
  display: inline;
  float: left;
  padding: 1.4em;
  margin: 20px;
  width: 200px;
  }
```

It certainly appears that way [**12.7**]. With this little addition, IE6 will properly set our `margin-left` to 20px. What's more, turning "warning" into an inline box has no adverse effects on its boxy layout. The CSS specification explicitly states that floats are always treated as block-level elements, and that applying `display: inline` to a floated element will have the same effect as `display: block`—that is to say, no effect at all. So while we're including `display: inline` to fix an IE6-specific issue, it doesn't invalidate our CSS or break any other browsers.

However, certain CSS bugs you'll encounter require decidedly hairier fixes. So if we need to patch our CSS for broken browsers, let's see if we can get a bit more strategic about it.

12.7
With the addition of
display: inline, our
margin snaps back into
place. But is this the best
way to fix bugs?

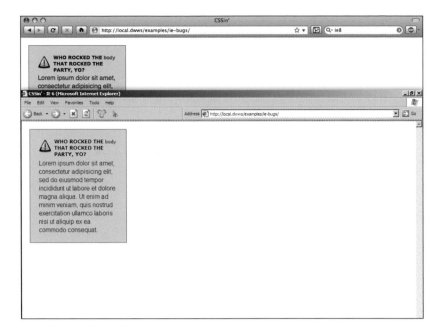

Spare the Rod, Hack the Browser

CSS hacks have a storied history in standards-based design, allowing design-ers to exploit bugs in a browser's CSS implementation to serve proper style rules to "good" browsers, while simultaneously feeding quirkier browsers a value their flawed rendering engine can understand. Here's an example:

```
#warning {
  background: #FCC;
  border: 1px solid #C00;
  float: left;
  padding: 1.4em;
  margin: 20px;
  width: 200px;
}

* html #warning {
  display: inline;
}
```

Meet the Star HTML (* html) hack (www.positioniseverything.net/
articles/poll/star-html.php). In plain English, the second rule's selector
translates to "select the element with an id of "warning" that's a descendant
of the html element, which is in turn the descendant of any element." Astute

readers will note that this rule doesn't make any sense: the html element is the root of a valid (X)HTML document, and can't be contained by other elements. So in theory, that second rule should never work. But prior to version 7, Internet Explorer thought there *was* some sort of invisible element above html, even if it wasn't in the markup. (I know it's completely nonsensical. Welcome to the special circle of pain that is IE6.)

Since this gibberish only makes sense to Internet Explorer 6 and lower, it allows us to pass special values to correct flaws in legacy versions of IE. Proper browsers that aren't hallucinating nonexistent HTML elements will ignore the rule altogether. And the added benefit? Although * html is completely non-sensical, the syntax is perfectly valid CSS. This allows us to quarantine our display: inline declaration within a separate rule, keeping our hack-free rule "clean" without invalidating our style sheet. Hacking never felt so good.

As the math-heads in the audience might've noticed, we might fix our doubled margin with a different tactic altogether:

```
#warning {
  background: #FCC;
  border: 1px solid #C00;
  float: left;
  padding: 1.4em;
  margin: 20px;
  width: 200px;
}

* html #warning {
  margin-left: 10px;
}
```

We're still using the Star HTML hack, but rather than correcting IE6's awful arithmetic, we're coddling it. We're telling old versions of IE to set a margin-left value of 10px, which will get doubled up to 20px, our desired value. This isn't a very practical approach to fixing this bug, since setting display: inline both corrects the issue *and* saves us from doing more of that nasty "math" thing. But if you ever needed to apply a corrective value to an especially challenging browser, this is an example of how a separate rule can help.

Note: For a fairly exhaustive list of CSS hacks, see www.centricle.com/ref/css/filters. You might want to keep a strong drink handy.

As hacks go, the Star HTML one is fairly mild. As I mentioned above, it exploits a browser-specific parsing bug without invalidating our CSS. But depending on the browsers you're trying to patch, the hack required might not be as forgiving. Furthermore, Star HTML isn't the only CSS hack out there. Depending on what bugs you're fixing, you might need to add in malformed (read: invalid) properties that address only the affected browsers. Or you'll add more valid-yet-nonsensical selectors like * html to your CSS, increasing the maintenance overhead as your style sheet grows in size.

I realize I'm painting a bleak picture. In truth, it's anything but. As we've said throughout this book, a properly built style sheet—when applied to a foundation of valid (X)HTML—will work in an overwhelming majority of today's browsers, while degrading gracefully in the browsers of yore. And once you're familiar with a given browser's idiosyncrasies, you'll find the need for hacking to be incredibly minimal; instead, you'll simply code around the problem areas, largely avoiding the need for messy hacks.

Keep 'em Separated: Conditional Comments

Let's look at the fix required to get IE to support 24-bit PNGs, thereby removing that gray background from our header's icon.

```
#warning h2 {
  background: url("alert.png") no-repeat 0 0.3em;
  color: #000;
  font: bold 0.75em/1.3 Verdana, sans-serif; /* 12px / 16px =
0.75em */
  margin: 0 0 0.3em;
  min-height: 40px;
  padding-left: 40px;
  text-transform: uppercase;
}

* html #warning h2 {
  background: none;
  filter: progid:DXImageTransform.Microsoft.
AlphaImageLoader(src="alert.png", sizingMethod="image");
}
```

Yikes. While our Star HTML hack might be valid CSS, the garbage we've wrapped it around certainly isn't. Behold AlphaImageLoader, a proprietary Microsoft *CSS filter* that fixes the lack of proper PNG transparency in legacy versions of IE. More information is available at Microsoft's developer site (msdn.microsoft.com/en-us/library/ms532969(VS.85).aspx), but it is not for the faint of heart nor the standards-minded: this workaround will invalidate your CSS, bulk up your code, and generally cause much gnashing of teeth. On the occasions when we need to work around a problem browser, it'd be nice if we could avoid a battalion of hacks that both invalidate our code and bloat our CSS. What's the alternative?

When we start building the XHTML/CSS for a Happy Cog project, the head of our templates often contains the following code:

```
<link rel="stylesheet" href="css/screen/main.css" type="text/
css" media="screen, projection" />
<!--[if IE]>
<link rel="stylesheet" href="css/screen/patches/win-ie-all.css"
type="text/css" media="screen, projection" />
<![endif]-->
<!--[if IE 7]>
<link rel="stylesheet" href="css/screen/patches/win-ie7.css"
type="text/css" media="screen, projection" />
<![endif]-->
<!--[if lt IE 7]>
<link rel="stylesheet" href="css/screen/patches/win-ie6-below.
css" type="text/css" media="screen, projection" />
<![endif]-->
```

Those odd-looking HTML comments are in fact conditional comments (msdn. microsoft.com/en-us/library/ms537512(VS.85).aspx), a proprietary Microsoft-only invention that builds some conditional logic into Internet Explorer's HTML parsing. When IE encounters a conditional comment, it evaluates the bit inside the square brackets; if the condition is met, then it parses the markup inside; if not, then it continues skipping down the page as though nothing had happened.

In the above example, all browsers get our primary, hack-free style sheet, main.css. But we're using conditional comments to serve win-ie-all.css to all IE browsers ([if IE]), win-ie7.css to IE7 only ([if IE 7]), and win-ie6-below.css to (you guessed it) versions of Internet Explorer less than 7 ([if lt IE 7]). If we needed to apply a patch to, say, IE8, we could add an additional style sheet thusly:

```
<link rel="stylesheet" href="css/screen/main.css" type="text/
css" media="screen, projection" />
<!--[if IE]>
<link rel="stylesheet" href="css/screen/patches/win-ie-all.css"
type="text/css" media="screen, projection" />
<![endif]-->
<!--[if IE 8]>
<link rel="stylesheet" href="css/screen/patches/win-ie8.css"
type="text/css" media="screen, projection" />
<![endif]-->
<!--[if IE 7]>
...
```

Now, IE8 is a fine, standards-compliant browser that likely needs no special care. But this illustrates the benefit of using conditional comments: namely, that our primary CSS file remains untouched and hack-free. To patch IE6, we can leave `main.css` alone, and simply write the following into `win-ie6-below.css` to fix our two CSS bugs:

```
#warning {
  display: inline;
}

#warning h2 {
  background: none;
  filter: progid:DXImageTransform.Microsoft.
AlphaImageLoader(src="alert.png", sizingMethod="image");
}
```

We're still resorting to IE-specific fixes (`display: inline` and the Love-craftian gibberish that is our `AlphaImageLoader` declaration), but our selectors are much more straightforward than before. By triaging our browser patches through conditional comments, we need not commit obscure parsing bugs to memory, wracking our brains to remember which hacks work with which browsers. Instead, we can simply write common-sense CSS selectors, using conditional comments to serve the style sheet only to the browsers that require it.

I realize that advocating the use of a "Microsoft-only invention" may cause anxiety, heartburn, and/or torch waving. However, the genius of conditional comments is that they're valid HTML: all non-IE browsers treat conditional comments as regular HTML comments, skipping over the code contained therein. But the decidedly nonstandard behavior that conditional comments produce in Internet Explorer has caused many standardistas to decry their use, suggesting that a reliance on such proprietary features belies the spirit of standards-based design.

And I can understand their reservations. However, I can't overstate the value of using conditional comments to surgically repair bugs in Internet Explorer. Furthermore, any IE-specific code you're required to use for bug fixing is concealed from the validator, tucked safely away behind an innocuous-looking HTML comment.

But we're not using conditional comments to trick the validator, to keep invalid CSS hidden from view. By quarantining CSS patches within these separate, IE-only files, we can lighten the bandwidth load for more standards-compliant browsers, and serve patches only to the broken browsers that need them. And rather than bulking up our primary style sheet with scores of browser-specific hacks, we've lightened our maintenance load. If we ever need to fix an IE7-specific issue, we don't need to scroll through the thousand-plus lines of our primary style sheet; instead, we can work within the file written specifically for that browser. Neat!

PNGs: Fixed with a Script

After working with `AlphaImageLoader` a bit, you might quickly notice its drawbacks. First and foremost, each element with a PNG background needs to have a corresponding `AlphaImageLoader` filter written to patch it. This means that you might find yourself writing a veritable truckload of rules like this:

```
#brand h1 a {
  background: none;
  filter: progid:DXImageTransform.Microsoft.
AlphaImageLoader(src="/-/img/logo.png", sizingMethod="crop");
  }

#brand h1 b {
  background: none;
  filter: progid:DXImageTransform.Microsoft.
AlphaImageLoader(src="/-/img/08.png", sizingMethod="crop");
  }
```

```
li.alert {
  background: none;
  filter: progid:DXImageTransform.Microsoft.
AlphaImageLoader(src="/-/img/alert.png", sizingMethod="crop");
  }
```

And let's face it: nobody wants to look at CSS like that. (Well, maybe you do. No judgments here.)

Furthermore, once you've applied `AlphaImageLoader` to an element, its background image stops behaving like a background image, ignoring the `background-position` and `background-repeat` CSS properties. This means that if you patch a background image with `AlphaImageLoader`, it will be anchored up in the top left corner of the element, and you won't be able to tile it. In fact, this is plaguing our little module [**12.8**]; zooming in on the header shows our `alert.png` is anchored up in the left- and topmost corner, happily ignoring our `background-position: 0 0.3em` property. The cheek.

12.8

On the left, a standards-compliant browser properly supports PNG transparency *and* **background-position**. On the right, IE6's **AlphaImageLoader**-patched image gets the transparency right, but fudges the positioning. It's OK if you want to cry a little.

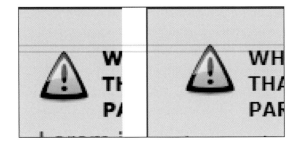

Thankfully, a relatively new JavaScript library called DD_belatedPNG (www. dillerdesign.com/experiment/DD_belatedPNG) provides much more flexibility than the `AlphaImageLoader` fixes ever could, converting the images into VML objects that not only display correctly in IE6 and below, but can be positioned or tiled as well. Simply download the file, and add the following to the `head` of your document:

```
<!--[if IE 6]>
<script src="js/DD_belatedPNG.js" type="text/javascript"></
script>
<![endif]-->
<script src="js/scripts.js" type="text/javascript"></script>
```

These two script elements function much as link elements do: we're referencing two external JavaScript files in a js/ directory, namely DD_belatedPNG.
js and scripts.js. The former is the library file we just downloaded, which we've
cordoned off with an IE6-specific conditional comment; the latter is a blank
file, in which we'll do our own custom JavaScript work. So open up scripts.js
and type in the following:

```
window.onload = function() {
  if (typeof DD_belatedPNG == "function") {
    DD_belatedPNG.fix("#warning h2");
  }
}
```

While we'll discuss JavaScript in a bit more detail toward the end of this book,
the above snippet does a few important things worth noting. The first line
(window.onload ...) instructs the browser to execute the code inside the
curly braces after the page has finished loading. Once that's happened, the
JavaScript checks to see if DD_belatedPNG has been loaded by the browser—
which will only happen if the user is browsing with IE6, thanks to the conditional comments in our markup. If that's the case, then the PNG fix will be
applied, and our little module is finally properly patched in IE6 [12.9].

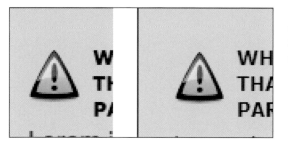

12.9
Our PNG is back in
line, and there's much
rejoicing.

CSS3: The New Hotness

The second version of the Cascading Style Sheets specification, CSS2, was finalized as a W3C standard in May 1998. That's right, 1998—the year that gave us *Armageddon* and Coldplay managed to produce the lovely little web standard we still use today. While it's taken more than a decade to finally see broad support for the spec among most of our browsers, it hasn't taken web designers that long to start pushing against the edge of the spec's limitations. We are, after all, an inquisitive lot, and after a decade of working with the language we're starting to ask for more.

Thankfully CSS3, the next major revision of the specification, is currently being written by the W3C. Work on the draft is far from finished, but you can currently review the status of its different component modules on the CSS Working Group's website (www.w3.org/Style/CSS/current-work). Now, some of you might be hesitant to read something as drearily dense as a specification. (Can't say I blame you.) But there's a legion of interesting features in there, more than we have space to list here. In fact, there's much in the CSS3 specification to love, features for which designers have been clamoring for years. Let's review a couple.

Alpha Channels and You

Wilson Miner, a San Francisco-based designer, has a great little website—his design is understated yet striking, founded upon a well-defined typographic grid that makes reading it a joy [**12.10**]. Looking under the hood at his style sheet, however, you'll quickly notice something interesting. Wilson's properties are peppered with rules that look like this:

```
body {
  background: #9178C4;
  color: rgba(30, 40, 30, 0.9);
  }
```

Throughout his style sheet, Miner has opted to declare his color values using rgba() notation, a new feature of CSS3's color module (www.w3.org/TR/css3-color/#rgba-color). If you've ever used rgb() to set colors in CSS, then three-fourths of this notation should look familiar to you. The first three numbers inside the parentheses are the red, green, and blue values of a color,

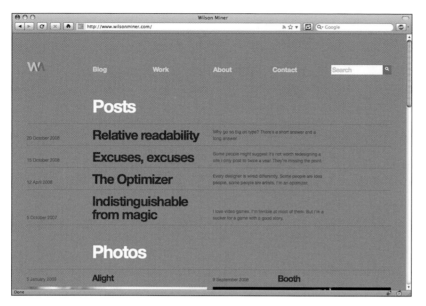

12.10
Wilson Miner's lovely little website (**www.wilsonminer. com**).

12.11
If Wilson's background changed, the **rgba()** transparency set on his type would stay the same.

set between 0 and 255. Each of the three values can be converted to one third of a hexadecimal color value, which in this case is #1E281E, a very dark gray.

The fourth value, however, is the interesting bit, allowing the user to set the color's alpha channel, specifying the transparency of the color. This value can range from 0.0 (completely transparent) to 1.0, which is fully opaque. Miner has used this fourth value to subtle yet stunning effect, setting his site's font color to rgb(30, 40, 30) (again, that's #1E281E for you hex-heads), but screened at 90% transparency (0.9). As a result, his text will automatically maintain its pleasing contrast if he ever changes his body's background color, without requiring him to update countless hex values throughout his CSS [**12.11**]. What's more, rgba() isn't limited to font colors. It can be applied to borders and background colors as well, allowing designers the flexibility to create subtle color overlays that can add additional depth to a design [**12.12**].

12.12
Here's an example of
a dropdown menu that
could benefit from some
`rgba()`.

The counterpart to `rgba()` is `opacity`. Both affect the alpha channel, but there's a subtle—and important—distinction between the two. While `rgba()` color notation changes the transparency of the color itself, `opacity` changes the transparency of an entire element, including its children. To see this in action, let's add an opacity property to our "warning" element from before:

```css
#warning {
  background: #FCC;
  border: 1px solid #C00;
  float: left;
  padding: 1.4em;
  margin: 20px;
  opacity: 0.7;
  width: 200px;
}
```

As with our `rgba()` example, opacity can be set to any value between `0.0` to `1.0` to completely hide or show an element, respectively. But as you see in our screenshot [**12.13**], this changes the opacity of the entire element, the text inside it, and even our alert icon. Powerful stuff, and the best part is that it's widely implemented: at the time of this edition's writing, Firefox 3+, Safari 3+, Opera 10+, and Google Chrome all support `rgba()` and `opacity`. So jump on in—the alpha channel's fine.

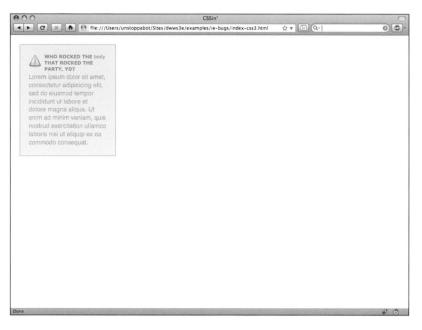

12.13
Setting **opacity** on our "warning" box changes its transparency, as well as that of its children. Good to know.

Un-Boxing the Boxiness

In the early days of web standards adoption, a common criticism lobbed against CSS-based design was that it felt boxy. And given our reliance on the box model for much of our early work—building designs that worked primarily through setting borders, margins, and background colors—the critique probably wasn't that off the mark. But then we discovered ways to introduce accents like rounded corners and drop shadows, in the hopes of imbuing our pages with some measure of depth.

However, some of us may have imbued a bit too much. Building those effects usually required lots of superfluous markup, mostly to provide our CSS with non-semantic hooks that created the illusion of a curved box or a shadow. And all too frequently, the methods we chose weren't that flexible. To create the drop shadow effect that Mitch from Sales was so keen on, we'd set a box's width to match the image of a shadow; changing the width of the box would usually require a host of style sheet edits, and new images to boot.

Note: Interested in learning more about pre-CSS3 techniques for creating rounded corners? As usual, the CSS-Discuss wiki is a great resource: check out `css-discuss.incutio.com/?page=RoundedCorners` and `css-discuss.incutio.com/?page=DropShadows` for links galore.

While these techniques are certainly time-tested and reliable, CSS3 dangles the promise of three wonderful-sounding alternatives before us: the `text-shadow`, `box-shadow`, and `border-radius` properties. A fine example of all three is available on www.10to1.be [**12.14**], designed by Tim Van Damme of www.madebyelephant.com. Thanks to `box-shadow` and `border-radius`, the subtle shadow beneath the header and the curved edges for important links are created with pure CSS [**12.15**]. Tim's even used `text-shadow` to create a light embossing effect on the site's copy [**12.16**], like so:

```
body {
  background: #222 url(../img/body.gif) repeat-y fixed 50% top;
  color: #86521E;
  font: normal 13px/20px "Lucida Sans", "Lucida Grande",
"Lucida Sans Unicode", Verdana, sans-serif;
  text-shadow: #f1e4bc 0 1px 0;
  }
```

Nary an image was sliced to create these effects, and no additional markup was stapled on to the site's markup. Behold the vision of CSS yet to come.

12.14
10to1.be tastefully applies various CSS3 properties to subtle yet striking effect.

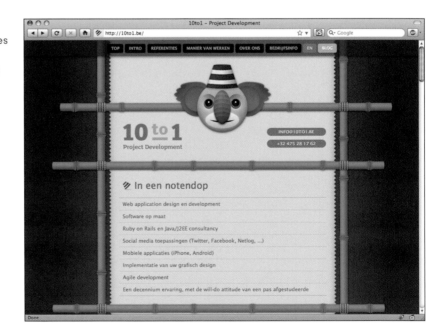

12.15
No PNGs were
exported in the
making of these
effects.

12.16
One little **text-shadow**
property on the **body**
element is all it takes
to produce this simple
embossing effect.

Let the Coder Beware

It's worth underscoring that large swaths of the CSS3 specification have yet to
be finalized. Some browser makers are waiting for the specification to mature
a bit more before implementing it, whereas others are including some CSS3
features quickly but cautiously. For example, if I wanted to use border-radius
in Safari 3 or higher, I'd include the following:

```
#warning {
  -webkit-border-radius: 1em 1em 1em 1em;
}
```

To get the same working in Firefox 3.5 and above, I'd simply add:

```
#warning {
  -moz-border-radius: 1em 1em 1em 1em;
  -webkit-border-radius: 1em 1em 1em 1em;
}
```

We can even collapse these properties further, much as we do with margin or
padding:

```
#warning {
  -moz-border-radius: 1em;
  -webkit-border-radius: 1em;
}
```

You'll find no mention of -moz-border-radius or -webkit-border-radius in
the specification, and you never will. Given the spec's unfinished state, these
browser-specific prefixes are a precautionary step taken by Apple and Mozilla;
once CSS3 has been finalized, the -moz and -webkit prefixes will be dropped
in favor of a proper border-radius. Until then, use these proprietary properties with care. You may even want to include them in a separate style sheet,
which will make it easier to remove them once the prefixes are dropped.

Note: At the time of this edition's writing, Opera and IE have not yet implemented `border-radius`. (Opera 10 has, however, implemented some of the spec's more stable features, such as `rgba()`, `text-shadow`, and the like.) What's more, Mozilla and Safari's implementations disagree in a few key areas. So as with all experimental properties, use at your own risk.

Furthermore, given the varied browser support for CSS3's different modules, it's worth creating fallbacks for non-CSS3-compliant browsers. For example, when setting color values with `rgba()`, adding a contingency color is easily done:

```
#warning {
  background: #FCC;
  background: rgba(255, 0, 0, 0.2);
  }
```

We've duplicated our `background` property, but for a reason: browsers that haven't implemented `rgba()` will apply the hex notation, and disregard the second `background`, thinking it to be malformed. In fact, Wilson Miner has done exactly that on his personal site. Viewed in an `rgba()`-aware browser, the transparency on the type subtly sparkles; but in IE and pre-10.0 versions of Opera, the colors have been flattened to the `rgb()` equivalents Miner provided [**12.17**].

12.17

In IE6 and older versions of Opera, the colors are noticeably less alpha-y.

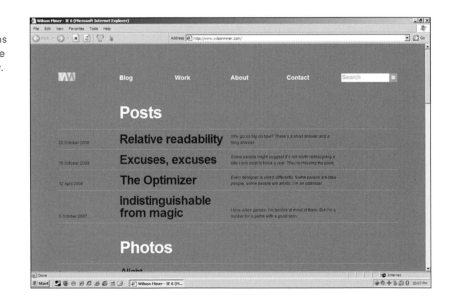

So with these fallbacks in place, we've taken steps to ensure our content's accessible to the widest audience possible. The design, however, will be noticeably (if subtly) different from browser to browser, depending on its level of CSS3 support. Is this a bad thing?

Rethinking "Support"

Predictably, in this rapid-fire adoption of new standards, some browsers haven't been able to keep up. So while there's a fair amount of excitement around the future of CSS, there's been significant debate around a rather old concept: namely, what does "browser support" mean today? A new, exciting CSS specification is being actively (if slowly) developed, and browser makers are quickly adopting the features most interesting to them; in certain cases, some browser vendors are creating custom extensions that they hope CSS3 will adopt [**12.18**]. Where, then, does that leave legacy browsers that simply can't support these features?

Of course, when the issue of support arises, IE6 is usually the browser that's at the heart of the discussion. Its creaky, flawed rendering engine has frustrated designers for much of its decade. And now that CSS3 and HTML5 are on the

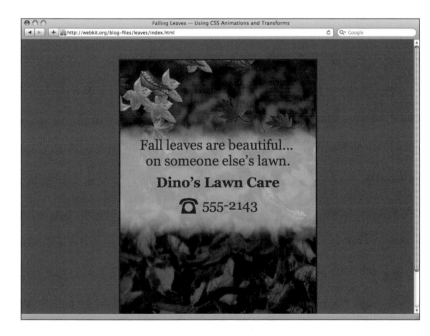

12.18
Check out **www.webkit. org/blog/324/ css-animation-2** in the latest version of Safari for information on Apple's proposed animation module for CSS. (That's right, animation.)

horizon, the tension between specification and reality has never been greater: on the one hand, we've exciting new languages emerging from the W3C; on the other, we've a browser that was released the year the Spice Girls disbanded.

Even if you're not experimenting with CSS3, IE6 can be frustrating to support. If legacy versions of IE are driving you to consider browsercide, you have a few different options:

- **Provide an alternate style sheet to legacy versions of IE.** Through the judicious application of conditional comments, it's possible to serve IE a different CSS file altogether, giving those users a different (read: reduced) experience. As mentioned in Chapter 1, Andy Clarke has come up with a style sheet he calls "Universal Internet Explorer 6 CSS," which presents a typographically exquisite experience to IE6 users, though it's one that's stripped of any layout or ornamentation (see an example at www.stuffandnonsense.co.uk/content/demo/2009/05/21/ forabeautifulweb.html).

- **Hide all styles from IE6.** The inverse of Andy's approach is to use conditional comments to conceal our CSS from IE6—full stop, do not pass go, do not apply any styles whatsoever to the antiquated browser. CSS guru Dan Cederholm recently blogged about this approach (www.simplebits. com/notebook/2009/02/13/iegone.html), and, with the help of his readers, settled on the following:

```
<!--[if gte IE 7]><!-->
<link rel="stylesheet" type="text/css" href="screen.css"
media="screen, projection" />
<!--<![endif]-->
```

The syntax is a bit hairier than our usual conditional comment, but the result is that IE6 and below interprets the entire block as one big HTML comment, thereby skipping over the link element altogether.

- **Use JavaScript to patch IE6's broken CSS support.** The now-confusingly named "ie7" JavaScript library (code.google.com/p/ie7-js/) was written by Dean Edwards before IE7 (the browser) was released, and is designed to bring older versions of IE into the realm of the proper CSS-compliant browser. Simply include the JS file, and a slew of CSS layout bugs will automatically repair themselves in IE5 and IE6.

- **Do nothing.** That's right, nothing. Rather than worry about IE6-specific hacks, conditional comments, and all that frippery, simply serve your hack-free code to all browsers. Of course, it may appear broken in older browsers, so you might want to make sure your client's CEO won't have a problem with this tactic.

The tactic you choose should be driven by data, research, and—most importantly—talking with your users. If a significant percentage of your audience is viewing the web through IE6 and IE7, that fact should help you determine which method to adopt. (It probably won't be "Do nothing.") In a recent blog entry (`blog.digg.com/?p=878`), Digg's user experience team outlined their process for dealing with IE6's special brand of awful. While Internet Explorer 6 was on the decline in their browser stats, it still occupied a sizable minority of their readership, as well as a sizable portion of their maintenance budget. As a result, they considered running a browser upgrade message on Digg, suggesting that IE6 users consider installing a better browser.

Before posting this message, though, Digg decided to poll their IE users, asking which browser version they used, and why. The results surprised the interviewers: Barely a quarter of respondents were satisfied with Internet Explorer 6 and used it by choice. Three out of four IE6 users on Digg said they weren't able to upgrade; in short, most of Digg's IE6 users stick with that browser *because they don't have a choice*. If they could, they'd upgrade. But many were unable to install software on their computer, whether limited by their OS or by workplace policies. So again: know thy audience and design accordingly.

Flash and QuickTime: *object*s of Desire?

Many of us embed multimedia objects such as Flash and QuickTime movies in our sites. There is no standards-compliant way of doing so that works reliably across multiple browsers and platforms. To understand how this can be, I must tell a tale of hubris and vengeance as floridly melodramatic as anything in Shakespeare or Italian opera. Well, OK, not quite that melodramatic, but close.

Embeddable Objects: A Tale of Hubris and Revenge

When the creators of the original Mosaic and Netscape browsers first seized on the brilliant idea of allowing designers to include images in web pages, they "extended" HTML by creating an `img` tag specifically for their browsers. The W3C did not approve. It advised web authors to use the `object` element instead. But millions of websites later, the `img` tag was still going strong—and support for the W3C's `object` element was nonexistent.

Then came the FutureSplash plug-in (later rechristened Flash) along with other multimedia elements such as Real and QuickTime movies. Again, the W3C suggested that the `object` element be used to embed such content in web pages. But Netscape invented the `embed` element instead—and as competitive browsers came onto the scene, they too supported Netscape's `embed` element.

In the view of Netscape and Microsoft, their customers expected the web to function as a rich multimedia space, and it was up to browser makers to fulfill that desire through innovation—not coincidentally gaining market share in the process.

In the view of the W3C, browser makers were creating their own elements and ignoring perfectly good (standard) specifications. And what was the point of creating useful, open specifications if W3C member companies paid them no heed? In the years to come, the W3C would wreak a bloody double vengeance on those who had ignored its beautiful standards.

(OK, OK, they didn't wreak a bloody double vengeance or anything of the kind. They simply did what their charter told them to do: established markup standards that made sense. But it's more fun to tell it this way.)

The Double Vengeance of W3C

The W3C's first act of revenge was to avoid including `embed` in any official HTML specification, in spite of the fact that hundreds of thousands of designers were using it on millions of sites. The `embed` element was not included in HTML 3.2. It was not added to HTML 4—or to HTML 4.01, *the sole purpose of which* was to include commonly used tags that were missing from HTML 4. And because XHTML 1.0 was based on HTML 4.01, `embed` was not part of XHTML, either. Therefore, any site that used `embed` could not validate as HTML or XHTML.

That is correct. You read that right. Millions of sites that embed multimedia cannot validate against a W3C spec because the W3C never deigned to recognize the `embed` element.

As if the wound still smarts, the W3C initially banished the humble `img` element from its now-defunct XHTML 2.0 specification. You want pictures? Use `object`. You want Flash? Use `object`. You want QuickTime? Use `object`. So said the W3C.

The trouble is, support for `object` is sketchy in some modern browsers and nonexistent in older ones. And designers are not going to stop using Flash or embedding other kinds of multimedia content simply because the W3C objects to the tags they use. When a designer believes in and uses web standards but needs to embed rich content, what can she do? Well, she can switch to HTML5, which supports `embed`. Or, if she's still authoring in HTML 4.01 or XHTML 1.0, she can try the methods described next.

Twice-Cooked Satay: Embedding Multimedia While Supporting Standards

In November 2002, Drew McLellan of allinthehead.com and The Web Standards Project conducted an experiment. In an article for *A List Apart* magazine, Drew discarded the bloated, invalid markup universally used to embed Flash content in web pages, replacing it with lean, compliant XHTML (www.alistapart .com/articles/flashsatay). He threw away the invalid `embed` element altogether and replaced cumbersome IE-style markup such as this:

```
classid="clsid:D27CDB6E-AE6D-11cf-96B8-444553540000"
```

…with compliant markup like this:

```
type="application/x-shockwave-flash"
```

The HTML that Flash generates when you publish a movie typically looks like this:

```
<object classid="clsid:D27CDB6E-AE6D-11cf-96B8-444553540000"
codebase="http://download.macromedia.com/pub/shockwave/cabs/
flash/swflash.cab#version=6,0,0,0" width="400" height="300"
id="movie" align="">
  <param name="movie" value="movie.swf">
  <embed src="movie.swf" quality="high" width="400"
height="300" name="movie" align="" type="application/x-
shockwave-flash" pluginspage="http://www.macromedia.com/go/
getflashplayer">
</object>
```

The HTML is obese and invalid, but it works for any browser in which the Flash plug-in has been installed. Drew honed it down to the following lean, clean, and valid XHTML:

```
<object type="application/x-shockwave-flash" data="movie.swf"
width="400" height="300">
  <param name="movie" value="movie.swf" />
</object>
```

Not only is Drew's version lean, clean, and valid; it also actually plays Flash movies in modern browsers. Alas, these movies do not stream in IE/Windows, due to who knows what bug. The lack of streaming is not a terrible problem if your Flash content is limited to a few kilobytes. It is a major problem if your Flash files are large.

Drew solved the IE/Windows streaming problem by using one small Flash movie to load a larger movie. It seemed that a standards-compliant way of embedding multimedia had at last been found. After testing Drew's "Flash Satay" method in every available browser and platform, *A List Apart* published the article.

A Fly in the Ointment: Object Failures

Regretfully, after the article was published, a fresh problem was discovered. Instead of the embedded Flash content, some visitors saw a blank text area. This happened mainly in IE/Windows browsers, although most IE users were able to view the Flash content as expected. Similar problems were reported with contemporary Linux versions of Konqueror (the forerunner of Safari) and Mozilla. As with the IE6 Doubled Float-Margin Bug described earlier in this chapter, the `object` bug affected an unknown percentage of users.

A Dash of JavaScript

In an effort to embed Flash content and still achieve (X)HTML validation, some designers next tried using JavaScript browser detection and `document` `.write` to sneak the invalid `embed` elements past the W3C validation testing service:

```
<!-- used to create valid xhtml with embed tag -->
<script type="text/javascript">
//<![CDATA[
if (navigator.mimeTypes && navigator.mimeTypes["application/
x-shockwave-flash"]){
document.write('<embed src="/media/yourflashmovie.swf" ...
```

This technique works; the Flash displays correctly in all JavaScript-capable browsers (unless the user has bought into the "JavaScript is the bogeyman of security risks" hype and turned off JavaScript), and the W3C validation service is fooled into thinking that your page's markup is kosher. But as the beginning of this chapter asserted, we don't strive for XHTML validation to win a gold star. Tricking the validation service is not the same thing as achieving compliance.

The community has since evolved methods that achieve compliance and work reliably. These methods typically combine Drew's object work with such evolving best practices of standards-based design as unobtrusive JavaScript (www.onlinetools.org/articles/unobtrusivejavascript) and progressive enhancement (www.hesketh.com/publications/progressive_ enhancement_paving_way_for_future.html).

A leading example is SWFObject (code.google.com/p/swfobject), a DOM script that offers multiple standards-friendly ways to embed Flash, without resorting to outdated, proprietary markup. We have used it on large client projects and can vouch for its effectiveness and reliability. Until all browsers support `object` the way the W3C hoped they would—or until HTML5 is finalized and universally supported in all browsers—such workarounds are all we have.

A Workaday, Workaround World

Workarounds like SWFObject and conditional comments help us begin fulfilling the promise of standards ("create once, publish everywhere") in spite of the fact that no browser is perfect and some are less perfect than others. In so doing, workarounds free us to improve our sites' content, design, and usability instead of wasting costly hours on proprietary, dead-end technologies.

But not everyone approves of workarounds, however practical or beneficial. In the view of some, if browsers don't fully or correctly support a given W3C spec, it's too bad for that browser's users—or the standard should simply be avoided. The problems with this perspective are many, including these:

- If you limit yourself to specifications that are completely and accurately supported by all browsers, guess what? You can't create a web page. Even HTML 3.2 is not universally and accurately supported in its entirety.

- Getting standards right takes time—and time is tight in competitive markets. Commercial pressures sometimes force engineers to release products before nailing every nuance of a particular specification. Occasionally they must release software knowing it is flawed. (IE6.0 contained bugs of which its engineers were aware, such as the float and box model bugs mentioned earlier in this chapter.) If we are too purity-conscious to use workarounds, our site's visitors will suffer needlessly.

- Specifications are occasionally vague in places, and some specs change after being published. Take CSS2. CSS2 was revised to CSS2.1 in 2002 because the original version contained a few obscure or non-workable ideas. When goal posts move, teams fumble. Likewise, in CSS3, we've seen how browser makers are cautiously implementing new but unstable features. Rather than commit to a changing spec, they've clearly marked these exciting new features as experimental. After all, the spec may yet change.

- Most of us must compensate for the flaws of older user agents, particularly if those flawed agents are still widely used.

There is nothing wrong with these techniques and much right with them; they allow us to use standards today instead of turning our eyes to a distant horizon filled with perfect browsing software. As browsers improve, and as old browsers fall into disuse, fewer workarounds will be needed, although we might continue to use them to ensure that our sites are as backward compatible as they are forward looking. In the next chapter, we'll conclude our brief survey of browser joys and sorrows by examining one of the most basic aspects of design—namely, the control of typography.

chapter thirteen

Working with Browsers Part III: Typography

Along with positioning and color, typography is an essential tool of design. Print designers spend years studying the history and application of type. They learn to distinguish between faces that, to the uninitiated, look almost identical, such as Arial and Helvetica [13.1]. They spend hours kerning headlines and copy-fitting text, working with writers to change the words to suit the layout. When these traditionally educated designers come to the web, with its limited tools and unpredictable outcomes, they have often been less well equipped to navigate its rocky shoals than those from a nontraditional design background.

In this chapter, we'll discuss principles of working with type as they apply to the web, and consider important differences between print typography and typography on the web. We'll examine text-sizing tools built into CSS, and common means of enforcing typographic hierarchies on websites. We'll study the compromises each CSS method imposes on designers seeking to deliver a polished layout that respects users' freedom and avoids accessibility problems. And we'll look at the promise of real fonts on the web.

13.1
Arial vs. Helvetica
(detail). (**www.
ilovetypography.
com/2007/10/06/
arial-versus-
helvetica**)

13.1
Arial vs. Helvetica
(detail). (**www.
ilovetypography.
com/2007/10/06/
arial-versus-
helvetica**)

On Typography

Whether trained as a designer or not, anyone charged with creating a usable web layout that encourages reading should generally follow these guidelines:

1. Limit yourself to two (or at most, three) fonts to avoid a distracting "classified ads" effect. Presenting a wide array of fonts on the same page is necessary if your site is a type foundry or font store, unwise if not.

2. Restrict color and use it according to a quickly user-discoverable scheme. For example, if #c30 *red* is your unvisited link color, don't use it to also style non-linked text, and don't also offer *green* unvisited links, as the reader is likely to be confused and may miss important links—or become frustrated clicking text that looks like a link, but isn't. Aesthetics will also likely suffer from the profusion of colors. Rare designers can violate guidelines 1 and 2 [**13.2**], but unless you have their skill, tread lightly.

3. Match font size to column width to create a readable *measure* (www. webtypography.net/Rhythm_and_Proportion/Horizontal_Motion/ 2.1.2). Measure is the number of characters per line of text. Too few, and the eye grows fatigued; too many, and the reader gets lost (www. markboulton.co.uk/journal/comments/five_simple_steps_to_ better_typography). A measure of 45 to 75 characters is considered appropriate for a single column of text set in a serif face; 40–50 characters is preferred when laying out multiple columns on a grid. Creating a suitable measure is straightforward in fixed-width layouts, tricky in liquid (www.maxdesign.com.au/presentation/liquid). Setting

`min-widths` and `max-widths` for content columns can help. For Jedi-level fluid-grid-design skills, see `www.alistapart.com/articles/fluidgrids`.

4. When designing pages with more than one column, use a grid to create pleasing and eye-aiding consistency and variety (`www.markboulton.co.uk/articles/detail/five_simple_steps_to_designing_grid_systems`). Layouts that exemplify grid-based design include *NYTimes* (`www.nytimes.com`), Silnt (`www.silnt.com/v4`), the website of designer Jason Santa Maria (`www.jasonsantamaria.com`), *Times Online* (`www.timesonline.co.uk/tol/news`), An Event Apart (`www.aneventapart.com`), and especially Khoi Vinh's Subtraction (`www.subtraction.com`), which made the grid safe for so many others. Facilitating grid-based websites is a chief impetus behind so-called "CSS frameworks" such as Blueprint (`code.google.com/p/blueprintcss`), hosted by Google. For what it's worth, web designers and front-end developers who choose *not* to use third-party frameworks include Eric Meyer, Dan Cederholm, Ethan Marcotte, Aaron Gustafson, Jason Santa Maria, Cameron Moll, and yours truly. This is not because we're show-offs. It's because the best CSS often arises from your design—just as the best design arises from your content, product, and intended use.

13.2
Jason Santa Maria's Happy Cog-produced design for AIGA breaks rules about limiting fonts and restricting colors according to a clear schema. If you are as talented, go for it. Otherwise, don't (**www.aiga.org**).

5. Design to encourage reading (www.alistapart.com/articles/indefenseofreaders). Oversized opening paragraphs, pull quotes, initial caps, and other staples of book and magazine publishing are easy to add to your website using lean CSS and semantic markup. They guide the eye, comfort the soul, and aid comprehension by providing a familiar setting in which to read.

6. Last and perhaps least, setting type to a baseline grid (www.alistapart.com/articles/settingtypeontheweb) can bring additional rhythm and harmony to your web layouts.

Kern and Learn

This book cannot teach you the exact art and subtle science of using type to communicate—only experience can do that—but these two classics are invaluable as teaching tools:

Ellen Lupton, *Thinking with Type: A Critical Guide for Designers* (2004: Princeton Architectural Press) (www.papress.com/thinkingwithtype)

Robert Bringhurst, *The Elements of Typographic Style, 2nd Edition* (2002: Hartley & Marks Publishers)

Every designer should read Lupton and Bringhurst, but how do we apply their lessons to the web? The Elements of Typographic Style Applied to the Web (www.webtypography.net) and *A List Apart* (www.alistapart.com/topics/design/typography) can help. So can reading Mark Boulton's *A Practical Guide to Designing for the Web* (www.fivesimplesteps.co.uk).

To further cultivate your love and knowledge of type on and *off* the web, Ilene Strizver's "Top Ten Type Resources Online" (www.creativepro.com/blog/typetalk-top-ten-type-resources-online) recommends these sites, and so do I:

- ilovetypography (www.ilovetypography.com)
- Typophile (www.typophile.com)
- Typographica (www.typographica.org)
- TypeCulture (www.typeculture.com)
- Type Directors Club Books on Typography (www.tdc.org/tdc/resources)

- TheFontFeed (www.fontfeed.com)
- The Elements of Typographic Style Applied to the Web (www.webtypography.net)
- TypeRadio (www.typeradio.org)
- *A List Apart* (www.alistapart.com/articles)
- Twitter (www.twitter.com) (to find new type resources)

A-B-Cs of Web Type

Before we dive into exciting new typographic developments on the web, let's take a look at the basics:

Platforms and Browsers, Raster and Rag

Windows, UNIX, and Macintosh operating systems come with different sets of installed fonts, at different default resolutions, and often with different default rendering styles—from traditional PC rasterization to sub-pixel anti-aliasing, such as appears in Mac OS X by default with the Quartz graphics model [**13.3**], and in Windows XP+, provided the user has turned on the Cleartype option.

Type designers argue about whether Quartz or Cleartype offers the better onscreen emulation of printed type. The consensus is that Mac OS Quartz rasterization more convincingly simulates printed text, because it is better at font

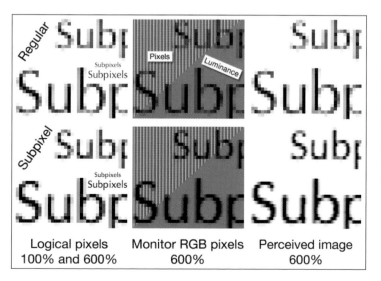

13.3
Subpixel anti-aliasing in Mac OS Quartz, magnified 600%, to show how color deviations at the edges of strokes create the impression of smooth, book-like type (**commons.wikimedia.org/wiki/File:Subpixel_demonstration_(Quartz).png**).

spacing, kerning, and so on—but that text set in Windows Cleartype may be easier to read at smaller sizes. Type designers like Font Bureau's David Berlow think the only way to produce adequate type on the web is to re-imagine classic fonts so as to better align their edges with the screen's pixels—a theory he and Roger Black have put into practice in the design of the Palm Pre operating system and on some websites (www.mit.edu).

Regardless of which font set and rasterization method may be "best," each affects page layout, denying the designer absolute control. And that's the point.

Then, too, the Lucida Sans that comes with Windows is not the same as the Lucida Grande that ships with Mac OS—and, of course, many fonts that ship with Macs don't ship with Windows, and vice-versa—nor do the two operating systems handle fonts in the same way. The old font size=3 thus means something different among operating systems, not only in size but also in appearance. Moreover, even on the same platform, each browser spaces out letters differently. Safari respects soft hyphenation while Firefox ignores it [13.4–13.5]. The same text in the same layout on the same platform may, therefore, "rag" differently when viewed in different browsers. (*Rag* is the irregular or "ragged" right margin you see in printed type set "flush left/rag right," and in most web type.) Although some of us obsessive types attempt to copyfit our words to our layouts, we can never guarantee print-like fidelity in all environments—and that's before taking the user's preferences into account.

The Unbearable Lightness of User Control

In addition to variance between platforms and browsers, the web differs from print in that, unlike a book or magazine, a web page can be visually adjusted by its readers' browser widgets, preferences, and plug-ins. Accommodating variant user preferences while delivering consistent design is tricky. It can also be difficult for traditionally trained designers to accept the very premise of user control. Some who create websites as a side-practice may not even be aware of common user preference variations. Thus designers from a print background frequently set type too small for comfortable reading. (You can even see this in several of the "Top Ten Type Resources Online" mentioned earlier.) Later in this chapter, we'll explore the trade-offs associated with size, and consider traditional and emerging best practices.

"We've got mail!" the old site cheerfully announces, complete with a meaningless header image. The image, like the header and navigation typography, is pixellated to convey "webbiness"—in case you forgot that you were looking at a website in a browser, I guess. "Got mail" is a play on America On-line (kids, ask your parents). "We" is the royal first person plural with which I used to write this site, despite being its sole author. I'd gotten into the habit of "we" from writing copy on entertainment sites for clients like Warner Bros. It made their sites, and mine, seem bigger. It was also an ongoing, self-deprecating joke, although not everyone got it.

13.4
Safari respects soft hyphenation (`www.zeldman.com/2009/08/05/past-blast`).

"We've got mail!" the old site cheerfully announces, complete with a meaningless header image. The image, like the header and navigation typography, is pixellated to convey "webbiness"—in case you forgot that you were looking at a website in a browser, I guess. "Got mail" is a play on America On-line (kids, ask your parents). "We" is the royal first person plural with which I used to write this site, despite being its sole author. I'd gotten into the habit of "we" from writing copy on entertainment sites for clients like Warner Bros. It made their sites, and mine, seem bigger. It was also an ongoing, self-deprecating joke, although not everyone got it.

13.5
Firefox, as of this writing, does not. For this reason and others, even on the same platform, the rag on this blog post differs from browser to browser. Thus do the gods make sport of our traditional art-directional desire to copy-fit words to suit our layouts.

A Short History of Web Type

Tim Berners-Lee, the inventor of the web and the founder of the W3C, viewed his creation as a medium for the easy exchange of text documents; therefore, he included no typographic control in the structured language of HTML. As described in Chapter 2, web designers initially used `tt`, `pre`, `blockquote`, and semantically meaningless paragraph tags to vary typefaces, achieve positioning effects, and simulate leading. They next began using GIF images of text set in Photoshop, a practice that continues to this day.

By 1995, with commercial sites springing up right and left and designers hacking HTML to ribbons, something had to be done to provide at least a few basic typographic tools. Netscape gave us the `font` element, whose attribute was size. You could specify numbers (font size=2) or relative numbers based on the user's default (font size=+1). Designers quickly abandoned paragraphs and other structural elements and controlled their layouts by combining font size with line break elements (br). Not to be outdone, Microsoft gave us font face.

Some readers of this book will remember those days and will also recall the problems—chiefly, those of platform difference. Windows assumed a default base size of 16px at 96ppi (pixels per inch). Mac OS, closely tied to print design, assumed a size of 12px at 72ppi based on the PostScript standard. Font sizes that looked dandy on one platform looked too big or too small on the other.

"Stupid Windows," said the Mac-based designers.

"Stupid Macintosh," said the Windows-based designers.

Points of Difference
Next came early CSS implementations such as that of IE3, thrusting the cross-platform problem into even greater relief. Points (pts) are a unit of print, not of the screen, but designers are familiar with points, and many chose to specify their web text using this unit. In the Windows world, 7pt type was 9px tall, which is the lowest threshold of legibility. On the Mac, 7pt type was 7px tall, making it illegible, and as useless as a beard on a baby.

In 1997, Microsoft.com chose 7pt type to ballyhoo the CSS prowess of their new IE3 browser for Windows and Macintosh. This was like inviting folks to a movie premiere and de-focusing the projector before screening. The type was equally illegible in IE and Netscape on the Macintosh, not because of browser problems, but because of platform differences. Todd Fahrner, soon to be the father of DOCTYPE switching (see Chapter 11), posted figure **13.6** on his personal site, annotating it to show that points were a useless unit of CSS in terms of screen design—although they are fine for print style sheets.

Fahrner also pointed out (sorry) that text set in points and pixels could not (at the time) be resized via the browser's built-in font-size adjustment widget. This was not because CSS1 considered points and pixels fixed units. (CSS1 does not define *any* sizing method as being non-resizable.) It was simply a decision

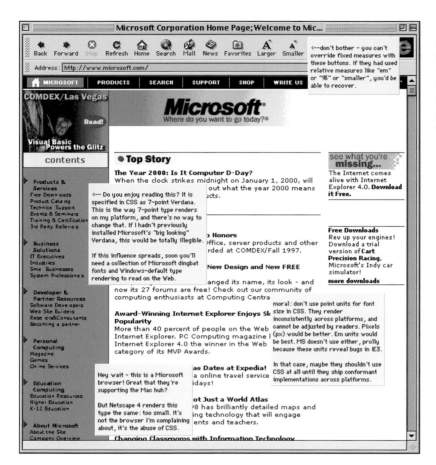

13.6
In this mid-1990s screenshot, Todd Fahrner documented problems of CSS misuse including screen type specified in points (`style.cleverchimp.com/font_size/points/font_wars.GIF`).

made by the first browser makers to begin supporting CSS. The user *could* reset type set in ems and percentages, but IE3, IE4, and Netscape 4 all suffered from bugs where type set in ems or percentages was concerned, making ems and percentages unreliable for design in those days. Fahrner would soon propose a solution to at least some of these problems.

At the time Fahrner voiced his concerns, the only size unit that worked the same way across browsers and platforms was the non-resizable pixel. Ten years later, the only entirely reliable unit is still the pixel. (Alas, IE/Windows still prevents users from scaling text set in pixels via Text Zoom. Universal Page Zoom, however, may make this moot, as we'll discuss later in this chapter when we consider the problem of text set in pixels.)

A Standard Size at Last

In an effort to transcend platform differences, the makers of Netscape and Microsoft's browsers and Mozilla put their heads together in late 1999 and decided to standardize on a default font-size setting of 16px/96ppi across platforms. By putting all platforms on the same page, as it were, browser makers and users could avoid the problems of cross-platform size differences and illegible text.

The 16px/96ppi Font-Size Standard

On a W3C mailing list in 1998, the plucky Todd Fahrner proposed standardizing on the 16px default used in Windows. All leading browser makers adopted his recommendation by 2000. Although Fahrner's concerns were practical in nature (he wanted to ensure that type could be read online), in the quotation that follows, he refers to something that might strike you as bizarre.

The framers of CSS1 were bound to a pet abstraction wherein the "average" length of a web user's arm was essential to defining the size of a pixel. *No, really.* Although the W3C has blessed us with many usable web standards, its members can sometimes follow their academic biases down the rabbit hole. Anyway, in advancing his idea about a standardized cross-platform font size, Fahrner was careful to cover the all-important arm length issue along with more pedestrian matters like usability and legibility. He wrote:

> Since before Mosaic, the default font-size value in all major browsers has been set at 12pt. I propose redefining the default as 16px…. The current default of 12pt rasterizes very differently across platforms. On Macs, it rasterizes into 12px (logical res fixed at 72ppi). On Wintel PCs, it rasterizes by default into 16px (logical res defaults to 96ppi) …All scalable font-size values… operate relative to this inconsistent base rasterization. For a designer, this means that the only way to suggest a [consistent cross-platform] font size is to use CSS pixel units, which are not user-scalable, and are thus not optimally user-friendly/portable….
>
> The appropriate corrective measure… is for Mac (and X11?) browsers to break with tradition and ship with the default value of "medium" text set at 16px, instead of 12pt. This should of course remain subject to user adjustment, but a consistent initial value will at least make the use of scalable font-size values less problematic for designers, as any variance

from the default will be due to express user preference rather than capricious legacy OS differences.

If designers tend to believe that 16px is too large as a base, why suggest it as the default?

One reason is pure expediency. The Mac is a smallish minority platform, though very strongly represented in the web design field. (I use a Mac!) It is unrealistic to expect that Windows/X11 browsers will change their defaults to match the Mac's rather quaint limitation to 72ppi logical resolution.

The 1996 CSS1 standard suggests a 1/90" value for a "reference pixel," extrapolated from a visual angle of 0.0227 degrees visual angle at arm's length. [User agents] are expected to scale pixels appropriately if the physical resolution is known to vary significantly from this value. A 1/90" reference pixel would suggest a rasterization of 12pt into 15px, rather than 16. 15 is, of course, much closer to 16 than to 12, however. Because no OS/UA currently assumes a 90ppi logical resolution (nor implements pixel-scaling) … the reference pixel value should be amended to 1/96". It's simple to preserve the suggested 0.0227 degrees visual angle by giving the reference user a longer arm's length.

Designers think that 16px is too large simply because they are used to the 12px base size of their Macs. Readability is 9/10ths familiarity.

```
lists.w3.org/Archives/Public/www-style/1998Dec/0030.html
```

Arms and the Pixel

Two years later, the first generation of significantly standards-compliant browsers embraced Fahrner's recommendation. In Internet Explorer, Netscape, and Mozilla, on both the Windows and Macintosh platforms, the default text size became 16px/96ppi, and increased legibility was enjoyed throughout the globe—except when some users changed it back, as discussed in the next section.

Fahrner's efforts eventually led the W3C to agree to a standard reference pixel size related to the 16px/96ppi concept in CSS2.1. In the excerpt that follows, you'll note that the W3C still remains concerned about the average length of a reader's arm:

> It is recommended that the reference pixel be the visual angle of one pixel on a device with a pixel density of 96dpi and a distance from the reader of an arm's length. For a nominal arm's length of 28 inches, the visual angle is therefore about 0.0213 degrees.
>
> —CSS 2.1 Working Draft, `www.w3.org/TR/CSS21/` `syndata.html#length-units`

While the standard reference pixel would seem to clear the way for a W3C standard user default size, the two are not officially related. The W3C has spoken to the first issue, but not to the second.

Netscape 6+/Mozilla (parent of Firefox), IE5+/Macintosh, and IE/Windows offered all users the same default font-size setting. Points, ems, percentages, and font-size keywords would work the same way across platforms (as long as the user did not change her preferences) and no user would be needlessly hurt because of a designer or developer's ignorance about platform differences. There were still bugs and inheritance problems in some browsers' implementation of percentages and ems, but the primary accessibility and usability hurdle had been cleared.

Missing the pt with Standard Reference px

Alas, browser makers don't explain why they do what they do, and web users don't study design issues (and why would they?). The benefit of a standard size temporarily evaporated as some users (and many designers) missed the point—literally.

For instance, an unknown percentage of Macintosh users, disgusted by text sizes they perceived to be huge and ugly, immediately switched their browsers back to the old 12px/72ppi setting, thus defeating the attempt at standardization and placing themselves once again in the position of being unable to read the text on many sites. On the web, the user is supposed to be in charge, and that remains true even if he doesn't realize what is in his best interest.

When these "switch back to 12px" fans happen to be designers, they might produce sites that look great on the Macintosh but appear to suffer from a glandular condition in the dominant Windows space. Many Macintosh-based designers misguidedly used 12px/72ppi, and their work (or their audience) suffered as a result. Today, thanks partially to wide dissemination of the first and second editions of this book, fewer Mac-based designers make this mistake. (It's also one reason this book continues to talk about these matters of ancient web history.)

Of course, some Windows users also find the 16px default too big for their liking and consequently set their browser to view all websites at a text setting below the norm. When Mac and Windows users do these things, it has no effect on sites that use pixels to specify type sizes, but it does cause problems for sites that use ems, percentages, and (to a lesser extent) CSS font-size keywords. We will examine these dilemmas as this chapter unfolds.

Sniffing Oblivion

Users who switched to smaller-than-standard type were simply making themselves more comfortable. They were not the only ones to miss the point of a standard size, nor should they have been expected to understand it. Many web professionals also missed the point, in part because Netscape and Microsoft did not publicize it.

In particular, a number of developers (we'll call them the Browser Quirks Brigade) had come to believe that browsers would always differ greatly in appearance and behavior and that the way to solve these differences was to combine browser detection with code forks and tag soup. They quickly did what they had been trained to do: sniff and fork.

Prior to 2000, instead of using pixels to ensure that text rendered at the same size on virtually any browser or platform, these developers had used points. Because points were (a) meaningless in terms of the screen and (b) implemented in vastly different ways between the two dominant computing platforms, these developers had created multiple point-driven style sheets, using JavaScript-powered platform detection to serve one point-driven style sheet to Windows users, another to Macintosh users. Often, it got far more complicated than that, but I haven't had my breakfast yet.

The Snake Vomits Its Tail: Conditional CSS

With the release in 2000 of standards-compliant browsers that supported the same default font size and resolution across platforms, web designers had the opportunity to abandon browser detection and point-driven, conditional

CSS. Instead, the Browser Quirks Brigade updated their scripts and banged out additional conditional CSS files. "Additional conditional" sounds funny, doesn't it? The results were anything but.

Instead of working as they were supposed to, these extended scripts and conditional files often defeated their own purpose, resulting in illegible or bizarrely formatted pages. Developers who created these little nightmares of non-usability were not stupid. Often, they were highly skilled professionals. Their clients forked over big bucks for needlessly complicated sites that never worked right and that required constant, expensive maintenance to continue failing in ever more complex ways at increasingly higher costs. It doesn't sound like what any sane being would desire, but it was (and on some large corporate sites still is) the norm. Agencies can, of course, ring the cash register by charging unwitting clients extra for constant, expensive maintenance, but that is not a good way to make money.

Nor is it sustainable. Eventually, coffers empty, budgets evaporate, and owner and visitors are stuck with an obsolete site as described in Chapter 1. With the shadow of doom upon them, in an effort to forestall the inevitable, some developers will slap a "Best viewed with…" banner on their front page. This is like popping a Surgeon General's warning on a pack of cigarettes and expecting it to turn into a jar of vitamins.

We can prevent such chaos when we understand that browsers support common standards and that the best solution is often the simplest. (That is, send all browsers the same style sheet and avoid pts except for print.)

Before leaving this section, let us note that a different kind of conditional CSS is sometimes not merely acceptable but *required* when you need outdated versions of IE to support sophisticated layouts and behavior. For examples, see Chapter 17.

Adventures in Font Size

In the *first* edition of this book, I spent a great deal of Chapter 13 moaning about the diabolical interaction between nonstandard sizes and non-scaling pixels.

Back then, a browser maker who shall go nameless (cough, Apple, cough) deliberately departed from the new 16px/96ppi standard on the grounds that big, horsey text was ugly. Since most users never change the default font size, if ems or percentages were used to size text, Apple browser users would see different text sizes than everyone else. Designers and clients can get fussy when that happens. Moreover, nearly all browsers in those days routinely botched nested percentages and ems.

In contrast, sizing text in pixels is straightforward—it's easy to set up visually and mathematically pleasing relationships such as 12px for body copy, 18px for line-height, and 24px for a headline. This is how one creates vertical grids that complement the horizontal layout grid. Such relationships *can* be created via ems and percentages, but the math is hairier, and the results are less predictable.

Plus, unless you also size your images in ems, you can't set up visually attractive and helpful correspondences between image size, headline size, column size, and so on. You *can* size images in ems, and sizing everything in ems is the golden gateway to *elastic* layout, in which *every element scales along with the user's text size* (www.alistapart.com/articles/elastic). Patrick Griffiths' "Elastic Lawn" in the CSS Zen Garden (www.csszengarden.com/?cssfile=/063/063.css&page=0) popularized the elastic layout; America On-Line was the first major site to implement the technique. But not all browsers and operating systems resize images well, although weak browsers can be helped along (www.unstoppablerobotninja.com/entry/fluid-images). In any case, Universal Page Zoom may make such hoop tricks moot, by treating *all* layouts as though they are elastic. We'll have more to say about that in a moment.

The Trouble with Pixels

The trouble with pixels traditionally comes down to this: In IE/Windows, users cannot resize text set in pixels. If you've used 9px type for your site's body text, many visitors will click their browser's Back button faster than you can say *squint*. Even 11px type might be too small for some, depending on the font chosen (11px Verdana and Georgia get fewer complaints than 11px Times, for instance), the monitor size and resolution, the visitor's eyesight, the degree of foreground/background contrast, and the presence or absence of distracting backgrounds. To a person who has less than 20/20 vision, the problem might be annoying. To one who is seriously visually impaired, it might be far worse than that. Wilson Miner has a fine entry on the importance of decently sized web type: www.wilsonminer.com/posts/2008/oct/20/relative-readability.

There is also the occasional CAD engineer who likes to surf the web on his 4,000×3000 32" workstation monitor and pepper web design mailing lists with angry letters about flyspeck-sized text. If he actually wished to solve his problem, he could use a browser that supported Text Zoom or Page Zoom. If he preferred to use IE6, he could switch on its option to ignore font sizes. He could even write a user style sheet like this one:

```
html,
body {
  font-size: 1em !important;
}
```

But he would rather complain about his problem than solve it in any of these ways, because for him this whole thing is a religious issue. (He also complains that the magazines he subscribes to are filled with inane coverage of celebrities and their marital problems. And he dislikes peanuts, yet he keeps eating them.) As a designer, you are responsible for your users' problems—even this guy's.

Here lies our dilemma. Pixels are preferable to ems and percentages as a delivery mechanism for consistent and accurate design rendering across platforms. They also facilitate the creation of mathematically and visually harmonious layouts. But the inability to scale pixel-based text in Internet Explorer causes too many problems for too many readers. For this reason, it has long been a best practice, among standards-based designers who care about accessibility, to set text size in ems or percentages, and *not* in pixels. Is that best practice, like diamonds, forever?

The world has long accepted, as immutable law, Microsoft's decision not to allow users to scale text set in pixels. Some of my WaSP colleagues and I felt differently. Having succeeded at persuading browser makers to support a standard font size, and having cheered as first IE5/Mac, then Mozilla/Firefox, and then Safari gave users the ability to scale any text (including text set in pixels) via Text Zoom, some of us lobbied hard for nearly a decade to get IE/Windows on the Text Zoom train. Alas, it never happened.

Page Zoom: Making Democracy Safe for Pixels

But something else *did* happen. Internet Explorer 7 introduced Page Zoom (a function long pioneered by Opera, to give credit where it's due). With Page Zoom, a user doesn't enlarge and reduce the size of text; instead she enlarges and reduces the entire layout [**13.7**, **13.8**, **13.9**]. Maybe it's something in the water, or maybe advanced standardistas were tired of racking their brains to prevent zoomed text from hornswoggling complex web layouts. Whatever the reason, in 2009 Firefox 3.5 and Safari 4.0 dropped Text Zoom in favor of Page Zoom [**13.10**, **13.11**].

Universal Page Zoom greatly simplifies the challenge of authoring bulletproof layouts, as user-resized text is the primary cause of borked page designs. With Page Zoom, you can have your complex layout—including musically sophisticated numeric relationships between image size, headline size, column width, and line-height—while ceding ultimate control of text size to your reader. And although browser makers might not have implemented Page Zoom with pixel text in mind, as IE6 fades and universal Page Zoom becomes the norm, designers who set text size via px will no longer be tied to the stone of shame.

How soon can you switch to px? In my view, you can do so as soon as your referrer logs tell you that the majority of your audience is using IE7 and higher. You needn't concern yourself with how many visitors use Safari, Firefox, and Opera, as text set in pixels has *always* been user-scalable in those browsers, one way or another. IE, as is so often the case, is our only problem here; and IE6 lies slowly dying as I write this.

13.7
Designer Cameron Moll's
Authentic Boredom in
IE8 (**www.cameronmoll.
com**).

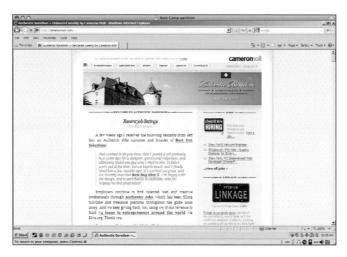

13.8
The same site with Page
Zoom applied.

13.9
The Page Zoom widget
in IE8.

13.10
Happycog.com in Safari 4.

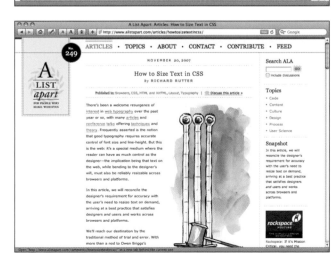

13.11
The same site with Page Zoom applied.

13.12
In "How to Size Text in CSS" (**www.alistapart. com/articles/ howtosizetextincss**) Richard Rutter refines his earlier pioneering work. Ironically, some *A List Apart* readers criticized the author for not advocating the 62.5% rule—unaware that he was the author of that rule.

Sizing With Ems: The Laughter and the Tears

Because of font scaling issues with pixels pre-IE7, accessibility advocates and standards-based designers—not to mention the creators of CSS1—have long agreed that ems are the way to go. The sentiment is typically expressed along these lines: "For accessibility, all `font-sizes` should be expressed in relative units throughout rather than in pixels." It's not uncommon to see sentences conveying this sentiment in design briefs and Requests for Proposal.

The 62.5% Solution

In 2004, developer Richard Rutter gave the world a 62.5% solution to the problem of the complex math inherent in em-based design (`www.clagnut.com/blog/348`). 62.5% of the 16px default size is 10px. Set the body to 62.5% and the rest of the math is easy (because it's based on 10):

```
body { font-size: 62.5%; }
p { font-size: 1.2em; line-height: 1.5; }
h1 { font-size: 2.4em; }
```

In the example above, p text is 12px tall (1.2 x 10px), its `line-height` is 15px (1.5 x 10px), and h1 headline text is 24px (2.5 x 10px). Easy-peasy!

Using Rutter's method, you can attain near-pixel-perfect control without running afoul of IE's unwillingness to scale pixels. Web designers were quick to seize on Rutter's brilliant idea, and it has become a best practice.

But the 62.5% method is not perfect. If the user has shrunk her default size, she and you will be out of luck—and that's a problem in ems-based design generally. It fails when a user has lowered his browser's default size, or when an IE/Windows user sets his browser's View: Text Size menu to "small" instead of "medium." Such changes make any text sized below 1em smaller than it is supposed to be and might make it too small for comfortable reading. (It might even be inaccessible.) Rutter himself later refined his technique farther, arriving at a near-perfect compromise between the user's need to resize text on demand, the designer's need for accuracy, and the risks posed by the user's control over the default font size [**13.12**]. I urge you to read his "How to Size Text in CSS" (`www.alistapart.com/d/howtosizetextincss`) and decide for yourself whether Rutter's updated ems-based techniques or pixel-powered layouts (made safe by Page Zoom) are most appropriate for your next web layout.

One other sizing method is worth discussing here:

The Font-Size Keyword Method

Little known and scarcely ever used, CSS1 (and later, CSS2) offered seven font-size keywords intended to control text sizes without the absolutism of pixels or the inheritance, cross-platform, and user-control hazards that come with ems and percentages. The seven keywords appear next, and their meaning will be obvious to anyone who has ever bought a tee shirt (www.w3.org/TR/CSS21/ fonts.html#font-size-props):

```
xx-small
x-small
small
medium
large
x-large
xx-large
```

For Love of Keywords

When you use ems or percentages, there is always the danger that their values will multiply, resulting in text that is too small or too large. By contrast, keyword values do not compound even when the elements nest. If the body, div, and p elements are all set to small, and p lives inside div, which lives inside body, the three smalls do not compound (as ems and percentages do), and the result is still legible. Moreover, the result is still small (not x-small or xx-small). Percentages and ems compound. Keyword values do not compound.

In addition, at least in Firefox and modern IE browsers, xx-small can never be smaller than 9px, which means it can never be illegible. Although 9px text might be hard for some users to read, that is not the same thing as illegibility.

Like ems, keywords are based on the user's default font size. Unlike ems (and unlike pixels in negative scaling Page Zoom), keywords never descend below the threshold of adequate resolution. If the user's default size happened to be 10px (unlikely, but possible), x-small would be 9px and xx-small would also be 9px. Obviously, in such a case, you would lose the size difference between x-small and xx-small, thus blurring the type hierarchy. But you wouldn't lose your readers by presenting them with illegible text.

Although less needed and less common today than when the first two editions of this book were published, font-size keywords remain a valuable tool for some page layouts. Using the Box Model Hack to serve false keyword sizes to 4.0 browsers, recommended in earlier editions of this book, is no longer necessary unless you are using a DOCTYPE that throws IE6 into Quirks mode (see Chapter 11).

I Want My Franklin Gothic!

Control over leading, margins, and type size is nice, but how about a little font action? Are we really limited to Times, Verdana, Arial, and the other few fonts installed by default on most Windows and Mac systems? Rhetorical questions usually imply that the answer is no. Indeed, CSS provides a mechanism by which we can embed real fonts as headlines or body text [**13.13**].

13.13
On the tenth anniversary of the publication of CSS, its co-author Håkon Wium Lie showed *A List Apart's* readers how to take web design out of the typographic ghetto, by harnessing the power of real fonts via **@font-face**.

CSS @font-face: Real Fonts on the Web

Headlines, of course, are often set in Photoshop in a nice typeface and then inserted on web pages via the `img` element. This time-honored method works (especially if you include appropriate `alt` text) but it is rather tedious.

For years, designers were limited to inserting pictures of fonts into their web pages, either as straightforward image files…

```
<img src="headline.gif" alt="Headline text goes here for people
who have images turned off." />
```

… or via CSS image replacement methods popularized in the first two editions of this book. (For more about image replacement, including the Phark `-9999px` method, see `www.mezzoblue.com/tests/revised-image-replacement`.)

Yet as far back as 1998, CSS2 provided a way to link to real fonts from your style sheet:

```
@font-face {
  font-family: "Watusi";
  src: url("http://www.example.com/fonts/watusi.ttf")
format("truetype");
  }
h1 { font-family: "Watusi", sans-serif }
```

Instead of static pictures of fonts, linked font files can be retrieved from the web and used to display HTML text. And not just for headlines, but for body copy, too. It's brilliant! It's magnificent! There are just two problems:

1. Unless they are specifically licensed for web use (and most fonts aren't), if you embed fonts you own on a web page, you may be violating your End User Licensing Agreement (EULA) with the font foundry. See `www .webfonts.info/wiki/index.php?title=Fonts_available_ for_%40font-face_embedding` for fonts that are licensed for web embedding.

2. While Safari (and other WebKit browsers, including Google Chrome), Opera, and Firefox support `@font-face` for TrueType (TTF) and OpenType (OTF) fonts, guess which browser does not? That's right, Internet Explorer. That's not because IE is technically inferior to the other browsers. Rather, it's because Microsoft does not wish to provide

technology that might infringe on the rights of type designers. Instead, Microsoft supports `@font-face` only for the Embedded OpenType (EOT) format—which Microsoft itself invented. EOT discourages the copying of copyrighted font files via encryption, "subsetting" (using only needed characters rather than the entire font), and other techniques. Microsoft has supported EOT—and proposed it as a W3C standard (`www.w3.org/Submission/2008/01`)—since IE4 was young. No other browser maker supports EOT. It's the perennial web standards problem, but until Microsoft joins the party, Jon Tan offers a commendable workaround (`www.jontangerine.com/log/2008/10/font-face-in-ie-making-web-fonts-work`).

If you visit `www.zeldman.com/dwws` (a mini-site for this very book), you'll see a web page using a web-licensed version of the Font Bureau's Franklin Pro Medium, embedded via `@font-face`, with fallbacks for Internet Explorer. View Source to see how easy it is to embed fonts via standard CSS, provided your license permits you to do so.

Embedded Font Standards: So Many to Choose From

As I write this, type foundries are on the verge of agreeing to standards that will protect their rights *and* enable designers to embed real fonts on their web pages via standard CSS (`www.zeldman.com/x/39`).

They are on the *verge*, but not there yet (`www.zeldman.com/x/16`). Competing proposals include Erik van Blokland and Tal Leming's .webfont (`lists.w3.org/Archives/Public/www-font/2009JulSep/0440.html`), a compressed format containing XML and font data; Ascender's EOT Lite (`www.ascendercorp.com/info/eot-lite-wrap-tool`), which dispenses with the chief objections to Microsoft's EOT while still working in IE (`www.readableweb.com/jeffrey-zeldman-questions-the-eot-lite-web-font-format`); and David Berlow's OpenType Permissions and Recommendations Table (`www.fontbureau.com/otpermtable`), a mechanism for showing that the designer has paid for the right to use a particular font on a particular domain. These methods work now. For instance, you can buy a web-licensed version of a Font Bureau font for 20% more than a non-web-licensed version, and embed it on a given domain via `@font-face`. It will be legally licensed, and it will work in Safari, Firefox, and Opera—but not in IE, unless you use Jon Tan's workaround. (I use a Berlow Font Bureau font at `www.zeldman.com/dwws`.)

Just as we experiment with JavaScript and advanced CSS on personal sites and pet projects, now is a good time to try `@font-face` (using licensed fonts, of course) on your blog and other non-critical projects. For that matter, as long as you license the font and use Tan's IE workaround, you can use real type on major projects. Hopefully, this year or next, type designers will agree to a standard, and Microsoft will get on the full `@font-face` train or lose market share to Chrome, Firefox, Opera, and Safari.

It's important that Microsoft support `@font-face` the way other browsers do not merely because of the principle (important in itself) that browsers should support web standards correctly and completely, but also because Microsoft's EOT format removes hinting and other niceties that make fonts look good onscreen. As long as Microsoft only supports EOT fonts, IE users will have substandard experiences when viewing real fonts online.

Meantime, if you prefer to wait until the font foundries work out their differences, you may wish to consider the following interim solutions.

sIFR—Accessible Type Replacement

In 2004, designer/coder Shaun Inman devised a method he modestly called Inman Flash Replacement, which allowed designers to replace XHTML text headlines with a font of their choice via JavaScript, Flash, and CSS (www. shauninman.com/plete/inman-flash-replacement). He submitted it to *A List Apart*, where, with dazzling foresight, we rejected it because it was not accessible. Soon after Inman self-published the technique, developers Tomas Jogin and Mark Wubben improved it, making its type scalable and accessible.

sIFR (www.mikeindustries.com/sifr), the improved Inman method, stands for *scalable Inman Flash Replacement*—the lowercase *s* is deliberate. In both IFR and sIFR, Flash and JavaScript replace short passages of HTML text with Flash movies of the same text set in a real font. The Flash movies are created on the fly. If JavaScript or images are turned off, the user "sees" the HTML text; text set in sIFR can also be copied and pasted.

Obviously sIFR is for headlines and short passages only.

sIFR has brought rich, accessible typography to thousands of sites. It's free and cool and has been blessed by accessibility experts Matt May and Joe Clark. Versions 1.0 and 2.0 are a pain to implement, and fail if the user has installed a Flash block plug-in—a drawback corrected by the superior version 3.0 maintained by Mark Wubben (`wiki.novemberborn.net/sifr3`). Almost every good designer I know has implemented sIFR at least once. Almost every man over forty I know has an annual colonoscopy. Those two sentences seem to be related.

Cufón—"Fonts For the People"

To ease the pain of implementing sIFR 1.0 and 2.0, Simo Kinnunen came up with an easier method of embedding fonts (`cufon.shoqolate.com/generate`). Cufón looks like it would be pronounced Coo-PHONE, and most people do pronounce it that way, but it actually stands for "CUstom FONts." (The accent is just there to look cool.) Documentation is available at `wiki.github.com/sorccu/cufon`.

Cufón does not require Flash or any other plug-in; browsers support it natively. It is fast, even when handling large amounts of text; is easy to set up; and it works in all major browsers. Cufón consists of two parts—a font generator, which converts fonts to a proprietary format, and a rendering engine written in JavaScript. To include a font, you load it via the standard `script` element. Cufón compresses well and works in …

- Internet Explorer 6, 7, and 8
- Mozilla Firefox 1.5+
- Safari 3+
- Opera 9.5+
- Google Chrome 1.0+

Before you get too excited, note that currently users cannot select text set in Cufón. This limits its usability and accessibility, and may be a sufficient reason not to use it. There are licensing concerns with Cufón as well, as the font's EULA needs to specifically allow web embedding. See the "EULA Licensing and Security" section of `www.cameronmoll.com/archives/2009/03/cufon_font_embedding`. Work is underway to make Cufón text selectable. Keep watching the skies.

Typekit and its Brothers

Until type designers agree to a standard and all browsers support `@font-face`, "middleman" platforms such as Typekit [**13.14**–**13.15**] and Typotheque [**13.16**– **13.17**] make real web fonts possible by handling licensing and technological hassles.

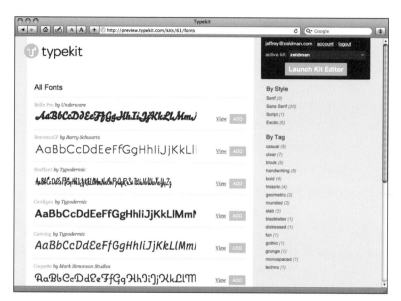

13.14
Typekit (**www.typekit. com**) lets designers embed real fonts on their web page without violating their end-user license. It works in all browsers.

13.15
The Typekit interface is easy to use, intuitive, and elegant.

13.16
Typotheque (**www. typotheque.com**) is a graphic design studio, a font foundry, and a platform for embedding fonts.

13.17
Typotheque considered (**www. forabeautifulweb. com/s/660**).

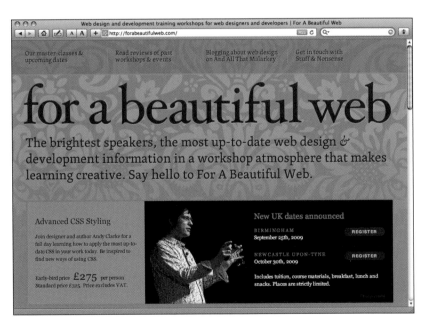

Here's how it works: First, companies like Typekit get font vendors to sign on. The companies agree to license their fonts through Typekit. Designers pay a monthly (or annual) fee to Typekit for arranging the license and hosting the fonts. Typekit also provides a technology solution, ensuring that the fonts show up in browsers that support standard font formats via `@font-face` (Safari, Firefox, Opera) as well as the one that does not (Internet Explorer). Worth noting is that Typekit is font-foundry-neutral, welcoming all, whereas Typotheque (at least initially) is a foundry-specific solution. The wizards at Clearleft have their own middleman platform in the works. All these solutions are currently in beta. As of this writing, pricing models for all but Typekit are unknown—and price is sure to have an impact on acceptance.

Moreover, no web font middleman offers every font you could wish for, and ultimately, designers will only choose a service that provides fonts they wish to use. Nor is it yet known whose technical solution will be best, whose font file will load fastest, how reliable each hosting platform will be as usage scales up, and so on. For designers and for these start-up platforms, these are exciting times indeed.

It remains to be seen whether a font-licensing standard and universal browser support for `@font-face` will kill the middlemen, or whether the middlemen will prove so successful that they delay or stifle the adoption of a font-licensing standard and allow Microsoft to shrug its shoulders indefinitely at supporting `@font-face` for anything beyond its proprietary EOT file format. There is also the possibility that the middlemen, by increasing acceptance of web fonts, will hasten the arrival of a licensing standard—and that this will, in turn, prompt Microsoft to support `@font-face` completely and correctly.

chapter fourteen

Accessibility: The Soul of Web Standards

This chapter's title is not fanciful or exaggerated. Accessibility is at the very core of standards-based design. Like semantic markup and CSS layout, the goal of accessible (or "universal") design is to make sure your content can be read, and your site can be used, by everyone—no matter what device they browse with, and regardless of physical ability. Wrongly perceived as dull and dismal, accessibility is actually where much of today's innovation is going on. If you enjoy browsing the web on your iPhone, for instance, thank the key technology that makes its interface possible: screen magnification, developed first as an aid to accessibility.

Accessibility is so closely linked to the other standards discussed in this book that in the 1990s, the W3C launched a Web Accessibility Initiative (WAI) to advise web builders on strategies for achieving it (www.w3.org/WAI/GL). WAI's chief task is to create guidelines for making web content accessible to people with disabilities. Not surprisingly, these guidelines are called Web Content Accessibility

Guidelines, or WCAG for short. WCAG 1.0 (www.w3.org/TR/WCAG10), published in 1999, offers fourteen guidelines as general principles of accessible design. WCAG 2.0 (www.w3.org/TR/2008/REC-WCAG20-20081211), the current standard, emphasizes "testable" principles and embraces dynamic, rich environments, such as Flash and Ajax, which WCAG 1.0 either abhorred or never dreamed of.

Many nations, especially in the European Union, use WCAG 1.0 or 2.0 as a *legal* standard for judging and enforcing the accessibility of sites. This is mostly pretty wonderful, as it enables the whole world to work with a single standard. The whole world doesn't always take advantage of the opportunity. The United States, for example, follows a unilateral specification called Section 508 instead of WCAG 1.0, possibly to avoid doing anything the French do.

Five Tips for Creating Accessible Websites

If the notion of making your site accessible seems overwhelming at first—or if reading WCAG 2.0 makes your head spin—simply strive to do these five things on every website:

1. Get Started

Just as fear of table-less layout once prevented thousands of developers from discovering standards-based design, many web slingers now fear that accessible design is too complex to master or too overwhelming a task to undertake. ("Our site is so messed up, I wouldn't know where to begin.") The longest journey begins with the shortest alt text. You make a web page accessible the same way you make it semantic: one p, one div, one form field at a time.

2. Use Logical Page Structures

Follow this book's core advice, and *structure your page semantically*, using h1, h2, p, and so on, as appropriate. Not only will this make your content easy for search engines to find, it will also enable visually disabled people who use screen readers to navigate your website's content.

Screen reader users navigate web pages by tabbing from h2 to h2 and from section to section, much as sighted users navigate by visually scanning. Non-semantic junk such as div class="headline" is unhelpful to screen readers and Google. Using h1–h6 instead makes your content findable and provides navigation for the blind.

When structuring your site semantically, pay particular attention to forms and tables, using techniques discussed later in this chapter—and in even more detail in this book's companion volume, *Developing with Web Standards*.

3. Provide Keyboard Access

Mice are nice for people with "normal" physical mobility. But many people cannot use mice. Keyboards and assistive devices are their gateway to online user experience. Use techniques discussed later in this chapter to code your site for keyboard access, and you welcome millions of people you would other-wise have locked out. Providing keyboard access is particularly important when Ajax is part of your user experience flow. If you're serving up lightboxes, in-page pop-ups, and other Ajax treats, keyboard access is a must.

4. Provide Alternatives

Information that is conveyed through a single sense, such as audio, requires an alternative (such as text).

5. Pick a Standard and Stick to It

Fumbling around in the dark is no way to create an accessible website. Picking a standard and following its guidelines is. Which standard should you choose? It almost doesn't matter, as long as you understand the guidelines and apply them to the best of your ability. (Unlike HTML, which is either valid or invalid, WCAG guidelines must be *interpreted*. My interpretation may differ from yours, yet we will both be "right" as long as people with disabilities can use our sites.)

WCAG 1.0 is a huge leap out of the dark, but it is also an aging specification, and it is not always as clear or as detailed as a standard should be. To clean up the parts that are vague, and to address changes in web development since WCAG 1.0 was new—to make it less about interpretation and more "scientific"— WAI developed WCAG 2.0 (www.w3.org/TR/UNDERSTANDING-WCAG20).

WCAG 1.0 offers three standardized levels of access, from the readily achieved (Priority 1), to one that requires slightly more work (Priority 2), to a master level (Priority 3). WCAG 2.0 also offers three levels. The point of the three levels is that accessibility, like the other forms of standards compliance discussed in this book, is a continuum rather than an all-or-nothing affair. Your first CSS site might have imperfect semantics and might even use a table or two as a layout container, but you would at least be trying. Likewise, with a small and reasonable effort, any of us—even those who are new to accessibility—can attain WCAG 1.0 Priority 1 conformance or something close to it. In so doing, we'll begin making our sites available to many of those whom we had previously locked out.

Must you choose a W3C standard? Is Section 508 a bust? On the contrary, in the U.S., conformance with Section 508 is mandatory for many websites. Here's a tip: If you attain WCAG 1.0 or WCAG 2.0 Priority 2 accessibility, you will also automatically achieve Section 508 compliance. Of course, if you prefer to work directly to the Section 508 guidelines, you certainly can. Like we said at the top, pick a standard, and begin applying it.

Access by the Books

Many well-intended accessibility books preach fire and brimstone. The smell of sulfur does not inspire designers. All too frequently, these books contain only visually ugly—or completely unrealistic—examples of accessible sites, along with impractical advice such as "never specify type sizes." Some authors in the field are hostile to design. Others have no experience in developing commercial sites. Designers might come away from these books believing that accessibility is irrelevant.

Other books, well researched and fueled by passionate insight, are worth the devotee's time, but are not recommended for the general web professional, because they are pitched at readers who live with one or more disabilities. In serving that readership, these books spend much time presenting alternate input methods and assessing the merits and demerits of alternative user agents. Nondisabled designers, who may already be uneasy about accessibility because of an unconscious anxiety about disability itself, are often not best served by such books.

I recommend the following:

- *Universal Design for Web Applications*, by Wendy Chisholm & Matt May (O'Reilly: 2009)

  The most up-to-date book on the subject, written by two renowned accessibility experts and standards gadflies, *Universal Design* covers all the basics of accessible web markup with a depth this chapter cannot. It explains how the rise of mobile devices necessitates that increasing and ever-more-sophisticated attention be paid to accessible design; discusses the changing legal environment; and explains (in English, even), such W3C documents as WCAG 2.0, ATAG (The Authoring Tool Accessibility Guidelines — www.w3.org/WAI/intro/atag.php), UAWG (www.w3.org/TR/WAI-USERAGENT), and WAI-ARIA (www.w3.org/WAI/intro/aria.php). What are those? ATAG tells the makers of web authoring software, such as Dreamweaver, how to ensure that their products are accessible to people with disabilities. UAWG guidelines do the same for makers of web browsers. And WAI-ARIA, "the Accessible Rich Internet Applications Suite, defines a way to make Web content and Web applications more accessible to people with disabilities. It especially helps with dynamic content and advanced user interface controls developed with Ajax, HTML, JavaScript, and related technologies."

  Chisholm and May spend a great deal of the book describing how to create accessible forms, and they also provide fantastic coverage of videos, scripting, rich internet applications, and more. This book is a must-have.

- *Building Accessible Web Sites*, by Joe Clark (New Riders: 2002)

  Part guidebook, part manifesto, Clark's tome is among the most compellingly written web design books ever: witty, opinionated, and truthful. In my strange line of work, I see most new design books and many new computer books. Few are complete, fewer still are entirely lucid, and with very few indeed do I feel that I am in the hands of a master communicator. I devoured Clark's book as if it were the latest Harry Potter novel, then read it again. Not only will you learn everything you need to know about common sense, practical accessibility from this book; you can actually read it for pleasure.

Building Accessible Web Sites covers it all, from the basics of writing usable `alt` attributes to the complexities of captioning rich media. Prior to writing this book, Joe Clark, whom the *Atlantic Monthly* called "the king of closed captions," had spent twenty years in the field of media access, and it shows. He is uniquely positioned to guide the reader clearly and confidently from the big picture to the smallest detail—offering phased accessibility strategies that fit any budgetary or time constraint, and straight talk that clarifies regulations and debunks myths. Moreover, Clark cares as much about design aesthetics as access, and he shows how the two are compatible. I recommend this book unreservedly. Sadly, *Building Accessible Web Sites* is now out of print. On the plus side, you can get a used copy cheap—or read the book online for free: `www.joeclark.org/book/sashay/serialization`.

- *Web Accessibility: Web Standards and Regulatory Compliance*, Jim Thatcher et al. (Friends of Ed, 2006)

  Written by multiple subject matter experts including Jim Thatcher, Shawn Lawton Henry (a WAI member and contributor to WCAG), *A List Apart*'s Andrew Kirkpatrick, and Bruce (Dr. HTML5) Lawson, this task-focused book tells you in specific detail how to deliver web content that fully complies with accessibility laws and regulations. It covers everything from accessible navigation and data input to accessible JavaScript, PDFs, and Flash. You'll learn how screen readers and other forms of assistive technology help people use, navigate, and create web content. Glossaries cover U.S. accessibility law in depth, worldwide accessibility laws and policies, and more. This book belongs on the shelf of every developer and site owner for whom accessibility is legally mandatory.

Among other benefits, reading these three books will help overturn many mistaken and sadly widespread ideas such as those we are about to discuss.

Widespread Confusion

Presented with the notion of accessibility, many otherwise savvy designers, developers, and site owners tend to spout meaningless aphorisms about serving their customers. Informed of accessibility laws such as U.S. Section 508 of the Rehabilitation Act, they often subside into what we may characterize as mental incontinence.

The Genius Puts His Foot in It

On more than one stage, lecturing to a professional audience, I have heard a highly respected fellow web designer respond to a spectator's accessibility question with nonsense like this: "We create cutting-edge branding work for the elite consumers our client is trying to reach. That accessibility stuff—that's a very small part of our market, and… uh… our client doesn't mind losing those few people. I mean, hey, our client makes high-definition wide-screen TVs. Blind folks aren't buying those this year (chuckle, chuckle)."

Actually, blind people might buy those TVs for a sighted partner or family member if the site allowed them to read the specifications and use the online ordering forms. Moreover, the overwhelming majority of visually impaired web users are not entirely blind or even close to it. Most who require access enhancements range from people with low vision to the color blind to the slightly myopic, and any of these might desire and be willing to purchase a high-quality, big picture television set.

The "Blind Billionaire"

Moreover, web crawlers are, in effect, blind users. And the Google search engine is the biggest blind user on the web. This "user" gives out recommendations in the form of search results to a metric ton of customers every day. Dish out appropriate content, well written and well structured, and you not only serve the blind folks in your audience, you also attract millions of sighted ones. Put another way, Google's aggregate readership makes the search engine much like a blind billionaire. How many sites would willingly say no to potential clients who have a few billion dollars to spend? Considered a third way, if you count all the disabled folks in America alone, it's something like the combined populations of the greater metro areas of Los Angeles and New York City. Would it be smart to exclude everyone living in and around those cities from your site? Of course it wouldn't.

Access Is Not Limited to the Visually Impaired

But access is not limited to the visually impaired. Motor impaired (partly or completely paralyzed) consumers might want to buy a nice television and might also prefer shopping online to hassling with a trip to a brick and mortar store. Many access enhancements are targeted to that group rather than to the cane-and-tin-cup cartoon that invariably springs to mind when the ill-informed contemplate accessibility. Access enhancements also help non-disabled consumers who are attempting to buy that spiffy TV while viewing the site on a smart phone.

In short, the designer or developer or site owner who says, "Blind people don't buy our products," is missing the point and the boat. He himself is blind to the true nature of the audience he needlessly rejects—including millions of non-disabled visitors who might have found his site via a search engine if the site had only made an effort to conform to access guidelines, and many others who would have ordered his product over their phone if only his site let them. Sadly, he is not unique in misunderstanding what access entails and whom it serves.

A Cloud of Fuzzy Ideas

Over the years, I have heard many misguided utterances flow from the lips of otherwise extremely clued-in web professionals, including these:

"That's our client's problem. If they don't include it in the RFP [Request for Proposal], we don't have to worry about it," said a lead developer at one of the largest and most famous of global web agencies shortly before it went bankrupt and its remnants were bought by a small company in Central Asia. By the way, he was wrong.

"Section 508? That's for the government. We're not government employees." I heard this one from a design agency whose client was legally mandated to provide access.

"One of our committee members is looking that over. We're supposed to get a white paper about it some time or other." A senior project manager at a U.S. government facility shared this insight with me one year after Section 508 became the law of the land.

"Well, we're a Dreamweaver shop," a designer informed me. "So that whole accessibility thing is handled in the new upgrade, right?" Yes and no. The latest version of Dreamweaver provides numerous accessibility enhancements, but you have to know how to use them. Merely opening Dreamweaver does not guarantee creating an accessible site, any more than using a Nikon camera guarantees taking a superb photograph.

The Law and the Layout

The volume of confusion was already high when the passage of Section 508 of the U.S. Rehabilitation Act cranked it up to 11. (Note: I write from an American perspective and use American examples in this section, but the same principles apply no matter where you are and no matter what your local laws might be. In most cases and most places, your local laws will come straight out of WCAG 1.0 or 2.0.)

Section 508 (`www.section508.gov`) requires that many sites accommodate people with disabilities ranging from limited mobility to a vast range of visual impairments, and it spells out what accessible means. (Hint: adding `alt` attributes to your images is not enough.) Faced with such a task, many web professionals conclude that accessibility means text-only pages or unattractive, "low-end" design. This isn't so.

All staples of contemporary web design are entirely compatible with 508 compliance; they simply require a little thoughtful care. As this chapter progresses, we'll examine some of what accessibility and Section 508 compliance specifically entails, and we'll explore how you can use intelligent judgment and available tools to make your site comply beautifully.

Section 508 Explained

Section 508 is part of the Rehabilitation Act of 1973, which is intended to end discrimination against people who have disabilities. Enacted by the U.S. Congress on August 7, 1998, Public Law 105-220 (Rehabilitation Act Amendments of 1998) significantly expanded 508's technology access requirements. The law covers computers, fax machines, copiers, telephones, transaction machines and kiosks, and other equipment used for transmitting, receiving, or storing information. It also covers many websites. (Yet it doesn't seem to have any effect on the keypads used at checkout counters. We have yet to find an accessible one, even when they use real buttons—which is rare.)

Section 508 became U.S. law on June 21, 2001. It directly affects Federal departments and agencies, as well as web designers who produce work for them. The law also applies to government-funded projects and to any states that choose to adopt it. Many have done so.

In a nutshell, Section 508 applies to the following:

- Federal departments and agencies (including the U.S. Postal Service)
- Deliverables from contractors who serve them
- Activities sponsored or funded by the Federal government
- Activities sponsored by states that have adopted the regulation

"Equal or Equivalent Access to Everyone"

Section 508 requires all websites under its jurisdiction to provide "equal or equivalent access to everyone," including the visually impaired, the hearing impaired, the physically disabled, and people who have photosensitive epilepsy.

Problems faced by these web users might surprise you. For example, small, non-resizable text can prevent people who have limited vision from reading your content. (See the discussion of the pixel problem in Chapter 13.) Tiny navigation buttons that have small "hit" areas can thwart those who have impaired motor skills. Blinking or flashing pages (yes, there are still plenty of those being created) can trigger life-threatening seizures in people who have epilepsy. The list goes on. The law explains many common access problems and suggests, but does not dictate, possible solutions.

Section 508 does not forbid the use of CSS, JavaScript, images, or even sad old table layouts. Nor does it prevent you from incorporating rich media such as Flash and QuickTime, as long as you follow certain guidelines discussed later in this chapter. Naturally, most 508-compliant (like most standards-compliant) sites will look spiffier in new browsers than in old ones. That's no problem under the law, because web users can upgrade their browsers simply by downloading the latest version, and most browsers are available for free.

Accessibility Myths Debunked

What have we learned so far? Conformance with accessibility guidelines not only makes your site available to millions of people who live with disabilities, but also helps you reach millions more, including customers who use mobile devices—and attract still more via search engines. Sounds pretty good. So why are so many designers, developers, and site owners confused about or hostile to accessibility guidelines and regulations? Primarily, they are confused or hostile because myths about access have long soiled the pool. Let's try to clear up some of these mistaken notions.

Myth: Accessibility Forces You to Create Two Versions of Your Site

Not true. If you design with web standards and follow guidelines, your site should be as accessible to screen readers, Lynx, mobile devices, and old browsers as it is to modern, compliant browsers. Standards and accessibility converge in agreeing that one web document should serve all readers and users. Even Flash and PDFs can now be made accessible. But explaining how is a job for someone else's book. (See *Web Accessibility: Web Standards and Regulatory Compliance* and the Adobe site listed later in this chapter.)

Myth: A Text-Only Version Satisfies the Requirement for Equal or Equivalent Access

Not true. Adaptive technology has come a long way, and almost anything on a conventional web page can be made fully or at least partially accessible, with no visible alteration to your layout. (Remember: the work takes place under the hood.) Shuttling disabled visitors off to a text-only site assumes that the color blind can't see at all, or that those who have limited mobility have no use for images. It also assumes that these users have no interest in shopping on your commerce site or participating in an online discussion forum. In short, the outdated text-only approach helps no one. Not only that, creating and maintaining text-only pages costs far more (and is far less reliable) than simply adding assistive tags and attributes to your site.

Myth: Accessibility Costs Too Much

Not true. What is the cost of adding a `label` to your web form, or of writing a table summary? What is the cost of typing a brief `alt` text for each image on your page? Such tasks can be accomplished in minutes. Higher-level conformance entailing specialized work can, of course, cost more than these simple tasks—but not necessarily. For instance, it takes some work to author closed captions for web videos or to caption live streaming media news feeds in real time. But it doesn't have to be tons of work or cost mountains of cash. For a handy guide on how it's done, read (who else) Joe Clark's "Best Practices in Online Captioning" (`www.joeclark.org/access/captioning/bpoc`).

With large sites whose content is updated by non-development (editorial) personnel, adding access to new pages is often as simple as updating the content management system to prompt for required attributes. (For example, the system can prevent content folks from uploading an image until they have entered `alt` text for that image.) On a dynamic site, it might be as easy as reworking the templates that generate pages on the fly. Adding access attributes to forms, structural summaries to table layouts, and making other, similar adjustments to global templates can be a one-time cost that pays off by welcoming new customers and occasionally waving garlic before the vampires of the legal profession.

"It's Not in the Budget"

I have this friend. He is always buying CDs he has no time to listen to and DVDs he has no time to watch. He rents a studio in case he feels like painting even though he hasn't painted in two years. He gets all the cable channels although he never watches TV because he is always going out to clubs. The only downside to his thrilling consumer lifestyle is a throbbing around his lower-left molar. He's had a toothache for two months but "can't afford" to see a dentist. You might say that my friend's priorities are out of whack, but his attitude is no different from that of many companies.

Those who complain about the cost of accessibility (and who also typically complain about the cost of web standards) are invariably the same people who waste thousands on browser detection, conditional scripts, conditional CSS, and even conditional HTML as described in Chapter 13. They think nothing of squandering cash money sending ten different style sheets to ten different browsers, all of which would be better served by a single CSS file. Instead of an open source content management system like Drupal (`www.drupal.org`) or a low-cost, standards-compliant one like ExpressionEngine (`www.expressionengine.com`), they'll spend millions on a bloated, proprietary framework that generates invalid markup and user-unfriendly URLs and requires constant maintenance by expensive specialists.

But cough up a few dollars on accessibility? "It costs too much," they claim.

Many companies that claim they cannot afford to implement even the most basic levels of accessibility nevertheless seem to have plenty of dough for backend development, streaming media, and needlessly complex JavaScript. If these expenses are considered part of doing business, the far tinier cost of providing access must be regarded in the same way.

Myth: Accessibility Forces You to Create Primitive, Low-End Designs

Not true. Images, CSS layouts, JavaScript, server-side technologies like PHP, and other staples of contemporary web design are perfectly compatible with WCAG Priority 1 and U.S. Section 508 compliance; they simply require care and judgment. You can also use plug-in-based technologies like Flash and QuickTime, as long as you follow the guidelines that pertain to them (discussed later in this chapter). All sites produced by Happy Cog in the past nine years encourage forms-based user interactivity and employ DOM-based scripts, CSS layouts, rich imagery, et cetera ad infinitum, yet they are accessible and handily pass online access conformance tests. So do sites by our colleagues at Clearleft, Erskine Design, and hundreds of others.

Important: as we'll soon see, passing online access conformance tests does not guarantee that your site is truly accessible or compliant. There are limits to the kinds of tests that software can perform; human judgment must temper and evaluate all such tests. On the other hand, failing WCAG Priority 1 or U.S. Section 508 tests is a pretty good sign that your site does not comply.

Myth: According to Section 508, Sites Must Look the Same in All Browsers and User Agents

Not true. How could they? Naturally, most 508-compliant sites will look better in new browsers than old. That's no problem under the law because web users can freely upgrade simply by downloading. Content must be both usable and accessible regardless of user agent or device. Visual design cannot be present in many of these environments, and need not look the same from one graphical browser to the next. Old-school methods intended to make sites look the same in all browsers and on all platforms are one reason the web still has so many inaccessible, invalid, hard-to-maintain sites.

Myth: Accessibility Is "Just for Disabled People"

Not true. Certainly, conformance can improve (or in some cases, provide for the first time) access for people who have major disabilities. But it will also help the following:

- Anyone who uses mobile devices, a market segment that is growing exponentially, and has eclipsed desktop use in Asia and Africa

- People who have temporary impairments and disabilities (for example, broken wrists)

- People who have minor, correctable vision problems, including aging baby boomers (a huge segment of the population)

- Those who are temporarily accessing sites away from their customary environment—for instance, via kiosks or feature-limited browsers in airports and other public places

- Site owners who want to reach any of these people rather than sending them to a competitor's site

- Site owners who want to benefit from search engines, the biggest "blind users" of them all (see "The 'Blind Billionaire'," earlier in this chapter)

Myth: Designers Can Freely Ignore Accessibility Laws if Their Clients Tell Them To

That remains to be seen. I know of no cases where web designers have been held liable for creating inaccessible sites—*yet*. But the U.S. Justice Department has gone after architects who violate the Americans with Disabilities Act, whether the client told them to "build it that way" or not. Web designers might someday face similar penalties. It's our job to educate clients (or bosses), not blame them, when we knowingly do the wrong thing. Besides, even if *you* get off the hook, do you really want your client being sued by users or harassed by the Justice Department?

In 2006, blind patrons sued Target, alleging that its website was inaccessible and thus in violation of anti-discrimination laws (`news.cnet.com/Blind-patrons-sue-Target-for-site-inaccessibility/2100-1030_3-6038123.html`). After delaying for months over stupidly simple fixes, Target got off the hook by revising its site on a rush basis. I wouldn't want to be the Target vice-president who had approved the previous, inaccessible version. I also wouldn't want to be the designer or agency head on the other end of the vice-president's phone call.

Accessibility Tips, Element by Element

The following guidelines offer approaches to bringing commonly used web page elements into conformance with WCAG or governmental accessibility guidelines.

Images

Leaving out `alt` text will cause users of Lynx, screen readers, and other non-mainstream browsers and devices to hear or see "[IMAGE] [IMAGE] [IMAGE]" or something equally unhelpful. Lack of `alt` texts will also be flagged as a WAI access error and an XHTML validation error. Use the `alt` attribute to the `img` element (`www.w3.org/WAI/GL/WCAG20/checkpoints.html`) to describe the content of each image. And we do mean *content*—not mere appearance.

Your Friend, the Null *alt* Attribute

For meaningless images, such as spacer GIFs (not that *you're* still using spacer GIF images), use `alt=""`, also known as the null `alt` attribute, or null `alt` text. Do not compound users' problems with literal `alt` text for meaningless images like `alt="pixel spacer gif"` or `alt="table cell background color gradient"`. Use the null `alt` attribute for images that are intended to create purely visual (nonmeaningful, nonsemantic) design effects. Or, better yet, put presentational imagery in your CSS, where it belongs.

Use *alt* Attributes That Convey Meaning to Your Visitors

Use `alt` attribute values that convey meaning to your visitors, rather than meaning to you and your colleagues. For instance, on a logo that also works as a link back to the home page, use `alt="Smith Company home page"` instead of `alt="smith_logo_rev3"` or `alt="Smith Company logo"`. To a visually disabled user, it is of scant interest to be told that an image she can't see is a logo. The fact that clicking the image will take her back to the home page is far more significant. If you feel you must, you can hedge your bets by writing something like this:

```
alt="Smith Company home page [logo]"
```

Alternately, because the purpose of `alt` text is to provide an alternative to be read when an image is not available, you might use *Smith Company [logo]* as your `alt` text, and *Smith Company home page* as `title` text on the link.

Resist "helpful" software that generates `alt` attribute values for you; this software will most likely generate useless `alt` texts derived directly from filenames:

```
alt="smith_logo_32x32"
```

In short, never send a robot to do a human being's job. In fact...

Don't Trust Software to Do a Human Being's Job

Don't assume that your `alt` attributes work if your page passes web-based accessibility tests. A page that uses `alt="mickeymouse"` for every image (or `alt=""` for every image) might pass these tests just fine. No software can tell if your `alt` texts are appropriate. And frankly, you wouldn't want to live in a world where software *could* make these kinds of judgments. If you don't know what I'm talking about, watch *2001*, *Blade Runner*, *The Matrix*, *Minority Report*, *Terminator*, or *The Brave Little Toaster*. Okay, maybe not so much *The Brave Little Toaster*.

The *alt* Tooltip Fandango

Some leading browsers (in other words, all old versions of Internet Explorer) misguidedly display `alt` attributes as tooltips when the visitor's cursor hovers over the image. Although millions of web users are accustomed to it by now, it is a horrible idea for many reasons. Chiefly, `alt` text is an accessibility tool, not a nifty tooltip gimmick. (The `title` attribute is fine for nifty tooltip gimmicks.) As mentioned two tips ago, the W3C explicitly states that `alt` text should be visible only when images cannot be viewed:

> The alt attribute specifies alternate text that is rendered when the image cannot be displayed... User agents must render alternate text when they cannot support images, they cannot support a certain image type, or when they are configured not to display images.
>
> —www.w3.org/TR/REC-html40/struct/objects.html#h-13.2

No browser should display redundant `alt` text that describes what the sighted visitor can already plainly see. But IE/Windows, for instance, did just that until IE8 came along. In their defense, Netscape/Windows did it first and the two were locked in an HTML arms race at the time, always trying to one-up or at least catch-up. This is not your problem, unless it misleads you into writing "creative" `alt` text that fails to do its primary job of explaining images to those people who can't see them.

No *alt* for Background Images

Access novices often ask if they need to write `alt` text for CSS (or HTML) background images. It is a logical and reasonable question, to which the answer is no. In fact, you couldn't do so if you tried. There are no `alt` attributes in CSS. (For example, there is no `alt` attribute for a background image placed on the body.)

If a background image conveys important meaning that is not provided by the page's text—for instance, if the page's sole text reads, "He was honest" and the CSS background image is a portrait of Abraham Lincoln—you might try including the words *President Abraham Lincoln* inside a `title` attribute on the `body` element, or use the `summary` attribute if a table was used to lay it out. A better option would be to include the image as content (i.e., as an `img`) with appropriate `alt` text. You could always use CSS to place the image behind the words, so it looks like a background.

Better still, you might ditch the whole idea. A picture of Lincoln with the words, "He was honest"? What kind of crummy web page is that?

Streaming Video

Where a plug-in is required, include one clear link to the required item.

If you use an image to link to a required plug-in, make sure it has appropriate `alt` text.

To enhance the accessibility of QuickTime (or some other multimedia format), use a captioning tool or a web standard like SMIL to provide descriptive text and captions equivalent to audio tracks. See `www.alistapart.com/articles/ smil` for a designer-friendly introduction to SMIL, then luxuriate in the aforementioned "Best Practices in Online Captioning" (`www.joeclark.org/ access/captioning/bpoc`).

Flash

Flash CS 4 meets many Section 508 requirements, including content magnification, mouse-free navigation, sound synchronization, text equivalents, and more. It can create accessible web content that works with Microsoft Active Accessibility to communicate with screen readers. Screen readers, sometimes incorrectly referred to as "voice browsers" or "text readers," are programs that translate on-screen content into audio, providing non-sighted users with an aural interface to their computer. The leading screen readers, Window-Eyes (`www.gwmicro.com/Window-Eyes`) and JAWS (`www.freedomscientific. com/jaws-hq.asp`), work happily with accessible Flash content. For a tutorial on creating accessible sites in Flash, visit `www.adobe.com/accessibility/ products/flash/tutorial`.

Additional tips:

- If you use JavaScript to detect the presence or absence of Flash, have a backup plan—that is, one clear link to the required item—for those who don't or can't use JavaScript. Also, if you use JavaScript to detect the presence or absence of Flash, for the love of Heaven, make sure you know what you're doing. The medium is littered with the corpses of broken browser and plug-in detection scripts and the bodies of web users caught in the crossfire. A good choice is SWFObject (`code.google.com/p/ swfobject`).

- Understand that despite your best, most sincere efforts, some people will not be able to access your Flash content.

Color

If you use color to denote information, such as the fact that certain text is a link, reinforce it with other methods—for instance, also bolding or underlining links, not just relying on color alone. If you've turned off underlining via CSS, consider making links bolder than normal text. If you do this, avoid using bold on non-linked text, lest you hopelessly confuse the color-blind user as to which bold text is hyperlinked and which bold text is simply bold. If the difference between linked and ordinary text is obvious even to a color-blind person (if text is black and links are white, to use the most extreme example), bolding or other differentiation schemes will not be necessary.

Avoid referring to color in your text. "Visit the Yellow Box for Help" is useless direction for those who can't see (or can't see that color).

Use care when creating harmonious color schemes, whose differences might not be apparent to those who have certain types of color blindness. Joe Clark devotes many readable and essential pages to this subject's details. His book is available online and at fine used bookstores everywhere.

You will also want to visit `www.vischeck.com`, which lets you see how your web pages appear to people with various types of color blindness.

CSS

Test your pages with and without style sheets to be certain they are readable either way. Don't worry about changes to graphic design with styles turned off, unless those changes render the site unusable.

Structured Markup Conveys Meaning When CSS Goes Away

If you author with well-structured (X)HTML, your page will work better even when styles are switched off or unavailable. Readers "get" semantic markup with or without CSS. As I keep saying, emphasize structure and avoid divitis. Markup like that shown next won't make much sense when CSS is unavailable to the user:

```
<div class="header">Headline</div>
<div class="copy">Text</div>
<div class="copy">Text</div>
<div class="copy">Text</div>
```

Don't Trust What You See in One Browser Alone

Write valid CSS and test it in multiple browsers. Don't write invalid CSS that happens to work in a particular browser. Bad CSS might make a page illegible. Not every web user knows how to turn off CSS, let alone how to override your CSS with user style sheets, and not every browser supports user style sheets at this time.

Take Care When Sizing Text

If you specify text size with ems or percentages, check your site with a smaller default font size (see Chapter 13). Avoid pixel-sized text if a majority of your audience uses IE6 (once more, see Chapter 13) *or* use DOM- or backend–driven style switchers to let users change text sizes (see Chapter 15).

Don't—I Repeat, Don't Trust Access Validation Test Results

Don't assume that your CSS is "safe" simply because your page passes online accessibility tests. A page that uses illegible 7px type might pass these tests.

Rollovers and Other Scripted Behaviors

Code to ensure that links work even when JavaScript is turned off. Test by turning off JavaScript in your browser.

Provide Alternatives for Non-Mouse Users

Folks who have impaired mobility can and do use JavaScript-capable browsers but might be unable to click or perform other mouse maneuvers. Provide
alternate code for these users:

```
<input type="button" onclick="setActiveStyleSheet('default');
return false;" onkeypress="setActiveStyleSheet('default');
return false;" />
```

In the preceding example, onkeypress is the non-mouse user equivalent to
onclick. The two lines of code coexist peacefully. The alternate code is invisible to the mouse user. Yes, coding the same function two ways adds a few bytes
to your page's overall weight. In this case, the fractional increase in bandwidth
pays off by welcoming disabled users instead of punishing them for being
disabled.

Of course, you *really* want to remove JavaScript event handlers from your
markup via unobtrusive DOM scripting, but that is a topic for Chapter 15.

Use noscript to provide for those who can't use JavaScript. Or better yet, use
progressive enhancement and ditch noscript altogether.

The interaction between scripted behaviors and accessibility can be quite
complex, and a full discussion is beyond the scope of this chapter. For more
information on working with JavaScript, read the books recommended in
upcoming Chapter 15.

Forms

At the outset of this chapter, I highly recommended three books. Each devote
an entire chapter to the ins and outs of creating accessible online forms. From
this coincidence, you might be tempted to conclude that the creation of accessible online forms can be somewhat involved. You would be correct.

Don't panic. Most tasks involved are simple and straightforward, such as associating form fields with appropriate labels (for instance, associating the text
area in a Search form with a "Search" label). It's just that there are a lot of little
tasks like that, and discussing them all exceeds this chapter's scope.

After you've built what you hope are accessible forms, test your work in Lynx
(lynx.browser.org) or JAWS. Users of older Macs will need Virtual PC

(www.microsoft.com/windows/virtualpc/default.mspx) or a real PC
to run JAWS. On an Intel-based Mac, you'll need Boot Camp (www.apple.
com/support/bootcamp), Parallels (www.parallels.com), Fusion (www.
vmware.com/products/fusion), or VirtualBox (www.virtualbox.org), plus
a Windows CD or virtual machine. You can also run VoiceOver (www.apple.
com/macosx/features/voiceover), an accessibility interface that's built into
Mac OS X (starting with Tiger). For Linux folks, a free screen reader is included
in the SuSE Linux 7.0 distribution (www.hicom.net/~oedipus/vicug/
SuSE_blinux.html), or you can pick up Speakup (www.linux-speakup.org/
speakup.html).

Image Maps

Avoid image maps if you can—and you generally can. When required, use
client-side image maps with alt text and provide redundant text links. Just say
no to old-fashioned, server-side image maps.

Table Layouts

Don't sweat this. Write simple table summaries as explained in Chapter 8, and
use CSS to avoid the need for deeply nested tables, spacer GIFs, and other such
junk, as explained in Chapters 8 through 10.

That's really it. Despite what you might have heard to the contrary, the use of
simple table layouts is not a major access hazard, is not illegal under WAI or
Section 508 guidelines, and will not condemn your soul to eternal torment.
OK, I'm not sure about the eternal torment part, but table layouts aren't illegal
under WCAG or Section 508 (though some of us may wish they were).

Tables Used for Data

Identify table headers and use appropriate markup to associate data cells and
header cells for tables that have two or more logical levels of row and column
headers. In a table that lists members of the cast of *The Music Man*, a typical
table header might be *Actor*, and table cells associated with it would include
Robert Preston, *Shirley Jones*, *Buddy Hackett*, *Hermione Gingold*, and so on.

A sighted person who is using a graphical browser will see the connection between *Actor* and the column of names directly below it. But screen
reader users require additional markup that connects the table header to its

associated data cells. View source at `www.w3.org/WAI/wcag-curric/sam45-0` `.htm` to see how the WAI group clarifies the connection between headers and their associated data cells.

Frames, Applets

Just say no.

Flashing or Blinking Elements

Just say no. Not just no, hell no. You might not have used `blink` or `marquee` since you were knee-high to a FrontPage template (if ever), but keep in mind that the ban on flashing and blinking elements applies to Flash and QuickTime content as well.

Tools of the Trade

If you use a visual editor to create web pages, several tools and plug-ins can simplify conformance with access guidelines:

Firefox Web Developer Toolbar

This fabulous, free menu and toolbar for Firefox provides numerous web development tools, many of them ideal for quick accessibility testing. Toggle CSS styles on and off, temporarily disable JavaScript and page colors, and more. The toolbar can be installed in Firefox or Mozilla on any platform that runs these browsers, including Windows, Linux, and Mac OS X (`www.chrispederick.com/work/webdeveloper`).

IE's Web Accessibility Toolbar

Provided by the Accessible Information Solutions (AIS) team of Vision Australia, this free toolbar (donations welcome) for IE/Windows makes it easy to check for various aspects of accessibility. Toggle CSS styles, replace `img` elements with their `alt` attributes, test animated GIFs to determine if they are in a "flicker rate" range that can trigger photosensitive epilepsy, and more (`www.visionaustralia.org.au/info.aspx?page=614`).

Loving Cynthia

Whether you use the products mentioned earlier or mark up and code your sites by hand like a macho macho (wo)man, the Cynthia Says portal should be your next stop (`www.contentquality.com`).

This fast, free service can test any page for access conformance, although the nuances require judgment and analysis. Both WAI and Section 508 rely on a manual checklist to ensure compliance. Unlike the W3C's markup and CSS validation services, the Cynthia Says portal's validation tests cannot provide you with an unconditionally clean bill of health or a list of mistakes to be fixed. Instead, you must interpret its output. That's where things get tricky. But it's also where they become educational and where you get to earn your paycheck as a knowledgeable designer, developer, or related web specialist.

Before Cynthia, there was Bobby, an online accessibility testing service featuring a happy British police officer as its mascot. (Bobby was later acquired by Watchfire, which changed the program to something called WebXACT, which didn't work well, and they eventually went out of business.)

Keeping Tabs: Our Good Friend, the *tabindex* Attribute

The `tabindex` attribute specifies the tabbing navigation order among active elements on the page. If you don't create a logical tab order, people who rely on tabbing (instead of the mouse) will simply tab from link to link in the order that links appear in your (X)HTML source. This might not be the most useful way to guide them through your site, particularly if your body text contains numerous links or long-winded navigation that occurs early in markup.

Like Skip Navigation, `tabindex` spares screen reader users from the worst aspects of serial navigation, enabling them to quickly skip to content that interests them. Whereas Skip Navigation leapfrogs long lists of links, `tabindex` provides shortcut serial access to various parts of the page—not unlike a DVD's chapter index, which lets movie fans skip ahead to the car chase or back to the love scene.

On commercial sites, after creating a tab order, you would test on real users. On personal or nonprofit sites, you might not have that luxury. When user testing is not an option, construct a user scenario, create a tabbing order based on that scenario, and wait to hear from your site's visitors who use `tabindex` whether you guessed right or not.

Planning for Access: How You Benefit

Although many sites are not legally required to provide access today, they might have to do so tomorrow. One thing we all know about laws is that they continually change. Another thing we know is that we are all subject to laws, whether we like them or not. Applying these enhancements to your site, even if you are not required to do so under today's laws, might protect you from expensive retooling should the laws change next year, and might also protect you from the cost (and bad publicity) of antidiscrimination lawsuits.

The Love You Make

Having trotted out the rationale behind many site owners' sudden interest in accessibility, let me hastily add that fear of lawsuits is the wrong reason to incorporate access into your design practice. These enhancements open any site to new visitors—and whose site could not use more visitors? Those locked out of other sites will be inclined to feel quite loyal to yours if you welcome them into it by making these adjustments to your markup. If other online stores block disabled visitors and nontraditional device users and *your* store welcomes them, guess who will be selling to those customers, and guess who won't be?

And don't forget, the more accessible your site is to disabled visitors and non-traditional internet device users, the more available its content will also be to Google, Bing, and all the other crawler-driven search engines and directories that send visitors your way. Conversely, the less accessible your site, the less traffic it will draw from Google and its brothers. Golly, I was trying to attain higher moral ground, and I still seem to have offered purely self-interested reasons for implementing accessibility. Here are two more:

1. Implementing access enhancements can deepen your understanding of design. Considering things like tab order can take you beyond a vision of design as the decoration of surface appearance ("look and feel") and into the realms of user experience, contingency design, and general usability. These are issues that web designers, user experience designers, information architects, and usability specialists think about anyway. Accessibility is just another aspect of considering how to best build our sites to meet diverse human needs. The more you consider accessibility, the more profoundly you will understand user experience and anticipate user behavior—making you a better designer.

2. Implementing access and honing a conformance strategy can sharpen your development skills and provide fresh perspectives you might never have considered otherwise. Learning the ways of WAI and the particulars of 508 will increase your value as a professional web designer, position your web agency as smarter and more clued-in than its competitors, and help your sites reach more people than ever before. That is what every site owner wants and what every designer or developer strives for.

Practicing accessibility will help your visitors reach their goals, yes; but it will also help you reach your own.

chapter fifteen

Working with DOM-Based Scripts

In the beginning, Netscape created JavaScript, and it was good. Then Microsoft begat JScript, and it was different. Vast armies clashed by night and the flames of DHTML threatened to engulf all. Salvation arrived with the birth of a standard Document Object Model (DOM), whose first manifestation was called DOM Level 1 (`www.w3.org/TR/1998/REC-DOM-Level-1-19981001`). And it was very good indeed. For the first time, the W3C DOM gave designers and developers a standard means of accessing the data, scripts, and presentation of which their sites were composed.

In the years since, the W3C has continued to update its DOM specs, and, at the urging of The Web Standards Project, browsers have come to support nearly all of the DOM Level 1 specification, although they sometimes differ in the ways they support it. In this chapter, we will meet the DOM and explore a few of its simpler uses as an aid to creating accessible, user-focused sites.

This will be a short chapter, not because the subject is light but because it is broad and deep, requiring way more space and time than I can provide here. Fortunately, two fine books do what the present chapter cannot:

DOM by the Books

- *DOM Scripting: Web Design with JavaScript and the Document Object Model* by Jeremy Keith (Friends of Ed, 2005) is the supremely readable, designer-friendly book we've all been waiting for. After gently introducing JavaScript and the DOM and covering emerging best practices, it moves on to a series of visually exciting and useful projects, each of which teaches how to think as well as how to do. A sample chapter (www.domscripting.com/book/sample) conveys the book's likable tutelage style. The author is a founder of Clearleft (www.clearleft.com), a British agency specializing in standards-based design, and a member of The Web Standards Project.

- *The JavaScript Anthology: 101 Essential Tips, Tricks & Hacks* by James Edwards and Cameron Adams (SitePoint, 2006) lists hundreds of ways to control web page behaviors via JavaScript (i.e., to use the DOM). The emphasis is on best practices that have arisen in the standards-based scripting community in the past few years—such as progressive enhancement (providing for users who don't have JavaScript) and unobtrusive scripting (separating structure and presentation from behavior—see sidebar). A chapter on JavaScript and accessibility is of particular interest; there's also good stuff about building web applications using Ajax. James Edwards and Cameron Adams are freelance coders hailing from the UK and Australia, respectively.

These books will show you how scripting can play a key role in creating accessible, standards-based sites. What follows in this chapter is a non-scripter's quick overview.

Unobtrusive Scripting

The "DOM by the Books" section of this chapter cites *unobtrusive scripting* (also known as *unobtrusive JavaScript* and *unobtrusive DOM scripting*) as a best practice in standards-based development. The idea is simple: separate behavior from the other two layers of web development (structure and presentation). Unlike the advertising popups, forced new windows, forced size changes, and other "in your face" JavaScript gimmicks of yore, unobtrusive scripting is user-focused and self-effacing. It is designed to enhance an already semantic and accessible markup structure, and to offer fallbacks if the user or device does not support JavaScript.

Though it has since disbanded, The Web Standards Project's DOM Scripting Task Force cited the following benefits to the practice:

- The usability benefit: An effect created by an unobtrusive DOM script does not draw the attention of the user. It is so obviously a good addition to the site that visitors just use it without thinking about it.

- The graceful degradation benefit: An unobtrusive DOM script does not draw the attention of its users when it fails. It never generates error messages, not even in old browsers. An unobtrusive script first asks, Does the browser support the objects I want to use? If the answer is No, the script silently quits.

- The accessibility benefit: The basic functionality of the page does not depend on the unobtrusive DOM script. If the script doesn't work, the page still delivers its core functionality and information via markup, style sheets, and/or server-side scripting. The user never notices that something is not there.

- The separation benefit: An unobtrusive DOM script does not draw the attention of web developers working on other aspects of the site. All JavaScript code is maintained separately, without littering files dedicated to XHTML, PHP, JSP, or other languages.

For more on the subject, see "Ten Good Practices for Writing JavaScript in 2005" by Bobby van der Sluis (www.bobbyvandersluis.com/articles/goodpractices.php).

What's a DOM?

Just what is the DOM? According to the W3C (www.w3.org/DOM), the DOM is a browser-independent, platform-neutral, language-neutral interface that allows "programs and scripts to dynamically access and update the content, structure, and style of documents. The document can be further processed, and the results of that processing can be incorporated back into the presented page."

In English, the DOM makes other standard components of your page (style sheets, (X)HTML elements, and scripts) accessible to manipulation. If your site were a movie, (X)HTML would be the screenwriter, CSS would be the art director, scripting languages would be the special effects, and the DOM would be the director who oversees the entire production.

A Standard Way to Make Web Pages Behave Like Applications

Although programming such usage exceeds the scope of this book, the most exciting aspect of DOM-driven interactivity is that it can mimic the behavior of conventional software. For instance, a user can change the sort order of tabular data by clicking on the header, just as she might do in an Excel spreadsheet or in the Macintosh Finder (the application that lets Macintosh users sort, copy, move, rename, delete, or in other ways process various files and folders on their desktops).

In recent years, this DOM-powered ability to mimic traditional software has facilitated a burst of standards-based web application development, creating new products and breathless excitement—not to mention a few buzzwords. But it didn't happen overnight.

Developers initially used DOM-driven interactivity to emulate software exclusively on the client side—that is, on the visitor's hard drive [15.1, 15.2, 15.3]. Manipulating data on the client side meant that the action would work even if the internet connection were terminated—an advantage at a time when less than half of U.S. web users enjoyed fast, always-on connections. Doing all the work on the user's hard drive instead of over the network also reduced strain on the server. More interestingly, these initial DOM demos introduced something new to the realm of HTML: the ability to respond to a user's action without forcing a page refresh. The stage was set for Ajax.

15.1
The DOM enables web pages to behave like desktop applications. In this early (2002) demo by Porter Glendinning, data is sorted by album title when the user clicks the Album header (**www. glendinning.org/ webbuilder/ sortTable**).

15.2
Clicking the header again reverses the sort order. The changed order is immediately visible on the original page. A separate "results" page is not needed.

15.3
Clicking the Rank header re-sorts the list in numerical order, still without loading a new page and without requiring server/ client processing or contact.

Although demos like the one shown in figures 15.1–15.3 were modest, their implications were bold, as they proved you didn't need Flash to create seamless interactivity on the web. In the first edition of this book, I predicted that, with browsers finally supporting the W3C DOM, web standards would soon introduce a new era of rich applications and user experiences. A couple of years passed without proving me right. My prediction was starting to look like last week's sushi.

Then Google introduced Gmail (`mail.google.com`), an online mail application built with CSS, XHTML, JavaScript, and the DOM, with a little Microsoft stuff thrown in.

Next thing you know, 37signals's Basecamp (`www.basecamphq.com`) had replaced Microsoft Project as the web professional's project management tool of choice. Then Mr. Garret published his essay on Ajax (Chapter 4). And just like that, DOM-powered interactivity was the hottest thing going since—well, since Gmail.

So Where Does It Work?

Albeit with some differences, the W3C DOM is supported by all of the following browsers:

- Mozilla 0.9 and higher (including Firefox and Camino)
- IE5/Windows and higher
- Safari
- Opera (since version 7)

This list is not exhaustive, as DOM support has only grown in recent years. Modern browsers also support `XMLHttpRequest` (`en.wikipedia.org/wiki/XMLHttpRequest`), a DOM technology enabling servers to respond to users' requests without a page refresh. While `XMLHttpRequest` began as a Microsoft invention, the W3C is in the process of turning it into an honest web standard (`www.w3.org/TR/XMLHttpRequest`).

Other than a few obsolete browsers, what is missing from the list? Many handheld devices and web phones do not yet fully support the DOM, and text browsers like Lynx never will. In many cases, you can compensate for those user agents' lack of DOM support the same way you've always compensated for non-JavaScript environments. (You *have* always compensated for non-JavaScript environments, haven't you?)

To support non-DOM-capable devices, do the following:

- Use `noscript` elements that provide alternative access (a hypertext link instead of a fancy button, for instance).

- Test in Lynx, as described in the discussion of accessibility and JavaScript in Chapter 14, "Accessibility: The Soul of Web Standards"

- Never, ever use bogus `javascript:` "links" that lead nowhere, such as `<a href="javascript:" ...>`. Instead, use the DOM to attach rich behaviors to your links or, if you must have those nasty `javascript:` links in your markup, use the DOM to insert them. This ensures that only JavaScript-aware devices will see them, so non-JavaScript-capable users aren't left out in the cold.

Please DOM, Don't Hurt 'Em

Supporting non-DOM-capable devices and users via unobtrusive scripting is not only a best practice, it's also the right thing to do in nearly all cases. It's particularly the right thing to do on content sites, traditional interactive sites, and sites that combine interactive and informational features. That covers most sites, probably including yours.

How It Works

Here's the situation: you're a web designer for a fairly large website, with content produced by a separate editorial department, a team removed from your own. One day, as you're catching up on RSS feeds, a member of the marketing department sidles up to your desk. Seems that the folks upstairs have been talking, and they'd like you to make a small change (their words) on the website: namely, all links that point to external websites should have a little icon appended to them [15.4]. They'd like this pushed out to every page on the site, including the hundreds and hundreds of previously published articles. And with that, the marketing person leaves you to think, thanking you for your help. (As she left, she might have said something about how the icons will heighten some combination of "synergy," "bricks-to-clicks," and/or "24/7/365 marketecture," but you might've misheard her.)

15.4

Our simple little
external.gif, which
we'll be inserting into
each external link. Hence
the name.

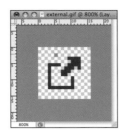

Given that the content team's unavailable to help with this—they're not half as tech-savvy as you are, and they're under a deadline crunch—it looks like it's up to you. How do we insert that little GIF into every external link on over a hundred pages?

Enter the DOM. Let's assume you've whipped up a quick HTML page, which has some test markup in the body:

```
<p>Here we have a selection of links: <a href="/about/">an
internal page</a>, <a href="http://yahoo.com/">an external
site worth visiting</a>, <a href="http://google.com/">another
external site</a>, and <a href="/contact/">one final internal
page</a>.</p>
```

Nothing fancy: it's a paragraph with four links inside it, two of which point to external sites. We can tell they're external because those anchor elements have `href` attributes that begin with `http` (this'll be important later). And what the heck: let's add a lick of style to it:

```
body {
  color: #303030;
  font: normal 100%/1.3 Helvetica, Arial, sans-serif;
  }

a {
  color: #36C;
  }

a img {
  border: none;
  margin-left: 0.1em;
  vertical-align: baseline;
  }
```

Nothing fancy, but this is just a simple test page, with some basic CSS applied [15.5].

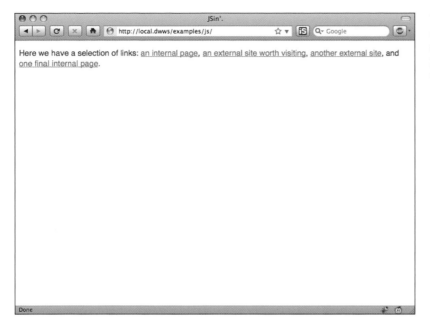

15.5
Our markup and
CSS awaits a layer of
JavaScript. The air is thick
with excitement.

Now, to the matter at hand: getting our hands dirty with a little JavaScript.
After consulting with some of the fine books listed above, we've put a bit of
JavaScript in the head of our document.

```
<script type="text/javascript">
function externalLinks() {
  var allLinks = document.getElementsByTagName("a");

  var icon = document.createElement("img");
  icon.setAttribute("src", "external.gif");
  icon.setAttribute("alt", "[external link]");

  for (var i = 0; i < allLinks.length; i++) {
    var oneHref = allLinks[i].getAttribute("href");
    if (oneHref && oneHref.indexOf("http") == 0) {
      var newImg = icon.cloneNode(true);
      allLinks[i].appendChild(newImg);
    }
  }
}

window.onload = externalLinks;
</script>
```

If you've never written a line of JavaScript, the above might feel a little over-whelming. Let's briefly walk through the important bits.

```
function externalLinks() { ... }
```

This first line inside our script element defines a JavaScript *function*, which we've named externalLinks. A function is a discrete chunk of JavaScript code, which only runs once another piece of JavaScript explicitly calls its name. (Think Pokémon, but geekier. OK, maybe just *as* geeky.) And in fact, that's what the final line of our JavaScript does:

```
window.onload = externalLinks;
```

This line simply invokes our externalLinks function as soon as our HTML's finished loading. No muss, no fuss.

```
var allLinks = document.getElementsByTagName("a");
```

Now that we've declared our function, we move to a slightly hairy-looking piece of JS. Let's look at the right-hand side of the equals sign (=) first, where we've employed our very first DOM method, document.getElementsByTagName(). And it's very descriptively named: if we insert the name of an HTML element between the parentheses, getElementsByTagName() will scour our document for each of those elements, and store it in a list (also known as a *collection*). So our document.getElementsByTagName("a") tells our JavaScript to take note of every anchor in our HTML, so that we can do something with it later.

The left side of our equals sign (var allLinks), while much shorter, is no less important. We've declared a *variable* called allLinks. Just like in mathematics (a field I won't pretend to know much about), variables are stand-ins for an actual value; with our allLinks variable declared, we've stored the results of our document.getElementsByTagName("a") query in memory. From that point on, we can refer to allLinks throughout the remainder of our function, without having to invoke document.getElementsByTagName("a") over and over again.

```
var icon = document.createElement("img");
icon.setAttribute("src", "external.gif");
icon.setAttribute("alt", "[external link]");
```

Next, we've created another variable called `icon`. This time, we're using `document.createElement()` to, well, create an HTML element—specifically, an `img` element, as per the `"img"` we wrote in the parentheses. The next two lines assign attributes to the element—a `src` attribute that points to our `external.gif` file, and an `alt` attribute that reads "[external link]"—but this element exists in the browser's memory (not the page... yet) and is referenced by our `icon` variable.

```
for (var i = 0; i < allLinks.length; i++) { ... }
```

This is a `for` loop, a fairly common JavaScript tool. Inside its parentheses, we've declared another variable (generically named `i`), which starts with an initial value of zero (`var i = 0`). Then, we're going to keep repeating the code inside its curly braces as long as the value of `i` is less than the number of anchors stored inside of `allLinks`. And on each loop, we're going to add one to the value of `i`. If `i` is ever equal to or greater than the length of `allLinks`, we'll stop looping and carry on.

If your head's reeling from the above paragraph, don't worry—I'm feeling a bit woozy, and I only typed the thing. Let's step through that in pieces, applying liberal amounts of plain English:

1. Working off our sample HTML document from above, our `allLinks` list, or array, has four items in it, one for each anchor in our page. Therefore, `allLinks.length` has a value of four.

2. When our JavaScript function begins to run, it encounters the `for` loop, assigning `i` a value of zero.

3. Then it asks itself if `i` (with its value of `zero`) is less than the length of `allLinks.length` (4).

4. Since zero is less than four, it proceeds on to execute the code inside the loop's curly braces.

5. When the code in the curly braces is done executing, the final bit of the loop increases the value of `i` by one (`i++`), setting it to a new value of `one` (0+1).

6. This will continue until the loop's run four times, once for each link in our document. At the start of the fifth run-through, `i` will have a value of `four`. When the JavaScript checks to see if the value of `i` (with its value

of `four`) is less than the length of `allLinks.length` (4), it'll slam down on the brakes: since four is not less than four (they're equal), it'll exit the loop, and stop executing the code inside it.

To sum up: our loop will run once for each anchor in our HTML, adding one to the value of `i` each time. Once the loop's run out of anchors, it'll simply stop running.

```
var oneHref = allLinks[i].getAttribute("href");
```

Inside the loop, we've declared a new variable called `oneHref`. As we step through each iteration of our loop, `allLinks[i]` will refer to a different a element in our list—`allLinks[0]` is the first link, `allLinks[1]` is the second link, and so on. So all we're doing here is getting the `href` attribute of the anchor we're currently looking at, and saving it for the next line:

```
if (oneHref && oneHref.indexOf("http") == 0) { ... }
```

Here we have a conditional statement, denoted by the appropriately inquisitive-sounding `if` at the beginning of the line. Inside the parentheses, the JavaScript is asking if there's a `oneHref` variable—which is true, if the anchor we're inspecting has an `href` attribute—*and* if that `href` attribute begins with `http` (`oneHref.indexOf("http") == 0`). In other words, is this an external link? If so, then the code inside the parentheses gets executed.

And finally, here's where the magic happens:

```
var newImg = icon.cloneNode(true);
allLinks[i].appendChild(newImg);
```

Inside our conditional `if` statement, we're doing two things: first, we're creating a variable called `newImg`, and using the `cloneNode()` method to duplicate our new image element (stored in the `icon` variable from before). Then, we're using `appendChild()` to take that new image, and, well, append it as a child of the current link. And remember: because this is contained within the conditional code that asks if the current link is external, then only external links will get our sexy little icons. And as we can see from our test HTML page, our JavaScript is working admirably [15.6]. Easy peasy.

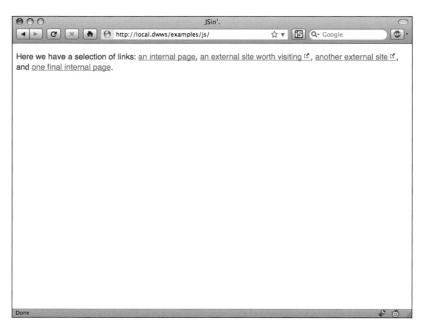

15.6
Our JavaScript function's finished, with our DOM-inserted images in place on external links only. Huzzah!

Checking for Support

However, there's one problem with our function. If our page is viewed in a browser that supports JavaScript but *not* the DOM, it'll produce an error. Asking an antiquated, non-DOM-aware browser to execute `document.getElementsByTagName()` or `document.createElement()` would be like walking up to some longtime friends and asking them the time of day in Esperanto: you'll get a couple of blank stares, and possibly a few inquiries about your mental health. Unless your friends speak Esperanto.

OK, so that's not the best analogy. Still, we need to safeguard our JavaScript against browsers that don't understand the DOM methods it uses. But rather than sniffing the User Agent string (a broken practice discussed way, way back in Chapter 1), we should simply ask the browser if it supports the DOM methods we rely upon—in this case, that's `document.getElementsByTagName` and `document.createElement`. And we can ask that question with minimal fuss, requiring only two extra lines of code:

```
<script type="text/javascript">
function externalLinks() {
  if (document.getElementsByTagName && document.createElement) {
    var allLinks = document.getElementsByTagName("a");
    var icon = document.createElement("img");
    icon.setAttribute("src", "external.gif");
    icon.setAttribute("alt", "(This is an external link)");

    for (var i = 0; i < allLinks.length; i++) {
      var oneHref = allLinks[i].getAttribute("href");
      if (oneHref && oneHref.indexOf("http") == 0) {
        var newImg = icon.cloneNode(true);
        allLinks[i].appendChild(newImg);
      }
    }
  }
}

window.onload = externalLinks;
</script>
```

The only change we've made is to wrap the contents of our function within a conditional statement. With that edit, our function will *only* run if the browser understands document.getElementsByTagName and document.create Element; if it doesn't, then the function will quit silently, and the links in our HTML will still function. *Voilà!* That's progressive enhancement at work.

Code Variants

In a global .js file, the code would look as it does previously. Using a global .js file is preferred as it reduces our workload, saves bandwidth by employing caching, and helps separate behavior from structure by letting markup be markup and a script be a script. To use a global .js file, we'll simply paste the script into an empty file (let's call it scripts.js), and add the following to the head of the document:

```
<script type="text/javascript" src="scripts.js"></script>
```

This effectively links scripts.js to our markup, much as link can be used to apply a style sheet to our (X)HTML. Once we've moved the JS to an external file, the functionality therein can be applied to ten or ten thousand pages, as long as they include the script above.

If we're just applying the JavaScript to an individual page, we would type it between <head> and </head>. In HTML 4.01 documents or XHTML 1.0 Transitional documents (or in XHTML 1.0 Strict documents served as text/html, if we're feeling saucy), the script would read as follows:

```
<script type="text/javascript">
<!--  //
function externalLinks() {
  ...
}

window.onload = externalLinks;
// -->
</script>
```

In XHTML Strict documents served as application/xhtml+xml, we would either use a global .js file or insert this:

```
<script type="text/javascript ">
// <![CDATA[
function externalLinks() {
  ...
}

window.onload = externalLinks;
// ]]>
</script>
```

A real discussion of what we can do with JavaScript is beyond the scope of this book. But I can't close this chapter without sharing at least one really nifty (and helpful) use of DOM-based interactivity.

Style Switchers: Aiding Access, Offering Choice

In Chapter 13, we discussed the impossibility of delivering web type without alienating at least some of your potential visitors, and lamented that sixteen years into the web's evolution as a medium, pixels were still the most reliable method of sizing type—yet also the most troublesome for IE users pre-version 7.0. What if you could offer your visitors a choice of user-selectable type approaches? What if you could even change your layout while you were at it?

According to CSS, you can. CSS allows you to associate any web page not only with a default (persistent) style sheet, but also with alternate CSS files. In the interest of enhancing accessibility, these alternate style sheets might offer larger type [15.7, 15.8] or a higher-contrast color scheme. Or they could completely change the site's appearance for purposes of what was once called "user customization."

The W3C recommends that browsers provide a means of allowing users to choose any of these alternate styles, and Gecko-based browsers like Mozilla Firefox do just that. But most browsers don't. The creative and accessibility benefits of alternate style sheets might have remained beyond reach forever. But in 2001, then-teenage web developer Paul Sowden solved the problem by taking advantage of the fact that alternate style sheets, like any other page component, are accessible to the DOM.

In a groundbreaking *A List Apart* article (www.alistapart.com/articles/alternate) Sowden wrote a JavaScript file (www.alistapart.com/d/alternate/styleswitcher.js) that enabled site visitors to load alternate styles at the click of a link, a form element, or any other interactive widget. After explaining how to use his script, Sowden released it as open source.

Tens of thousands of designers have since used the code to solve accessibility problems, explore creative effects, or both. Among other things, Paul Sowden's *ALA* style switcher helped inspire Dave Shea's beloved CSS Zen Garden. Besides finessing font sizes and swapping skins, style switchers can also drive *zoom layouts* (www.alistapart.com/articles/lowvision) intended to help users with low vision.

15.7
New York magazine
(**www.nymag.com**),
which will be discussed
in greater detail in
Chapter 17, uses a DOM-
based style switcher
on certain pages to let
users change font sizes.
See it in action at **www.
nymag.com/guides/
fallpreview/2009/
politics/58456**.

15.8
The same page with big-
ger text, applied through
a careful mixture of
JavaScript and CSS.

Learn to Love Your (JavaScript) Library

As we noted earlier, the past few years have really seen a marked rise in JavaScript's popularity. Not long ago, JavaScript was the ugly stepsister, relegated to the realm of form validation and obnoxious popup window scripts. But today, clients and companies are asking for rich, JavaScript-driven interfaces to be built online. As a result, design teams have demanded ways to cut down on some of the rote tedium associated with DOM scripting, so that they might build those robust interfaces more quickly and easily.

Enter JavaScript libraries, stage left. A library provides a framework that abstracts out some of the more tedious bits of DOM scripting, while simultaneously addressing some of the few remaining cross-browser disagreements that still exist between different browsers' DOM implementations. And the options for good JavaScript libraries are legion, including such names as Prototype (www.prototypejs.org), Dojo (www.dojotoolkit.org), MooTools (www.mootools.net), and Scriptaculous (script.aculo.us).

But for now, let's take a look at jQuery [**15.9**], a popular JavaScript library that we'll be using in Chapter 17. Because it uses CSS-like selectors for its interface, I find it's incredibly easy for more design-savvy people to tinker with. For example, if I wanted to select all the anchors in my document, I'd simply write:

```
$("a");
```

To select all the anchor elements with a class of "alert", I can write:

```
$("a.alert");
```

Or, if we wanted to revisit our earlier function, we could bust out:

```
$("a[href]^='http'");
```

Looks a little more complex, but jQuery's documentation (docs.jquery.com) can be an incredible boon in cases like this (docs.jquery.com/Selectors/attributeStartsWith#attributevalue). Here, we've simply selected all the anchors whose href attributes begin with http.

And once you've gotten that collection of elements, you can then alter them with additional jQuery methods. I can add a new class to those external links:

```
$("a[href]^='http'").addClass("external");
```

15.9
The jQuery homepage.
(**www.jquery.com**).

Or insert an image in each one:

```
$("a[href]^='http'").append('<img src="external.gif" src="(This
is an external link)" />');
```

Or (and this is where you can tell I've gone mad with power) I can do both, simply by "chaining" the two methods together:

```
$("a[href]^='http'").addClass("external").append('<img
src="external.gif" src="(This is an external link)" />');
```

In fact, we can rewrite our previous function with only a few lines of jQuery, using its terse, CSS-like syntax.

```
<script type="text/javascript>
$(document).ready(function() {
  $("a[href^='http']").append('<img src="external.gif"
src="(This is an external link)" />');
});
</script>
```

That's it. Our JavaScript has been reduced to just three lines, whereas before we wrote well over a dozen. And the functionality is exactly the same: as soon as the page has finished rendering, we've selected all the external links and appended an img element to the contents of each one.

However, there is a slight trade-off to consider: in order to avail ourselves of a JavaScript library's interface, we need to include the library itself:

```
<script type="text/javascript" src="jquery.js"></script>
<script type="text/javascript>
$(document).ready(function() {
  $("a[href^='http']").append("<img src=\"external.gif\"
src=\"(This is an external link)\" />");
});
</script>
```

This will add some weight to our page. jQuery's codebase, for example, is 20 kilobytes. This is far from a prohibitive amount—it's lighter than most image files—but you should take this additional bulk into consideration when planning your JavaScript strategy. If all you need is a simple function or two, some hand-spun DOM scripting might make more sense; if it's a rich, highly interactive interface you're building, then pick your favorite JavaScript library and start coding away.

How Will You Use the DOM?

This chapter has offered merely a teasing taste of what the DOM can do and how it is being used in sometimes simple, sometimes sophisticated ways on commercial, personal, and public sector sites. You can use the DOM to create rich internet applications, deliver creative effects, enhance accessibility, and more. In the hands of an experienced programmer, the DOM offers the power to create standards-based software that works for anyone who has access to a modern browser. But even if you're a capital-*D* Designer who hates to code, you can use it to add accessibility options to your site. So ask not what the DOM can do for you—ask what you can do with your DOM.

chapter sixteen

A Site Redesign

Let's put our knowledge of standards-based design to the test by redesigning a website. The site in question is zeldman.com, online since May 1995. Essential to the site is "The Daily Report," one of the oldest continuously published blogs.

Before redesigning, it's wise to see what your colleagues are up to. We call this a competitive audit when we conduct it on behalf of a client or an in-house employer; when we do it for ourselves, we call it "seeking inspiration." My audit revealed what I already knew: for over a year, my blogging colleagues had been busting out of the shackles of the 800 x 600 blog layout, creating wide, multi-column layouts [16.1–16.4] inspired by Josef Müller-Brockmann, author of *Grid Systems in Graphic Design* and father of the modern layout.

Designed for a world of 1024-pixel (and wider) monitors, this popular approach to web layouts typically contains eight or more equal grid columns [16.1] that combine to form master columns of various widths, bringing consistency and variety to the reading experience. To allow for margins and browser chrome, a 1024px grid layout is

960px to 970px wide. Khoi Vinh, design director of nytimes.com, promoted the wide grid on his personal site, subtraction.com. *A List Apart* made it safe for webzines. Cameron Moll created a background image to help designers create modular grids that fit neatly into 960px of horizontal screen space (`www.cameronmoll.com/archives/2006/12/gridding_the_960`). The world of web designers was (and is) cuckoo for wide screens and whitespace.

16.1
Khoi Vinh explains how to use a background image to help verify the alignment of a grid-based 1024 layout (**www.subtraction.com/2004/12/31/grid-computi**).

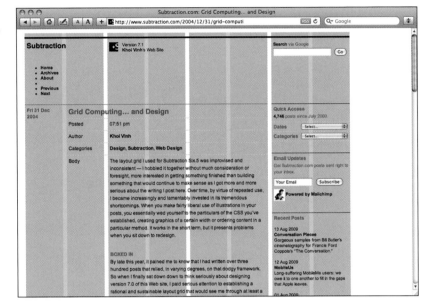

16.2
Grid-based 1024 layout at Naz Hamid's Weightshift (**www.weightshift.com/about**).

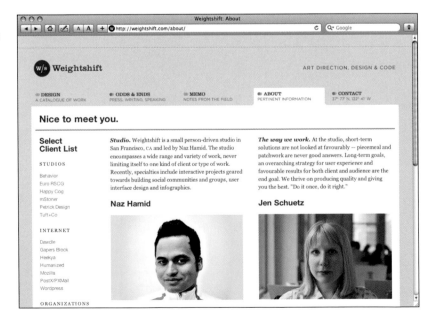

16.3
Grid-based 1024 layout by Jason Santa Maria (**www. jasonsantamaria.com/ articles/ whats-golden**).

16.4
Grid-based 1024 layout on Veerle Pieters' personal site (**veerle. duoh.com**).

16.5
2004, a drop-shadow Odyssey (AKA the previous look and feel at zeldman.com).

Was a grid-based 1024 layout in my site's future? The blog's previous redesign [**16.5**], created for the second edition of this book, had all the hallmarks of the year in which it was made: subtle drop-shadows inspired by then-new Mac OS X; soft pastel colors signifying the maturation of the no-longer-wild web; and a narrow measure that fit into an 800 x 600 viewport yet looked natural at 1024 x 768 and higher. If I wanted to bring zeldman.com up to 2009 spec, surely all I needed to do was remove the background color, add Twitter, Flickr, and other social networking site feeds, and plunk all that social networking goodness into a widescreen, modular grid layout.

Out of the Past

It was a good plan and would be an appropriate strategy for many sites. For instance, it would be perfect for a portfolio site, for a site by an expert designer who only dabbles in writing, or for the site of a writer-designer who creates web applications and wants to show them off on his front page. But people don't come to my site to check out my portfolio or Flickr feed. They come to read. And that single fact guided me toward a design solution.

Given my site's purpose, the right layout would be one that encouraged reading and removed anything that distracted from reading. In a perfect world, there would just be text, as in a book. No navigation, no sidebar, no links, no buttons. That, of course, was not possible. But the new design should focus the visitor's attention clearly and unmistakably on the writing. There might well be an underlying grid, but it would probably not be 1024 x 768, as more than two columns (one content column, one sidebar) would not be necessary for the reading portion of the page, and a readable measure required a narrower page. As a bonus, my redesign would look good on an iPhone—the device that was bringing beauty and usability to the mobile experience and driving a new generation of smart phones.

Furthermore, if reading and an old-fashioned 800-pixel-wide layout were essential, then perhaps instead of modernizing the site, I should seek inspiration from its past. The site had gone through many design permutations in its fourteen-year history [**16.6, 16.7**], but its most characteristic look and feel—the "famous" one, the one most people thought of when they thought of my site— was a stripped down, high-contrast look from the end of the 20th century: white foreground, black text, reddish-orange background and accessories [**16.8, 16.9**]. This old look was synonymous with zeldman.com for many people, and helped define "what a blog looks like" for many more. What if I were to resurrect that cheesy old design, but add typographic niceties made possible by improved CSS support in browsers? Other parts of the page might end up doing the modular grid mambo, but the core of the page would look like a better-dressed version of 1999.

It sounded like a plan.

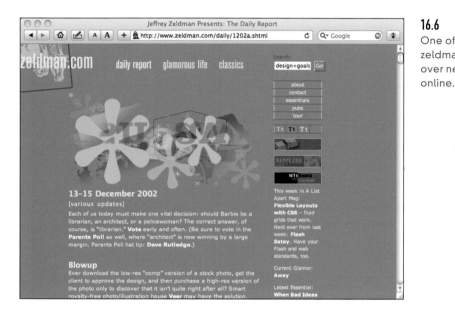

16.6
One of dozens of looks zeldman.com sported over nearly fifteen years online.

16.7
And another.

16.8

The look …

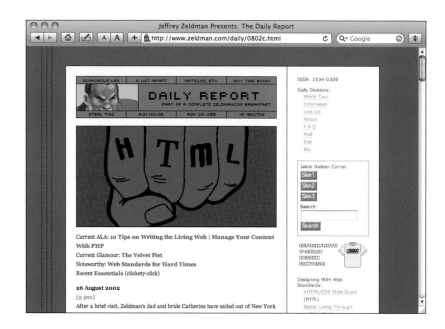

16.9

… for which zeldman.com was best known would become the inspiration for a retro-themed, yet modern and readable, redesign.

Designing from the Content Out

Instead of sketching the entire page in successive iterations to define its over-all look and feel, I decided to design the core of the page first.

If the site's content was going to drive its design—which is always a good idea—I was determined to design with real content, just as we do on Happy Cog client projects. Nothing is better than a site that's designed to serve specific words, themes, and messages; nothing's worse than a beautiful template that, when you dump words into it, turns out to hinder the site's communication. OK, some things are worse. Stepping on a jellyfish, for instance. But in our field, few things are sadder than a beautiful yet inappropriate design. Working with real content helps prevent that.

Since I was working with real content, I decided to design in code instead of with paper, pencil, and Photoshop. I concerned myself only with the middle of the page, where the content would live. I didn't worry about what the masthead would look like, or how the footer should function. I simply copied real content from my existing site with real markup that I knew was structurally and semantically sound, pasted it into a text editor, and saved it as a new HTML file.

Without opening Photoshop, I designed a 770px grid in my head—550px for the site's main content, 220px for sidebar stuff—and did a quick sketch to check my arithmetic [**16.10**]. In my new HTML file, I wrote CSS to lay out the two

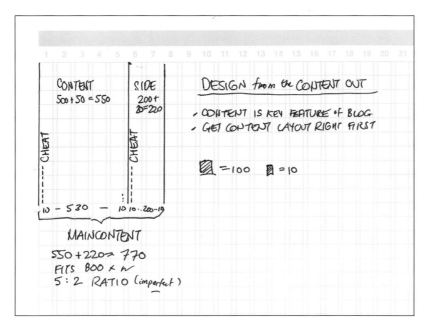

16.10
A quick sketch verifies the arithmetic behind our layout grid. We'll need these numbers to write our CSS.

sections, "maincontent" and "sidebar". The code for the initial layout of the site's middle section looks like this:

```
html {
  min-width: 770px;
   }

div#wrapper{
  width: 770px;
  margin: 0 auto;
  padding: 0;
  text-align: left;
  }

div#maincontent {
  float: left;
  margin: 0;
  padding: 0;
  width: 550px;
  }

div#sidebar{
  float: left;
  margin: 0;
  padding: 0;
  width: 220px;
  }
```

The html declaration establishes that the page will be 770px wide and provides a hook for backgrounds and styles if needed. The "wrapper" inside html encloses the two floated columns ("maincontent" and "sidebar"), centers the layout, and establishes that the text is aligned left. As you can clearly see, the main content area is 550px wide, and the sidebar is 220px—just like we planned.

A Little Air

Columns need gutters between them or the text they contain won't breathe. With padding added to create breathing room, the code for the layout of the middle section reads like this:

```
html {
   min-width: 770px;
     }

div#wrapper{
   width: 770px;
   margin: 0 auto;
   padding: 0;
   text-align: left;
   overflow: visible;
   min-height: 1000px;
   }

div#maincontent {
   float: left;
   margin: 0;
   padding: 0 30px;
   width: 490px;
   }

div#sidebar{
   float: left;
   margin: 0;
   width: 180px;
   padding: 0 20px 36px;
   }
```

The result [16.11] is nothing to sing about, but we can verify that our layout is centered and that there are two columns whose widths form an approximate 5:2 relationship—just as we desired—with nice gutters between.

To help the layout look great on an iPhone, we add this viewport-controlling meta element to the head:

```
<meta name="viewport" content="width=770" />
```

16.11
The basic layout with real content (www.zeldman.com/dwws/1.html).

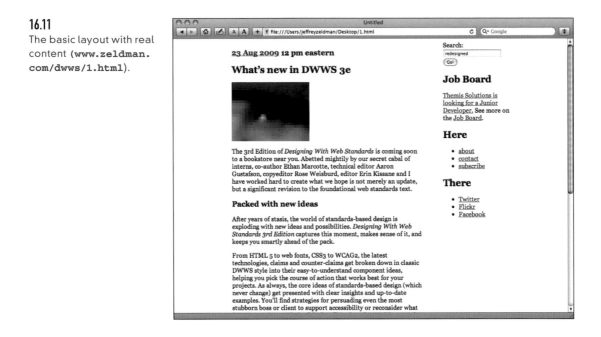

Setting the viewport to 770px ensures that the iPhone will zoom in on the site as we wish. For more iPhone tips, see Craig Hockenberry's "Put Your Content in My Pocket" (www.alistapart.com/articles/putyourcontentinmypocket).

Fonts, Intros, and Drop Caps

Next, we try the layout with different (but still real) content, and begin adding color and typographic details [**16.12**, **16.13**] to our CSS:

```css
/* Set out the main layout divisions */

html {
  min-width: 770px;
  background: #f9f8f3;
  }

div#wrapper {
  color: #222;
  background: #f9f8f3 url(/i/z3bg.gif) top left repeat-y;
  width: 770px;
  margin: 0 auto;
  padding: 0;
```

```
    text-align: left;
    overflow: visible;
    min-height: 1000px;
    }

div#maincontent {
    float: left;
    margin: 0;
    padding: 0 30px;
    width: 490px;
    }

div#sidebar{
    float: left;
    margin: 0;
    width: 180px;
    padding: 0 20px 36px;
    font-family: "Helvetica Neue", Arial, Helvetica, sans-serif;
    }
```

We have given our site a reddish-orange background and established that all sidebar content will be set in Helvetica Neue unless we say otherwise. There's not much code here, but every line works hard.

16.12
Real content gets dumped into the layout. Before styling type, we futz with margins and gutters.

16.13
Color has been added, gutters are in place, text is styled (and a hierarchy established), and a simple graphic element adds brand character.

Speaking of Helvetica Neue, let's make sure that the entire site is set in that face unless specific elements are styled otherwise. While we're at it, we'll use a faux background image [**16.14**] to prevent the site's reddish orange background color from "flashing" on long pages viewed over slow connections:

```css
body {
    text-align: center;
    margin: 0;
    padding: 0;
    border: 0;
    background: #c30 url(/i/ff-flash-fix.gif) top center
repeat-y; /* this will fix the flashing */
    color: #333;
    font: 11px/18px "Helvetica Neue", Arial, Helvetica,
sans-serif;
    }
```

Helvetica's great for headlines, subheads, and small sidebar text, but we'll want something more book-like for longer copy passages. Georgia is a fine choice:

```css
p {
    margin: 0 0 9px 0;
    line-height: 1.4;
    font-family: Georgia, "Times New Roman", Times, serif;
    }
```

16.14
A faux background
image adds background
color and thin vertical
rules to the background
of the wrapper.

Merrily we go through our markup, identifying elements and assigning
Georgia to them when we desire. The pattern we're using is simple: identify,
then style. When absolutely necessary, use specific selectors to target particular bits. If some list items, for example, will require Georgia while others need
Helvetica, we use descendant selectors to make sure the right element gets the
right style.

```css
div#maincontent div.endpost ul li {
   font-family: Georgia, serif;
   list-style: square outside;
   line-height: 18px;
   padding: 0 0 0 6px;
   margin: 0 6px 6px 15px;
   }

div#maincontent div.endpost ol li {
   font-family: Georgia, serif;
   font-size: 14px;
   line-height: 1.4;
   }

div#sidebar ul li {
   font: 13px/21px "Helvetica Neue", Arial, Helvetica,
sans-serif;
   letter-spacing: 2px;
   }
```

We won't look at every rule in the CSS (you can check it for yourself at www.
zeldman.com/wp-content/themes/zeldman-v2/style.css) but you get the
idea. Using real content and real markup gives us paragraphs, ordered and
unordered lists, definition lists, and other bits of structured content that need
to be styled, and may also need to have their size, line-height, margins, and
other details adjusted. Futzing with these details in CSS is no different than
doing so in InDesign or Photoshop—except that in CSS, unlike in Photoshop,
styles persist and cascade.

Drop That Cap!

In books and magazines, art directors often set a chapter or article's introductory paragraph larger than the paragraphs that follow; the big type catches the eye and leads into the story. A drop cap adds to the eye-catching effect that helps capture the reader's attention and lure her into engaging with the writer's words. Let's create an "intro" paragraph style, and a drop cap style as well:

```
body div#maincontent p.intro {
   font-size: 18px;
   line-height: 1.4;
   font-style: normal;
   font-weight: normal;
   }


/* IE7 and IE6 false value hacks on span.drop courtesy Paul of
hell.com */


span.drop {
   display: inline;
   float: left;
   margin: 0;
   padding: .25em .08em 0 0;
   #padding: 0.25em 0.08em 0.2em 0.00em; /* override for
Microsoft Internet Explorer browsers*/
   _padding: 0.25em 0.08em 0.4em 0.00em; /* override for IE
browsers 6.0 and older */
   font-size: 3.2em;
   line-height: .4;
   text-transform: capitalize;
   color: #c30;
   }
```

And here's the markup that makes it go:

```
<p class="intro"><span class="drop">T</span>his paragraph will
be bigger than the others, and the letter "T" will be styled as
a drop cap.</p>
```

Do we need a paragraph class of "intro"? For that matter, do we need a span of class "drop"? Firefox, Safari, and Opera support the first-child and first-letter pseudo-classes of CSS2.1, and thus let us style these elements without resorting to additional classes. Alas, Internet Explorer prior to version 8.0 does not. Whether to let IE users do without stylistic flourishes or not is a choice each designer must make for each design. (On some projects, of course, the client has a say as well.) Although most of my readers use Firefox and Safari, I decided to play it safe and use the extra `classes`. Doing so not only let IE 7 users in on my minimal design's minimal "fun," it also gave me control over when and when not to use intro paragraphs and drop caps.

Hackety Hack

Speaking of Internet Explorer, we won't even talk about why it gets the drop caps wrong, and requires hacks to trick it into displaying them as other browsers do. The saddest part of standards-based design is that we still have to account for browser differences—and mostly for IE. We don't do much of this, and we no longer do it in markup or with front- or back-end scripts; standards hacks are thankfully confined to an adjustment or two in your style sheet, or to separate IE style sheets, linked via conditional comments.

Note that hacks should always be annotated, so you or your successors can remember why you put them there, and take them out when bad versions of IE finally die. Annotations also provide credit to those who discovered and solved the problem, and links for other developers who may be scrutinizing your CSS to figure how you licked a problem they're experiencing on their site. Sharing is caring.

The Song Remains the Same

There are plenty of typographic details in the body of this site, but they all follow the same basic design pattern (or, if you prefer, work pattern) that we have established. Let's review:

1. Specify an element and style it.
2. Specify elements as generally as you can (i.e., style `h2` rather than `h2.subhead` or, heaven forbid, `h2.bigredletterz`).
3. If your styles bleed over into unwanted areas—for instance, if your `h2` content styling inadvertently bleeds over into the `h2` subheads in your sidebar—use descendant selectors to target specific elements while avoiding classitis:

   ```
   #maincontent h2 { font-size: 24px; }
   ```

Footer Fetish

Having laid out and styled our site's primary content, it's time to get to the bottom of things. Derek Powazek (www.powazek.com) was probably the first web designer to break the rule that "nothing important goes below the fold" and to use his blog's footer as a bold place filled with rich content. His innovation caught fire. Dan Cederholm [**16.15**], Jason Santa Maria [**16.16**], and Veerle Pieters [**16.17**] are among the modern web designers whose blogs are rich in footer love. Inspired by their originality, I decided to steal the idea for my site. It was kind of an obvious move. Having removed extraneous links and promotions from my redesigned site's sidebar in order to foster a deeper reading experience, I needed to put all those promotional elements *someplace*. The footer is a good someplace, and it allowed me to break up the grid a different way from the blog-like middle section of the page [**16.18**].

Our footer is divided into two components: two rows of promotional banners with descriptions at the top (the fancy footer stuff) followed by copyright information and so on (the standard footer stuff that used to get wrapped in the address element, and may be treated that way again in HTML5).

16.15
The footer at Dan Cederholm's site (**www. simplebits.com**).

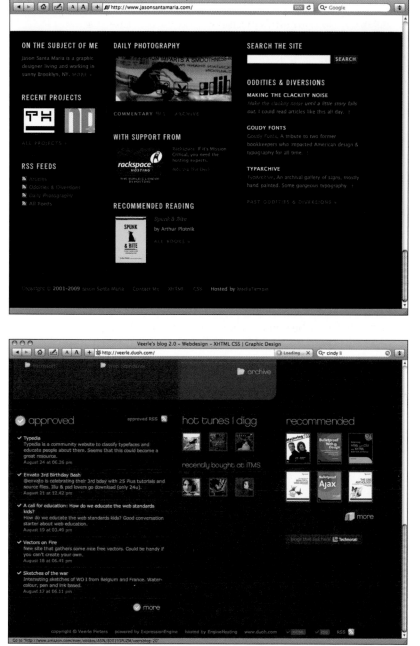

16.16
The footer at Jason
Santa Maria's site (**www.
jasonsantamaria.com**).

16.17
The footer at
Veerle Pieter's site
(**veerle.duoh.com**).

16.18

The footer at zeldman. com.

Let's take a look a what's going on in the footer's markup, starting with the "fancy" stuff. (The examples have been simplified to remove PHP, JavaScript, and numerous other bits that are not germane to the present discussion.)

```
<div id="footer">

<div class="first">
<a href="http://www.aneventapart.com/" title="Daniel Mall makes
Flash and web standards play nice at An Event Apart, for people
who make websites.">
<img src="/secret/danmall.jpg" alt="Daniel Mall makes Flash and
web standards play nice at An Event Apart, for people who make
websites." /></a>
<p>Daniel Mall weds Flash to web standards at
<a href="http://www.aneventapart.com/">An Event Apart</a>,
for people who make websites. (Photo &copy;
<a href="http://www.flickr.com/photos/pete-karl/">Pete Karl
II</a>.)</p>
</div>

<div>
<a href="http://www.alistapart.com/" title="Now in A List
Apart, for people who make websites.">
<img src="http://www.zeldman.com/wp-content/themes/zeldman-
v2/i/ala.jpg" alt="Now in A List Apart, for people who make
```

```
websites." /></a>
<p>In <a href="http://www.alistapart.com/issues/290">ALA No.
290</a>, build respect for content strategy, Motown style;
produce modular, reusable JavaScript the MVC way.</p>
</div>

<div>
<a href="http://www.happycog.com/design/krylon/" title="Happy
Cog redesigns Krylon.">
<img src="/secret/krylon.jpg" alt="Krylon" /></a>
<p><a href="http://www.happycog.com/design/krylon/">
Happy Cog&#8217;s redesign</a> of Krylon, the aerosol paint
leader, puts creative projects and products front and center.</p>
</div>

<hr />

<div>
<a href="http://www.webassist.com/professional/etc/"
title="Improve your web markup with Jeffrey Zeldman's Web
Standards Advisor."><img src="http://www.zeldman.com/i/
webassist.jpg" alt="Jeffrey Zeldman's Web Standards Advisor"
/></a>
<p><a href="http://www.webassist.com/professional/products/
productdetails.asp?PID=255&amp;WAAID=889">Improve your markup</
a>. Validate HTML, CSS,  microformats for single pages or entire
sites. Get advice on page structure, headings, ID, class, and
more. </p>
</div>

<div>
<a href="/talent/" title="Taking Your Talent to the Web - a free
downloadable book."><img src="http://www.zeldman.com/wp-content/
themes/zeldman-v2/i/talent.gif" alt="Taking Your Talent to the
Web" /></a>
<p>Rated Five Stars at Amazon.com since the day it was
published, this classic text on transitioning from print art
direction to web design is now a <a href="http://www.zeldman.
com/talent/">free downloadable book</a>.</p>
</div>

<div>
<a href="/dwws/" title="Designing With Web Standards - 3rd
edition coming soon."><img src="http://www.zeldman.com/
```

(continues on next page)

```
wp-content/themes/zeldman-v2/i/dwws.png" alt="Designing With
Web Standards" /></a><p>Create search-friendly sites that load
faster, reach more users, and cost less to design, update, and
maintain. <a href="/dwws/">Read about the third edition</a>,
coming this year.</p>
</div>

</div>
```

Wow, that's a lot to look at, but all that's happening is that there are six page subdivisions in a container called "footer." A glance at the CSS (below) explains the rest—or will, once you've read the paragraphs that follow.

```
div#footer {
  clear: both;
  border: 0;
  border-top: 1px solid #666;
  border-bottom: 12px solid #09f;
  background: #000;
  color: #dddcd8;
  width: 760px;
  padding: 36px 0 12px 10px;
  margin: 0;
  }

hr {
  clear: both;
  visibility: hidden;
  height: 1px;
  }

div#footer p {
  font: 11px/18px "Helvetica Neue", Arial, Helvetica, sans-
serif;
  margin: 6px 0 21px 0;
  }

div#footer p#credits        {
  clear: both;
  background: transparent url(/i04/author.gif) center left
no-repeat;
  line-height: 18px;
  margin: 0 0 0 20px;
  padding: 0 0 0 48px;
  }
```

```
div#footer div {
  float: left;
  width: 210px;
  padding: 0;
  margin: 0 0 0 30px;
  min-height: 190px;
  }

div#footer div.pleasure {
  width: 100px;
  margin: 0;
  padding: 0;
  }
```

As you can see, the footer clears the floated elements that precede it ("main-content" and "sidebar"), for reasons explained in Chapter 10. Each `div` inside the footer floats; each is 210px wide, with 30px of left margin to create gutters. Let's look at just one `div` from the fancy part of the footer, so we feel less overwhelmed:

```
<div>
<a href="http://www.alistapart.com/" title="Now in A List
Apart, for people who make websites."><img src="http://www.
zeldman.com/wp-content/themes/zeldman-v2/i/ala.jpg" alt="Now
in A List Apart, for people who make websites." /></a><p>In
<a href="http://www.alistapart.com/issues/290">ALA No. 290</
a>, build respect for content strategy, Motown style; produce
modular, reusable JavaScript the MVC way.</p>
</div>
```

When you look at just one, it's obvious that these little units are about as simple as HTML gets. We have a linked image, followed by a paragraph of explanatory text. The paragraph falls below the text because it is constrained by the width of the containing `div`. The `div` floats to the side of the `div` that follows it, which floats to the side of the third. The first three `div`s fill the width of the first line. The `hr` clears the floats, letting the second line begin.

I justify the `hr` semantically on the grounds that it creates a horizontal rule separating two groups of related items—a horizontal rule that will appear in non-graphical environments, conveying the slight separation between the two rows of three items. I think of it as a printer's mark, which conveys a page-structure semantic.

You could certainly argue the point; the alternative would be to wrap each row in an additional enclosing `div`. That is what most standardistas would do, but to me it borders on divitis, and the `hr` is actually cleaner. Of course, an old-school web designer would use table cells to create these effects, but we know why we don't want to do that. Isn't it beautiful that we can easily create CSS as tight as any table layout, and use it to style lean, semantic, search-engine-friendly markup? You bet it is!

The standard footer markup that follows the two promotional rows isn't worth our time to investigate here. It's the usual copyright and author information that used to get wrapped in `address` tags when the web was new (and will return as `address` elements in HTML5). There are links to HTML and CSS validation services, so my readers can annoy me when I forget to close a `li` in a blog post. I started adding HTML and CSS validation links to my footer in the 1990s, and while some consider the practice quaint, I'll likely keep doing it until most site owners recognize the importance of proper markup, and most websites are valid.

Head Out

The chief interest in the masthead [16.19] is what it isn't. The first edition of this book introduced Fahrner Image Replacement, a technique whereby pictures of type appear in visual browsers but remain selectable and accessible as text. Mike Rundle's Phark Image Replacement—the now-famous -9999px hack—succeeded Fahrner Image Replacement and solved its accessibility problems (`phark.typepad.com/phark/2003/08/accessible_imag.html`). Past zeldman.com mastheads used these image replacement techniques to serve the site's name and theme-line as an `h1` headline in markup and as a type logo onscreen, and past editions of this book explained these techniques in detail. Fahrner begat Phark, Phark begat sIFR, sIFR begat Cufón, and we are now entering the time of real fonts on the web. However, for this redesign, I simply used a GIF image for my masthead:

```
<div id="header">
<h1>
<a href="/" title="Jeffrey Zeldman Presents: Web design news
&amp; information since 1995">
<img src="http://www.zeldman.com/wp-content/themes/zeldman-
v2/i/masthead.gif" alt="Jeffrey Zeldman Presents: Web design
news &amp; information since 1995." /></a>
</h1>
</div>
```

6.19
Masthead over blog post in finished zeldman.com design (**www.zeldman. com/x/57**).

Among other things, using image replacement would have given me the ability to serve a smaller masthead image to underpowered, small-screen mobile devices that support handheld CSS. But not-so-smart phones tend not to support handheld CSS; and quite-smart phones at all price levels are now flooding the market. Therefore it seemed sensible to stick with an old-fashioned GIF image, supported by `alt` and `title` text.

Likewise, prior designs used CSS Sprites (www.alistapart.com/articles/ sprites) to create beautifully typeset, dynamic navigation with multiple roll-over states, all with a single image file and a few lines of CSS. But for this reading-focused redesign, I dispensed with fancy navigation, and thus with these techniques. These techniques are an indispensable part of any standards-based designer's tool kit. I just had no cause to use them here.

Details, Details

With a super-simple, neo-retro design, it's all about the details. I set line-heights and margins so as to reinforce a vertical baseline grid, using a technique derived from Wilson Miner's method (www.alistapart.com/articles/

settingtypeontheweb). And I set off "author" comments from reader comments [**16.20**] via simple markup and CSS:

```
<li class="comment zeldman_speaks">

...

div#maincontent ol.commentlist li.zeldman_speaks {
        background-color: #f9eae1;
}
```

There are lots of little details. I finessed several with reader input during a public beta, and continue to fine-tune the design to this day. Rarely has so much effort gone into something so ordinary. Then again, the greatest joy of designing a site that you own or maintain is that you can keep finding and correcting your aesthetic and usability blunders. (If you're like me, the longer you live with a design, the more you recognize its faults.) And this of course is what's so great about CSS. Instead of lamenting that I picked the wrong background color for a given page element, revealing my profound lack of talent and taste to the world, I can change the color in an imported style sheet, and improve the whole site in one go.

At least, until the next time I redesign.

16.20

With one **class** and one rule, "author" comments are set off from reader comments.

chapter seventeen

NYMag.com:
Simple Standards,
Sexy Interfaces

Founded in 1968 by Clay Felker and Milton Glaser, *New York* is one of the country's oldest lifestyle magazines. Its website (www. nymag.com) **[17.1]** is one of my favorite examples of editorial design done so very well: the site's vibrant palette and bold typography perfectly complement the magazine's brassy-but-refined brand, infusing its pages with a personality that makes reading a joy. What's more, the site's interface attains a level of complexity rarely seen on the average editorial site; a few minutes' exploration will reward the curious reader with some interface design thinking that is at once intricate yet intuitive, complex but compelling.

New York's Agenda (www.nymag.com/agenda) exemplifies the magazine's general interface finesse. Produced by design director Ian Adelman and the nymag.com design and user experience team, the Agenda is a rather simple-sounding application: it's a calendar, frequently updated by *New York*'s culture editors with a few choice events highlighted for the week ahead. But as you can see from

17.1
The *New York*
(**www.nymag.com**) home
page: luscious but
legible.

17.2
Meet the Agenda calen-
dar, which we'll be building in this chapter.

clicking around the Agenda [17.2], its designers weren't content with producing a simple, static calendar. Instead, the different columns are collapsed by default, concealing information until the user clicks upon a particular cell; once they've done so, the column expands, revealing the information the user requested. It's a clever spin on a rather straightforward task, and as we'll see throughout this chapter, it's powered solely by web standards.

We'll end this book not by plumbing the depths of another CSS layout, as we did in the previous chapter, but by narrowing our focus a bit: instead of plotting a page's columns or establishing a typographic grid, we'll focusing solely on recreating the calendar itself. But the bar hasn't been lowered just because our canvas has gotten smaller. Instead, this simple-looking calendar belies a complex, standards-rich framework that powers its interface, and we can learn much from reengineering it.

Taking Inventory

Looking at the mockup provided to us by the magazine's design team, we can see that the interface is thoroughly documented in the comp: by default, the page's first column is expanded [17.3], but a column's visual state should change upon being hovered over [17.4]. And finally, when a cell is clicked, all open columns should collapse, and the clicked column should expand in its place [17.5].

Obviously, this is a bit more complex than the other interfaces we've built to date. But thankfully, our usual tactics will see us through: before we start worrying about the finer points of the Agenda's interface, we need to take a content inventory and establish our markup foundation. So let's dive right in: what's the most appropriate HTML to use for building a calendar?

When I was becoming acquainted with the value of semantic markup, my first plan might have been to use a rats' nest of divs, one for each cell, with some fiendishly overwrought CSS simulating the rows and columns of a calendar. Or perhaps I would have thought to use an ol element, as its individual lis feel more meaningful than the semantically worthless div. However, I would have eventually discarded both options, as the HTML specification already has a more robust alternative for us to use: namely, the table element.

17.3
The initial view of the
Agenda, with the first
column expanded by
default.

17.4
Hovering over a column
introduces a subtle shift
in the design.

17.5
"Clicking a column"
brings more information
into view.

I realize that after sixteen chapters decrying the use of tables for modern page layouts, the last sentence might seem to be a kind of heresy. Perhaps you're even readying the torches and pitch, looking to storm my proverbial castle in search of a retraction. But if you can, hold the angry mob for one moment: while the **table** element is an awful tool for page layout, it is far from semantically worthless. In fact, the **table** element was designed was designed for marking up tabular data, such as spreadsheets, a conference schedule, and, yes, calendars.

Maybe you're still feeling a bit skeptical about my sudden bout of table boosting. In that case, let's take a broad look at the content types in our mockup, and see how well a table will work for our purposes. First, we'll start with an empty **table** element, and id it descriptively.

```
<table id="agenda-week">
</table>
```

17.6
The headers of our
calendar will translate
nicely into a series of **th**
elements, wrapped in a
thead.

17.6
The headers of our
calendar will translate
nicely into a series of **th**
elements, wrapped in a
thead.

Right at the top of our mockup, there's a row of headers [**17.6**], each cell displaying, when expanded, the day and date for the column. For that, we can use thead, which is a *row group* element (www.w3.org/TR/html401/struct/tables.html#h-11.2.3) composed of a row (tr) of table header cells (th). Quite a mouthful, but the markup's pretty straightforward:

```
<table id="agenda-week">
  <thead>
    <tr>
      <th scope="col">Today: 6/10/09</th>
      <th scope="col">Wednesday: 6/11/09</th>
      <th scope="col">Thursday: 6/12/09</th>
      <th scope="col">Friday: 6/13/09</th>
      <th scope="col">Saturday: 6/14/09</th>
      <th scope="col">Sunday: 6/15/09</th>
      <th scope="col">Monday: 6/16/09</th>
    </tr>
  </thead>
```

Tip: The scope attribute for th elements accepts two values, col and row, which designates whether the th applies to a column or row of data. For more on the semantic secrets of tables, Zoe Gillenwater's article on the topic (www.communitymx.com/content/article.cfm?cid=0BEA6) is highly recommended.

At the bottom of our calendar, there's a row of cells that link to all events for a given day [**17.7**]. For that, we'll use another row group element, tfoot, which simply contains a tr chock full of td elements. A word of warning, though: despite what its name (and position in our comp) would imply, the tfoot somewhat counterintuitively follows the thead in a valid table:

```
</thead>
<tfoot>
  <tr>
    <td>All of Today's Picks</td>
    <td>All Wednesday Picks</td>
```

```
      <td>All Thursday Picks</td>
      <td>All Friday Picks</td>
      <td>All Saturday Picks</td>
      <td>All Sunday Picks</td>
      <td>All Monday Picks</td>
    </tr>
</tfoot>
```

17.7
A footer row becomes a
tfoot. These names are
catchy, no?

Have no fear: desktop browsers will correctly position the contents tfoot
at the bottom of its containing table, with no added CSS hackery required
from us.

With the calendar's header and footer translated into table-ese, the events—the
meat of the Agenda—are the only elements left to translate into HTML [**17.8**].
For those, we'll be using the third and final row group element, tbody, which
comprises one tr for every row of events to be displayed. And each of those
rows will contain one td for every day of the week, like so:

```
  </tfoot>
  <tbody>
    <tr>
        <td>Event</td>
        <td>Event</td>
        <td>Event</td>
        <td>Event</td>
        <td>Event</td>
        <td>Event</td>
        <td>Event</td>
    </tr>
    <tr>
        ...
    </tr>
  </tbody>
</table>
```

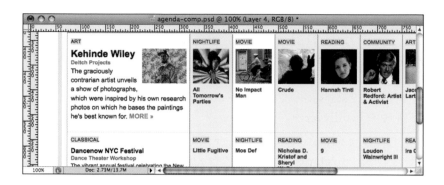

If you've ever slung a table in your career, then you probably recognize the core elements (tr, th, and td) we've been using to mark up the calendar. The three row group elements—thead, tfoot, and tbody—might be less familiar to you, but they give much-needed structure to our table, allowing our CSS to easily distinguish, say, header cells from footer cells, without peppering our markup with extraneous classes or ids. But more importantly, they're the best fit for describing our content *semantically*, proving that table really is the best element for the job.

With the broad underpinnings of our table's structure in place, we're almost ready to begin moving from markup to CSS. But how exactly are we supposed to style something as dynamic as this calendar?

From Inventory to Strategy

To find our answer, we'll need to revisit the design once more. But this time we'll try a slightly different kind of inventory; rather than surveying the different content types, let's catalog the different visual states, so that we can better understand the CSS needed to style them. We're not worrying about *how* to get these states to change—how to expand a column when a user clicks on a cell, or how the background colors will change—but just taking note of the design details in each instance.

Let's dive right in:

1. Starting from the top, we can see that the header cells [**17.9**] have three basic states. The *default* state shows only the name of the day, graphically set in a lovely typeface that sits on a very pale blue background. And at the top of the cell, there's a very faint "EXPAND" graphic that provides a nice visual cue for the user. But in the second state—the *over* state—that

background graphic becomes significantly darker, and the kerning gets much wider. The background of the cell also lightens up considerably, moving from the desaturated powder blue to a full white. And finally, when the user has clicked on a cell, there's the *open* state: the white background stays, the "EXPAND" cue disappears, and the date appears in delightfully large text.

2. Moving down to the footer, our three basic states still apply [**17.10**]. The default display is still a light, pale background, with the link text aligned to the left. And as before, the background brightens up when the user hovers over the column. Finally, the link text gets noticeably larger when the cell is in its open state, and is centered horizontally.

3. The calendar's events [**17.11**] contain quite a bit more information, but we're still dealing with three basic modes. We have the same background color shifts as before, but in the default and over states, only the event's category ("Reading," "Play," "Movie," and so on) and title are shown. In the cell's open state, however, all of the event's information is displayed: venue and summary come into view, a "MORE" link is displayed, and the title becomes noticeably larger.

4. In the first row, there is a slight variation in event styling [17.11]. In the default and over states, an image sits between the event's category and headline. When the cell is in its open state, however, the image floats off to the right. Furthermore, the open-state version of the event's title is set at a slightly larger size than other rows' events.

So no matter which aspect of the calendar we look at, we're still dealing with three basic visual states: default, over, and open. Of course, the design of each state varies significantly between the header, footer, and body of our calendar, but this three-state model is intact throughout.

With the exception of the footer, two of the states (default and over) display significantly less information than their corresponding open state. And therein lies the strategy we've been looking for: our table's markup should contain *all the content that could possibly be shown to the user at any given time*. We'll then use CSS to selectively hide, show, or just restyle bits of content, depending on what state the cell is in. So while the (X)HTML for each cell will be for its open state, we'll use CSS to change the display of that HTML to match our design, producing the default and over states.

17.9

The different visual states in our calendar's header.

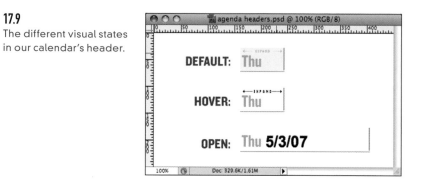

17.10

The visual states in our footer cells.

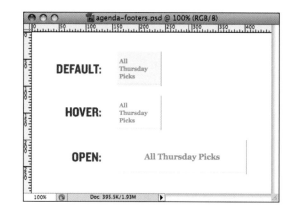

17.11

The different styles for our events. Note the slight differences between the events in the first row and those in subsequent rows.

Once More Into the Markup, Dear Friends

Our table's not quite finished, alas. While the high-level elements are in place, the content inside our `th`s and `td`s is, to put it mildly, rubbish. So let's wrap up our content inventory by looking at the three different types of cells in our table, and make that markup a bit more intelligent. And following our new strategy, we'll only be referencing the open state as we craft our XHTML; CSS will take care of the other two modes after we've finished our markup.

Looking a bit more closely at our design [**17.12**], we can see that the headers' open state has two elements we'll need to include in our markup: the blue label for the day, and the corresponding date in CSS-styled HTML text. With that inventory in place, let's flesh out the markup accordingly:

```
<thead>
  <tr>
    <th scope="col">
      <h3><img src="day-today.png" alt="Today:" />
<b title="May 1, 2007">5/1/07</b></h3>
    </th>
    <th scope="col">
      <h3><img src="day-wed.png" alt="Wednesday:" />
<b title="May 2, 2007">5/2/07</b></h3>
    </th>
    <th scope="col">
      <h3><img src="day-thu.png" alt="Thursday:" />
<b title="May 3, 2007">5/3/07</b></h3>
    </th>
    ...
    <th scope="col">
      <h3><img src="day-mon.png" alt="Monday:" /> <b title="May
7, 2007">5/7/07</b></h3>
    </th>
  </tr>
</thead>
```

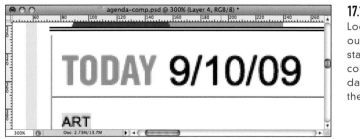

17.12
Looking more closely at our headers in the open state, we can see that they contain an image and a date. We'd best update the markup to match.

Moving into the th elements themselves, we know that our day labels need to be images, so we've done exactly that: each one has been turned into an img element, with an alt attribute containing the image's text. Then, for the date itself, we've wrapped it in a non-semantic b element; as we'll see in the next section, we need a special hook in our markup so that our CSS can distinguish that text from the image beside it. And finally, we've wrapped our content in an h3 element. It is a headline, after all, and it's preceded by an h1 and an h2 in the page's source.

Tip: Why not use a span, you ask? Well, a span would be perfectly acceptable for our date, since we're looking for a bit of nonsemantic cruft. However, I find that I usually resort to b or i first, simply because there are fewer characters. Which translates into less code in your template, and lower bandwidth costs for your clients and their users. Good times.

As always, we're not worrying about how our content needs to look, but how best to describe it; we've chosen the most semantically appropriate markup for our design. And for our footer, the semantics are much more straightforward. Inside each cell of our tfoot, we'll simply wrap the text in an anchor:

```
<tfoot>
  <tr>
    <td><a href="#">All of <i>Today&#8217;s</i> Picks</a></td>
    <td><a href="#">All <i>Wednesday</i> Picks</a></td>
    <td><a href="#">All <i>Thursday</i> Picks</a></td>
    <td><a href="#">All <i>Friday</i> Picks</a></td>
    <td><a href="#">All <i>Saturday</i> Picks</a></td>
    <td><a href="#">All <i>Sunday</i> Picks</a></td>
    <td><a href="#">All <i>Monday</i> Picks</a></td>
  </tr>
</tfoot>
```

With our tfoot finished, let's tackle the events, the meat of our calendar.

```
<td>
  <h4><b>Reading</b></h4>

  <dl>
    <dt><a href="#"><i><img src="img/pics/girl.jpg" alt="" />
</i>Tribeca Film Festival</a></dt>
    <dd class="venue">Multiple venues</dd>
    <dd class="summary">
```

```
    <p>There are more than 50 short films... <a class="more"
href="#">More &raquo;</a></p>
    </dd>
  </dl>
</td>
```

Looking at the design [17.11], we can see that events—whether they appear in the more prominent first row, or in subsequent rows—share the same types of content. There's the category for the event, which we've marked up in an h4 (with another one of those irritatingly nonsemantic b elements), since it's effectively subordinate to the h3 we coded in our thead. For the event itself, however, we've opted to use the dl element: the dt lists the title for the event, while various descriptively classed dd elements contain the venue and event summary information.

And with that, our table's finally finished. Not only do we have the major structural zones cordoned off by the thead, tfoot, and tbody elements, but we've appropriately marked up the content inside them as well. Of course, our table's not going to win any beauty pageants [17.13]. But with this homely-looking markup finally finished, we can start a proper CSS makeover.

17.13
Our unstyled but semantically rich Agenda calendar. Lovely, no? (OK, no.)

From Angle Brackets to Curly Braces

First, let's establish some basic design parameters:

```
body {
  background: #FFF;
  color: #000;
  font: normal 100% Arial, Helvetica, Geneva, Verdana,
sans-serif;
  }

a {
  color: #05A7D4;
  text-decoration: none;
  }

a:hover {
  text-decoration: underline;
  }

a.more {
  font-weight: bold;
  text-transform: uppercase;
  white-space: nowrap;
  }

#agenda-week {
  border-collapse: collapse;
  clear: both;
  font-size: 0.625em; /* 10px / 16px = 0.625em */
  margin-left: 2px;
  width: 764px;
  }

#agenda-week p {
  margin-top: 0;
  }
```

We've already drastically changed the display of our page with these few short rules [17.14]. We've established default color and type characteristics on our body element, which will be inherited by all other elements in our document (until we override them, that is). We've done the same for our document's links, establishing color and text-decoration properties that will be applied throughout to our entire design.

17.14
A light touch of CSS, and
our table's looking a
little less modest. If only
a little.

Toward the end of the above code block, we've narrowed our focus a bit to just #agenda-week. We're setting a relative font size on the **table** element itself, which is calculated relative to the body's font-size of 100%, and roughly equates to 10px. But more importantly, we've established some basic constraints for our table: we've limited its width to 764px, applied some margins, and cleared it of all preceding floats.

Tip: We've declared this 0.625em rule not because we want to set our type at miniscule sizes [17.14], but because we're not that great at complex math: with this baseline set, we can easily calculate relative font sizes. (For more on this, see the discussion of the 62.5% technique in Chapter 13.)

Now, it's obvious that our lightly styled table has some way to go until it matches our design. With these basic parameters in place, let's revisit the three different states we catalogued a few pages ago: the default, over, and open states. In fact, let's experiment a little by applying a class of "open" to the first cell of every row in our table, no matter whether it's in the thead, tfoot, or tbody.

```
<table id="agenda-week">
  <thead>
    <tr>
      <th class="open" scope="col">...</th>
      <th scope="col">...</th>
      <th scope="col">...</th>
      ...
    </tr>
  </thead>
  <tfoot>
    <tr>
      <td class="open">...</td>
      <td>...</td>
      <td>...</td>
      ...
    </tr>
  </tfoot>
  <tbody>
    <tr>
      <td class="open">...</td>
      <td>...</td>
      <td>...</td>
      ...
    </tr>
    ...
  </tbody>
</table>
```

Now, let's add the following rules to our style sheet:

```
#agenda-week th,
#agenda-week td {
  padding: 1em 1px 1em 7px;
  text-align: left;
  vertical-align: top;
  width: 72px;
}

#agenda-week th.open,
#agenda-week td.open {
  width: 242px;
}
```

Our first rule establishes some basic parameters for all th and td elements in our calendar—their default state. From there, we've then created an exception, applying a wider width to all cells with a class of "open."

While it's a subtle change [17.15], we finally have the model for finishing up the rest of our CSS. We can actually translate those different modes into class names, which we can attach to our ths and tds, changing the display of those cells conditionally. To play this out a bit further, let's add two more rules:

```
#agenda-week th h3 b {
  left: -1000em;
  position: absolute;
  }

#agenda-week th.open h3 b {
  position: static;
  }
```

Another small change, but we'll take it [17.16]. We've established a default rule for the non-semantic b elements wrapped around the dates in our thead's h3s: namely, we're positioning them off to the left of the browser window, effectively hiding them from view. But when the "open" class is applied to a cell, as it is in the first column of our table, the element's positioning information is removed, and the date is brought into view.

We can even apply this visibility toggle to the calendar's events. Remember that each event is a dl element, with dd elements marking up the venue and summary information. Since we want to suppress the display of those dds by default, we can simply add to our last snippet of CSS:

```
#agenda-week th h3 b,
#agenda-week td dd {
  left: -1000em;
  position: absolute;
}

/* "Active" elements */
#agenda-week th.open h3 b,
#agenda-week td.open dd {
  position: static;
}
```

17.15
By translating our three visual states into **class** names, we can change the presentation of certain parts of our table.

17.16
We've hidden the date by default, but shown it on cells marked as "open."

Our events are finally beginning to fall in line with our design spec. Lovely.

And lo, our calendar shapes up a bit further [**17.17**]. With a `class` toggle, we're now controlling the display of the venue and summary information for each event through a simple style rule.

Method, Meet Madness

As there are more subtle typographic rules to the calendar than we've time to explore here, let's fast forward past a few hundred lines of CSS. We've added background graphics for the cells' borders and for the `thead`'s EXPAND cues, and finely tuned the page's typography. And with our "open" `class` applied to cells in the first column, our template is finally matching the intended design: the open column's event information is displayed, as is the date at the top, and the column's footer is appropriately centered. The other, `class`-free columns get no such love [**17.18**]. Of course, if we remove that `class`, then the table lapses back into the default mode, according to the style rules we've used to define that state [**17.19**].

17.18
After fleshing out various typographic rules in our CSS, we see that our basic **class** toggle has held up well.

17.19
If we remove that **class** value, however, things look decidedly less interesting.

What's more, we've extended our toggle to include an "over" `class`, which corresponds to the design's over state; adding it to every cell brightens up our table considerably [**17.20**]. And if we're feeling really nutty, we could apply the "open" `class` to every cell in the table, with decidedly awkward-looking results [**17.21**].

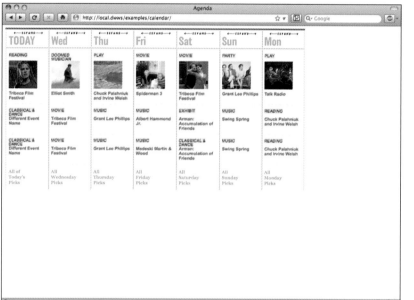

17.20
Adding a **class** of "over" to every cell applies the CSS rules for that state.

17.21
If we added **class="open"** to every cell, they all open. Not that you'd ever want to do this, mind you.

So if our style inventory's done, then why aren't we rejoicing? (Or, at very least, ending the chapter?) While our three-way `class` toggle is working beautifully, and our table looking quite pretty as a result, we've just been manually adding `classes` to the calendar's cells. This is less than ideal, and far from interactive: what we need is some mechanism for adding the "over" `class` as the user mouses over column, or clicks on a collapsed cell to change its `class` from "over" to "open." How do we change our markup dynamically?

Word to Your DOM

If the DOM were a superhero, we'd be playing its theme song as it flew to the rescue. While (X)HTML and CSS are the weapons of choice for describing and styling our content, they fire blanks when it comes to interaction. For that, we'll need to rely on DOM scripting via JavaScript, which will allow us not only to detect when a user hovers over or clicks on a cell, but to change the `class` name of that cell accordingly.

Meet the *colgroup*

However, we don't want to change just an individual cell. Hovering over a `td` or `th` should light up the cells above and below it in the column, and clicking on a cell should expand the whole column. So while our `table`'s XHTML is perfectly sound, we'll need to make some slight markup edits before our JavaScript can identify a cell as being associated with a particular column.

```
<table id="agenda-week">
  <colgroup>
    <col id="day-today" title="Today's events" />
    <col id="day-wed" title="Wednesday's events" />
    <col id="day-thu" title="Thursday's events" />
    <col id="day-fri" title="Friday's events" />
    <col id="day-sat" title="Saturday's events" />
    <col id="day-sun" title="Sunday's events" />
    <col id="day-mon" title="Monday's events" />
  </colgroup>
  <thead>
```

Before the start of our `thead`, we've added a `colgroup` element (www.w3.org/TR/html401/struct/tables.html#h-11.2.4), which contains seven `col` elements—one for every column of our table. While tables fall into a natural horizontal rhythm of rows (`tr`) and cells (`th` or `td`), `colgroup` and its child cols let us create a vertical grouping of those cells into columns. We've added a title to each col, which we've done as an accessibility feature: if a user visits our calendar with a speaking browser, they could invoke a command to have the column's title read aloud, no matter how deep the cell they're currently reading is nested.

However, we still need to associate our table's cells with their respective col element. To do so, we'll add a headers attribute to every th and td in our table, setting each to the id of the col in which that cell resides.

```
<thead>
  <tr>
    <th class="first" scope="col" headers="day-today">
      <h3><img src="img/day-today.png" alt="Today:" />
<b title="May 1, 2007">5/1/07</b></h3>
    </th>
    <th scope="col" headers="day-wed">
      <h3><img src="img/day-wed.png" alt="Wednesday:" />
<b title="May 2, 2007">5/2/07</b></h3>
    </th>
    <th scope="col" headers="day-thu">
      . . .
```

This is the only change we'll need to make to our markup, and it won't affect the display in the least. We've simply bolstered our table's semantics, with our headers creating a vertical association between all the cells in a given column. With this edit, our scripting work can finally begin. These headers attributes will allow our JavaScript to quickly survey the table when a user interacts with a cell, and update the class of all cells in, say, the "Wednesday" column. So let's remove all classes from our markup, setting our table back to its default state [17.19], and begin our JavaScript work.

Jumping Into jQuery

When the Agenda calendar was first built, reams of custom JavaScript were used to power its interactivity. For the sake of this chapter (and your attention span), we'll instead re-engineer the same functionality using the jQuery library (www.jquery.com), first discussed in Chapter 15. Let's add the following to the head of our HTML document:

```
<script type="text/javascript" src="js/jquery.js"></script>
<script type="text/javascript" src="js/scripts.js"></script>
```

In our first `script` element, we've linked to the jQuery library file that we've downloaded and placed in a `js/` directory. The second file, `scripts.js`, is currently blank, but that's where we'll be doing all of our calendar scripting.

Tip: Google actually provides free hosting of several popular JavaScript libraries, including jQuery. So if you find yourself frequently working with jQuery, you might consider linking directly to the file like so:

```
<script type="text/javascript" src="http://ajax.googleapis.com/
ajax/libs/jquery/1.3.2/jquery.min.js"></script>
```

Linking to Google's servers saves bandwidth from your end, but also helps your users: if they've visited another site that's using Google's hosted version of jQuery, it's probably cached in their browser, thereby saving them an extraneous download on your site. More information on Google's JS hosting can be found at `code.google.com/apis/ajaxlibs/documentation`.

With our jQuery in place and `scripts.js` at the ready, let's open up the latter and add in a few lines:

```
$(document).ready(function() {
  var aCells = $("#agenda-week th, #agenda-week td");
});
```

The first line of code (`$(document).ready(...)`) simply directs jQuery to execute all the code found within the parentheses once the page's DOM has finished rendering in the browser. At the moment, all that JavaScript does is declare a variable named `aCells`, using jQuery's CSS-like selector syntax (`$("#agenda-week th, #agenda-week td")`) to create a list of all the `th` and `td` elements in our table. By storing them in a variable, we're simply saving that list for future reference. However, we're not actually doing anything with that variable; we've just declared it for later use. Reloading the page doesn't produce any noticeable changes, as our page is in its default state, its columns still collapsed [17.19].

I know, I know. This feels like more of a whimper than a bang. But with this collection of cells stored in memory, we can start manipulating them with JavaScript. Let's start with a simple edit to `scripts.js`:

```
$(document).ready(function() {
  var aCells = $("#agenda-week th, #agenda-week td");

  aCells.filter("[headers=day-today]").addClass("open");
});
```

In this new line, we're asking jQuery to select a subset of the table's cells (as stored in our `aCells` variable) that have a `headers` attribute set to "day-today" (`aCells.filter("[headers=day-today]")`). Once all those cells have been collected, we're then adding `class="open"` to each element (`.addClass("open")`). If we reload our page, the change is noticeable. jQuery's followed our instructions dutifully, adding a `class` of "open" to every table cell with a `headers` value of "day-today," expanding the first column of our table as the "open" rules in our CSS are applied [17.22]. This might *look* the same as our earlier `class` experiments, but remember: `class="open"` doesn't actually exist in our markup. Instead, we're using JavaScript to scour the `table` for a specific `headers` value, and apply the markup for us.

With this single line, we have a strategy in place for finishing up our JavaScript. Our `aCells` collection contains all of the cells in our table, each column semantically tagged with the appropriate `headers` attribute that corresponds

17.22
While this might look like our earlier expanded calendar, this one's got the DOM behind it.

to a given column. So when a visitor uses a mouse to interact with a cell, we can employ its headers attribute as a key to search out all other th or td elements in that column. Once we've found all the cells that match that headers value, we can then use JavaScript to change their class accordingly. Let's begin by defining what happens when a user puts her mouse over a cell.

```
$(document).ready(function() {
  var aCells = $("#agenda-week th, #agenda-week td");

  aCells.filter("[headers=day-today]").addClass("open");

  aCells.mouseover(
    function() {
      aCells.removeClass("over");
      aCells.filter("[headers=" + $(this).attr("headers") +
"]").addClass("over");
    }
  )
});
```

Here, we've attached an event handler to our aCells array, aCells. mouseover(...), instructing jQuery to execute the code inside the parentheses whenever the user puts her mouse over any cell found within aCells. And once she hovers over any of the th or td elements in our calendar, two separate things happen:

1. First, we remove the "over" class from all the cells in our table (aCells. removeClass("over")).

2. Next, we simply tweak the code that expanded the first column. Instead of looking for a specific headers value (aCells.filter("[headers=day-today]")), we're using $(this) to refer to whatever th or td element the user's currently hovering over. We can then search for all the cells with matching headers attributes (aCells.filter("[headers=" + $(this).attr("headers") + "]")), and change their class to "over" (.addClass("over")).

And as you can see, it's working beautifully: if we put the cursor over any non-expanded cell, then the "over" class is applied to the column, and the CSS changes that its display accordingly [17.23].

17.23
Our JavaScript is now applying **class="over"** to an entire column whenever the user hovers over a cell.

We'll also need to deactivate a column if the user mouses off it, which is a simple variant of our `mouseover()` code:

```
$(document).ready(function() {
  var aCells = $("#agenda-week th, #agenda-week td");

  aCells.filter("[headers=day-today]").addClass("open");

  aCells.mouseover(
    function() {
      aCells.removeClass("over");
      aCells.filter("[headers=" + $(this).attr("headers") +
"]").addClass("over");
    }
  ).mouseout(
    function() {
      aCells.removeClass("over");
    }
  );
});
```

After we have added those three lines, the "over" `class` will be removed from every cell in our calendar whenever the user's mouse moves off a cell, or off the table altogether. (Unfortunately, this is a little hard to demonstrate in a book. But trust us, it totally works.)

So by now, mouse movement is fairly well handled: we have the mouseover and mouseout events coded, and presentational classes applied or removed from our calendar accordingly. All that's left is to define the behavior when our user clicks on a cell.

```
$(document).ready(function() {
  var aCells = $("#agenda-week th, #agenda-week td");

  aCells.filter("[headers=day-today]").addClass("open");

  aCells.mouseover(
    function() {
      aCells.removeClass("over");
      aCells.filter("[headers=" + $(this).attr("headers") +
"]").addClass("over");
    }
  ).mouseout(
    function() {
      aCells.removeClass("over");
    }
  ).click(
    function() {
      aCells.removeClass("open");
      aCells.filter("[headers=" + $(this).attr("headers") +
"]").addClass("open");
    }
  );
});
```

As before, we're simply reusing the syntax we used in the mouseover() handler, with one small (but critical) modification. Rather than applying the "over" class with our JavaScript, we're now appending class="open" to every element in aCells that matches the headers attribute of the cell we clicked on. So not only can we open the first column by default [17.22] and then hover over another column to change its state [17.23], but we can click on another cell to expand that column, finally completing the Agenda calendar in full [**17.24**].

17.24
Once we've written a click event handler, the columns expand properly when a user clicks on a cell.

Standards for All Seasons

In this chapter we've reinforced the powerful simplicity of designing with web standards. We've created an intriguing, intuitive interface atop a foundation of valid, semantically rich XHTML, with smatterings of CSS and JavaScript to breathe life into those staid-looking angle brackets. What's more, the calendar loads quickly, and degrades gracefully if a user's unable to view style sheets, or doesn't have JavaScript available to her. It meets our design goals and our client's needs, and so our chapter ends here.

There is obviously much more to the calendar, and indeed, to the rest of *New York's* site, than can be covered in a chapter like this one: there are the nuanced graphics that shift between one visual state to the next; the complex CSS framework that controls the alignment of the magazine's beautiful photography; all the little interlocking rules that control the finer points of the site's composition and typography. I urge you to visit nymag.com to discover these for yourself.

Of course, *New York's* design and content has evolved considerably since the Agenda was built, and will naturally continue to evolve in the months and years to come. But that's another story, and it's time to stop listening to me and start thinking about the stories you want to tell.

Index

`*  html` (Star HTML) hack, 240–242
& (ampersand), encoding of, 125
&#8217, 45
< (less-than sign), encoding of, 125
> (greater-than sign), encoding of, 125
`@font-face` selector, 172, 286–289
`@import rule` (CSS), 179, 180–181
37signals' Basecamp, 98, 99, 326
62.5% solution to em-based design, 283, 284
1024-pixel grid layout, 341–344

A

A List Apart
    baseline grids, article on, 268
    CSS layout of, 53–56
    designing to encourage reading, article on, 268
    Flash embedding, article on, 259–260
    fluid-grid designs, article on, 267
    iPhone tips, article on, 350
    page layout adjustments, 157
    Sowden's JavaScript file, 336
    style switching, article on, 336
    as top-ten resource, 269
    typography, articles on, 268
accessibility
    background images, 311
    books on, 298–300
    color, 312
    costs of, 305–306, 306–307
    CSS and, 313
    data tables, 315–316
    Flash, 311–312
    forms, 314–315
    guidelines for, 295–296, 297
    image maps, 315
    images, 309–310
    importance, 302
    JavaScript and, 313–314
    keyboard access and, 297
    legal basis for, 296, 298, 303–304
    legal liability and, 308
    myths on, 305–308
    planning for, 318–319
    search engines and, 301, 302, 308, 318–319

accessibility (*cont.*)
    semantic markup and, 296–297
    size of audience for, 301
    streaming video, 311
    table layouts, 315
    text size and, 313
    validation websites for, 316–317
    visual editor plug-ins, 316
    web crawlers and, 301
accessibility attributes, 48
"Accessible Drag and Drop with WAI-Aria"
    (Opera), 148
Accessible Informations Solutions (AIS), 316
Accessible Rich Internet Applications Suite
    (WAI-ARIA), 299
Adams, Cameron, 322
Adelman, Ian, 365
Adobe ColdFusion 8, 101
Adobe Dreamweaver
    accessibility enhancements, 303
    case conversion, 120
    classitis and, 160
    DOCTYPE switching and, 220
    standards support, 90–91
    tag closing by, 124
    XML and, 73
Adobe Dreamweaver MX, 91
Adobe Flex, 136
Adobe Illustrator, SVG graphics creation, 84
Adobe InDesign, XML and, 73
AIGA website, 267
AIS (Accessible Informations Solutions), 316
Ajax, 81, 326
Allen, Dean, 101
Allsopp, John, 88, 132, 144
Almost Standards mode (Gecko browsers),
    222, 223, 225, 226. See also Quirks
    mode; Standards mode
alpha channel (color transparency), 248–251
AlphaImageLoader declaration, 242–243,
    244, 245–246
alt attribute
    accessibility and, 48, 125, 305, 309–310
    for background images, 311
    proper use of, 310
Amazon website, 19, 79, 82
Ambient Findability (Morville), 112
America On-Line, 279

ampersands, encoding of, 125
An Event Apart website, 267
anchor links, 107
Anderson, Chris, 70
Andrew, Rachel, 91
Anuff, Joey, 34, 36
Apache, 96
APIs, 82
Apple. See also Macintosh/Mac OS; Safari
    Dashboard Widgets, 84
    web standards, embrace of, 9
Apple browsers. See Macintosh-based
    browsers
applets, 316
Arial, Helvetica versus, 266
arm length, pixel size and, 274, 275–276
article element, 141
aside element, 142
ATAG (Authoring Tool Accessibility
    Guidelines), 299
Atom, 77
attribute values
    description of, 146
    quoting of, 122–123
    requirement for, 123
attributes. *See also* names of individual
    attributes
    case sensitivity, 120–122
    for elements, 146
    spacing of multiple, 122–123
audio element, 140
Authentic Boredom website, 282
Authoring Tool Accessibility Guidelines
    (ATAG), 299
authoring tools, 90–92
auto value, 207

B

b element, 133
background images
    accessibility and, 311
    flashing of, on long pages, 352, 353
background property, 48, 233
backwards compatibility, 24, 27–31
bad URL syndrome, 102
bandwidth
    accessibility and, 314
    code forking and, 21, 22

condensed versus compressed markup, 26
CSS coding and, 24, 25, 48, 167, 179
divs and, 161–162
global .js files and, 314
HTML and, 109, 123
structured markup, savings from, 149
wasted, 43
BareBones BBEdit, 120
Basecamp (37signals), 98, 99, 326
baseline grids, 268, 363
BBC, RSS and, 79, 80
BBEdit, 124
BBTidy, 121
behavior, standards for, 47
Berlow, David, 269–270
Berners-Lee, Tim, 4, 34, 271
"Best Practices in Online Captioning"
        (Clark), 306, 311
"Beyond DOCTYPE: Web Standards, Forward
        Compatibility, and IE8" (Gustafson), 90
Bickner, Carrie, 73
Birbeck, Mark, 76
Black, Roger, 269–270
blinking elements, 316
bloated markup, cost of, 24–26
block boxes, 186
block status, 198
blockquote element, 130
Blueprint (CSS framework), 267
Boot Camp, 315
border (of boxes), 187–189, 190
border property, 47, 187, 190
border-radius property, 252–253
Boulton, Mark, 268
box model (page layout), 187–190
box-shadow property, 252
boxes, rounded corners for, 251–253
br element, 107, 124, 272
Bray, Tim, 71, 76
Bringhurst, Robert, 268
Browser Archive, 235
Browser Bugs at CSS-Discuss website, 238
browser sniffing, 16–17, 27
browser-specific coding, cost of, xvi
browser testing, 234–235
browsers. See also DOCTYPE switching;
        standards-compliant browsers;
        Standards mode; typography; and
        names of specific browsers

CSS implementation bugs, example of,
        230–235
CSS implementation bugs, hacks for,
        240–242
CSS implementation bugs, web resources
        for, 238
HTML 4.01 test suite for, 85–87
standard error handling, 136
standards support, 15–16, 19, 90, 218
XML and, 105–106
XML prolog, support for, 118–119
Budd, Andy, 190
bugs, in CSS interpretation
        double float-margin bug, 230–237,
                239–240
        hacks for, 240–242
        list of hacks for (website), 241
        PNG bug, 237, 242–247
        web resources for, 238
Building Accessible Web Sites (Clark),
        299–300
Building Findable Websites (Walter), 112

C

CakePHP, 96
Camino, 51, 219
Camino browser, 15
Campbell-Ewald, 57, 58
"Can HTML5 Make Accessibility Usable?"
        (Opera), 148
canvas element, 136, 137
Canvas Tutorial website, 148
case sensitivity of CSS selectors, 170
Cederholm, Dan, 256, 267, 356
Çelik, Tantek, 219
character set declaration, 117–118, 127
characters, Unicode encoding for, 45
Chicago Crime website, 82, 83
Chimera, 219
Chisholm, Wendy, 299
Chrome (Google)
        Cufón and, 290
        HTML5 support, 140
        problems with, 13
        rgba( ) and opacity support, 250
        as standards compliant browser, 7, 14

Clark, Joe
  "Best Practices in Online Captioning,"
    306, 311
  blog by, 133
  Building Accessible Web Sites, 299–300
  on color and accessibility, 312
  Failed Redesigns campaign, 43
  on sIFR, 289
Clark, Richard, 148
Clarke, Andy, 15, 256
class attribute
  in page layout process example, 196,
    203–204
  using, 151, 152–153
class selectors, 176–177
classitis, 158–161
clear property, 213
Clearleft design agency, 293, 322
Cleartype, 269–270
CMSs, standards compliance, 92
Coda, 124
code element, 231
code forking, 21–24, 22, 57
coding. See markup
col element, 386–387
ColdFusion 8 (Adobe), 101
colgroup element, 386–387
color blindness website, 312
colors
  accessibility and, 312
  CSS specifications for, 168–169
  hex shorthand for, 195
  rgba( ) notation, 248–250, 254
  of text, 266
comments
  conditional, 243–245, 256
  double dashes within, 125
compatibility
  backwards, 24, 27–31
  forward, 6, 57, 59, 229–230
competitive audits, 341
conditional comments, 243–245, 256
conditional CSS files, 278
consumer software, XML and, 73
content, hiding, using CSS, 373, 381–383
content area (in boxes), 187–189
content inventories, 191, 201–203
Content Type meta element, 119, 127
controls attribute, 140

costs
  of accessibility, 305–306, 306–307
  of bloated markup, 24–26
  of file transfer bandwidth, 25
Craig, James, 133
create once, publish everywhere (forward
  compatibility), 6, 57, 59, 229–230
Creative Commons licensing, 82
CSS (Cascading Style Sheets). *See also* page
  layout
  accessibility and, 313
  benefits of, 167
  best practices using, 183
  browser bugs, example of, 230–235
  browser bugs, hacks for, 240–242
  browser bugs, web resources for, 238
  conditional, 277–278
  CSS2, finalization date, 248
  declarations, 168–170
  descendant selectors, 173–175, 176
  double float-margin bug, 235–237,
    239–240
  embedded style sheets, 180
  filters, 242–243
  frameworks, 267
  hacks in, 240–242
  id element and, 162
    id selectors, 174–176
  inheritance, 172–173
  inline styles, 182
  overview, 166
  PNG bug, 237, 242–247
  reference books for, 168
  selectors, 168–178
  style sheets, 16, 179–182
  styling elements using, 130–132
  text size and, 272–273
  used for layout, 128
CSS-Discuss website, 238, 251
CSS layout, acceptance of, 149–150
CSS Sprites, 363
CSS Validation Service (W3C), 104, 183
CSS Working Group website, 248
CSS Zen Garden website, 279, 336
CSS2.1, 47
CSS3
  browser support for, 90, 255–257
  contingent implementations of, 253–255
  CSS Working Group website, 248

rgba( ) notation, 248–250, 254
website for, 47
Cufón, 290
Cynthia Says portal, 316–317

D

Dash, Anil, 52, 322
Dashboard Widgets (Apple), 84
dashes, double, within comments, 125
data tables, accessibility and, 315–316
datagrid element, 147
dd element, 377
dd tags, 45
DD_belatedPNG (JavaScript library),
    246–247
declarations (in CSS), 168–170
default text size, 272, 274–277
definition data tags, 45
definition list tags, 45
descendant selectors (in CSS), 173–175, 176,
    353, 355
design. *See also* CSS; CSS3; New York
    magazine Agenda; standards;
    typography; Zeldman website
    best practices, using CSS, 183
    pattern for, 355
    before standards, cost of, 37–38
    using grids, 267
    using real content, 347
Developing with Web Standards (Allsopp),
    144
Digg user experience team, 257
digital cameras, XML and, 73
dir attribute, 146
disabilities, people with. See accessibility
display property, 197–198
div element, 140–141, 150–152
divitis, 160–162
Django Web framework, 82
dl element, 45, 377
DOCTYPE declaration
    Frameset, 116
    in HTML5, 136–137
    incomplete, Quirks mode and, 224
    location for, 116
    types of, 113–114

DOCTYPE switching
    Almost Standards mode, 223
    basics, 220–221
    complete and incomplete DOCTYPEs,
        223–226
    Gecko browsers and, 222
    Internet Explorer 8, 221–222
    introduction to, 218–219
documents, well-structured, 128
Dojo JavaScript library, 338
DOM (Document Object Model), 47, 321, 324
DOM-based scripts. *See also* JavaScript
    accessibility and, 314
    books on, 322
    browsers supporting, 326–327
    code variants, 334–335
    description of, 324–326
    DOM support, checking for, 333–334
    JavaScript libraries, 338–340
    for *New York* magazine Agenda, 386–393
    non-DOM-capable devices, supporting,
        326–327
    placement of, 334–335
    style switchers, 335–337
    unobtrusive scripting, 322
    working with, 327–337
DOM property, 219
DOM *Scripting: Web Design with JavaScript
    and the Document Object Model* (Keith),
    322
DOM Scripting Task Force, 323
.NET 2.0, 101
double dashes, within comments, 125
double float-margin bug, 235–237, 239–240
"Doubled Float-Margin Bug" (Position is
    Everything), 239
Dreamweaver. See Adobe Dreamweaver
Drupal, 306
dt element, 377
dynamic web pages, semantic structure and,
    98, 101

E

eBay website, 19
Ecma (European Computer Manufacturers
    Association), 127
ECMAScript (standard JavaScript), 4, 47

Edwards, Dean, 137, 256
Edwards, James, 322
Eisenberg, J. David, 77
"Elastic Lawn" (Griffiths), 279
elastic layout, 279
elements. *See also* attributes; names of
       individual elements
    case sensitivity, 120–121
    closing, 124–125, 138, 139
    nesting, 146
    omission of, 145–146
    semantics of, 128
*The Elements of Typographic Style, 2nd
       Edition* (Bringhurst), 268
The Elements of Typographic Style Applied
       to the Web (website), 268, 269
em-based design (typography), 279, 284–285
em element, 133
embed element, 258–259
embedded fonts, 288–293
embedded objects, 46, 258–262
Embedded OpenType (EOT) fonts, 288, 289
embedded style sheets, 180–181
empty tags, closing of, 124–125
European Computer Manufacturers
       Association (ECMA), 4, 127
EveryBlock, 82, 83
Evolt.org Browser Archive, 235
Expression Web Designer, 91–92
ExpressionEngine, 306
Extensible Markup Language. *See* XML
Extensible Stylesheet Language
       Transformation (XSLT), 76–77
external style sheets, 179

F
Fahrner, Todd, 218–219, 272, 274–275
Fahrner Image Replacement, 362
failed redesigns campaign, 43
faux background images, 352, 353
Felker, Clay, 365
figure element, 142
file transfer bandwidth, cost of, 25
FileMaker Pro, XML and, 73
findability, 70
Firefox. *See also* Gecko-based browsers
    CSS3, support for, 252, 254
    Cufón and, 290

first-child and first-letter support, 354
@font-face support, 287
HTML5 support, 137, 140
market share, 30
new coding for, 15
Page Zoom and, 281
RDF usage, 76
rgba( ) and opacity support, 250
soft hyphenation and, 270, 271
as standards compliant browser, 7–8, 14
standards support, 90
style switching, support for, 336
SVG support, 84
text size keywords in, 285
user agent string, 17
web developer toolbar, 316
XMLHttpRequest and, 79, 81
first-child pesudo-class, 354
first-letter pesudo-class, 354
Flash objects
    accessibility and, 311–312
    browser support for, 258–261
    text replacement using, 289
"Flash Satay" (McLellan), 259–260
flashing elements, 316
Flex (Adobe), 136
Flickr, 65, 79, 82
float property, 198–200, 209–213
fluid-grid design, 267
font element, 36, 271–272
@font-face selector, 172, 286–289
font property, 195
font-size-adjust property, 172
fonts. *See also* text size; typography
    embedded, 288–293
    real font files, linking to, 287–289
    specifying, in CSS declarations, 171–172
    use of multiple, 266
footer element, 140, 142, 212–214
Ford, Paul, 76, 133
forms, accessibility and, 314–315
forward compatibility, 6, 57, 59, 229–230
frames, 316
Frameset DOCTYPE, 116
"From Switches To Targets: A Standardista's
       Journey" (Meyer), 90
Fusion, 315
FutureSplash (Flash), 258

G

Garrett, Jesse James, 81, 326
Gecko-based browsers. *See also* Camino;
    Firefox; Mozilla browser
    complete DOCTYPEs and, 225, 226, 227
    new coding, 15
    problems with, 13
    standards support, 219, 222
    style switching, support for, 336
    XHTML 1.0 Strict versus Transitional in,
        223
generic values for font specifications, 171
GeoLocation API, 136, 137
Gillenwater, Zoe, 370
Glaser, Milton, 365
Glendinning, Porter, 52, 325
global .js files, 334
Gmail, 326
GNU licensing, 82
Google. *See also* Chrome
    Gmail, 326
    JavaScript hosting, 388
    web standards, embrace of, 9
"Google Bets Big on HTML5" (O'Reilly), 148
Google Maps, 82
greater-than signs (>), encoding of, 125
Grid Positioning Module, 210
Grid Systems in Graphic Design (Müller-
    Brockmann), 341
grids (in page design), 267, 279, 341–342,
    344
Griffiths, Patrick, 279
Gruber, John, 101
Gustafson, Aaron, 90, 267

H

h1 element, 129–130, 131
hacks
    for CSS interpretation bugs, 240–242
    for Internet Explorer, 355
Hamid, Naz, 342
Hansson, David Heinemeier, 98
Happy Cog
    AIGA website, 267
    Housing Works website, 177–178
    A List Apart website, 53–55
    MICA website, 48, 49
    website, Page Zoom and, 283

header element, 140, 141
headers attribute, 387
headline (h1, h2, h3...) elements
    accessibility and, 296–297
    divs and, 161
    header element and, 141
    in page layout process example, 204–205
    real fonts and, 287
    in semantic markup, 46, 128, 129–131
Helvetica, Arial versus, 266
Henry, Shawn Lawton, 300
hexadecimal color specifications, 169
Hickson, Ian, 87, 89, 135
Hickson Uncertainty Principle, 138
hiding content, hiding, using CSS, 373,
    381–383
Hilton's hotel search website, 41–42
hlink element, 107
Hockenberry, Craig, 350
Holovaty, Adrian, 82
Holzschlag, Molly, 91
HomeSite, 124
Honorable Mentions-IE Blog website, 238
Hook Mitchell website, 38–41, 48
horizontal centering, using auto value, 207
Housing Works website, 177–178
"How to Size Text in CSS" (Rutter), 283, 284
hr element, 361
href element, 107
HTML (Hypertext Markup Language). *See
    also* HTML5
    design tools, lack of, 34
    layout effects using, 36
    portability, 46
    reasons for using, compared with
        XHTML, 109–110
    typographic control and, 271
    XHTML, comparison with, 104–106
    XML, comparison with, 71–72
HTML, conversion to XHTML 1.0
    attribute values, quoting of, 122–123
    attribute values, requirement for, 123
    case sensitivity, 120–122
    character encoding, 126–128
    character set declaration, 117–118, 127
    comments, double dashes within, 125
    DOCTYPE declaration, 113–114, 116
    encoding less-than signs and
        ampersands, 125

HTML, conversion to XHTML 1.0 (*cont.*)
  namespace declaration, 117
  strict *versus* transitional, 115
  summary, 126
  tags, required closing of, 124–125
  XML prolog, 118–119, 127
HTML4.01, 44, 85–87, 108
HTML5
  additional resources for, 147–148
  b and i elements in, 133
  browser support for, 137–138
  creation of, 87–89
  creators of, 135
  DOCTYPE statement, 225
  elements in, complete list of, 137
  embed tag, support for, 259
  extensibility, lack of, 144–145
  links in, 147
  new elements in, 140
  new features in, 136–137
  page structure semantics, 140–145
  specifications for, 145–147
  syntax, dual types of, 138
  validation services for, 104, 138–139
  web applications and, 136
  XHTML versus, 108, 138–139
HTML5 Super Friends, 142
HTML Tidy, 101, 120, 121, 123
"HTML5: A Story in Progress"
  (Burningbird), 148
"HTML5: Could it Kill Flash and
  Silverlight?" (Infoworld), 148
"HTML5: Features You Want Desperately But
  Still Can't Use" (YouTube), 148
HTML5 Doctor (website), 148
HTML5 Gallery (website), 148
HTML5 Reset Stylesheet (website), 148
Hunt, Lachlan, 88, 140
Hutchinson, Grant, 50, 52
Hyatt, Dave, 238

I

i element, 133, 146
id attribute, 150, 152–154, 162, 203–204
id selectors, 174–176
IE3, text size and, 273

IE4
  standards, lack of support for, 16
  text size and, 273
IE5 Macintosh Edition, 219
IE5.5, Quirks mode, 222
IE6
  bugs in, 235–241, 262
  designing for, 62, 64
  DOCTYPE switching, support for, 219
  Quirks mode, 225
  standards, lack of support for, 14–15
  support for, 255–257
IE7
  designing for, 62
  as standards compliant browser, 14, 89
  style elements for, 354–355
IE7 JavaScript library, 256
IE7 Standards mode (IE 8 Compatibility
  View), 222
IE8
  Almost Standards mode, 222
  HTML5 support, 137, 138
  rendering modes, types of, 221–222
  stability, 239
  as standards compliant browser, 7–8, 14,
    89
  web standards and, 221–222
Illustrator (Adobe), SVG graphics creation,
  84
ilovetypography website, 268
image management software, 73
image maps, accessibility and, 315
image replacement, 287, 362–363
images
  floating of, 199
  Gecko treatment of, 223
  min-height property and, 233
  PNG bug, 237, 242–247
  sizing of, 279
img element
  alt attribute for, 309
  closing of, 124
  headlines and, 287
  origins of, 258
  XHTML2.0 and, 107
@import rule (CSS), 179, 180–181
InDesign (Adobe), XML and, 73
inheritance (in CSS), 172–173, 194, 196
inline boxes, 186

inline CSS and scripting, 162–163
`inline` status, 198
inline styles, 182
Inman, Shaun, 97, 289
Inman Flash Replacement, 289
International Standards Organization, 127
Internet Explorer browsers. *See also* entries
    beginning "IE"
  complete `DOCTYPES` and, 225, 226, 227
  conditional comments, 243–245
  CSS3, support for, 254
  Cufón and, 290
  default text size, 276
  DOM support, 326
  early versions, problems of, 13, 19
  `first-child` and `first-letter`
    support, 354–355
  Flash objects in, 260
  `@font-face` support, 287–289, 293
  hacks for, 355
  market share, 30
  Page Zoom, 281–283
  pixel text size, problem of, 280–281
  text size keywords in, 285
  web accessibility toolbar, 316
  web standards and, 89–90
  XML prolog, support for, 118–119
  XMLHttpRequest and, 79, 81
Internet Explorer Collection, 235
Internet Explorer/Macintosh, default text
    size, 276
"Introduction to RDFa" (Birbeck), 76
iPhone, viewport meta element, 349–350
iPhoto, XML and, 73
ISO 8859 encoding, 127
iTunes, XML and, 73
iTV Production Standards Initiative, 75

J

JavaScript. *See also* DOM-based scripts
  accessibility and, 313–314
  Cufón and, 290
  Flash objects and, 261, 312
  global `.js` files, 334
  id naming, 154
  ie7 JavaScript library, 256
  inline, problem of, 162–163

  libraries, 338–340
  multi-threaded, 136
  for PNG bug correction, 246–247
  sIFR and, 289
  standard (ECMAScript), 4, 47
  unobtrusive, 261
`javascript:` links, 327
The JavaScript Anthology: 101 Essential Tips,
    Tricks & Hacks (Edwards and Adams),
    322
JAWS (screen reader), 312, 315
Jogin, Thomas, 289
jQuery JavaScript library, 338–339, 387–392
JSON, 81

K

Keith, Jeremy, 90, 322
keyboard access for accessibility, 297
keywords, for font-size, 285–287
Kinnunen, Simo, 290
Kirkpatrick, Andrew, 300
KPMG website, 28–30

L

Lawson, Bruce, 300
layout. *See* page layout
`legend` element, 142
less-than signs (<), encoding of, 125
li element, 130, 132
Libby, Dan, 77
libraries, JavaScript, 338–340
Lightbox, 181
line break (`br`) element, 107, 124, 272
`line` (`l`) element, 107
line measure (characters per line), 266
`link` element, 179
links, in HTML5, 147
liquid layouts, line length and, 266
lists, 131–132, 151
location awareness, 136
long-tail marketing, 70
`ltr` attribute value, 146
Lupton, Ellen, 268
Lynx browser, 40, 314, 326, 327

M

Macintosh. *See also* OS X; Safari
    default text size and, 272–276, 279
Macintosh Finder, 324
Macromates TextMate, 121
Marcotte, Ethan, 267
`margin` property
auto value, 207
    in box model, 187
    shorthand for, 189–190, 194, 207
margins (of boxes), 187, 188
Markdown (quasi-markup language), 101
markup. *See also* HTML; XHTML; XML
    bad, problems of, 102
    common errors in, 158–161
    compression of, 26
    embedded objects in, 46
    improving, 149–163
    inline CSS and scripting, 162–163
    modern, 95–110
    non-standards compliant, 20, 21–24,
        24–26
    of page versus content, 128–129
    semantic, 46
    semantic, and reusability, 155–158
    for single browsers only, 28, 30
    standards compliant, 24–25
    structural, 128–133
    validation services, 103–104, 183
    validity, 46
markup languages, 44–46
Maryland Institute College of Art (MICA),
    48–49
Matsumoto, Yukihiro, 98
`max-width` attribute, 267
May, Matt, 289, 299
McLellan, Drew, 91, 259–260
measure (characters per line), 266
`meta` element, 119, 221
Meyer, Eric, 55–56, 90, 130, 238, 267
MICA (Maryland Institute College of Art),
    48–49
microdata, 147
microformats, 72
Microsoft. *See also* Internet Explorer
    CSS, support for, 218
    Embedded OpenType (EOT) fonts, 288
    JScript, 321

test suites, 85–87
    web standards, support for, 218
    web standards, use of, 50
Microsoft Active Server Pages .NET 2.0, 101
Microsoft Expression Web, 124, 160
Microsoft Office, XML and, 73
Microsoft Silverlight, 136
middleman font platforms, 291–293
MIME types, HTML5 and, 139
`min-height` property, 233
`min-width` attribute, 267
Miner, Wilson, 248, 249, 254, 280, 363
Mint website, 97
mobile devices
    accessibility and, 308
    image replacement and, 363
    websites viewed on, 65
Mobile Safari, HTML5 support, 137
modern browsers. See standards-compliant
    browsers
`mod_gzip` module, 26
Moll, Cameron, 282, 342
Moon's Designs, 35
MooTools JavaScript library, 338
Morville, Peter, 70, 112
Mosaic, 27
motor impairment, accessibility and, 302
Movable Type, 78, 81
`-moz-border-radius` property, 253
Mozilla. *See also* Firefox; Gecko-based
    browsers
    default text size, 276
    `DOCTYPE` switching and, 219
    DOM support, 326
    web developer toolbar, 316
Mozilla Foundation, 87
MSN, web standards, embrace of, 9, 10
MSN Game Zone, 18
Müller-Brockmann, Josef, 341
Multi-Safari, 235
multimedia elements, 140, 258–262. *See also*
    Flash objects; QuickTime
MVC frameworks, Rails, 98
MySQL, PHP and, 96
myths on accessibility, 305–308

N

names, structural, 151–152
namespace declaration (XHTML), 117
  nav element, 142, 151
Netscape
  CSS compliance, 51, 53
  default text size, 276
  divs and, 161
  DOCTYPE switching and, 219, 222, 225, 226
  early versions, problems of, 19
  embed element, 258
  font element, 271–272
  inheritance and, 173
  JavaScript, creation of, 321
  Microsoft, competition with, 86
  RSS and, 77
  standards support, 7, 16, 19, 218
  table-based layouts, support for, 27
  tt tags and, 36
Netscape 1.0, 27
Netscape 4
  standards, lack of support for, 16
  text size and, 273
  Web Standards Project website in, 51
New York magazine
  complex design of, 365, 366
  style switching, 337
New York magazine Agenda
  about, 365, 367
  behavior of, 367–369
  body of, 371–372
  content inventory for, 367
  CSS coding for, 378–386
  events, coding of, 376–377
  footer for, 370–371, 376
  headers for, 370
  illustration of, 366
  scripting for, 386–393
  table element for, 367, 369
  table markup for, 375–377
  visual states, 372–374
New York Times
  grid design, 267
  mobile *versus* desktop browser version, 65
  RSS and, 79

Newton handheld, 52
Nielsen, Jakob, 64
noscript element, 314, 327
null alt attribute, 309

O

object element, 107, 258, 259
obsolescence
  backwards compatibility, 27–31
  bad markup, 19–20
  bloated markup, cost of, 24–26
  browser version problem, 16–19
  code forking, 21–24
  modern browsers, differences from older versions, 15–16
  modern browsers and web standards and, 14–15
  problem of, 3–5
  version problem, 16–19
Ogg codec, 140
opacity property, 250–251
OpenOffice, XML and, 73
OpenType (OTF) fonts, 287
Opera browsers
  complete DOCTYPEs and, 225, 226
  CSS3, support for, 254
  Cufón and, 290
  DOM support, 326
  first-child and first-letter support, 354
  @font-face support, 287
  HTML5 support, 137, 140
  new coding for, 15
  Page Zoom, 281–283
  problems with, 13
  rgba( ) and opacity support, 250
  standards support, 7–8, 14, 90
  user agent string, 17
  version 10, user agent string problem, 17
  XMLHttpRequest and, 79, 81
Opera Mini, 7, 30
Opera Software company, 87
operating systems, fonts and, 269–270
Optima System PageSpinner, 120, 124
order, in font specifications, 171

OS X
    default text size and, 272–276, 279
    Quartz graphics model, 269–270
    Voice Over, 315
    XML and, 73
outlines, content structure and, 129

P

padding
    in boxes, 187–188, 190
    between columns, 349
padding property, 187, 190
page flow
    boxes and, 186
    floated elements in, 200, 209, 213
    img elements in, 197
page layout. *See also* CSS; HTML; XHTML;
        XML
    box model, 187–190
    content inventories, 191, 201–203
    elastic, 279
    Grid Positioning Module, 210
    page flow, 186
    standards and, 185–215
    standards-compliant code for, process
        example, 191–214
    using floats for, 209–212
page structure
    elements for, in HTML5, 140–142
    language for, 88
    presentation, separation from, 130–131,
        157–158
Page Zoom, 281–283
page zoom, and typography, 281–283
PageSpinner, 120, 124
Palm Pilot, 52
Palm Pre, type design on, 270
Panic Coda, 120
Paoli, Jean, 71
Parallels, 315
personal information managers, 73
personal publishing tools, 81–82
Phark Image Replacement, 362
PHP, description of, 96
Pieters, Veerle, 343, 356, 357

pixels
    defining size of, 274–276
    text size and, 273, 279, 280–281
PNG bug, 237, 242–247
PocketPC, 52
podcasts, 70, 77
points (print size unit), 272–273, 277
Position is Everything website, 238, 239
poster attribute, 140
"The Power of HTML5 and CSS 3" (Starr),
        143–144
Powzaek, Derek, 356
A Practical Guide to Designing for the Web
        (Boulton), 268
presentation, separation from structure,
        130–131, 157–158
presentation languages, 47
presentational hacks, 102–103
"A Preview of HTML5" (Hunt), 88, 148
print style sheets, 55–56
printer-friendly pages, 53, 55–56
progressive enhancement, 62, 64, 261, 314,
        334
properties. *See* names of individual
        properties
Prototype JavaScript library, 338
Public Law 105-220 (Rehabilitation Act
        Amendments, 1998), 303
publishing tools, 90–92
"Put Your Content in My Pocket"
        (Hockenberry), 350

Q

QuarkXPress, XML and, 73
Quartz graphics model, 269–270
QuickTime, 258, 311
Quirks mode. *See also* Almost Standards
        mode; DOCTYPE switching; Standards
        mode
    browsers' actions in, 220
    Gecko browsers, 222
    IE5/Macintosh and, 219
    IE6, 225
    IE8, 222
    triggers for, 109, 224, 227

R

rag (ragged right margin), 270, 271
Raggett, Dave, 121, 142
Rails, 98
RDF (Resource Description Framework), 76, 105
RDFa, 76
Real (multimedia player), 258
recovery.gov website, 43
rel attribute, 147
Resource Description Framework (RDF), 76, 105
RGB color specifications, 169
rgba( ) notation, 248–250, 254
rich internet applications, HTML5 and, 109
Rich Site Summary (RSS), 70, 77–79, 105
Rosam, David, 82
rounded corners for boxes, 251–253
row group elements, 370
RSS (Rich Site Summary), 70, 77–79, 105
rtl attribute value, 146
Ruby, Sam, 135
Ruby on Rails, 98–99
Rundle, Mike, 362
Rutter, Richard, 283–284

S

Sacui, Al, 25
Safari
    border-radius property, support for, 252
    Cufón and, 290
    DOM support, 326
    first-child and first-letter support, 354
    @font-face support, 287
    HTML5 support, 137, 140
    Page Zoom and, 281
    problems with, 13
    rgba( ) and opacity support, 250
    soft hyphenation and, 270, 271
    as standards compliant browser, 7–8, 14
    standards support, 90
    user agent string, 17
    XMLHttpRequest and, 79, 81
Santa Maria, Jason
    grid-based layout by, 343
    A List Apart website, design for, 54

website, 80, 267
    website footer, 356, 357
scalable Inman Flash Replacement (sIFR), 289–290
Scalable Vector Graphics (SVG), 76, 84, 105
scope attribute, 370
screen magnification, 295
screen readers
    description of, 311–312
    early, 37
    form testing using, 314–315
    structural HTML elements and, 155
    website testing using, 40
Scriptaculous JavaScript library, 338
scripting languages, 101. See also DOM-based scripts; PHP
search engine optimization (SEO), 70–71, 131, 155
search engines, accessibility and, 301, 302, 308, 318–319
Section 508 of the Rehabilitation Act (accessibility standard), 296, 298, 303–304
section element, 140–141
selectors (in CSS)
    about, 168–170
    class selectors, 176–177
    combining, 177–178
    descendant, 173–175, 176
    grouping of, 172
    in page layout example, 193
semantic markup
    accessibility and, 296–297
    reusability and, 155–158
semantics
    of elements, 128
    of HTML5 page structure, 140–145
"Semantics in HTML5" (Allsopp), 88, 148
semicolons, in CSS declarations, 169
SEO (search engine optimization), 70–71, 131, 155
server-side scripting languages
    ColdFusion 8, 101
    description of, 96
    .NET 2.0, 101
    JSP, 101
    PHP, 96
    Ruby on Rails, 98–99
    standards-compliant templates and, 101

Sharp, Remy, 137
Shea, Dave, 336
shorthand
    background property, 233
    benefits of, 190
    font property, 195
    hex colors, 196
    margin property, 189–190, 194, 207
    zero values, 190
Siegel, David, 36
sIFR, 181, 289–290
Silnt website, 267
Silverlight (Microsoft), 136
Simple Object Access Protocol (SOAP), 82
Sivonen, Henri, 139
size attribute, 271–272
Skip Navigation, 317
slow load times, 64
Smartronix, Inc. website, 43
SMIL (Synchronized Multimedia Integration
    Language), 105, 311
social networking sites, 79, 81
soft hyphenation, 270
Sowden, Paul, 336
span element, 150, 376
Speakup (Linux screen reader), 315
Sperberg-McQueen, C. M., 71
Spolsky, Joel, 119
standard object models, 47
standards. See also standards-compliant
    browsers
    advocating for, 61–67
    benefits of, xvi-xvii, 31–32, 48–49, 53, 56,
        58–59
    browser support for, 90
    as continuum, 6
    definition, 6–7
    future of, 85–92
    Gecko and, 222
    Internet Explorer 8 and, 221–222
    page components and, 44
    page layout and, 185–215
    trinity of, 44–47
    workarounds, 262–263
standards bodies, 4
standards-compliant browsers
    description, 7–8
    earlier versions, differences from, 15–16
    web standards and, 14–15

Standards mode. See also Almost Standards
        mode; DOCTYPE switching; Quirks
        mode
    complete DOCTYPE statements for ,
        223–225
    description of, 220
    Gecko browsers and, 222, 225, 226
    IE 5 Macintosh Edition and, 219
    IE8 and, 221–222
    triggers for, 227
Star HTML hack, 240–242
Starr, Jeff, 143–144
Steadman, Carl, 34, 36
streaming video, accessibility and, 311
Strict DOCTYPE, 223–224
Strizvers, Ilene, 268
strong element, 133
structural markup, 128–133
structural names, 151–152
structure, standards for, 44–46
style sheets (CSS files), 16, 179–182. See also
        CSS
style switchers, 335–337
subpixel anti-aliasing, 269
Subtraction website, 267
Suck website, 33–34, 36–37, 48
Surfin' Safari website, 238
SuSE Linux distribution, screen reader in,
        315
SVG (Scalable Vector Graphics), 76, 84, 105
SWFObject, 261, 312
Symfony, 96
Synchronized Multimedia Integration
        Language (SMIL), 105, 311

T

tabindex attribute, 317
table element, 367, 369
tables
    body, 371–372
    footers, 370–371, 376
    headers, 370
    row group elements, 370, 371
    semantic markup and, 156
    summaries, 315
    table element, 367, 369
tags. See attributes; elements

Tan, Jon, 289
Target website, 308
Tasman rendering engine, 219
tbody element, 371–372
templates, XHTML 1.0 Transitional, 191–192
test suites, 85–87
text browsers, 40
text-indent property, 194
text-only websites, accessibility and, 305
text-shadow property, 252–253
text size
    accessibility and, 304, 313
    changing, 157
    conditional files and, 278
    default, 272, 274–277
    early CSS implementation and, 272–273
    keywords for, 285–287
    page zoom and, 281–283
    points and, 272–273
    size attribute, 271–272
    user control of, 270, 274–275
text-transform property, 233
Text Zoom, 219, 273, 281
Textile (quasi-markup language), 101
TextMate, 121, 124
tfoot element, 370
Thatcher, Jim, 300
thead element, 370
TheFontFeed website, 269
"They Shoot Browsers, Don't They?" (Keith), 90
Thinking with Type: A Critical Guide for Designers (Lupton), 268
Thomas, Matthew Paul, 133
Times Online website, 267
TinyMCE, 101
title attribute, 48, 125, 310
"Top Ten Type Resources Online" (Strizver), 268
Topics: Code: HTML and XHTML website, 148
TrueType (TTF) fonts, 287
tt tags, 36
Twitter, 98, 100, 269
type, baseline grids and, 268
Type Directors Club Books on Typography website, 268
TypeCulture website, 268
Typekit, 291, 293

TypeRadio website, 269
Typographica website, 268
typography
    additional resources for, 268–269
    basics of, 269–271
    Cufón, 290
    design pattern for, 355
    em-based design, 279, 284–285
    font sizing, 271–281
    general guidelines, 266–268
    page zoom and, 281–283
    real web fonts, 287–289
    sIFR, 289–290
    size standardization, 274–278
    Typekit, 291, 293
    Typotheque, 291–293
    web type, history of, 271–273
Typophile website, 268
Typotheque, 291–293

U

UAWG guidelines, 299
ul element, 151
Ulead Glow Frame tutorial, 35
Unicode Consortium, 126
Unicode encoding, 45, 126
universal design. See accessibility
Universal Design for Web Applications (Chisholm and May), 299
"Universal Internet Explorer 6 CSS" (Clarke), 15, 256
Universal Page Zoom, 273, 279, 281–283
unobtrusive scripting, 322
URLs, correcting bad, 102
U.S. Navy website, 57, 58
USA Today, RSS and, 79
user agent (UA) strings, 17
user style sheets, 313
users. See also accessibility
    control of text size, 270, 274–275
    loss of, through single-browser coding, 28, 30
"Using XML" (Eisenberg), 77

V

validation of markup
    Cynthia Says portal, 316–317
    description of, 46
    Flash objects and, 261
    HTML5 and, 138–139
    validation services, 103–104, 183
the Validator (W3C Markup Validation
        Service), 103–104, 183
Van Damme, Tim, 252
vCard, 147
version problem (websites), 16–19
"Version Targeting: Threat or Menace?"
        (Zeldman), 90
video element, 136, 137, 140
viewport meta element, 349–350
Vinh, Khoi, 267, 342
Virtual Box, 315
Virtual PC, 314–315
Vischeck website, 312
visibility toggle, 373, 381–383
Vision Australia, 316
Visual Basic Studio, 92
visual editors, 160, 316. See also names of
        specific programs
visual elements, structure and, 133–134
visual experiences, acceptability of range of,
        63–67
VoiceOver, 315
Volkswagen website, 21, 22–24

W

W3C (World Wide Web Consortium)
    description, 4
    on DOM, 323
    DOM specifications, 321
    embed tag, lack of support for, 259
    img tag, lack of support for, 258, 259
    object element and, 258–259
    test suites, 85–87
    validation services, 103–104
    Web Accessibility Initiative, 295–296
W3C HTML Working Group, 135
WAI (Web Accessibility Initiative), 295–296
WAI-ARIA (Accessible Rich Internet
        Applications Suite), 299

Walsh, Jo, 76
Walter, Aarron, 112
Washington Post website, 157
WaSP. See Web Standards Project
Web 2.0 applications, 81
*Web Accessibility: Web Standards and
        Regulatory Compliance* (Thatcher), 300
Web Accessibility Initiative (WAI), 295–296
web applications, HTML5 and, 136
web browsers. See browsers
Web Content Accessibility Guidelines
        (WCAG), 295–296, 297
web crawlers, accessibility and, 301
Web Design Group, markup validation
        service, 104
Web Hypertext Application Technology
        Working Group (WHATWG), 4, 87, 135
web pages, application-like behavior,
        324–326
web services, 82–84
web standards. See standards
Web Standards Advisor (Zeldman), 121
Web Standards Project (WaSP)
    cofounder of, 218
    description, 7
    DOM Scripting Task Force, 323
    Dreamweaver Task Force, 91
    mentioned, 85
    website portability, 50–53
web type, history of, 271–273
WebKit, 7, 30, 140
-webkit-border-radius property, 253
websites, obsolescence, 3–5
Weightshift website, 342
Weinman, Lynda, 36
well-structured documents, 128
"What Is RDF?" (Bray), 76
WHATWG (Web Hypertext Application
        Technology Working Group), 4, 87, 135
White House website, 58
whitespace, in CSS rule sets, 170
Wikipedia, web standards, embrace of, 9, 10
Wilson, Chris, 135
Window-Eyes (screen reader), 312
Windows. See also Internet Explorer
    browser default text size, 272
    Cleartype, 269–270
Winer, Dave, 77
Wired News, 79

Wium, Håkon, 285
WordPress
    RSS and, 78
    web standards, embrace of, 9, 11
    XML-RPC and, 81
WordPress CSS Codex-Fixing Browser Bugs
    website, 238
workarounds, benefits of, 262–263
World Wide Web Consortium. *See* W3C
Wubben, Mark, 289, 290
WYMEditor, 101

X

XHTML
    attribute values, 122–123
    books on, 112
    case sensitivity, 120–122
    character encoding, 125, 126–128
    character set declaration, 117–118
    complete DOCTYPEs, list of, 225–226
    conversion tools, 121
    converting to, 113–128
    description of, 104–106
    DOCTYPE declarations and, 113–114, 116
    double dashes, 125
    drawbacks, 74
    embed tag, lack of support for, 259
    HTML5 versus, 138–139
    namespace declaration, 117
    overview, 106
    reasons for using, compared with HTML,
        109–110
    rules summary, 126
    Strict versus Transitional, 106, 115, 223
    structural markup and, 128–133
    tags, required closing of, 124–125
    template for XHTML 1.0 Transitional,
        191–192
    validation, Flash objects and, 261
    version 2.0, 89, 107–108
    XML and, 84
    XML prolog, 118–119
XHTML1.0
    about, 105
    browser support for, 108
    portability, 45–46
    stability, 138
    website for, 44

XHTML5, 138
XML (Extensible Markup Language). *See
    also* XHTML
    applications, 72, 85, 105
    benefits of, 74, 75
    HTML, comparison with, 71–72
    personal publishing tools and, 81–82
    RDF, 76
    RSS 2.0, 70, 77–79
    SOAP, 82
    in software, 73
    SVG and, 84
    XML-RPC, 81
    XMLHttpRequest, 79, 81
    XSLT, 76–77
XML prolog, 118–119, 127, 225
XML-RPC, 81
XMLHttpRequest, 79, 81, 326
XSLT (Extensible Stylesheet Language
    Transformation), 76–77

Y

Yahoo website, 79, 96
Yellow Pages website, 98, 100

Z

Zeldman, Jeffrey, 90, 121
Zeldman website
    author comments in, 363, 364
    drop caps in, 354–355
    embedded font example, 288
    footer, 356, 358–362
    grid layout, 341–344
    header, 362–363
    images of, 350, 352, 3351
    main content, design for, 347–353
    old versions, images of, 343, 345–346
    purpose, 344
Zend, 96
zero value, shorthand for, 190
zoom layouts, 336

Get free online access to this book for 45 days!

And get access to thousands more by signing up for a free trial to Safari Books Online!

With the purchase of this book you have instant online, searchable access to it for 45 days on Safari Books Online! And while you're there, be sure to check out Safari Books Online's on-demand digital library and their free trial offer (a separate sign-up process). Safari Books Online subscribers have access to thousands of technical, creative and business books, instructional videos, and articles from the world's leading publishers.

Simply visit www.peachpit.com/safarienabled and enter code NZYSOXA to try it today.